Radio Rides th

Radio Rides the Range

A Reference Guide to Western Drama on the Air, 1929–1967

Edited by *Jack French and David S. Siegel*

Foreword by Will Hutchins

McFarland & Company, Inc., Publishers
Jefferson, North Carolina, and London

LIBRARY OF CONGRESS CATALOGUING-IN-PUBLICATION DATA

Radio rides the range : a reference guide to western drama on the air, 1929–1967 /
edited by Jack French and David S. Siegel ; foreword by Will Hutchins.
p.   cm.
Includes bibliographical references and index.

ISBN 978-0-7864-7146-1
softcover : acid free paper ∞

1. Radio programs—United States—Catalogs.
I. French, Jack, 1936– editor of compilation.
II. Siegel, David S. editor of compilation.

PN1991.9.R33 2014   791.44'65878—dc23   2013037402

BRITISH LIBRARY CATALOGUING DATA ARE AVAILABLE

Cover images © 2014 Photodisc

Manufactured in the United States of America

*McFarland & Company, Inc., Publishers
Box 611, Jefferson, North Carolina 28640
www.mcfarlandpub.com*

To the memory of the American Indians and
the ordinary and extraordinary men and women
whose true-life exploits settling the western frontier
captured the imagination of generations of radio listeners

Table of Contents

Acknowledgments

Assembling this guide of more than 100 dramatic western radio programs broadcast over more than three decades could not have been done without the support, assistance and contributions of many individuals.

Our thanks go first to the twenty vintage radio historians, writers and collectors who agreed to contribute individual sections for this book, spending countless hours listening and re-listening to series episodes, digging through old newspapers, magazines and other archival information and tracking down the availability of actual program scripts. And to Will Hutchins for sharing his early experiences listening to radio with us in a nostalgic Foreword.

For their tireless research, especially unearthing information about so many lesser known programs, we are grateful to Karl Schadow and Irene Heinstein. Without their work many of the programs we've been able to document in this volume would remain buried and possibly forgotten forever.

We are also indebted to J. David Goldin and Jerry Haendiges for making rare audio copies of programs in their private collections available to our contributors; to Doug Hopkinson and Larry Jaenett for their efforts uncovering audio copies of *The Lone Indian* series; and to Janet McKee of the Recorded Sound Reference Center at the Library of Congress who made audio copies of several rare programs available to the editors.

Thanks also to Jeanette Berard of the American Radio Archives at the Thousand Oaks Library, Thousand Oaks, California; Michael Henry at the Library of American Broadcasting, University of Maryland, College Park, Maryland; Kent Coffman of Kellogg's; and Gordy Spiering of the Milwaukee Area Radio Enthusiasts for providing many of the photographs in the book.

The information for one of the series included in this book, *The American Trail*, came from an unlikely research source for radio historians: the Veterans of Foreign Wars. And for their help unearthing the information about this program, we gratefully acknowledge the assistance of Cara Day, director of communications, and Michelle Strausbaugh, editor of the *Ladies Auxiliary VFW Magazine*.

Two other special sources of information were especially helpful: the Wyoming Room of the Sheridan Fulmer Public Library of Sheridan, Wyoming, and the assistance of Judy Slack and Bill Emery, who helped one of the book's contributors locate a script for *Dr. Frackelton's Stories of Cheyenne & Crow Indians*, and Caroline Yellowtail Houston who was instrumental in the translation of the Crow phrase used in that radio program, and

Aisha Pohoata of the Arizona State University Archives for assistance locating documents relating to *Phoenix Sun Valley Ranch Chuck Wagon* and *Tales of Pioneer Days.*

We also want to acknowledge the assistance of Bobb Lynes who assembled the list of western scripts available in the SPERDVAC library; Ron Sayles who provided background information on vital statistics such as birth and death dates for several radio performers; Melanie Aultman and Mark Anderson for their editorial assistance.

Finally, the editors would like to acknowledge the support and assistance of two individuals without whom this book would not have been possible: Cathy French for her technical support and assistance compiling and transferring electronic files and Susan Siegel for her assembling the book and preparing our manuscript for publication.

Foreword
by Will Hutchins

I'm glad I grew up on radio. As a wee lad, I'd take the bus to Hollywood and scrounge for tickets to see my idols of the airwaves in action. One time I sat beneath an overhanging mike at CBS and laughed my head off. Next day my school chums told me they'd heard me on *Burns and Allen*—my show biz debut.

Nighttime was magic time. Radio on, I'd lie in the semi-dark, listening. The amber hallway light kept the goblins away. I was transported to another dimension, the theatre of the mind. Radio provided story, actors, music and sound effects—I provided the rest. Budgets of my radio shows were limitless, for my dreams were boundless.

Tommy Cook and I went to different schools together. On Saturdays of yore, I'd cheer for ol' Tom as he volleyed and thundered on the tennis courts of Griffith Park. Then I'd bike over to the Atwater Theater and cheer some more when Tommy as Little Beaver and Don Barry as Red Ryder on the screen, foiled the schemes of the evil Ace Hanlon. Tommy's night job was playing Alexander Bumstead on the *Blondie* radio show.

I remember growing up in a gentler, carefree, smog-free Los Angeles where you knew all your neighbors for blocks around and Saturday movie matinees cost a dime. I'd whoop and holler as my cowboy heroes rode across the silver screen, guns a-blazing. I loved Hoot, Hoppy, Smiley, Andy, Gabby, Tex, Roy, Gene, Johnny Mack, and Don "Red" Barry, Lash, Durango Kid, and all the rest.

Many years later I hired on at the Warner Bros. "ranch" in Burbank, just one feller in a stable full of television cowboys. Clint "Cheyenne" Walker was our foreman. He trail-blazed the way for us; he was the king, the backbone of Warner Bros. Television. And there were the stars of *Maverick*, *Bronco*, *Colt .45*, and *Lawman*, none of whom ever went on location; every darn outdoor scene was shot in wild-west Warner Bros. fashion—meaning in their back lot.

For some reason I reminded my bosses of Will Rogers, so quicker than a fast draw they changed my name from Marshall Lowell Hutchason to Will Hutchins. My real name was too long, they insisted. (Soon after, they hired Efrem Zimbalist, Junior.) For all my years as *Sugarfoot* (1957–1961), we were always boxed into musty sound stages or the cramped back lot we shared with all the other Warner Bros. westerns. Once I lost control of a few head of cattle and rode them down the main western street into the middle of a scene being filmed for *Maverick*.

Occasionally, the producers would toss in some stock footage from the Warner Bros. film library to give the illusion of a higher budget. Then I'd get to dude-up in assorted outfits to match the stock shots. Over the years, I had the privilege of wearing Walter Brennan's shirt, Errol Flynn's coat, and Humphrey Bogart's pants. I never felt comfortable in my own duds, somehow reminding me of *Buster Brown*.

The roughest, toughest gang in the west was not the James Gang, nor the Dalton brothers, and not the Younger brothers either — it was the Warner brothers! They rode us hard and put us away wet. After a grueling week of 14-hour days in the 1950s, they'd send us western actors out on weekends for personal appearances for which Warners was paid handsomely and we were paid ugly.

Despite all the projections of Warner Bros., the emerging star turned out to be Bugs Bunny, the superstar of the lot, coming out of the small bungalow which was the home of the Warner Bros. animated cartoon department. Not long after *Sugarfoot* bit the dust (he flunked his bar exam), the entire Warner Bros. television department went down the tube, followed shortly thereafter by most TV westerns.

But I returned to those thrilling days of yesteryear when in 1998 my lovely wife, Babs, and I found the Friends of Old Time Radio (FOTR) Convention in Newark, New Jersey. (Or did they find us?) No matter — it was paradise! I now met all my boyhood heroes and heroines up close and personal. Shucks, those radio folks welcomed me with open arms — great people. Such camaraderie. The radio stars of yore were now in their 60s, 70s, 80s, even 90s, but their voices still rang clear and true, evoking countless memories. Radio actors can be of any age, color, height, or look — the voice is still all! What's more, I got to work with them as well since I was enlisted to fill in on four radio show re-creations... sort of like a utility infielder. Worked a few rodeos, never worked radio — easy roper, interloper, Sugarfoot.

One of my roles was in "The Return of the Cavendish," the 20th anniversary show of *The Lone Ranger*. I played a Western Union messenger and was seated on the stage next to Fran Striker, Jr., son of the show's creator and writer. When the magnificent voice of Fred Foy intoned "From out of the past come the thundering hoofbeats of the great horse, Silver" and the *William Tell Overture* soared, accompanied by hoofbeats and gunshots, well, I was a kid again.

In this re-creation, John Hart was a stalwart Lone Ranger, backed up by Dick Beals, Jackson "Cisco Kid" Beck, sweet Elaine Hyman, and Earl George, a Tonto for the ages; most were WXYZ alums. Sound effects experts Ray Erlenborn and Bob Mott played Silver and other sundry animals as needed. And of course, the Ranger and Tonto grunted every time they got off their horses.

Babs and I moseyed back to the FOTR convention several times. That's where I met up with David S. Siegel and Jack French; in fact, Jack appeared in one of the re-creations with me. Both these guys are diligent old-time radio historians, whose research abilities match their writing skills. The two of them love radio westerns as much as I do, so I was downright pleased when they asked me to write the foreword to their book.

They've corralled a posse of radio historians and western experts who wrote individual sections on the western series they've researched the most. Each one of these knowledgeable fellers and gals have nailed down the complete history of the shows they know best, so I reckon this volume will inform and entertain everyone. Most of their efforts were aimed at the more popular and durable series: *The Lone Ranger, Tom Mix, Red Ryder, Gunsmoke,*

Bobby Benson, Sky King, Melody Ranch, etc. They've covered all the kids' cowboy shows as well as the adult westerns (where all the horses are over 21).

But don't fret — David and Jack have not sashayed away from the obscure and almost-forgotten western series, some of them either regional or merely syndicated. So in this book, you can take a look-see at summaries of *Cactus Kate, Old Dodge Dramas, Boots & Saddles, Justice Rides the Range*, and *Pistol Pete Rice*, along with a passel of other little known western dramas. Some of the nuggets that David and Jack uncovered have amazed even me. Did you know that Chet Huntley of television news fame was the romantic lead in a mid–1930s Oregon radio western called *Covered Wagon Days*? (I shore didn't.)

In my life, I've had the honor of working with some mighty fine folks: childhood heroes, character actors, cowboys, stunt people, wonderful crews, directors, producers, and my secret loves, my leading ladies. I'm proud I got to hit the saddle and go on that glorious, wild ride across America's small screens, guns a-blazing, for westerns are eternal. They're our heritage. That ol' campfire flame of frontier days keeps flickering. There will always be a fascination for the wide open spaces, the winning of the West. It's our great melancholy land's mysterious longing for its receding past. The West shall rise again! And so shall the yeast!

Preface

The cowboy is the most romanticized, and possibly most misrepresented, character in American popular culture. His actual time on history's stage was very brief, barely two decades, from 1870 to 1890. The large cattle drives from Texas to the railheads in Kansas and Nebraska were brought to an end with the near-arctic storms of the winter of 1886-1887. They buried the prairie expanse in mountains of snow and sub-zero temperatures which killed thousands of cattle. Another factor that contributed to the cowpunchers' decline was the invention and wide acceptance of Glidden's barbed wire, which gradually ended the open range tradition.

But the cowboy remained in the forefront of the American psyche through his presence in the dime novels, pulp magazines, silent films, popular songs, wild west shows, and even the western costumes worn by juveniles. The cowpuncher and his horse were joined in most of these venues by the Indians of the Great Plains, the U.S. Cavalry, railroad men, gold miners, and a host of heroes and villains from an era that had passed away in the emerging West, but still filled the hearts and minds of most children and many adults.

So it was logical that in the late 1920s, when the fledgling radio industry gradually discontinued the practice of filling the airwaves with free recitals and lectures from unpaid volunteers and began to present dramatic programs, the heroes on horseback would be popular. By the mid–1930s, western radio drama, both transcribed and produced live, could be heard throughout the country. Through the 1940s and 1950s, and up to the ascendancy of television, western radio drama continued to attract large audiences of all ages.

Evidence of the widespread popularity of radio westerns may be established by three, albeit imperfect, measurements: the number of stations carrying them, the ratings they logged, and the requests for their radio premiums. For example, *Tom Mix* was aired on 298 Mutual stations in 1946 and on 375 stations the following year. To get an approximation of the number of listeners, one can examine the Crossley or Hooper ratings for a specific period and multiply that times the number of homes with a radio. During the 1934-35 season, *Bobby Benson* averaged an 8.8 rating which would translate into 1,795,200 listeners for each program. In the second half of 1945, *Tom Mix* averaged about the same, 1,754,300. The highest ratings number received by a western show occurred in the 1950-51 season of *Hopalong Cassidy*, when that show had nearly four million listeners.

Regarding radio premiums (as cited in Marilyn Boemer's *The Children's Hour*), a 1936 study of 3,000 children by Azriel Eisenberg found that they had received 1,726 various premiums by sending in proofs of purchase. The success of a program and the loyalty it inspired could, in part, be judged by the number of radio premiums it distributed over the years. From 1933 to 1950, Ralston Purina sent their **Tom Mix** listeners over 70 different premiums, including photos, badges, rings, toy guns, western attire, knives, flashlights, etc. Literally hundreds of thousands of these items, including premiums from other western programs, were eagerly sought by youngsters of that era. The record for the greatest number distributed for a single item was achieved by the somewhat incongruously named "Lone Ranger Atomic Ring," available for 15 cents and a Kix cereal boxtop. From 1948 to 1957 approximately six million rings were mailed to requesters.

Despite the historic popularity of western drama, there has never been one volume to encompass them all. There have been several books published which covered a single series, including William Harper's book on **Straight Arrow**, Bernard Drew's on **Hopalong Cassidy** and the one devoted to **Gunsmoke** by SuzAnne and Gabor Barabas. There have been at least six books published about **The Lone Ranger**. Nevertheless, there has not been one inclusive reference book to cover all western drama and your editors were determined to fill that void in broadcast history.

In our early discussions about the parameters of this book, the editors worked out which programs we would include and which ones we would not. Many people have different definitions for "the West." After all, when editor Horace Greeley reportedly said, "Go west, young man, go west," he was referring to Ohio. We decided that for the purposes of our book, "West" meant, with only a few exceptions, "west of the Mississippi River."

That decision dictated that programs about western frontiersmen in coonskin hats, e.g. Daniel Boone or Davy Crockett, would not find a place in our book. Likewise, radio's Indian fighters who confronted the Iroquois and Mohawk tribes in the East or in Canada would not be included within these pages, while those programs about frontiersmen who fought the Sioux, Apache, and Cheyenne on the Great Plains would be.

An additional refinement of our definition of the West involved excluding those programs whose heroes inhabited the "northwest." While many radio series (both in the United States and Canada) broadcast the real, and fictional, exploits of the Royal Canadian Mounted Police, they will not appear in this book. Granted, this was an arbitrary decision by the editors since the Mounties chased outlaws, fought claim-jumpers, and dealt with friendly and hostile Indians. One broadcast observer even claimed that any radio script from **The Lone Ranger** series could be changed to one of *Sgt. Preston of the Yukon* merely by adding snow. Nevertheless, radio's scarlet-clad stalwarts are not in this book. Nor are radio's forest rangers, such as *Mark Trail* and *Ranger Bill*, who despite occasional forays against cattle rustlers, spent most of their time fighting forest poachers and illegal fishing while protecting woodland creatures.

Another category of the western genre that we have not included is the program which exclusively consisted of music, of which there were a multitude of shows. Some of these all-music programs featured western stars who were actors on dramatic programs: Tex Ritter, Joe "Curley" Bradley, Gene Autry, etc. But we, as editors, justifiably felt that all these country and western musical shows would be better served in a book solely devoted to them.

There were five types of western dramas from the late 1920s to the mid–1960s in U.S. broadcast history and all are covered in this book:

1. **Anthology Programs.** These shows had no re-occurring lead roles nor any fixed geographic location in which their stories were set. They featured different characters, either historical or fictional, in each program using a variety of frontier regions and various time periods. Examples of these programs would be: *Empire Builders*, *Frontier Fighters*, and *When the West Was Young*. These programs attracted primarily a mature listening audience. Regardless of the frequently high production values, it was sometimes difficult for some of these series to build audience loyalty in the absence of a permanent central hero.

2. **Juvenile Adventure Programs.** These were usually 15 minute shows with two or three continuing characters (frequently an adult male hero, a geezer sidekick, and a juvenile tagalong) in every episode. They were short serial adventure and mystery programs until about 1949 when they evolved into half hour shows, each of which concluded their story in 30 minutes. Most of their heroes resembled the Lone Ranger, whom a child psychologist described as being: "In all his idealism, he is soberly factual, concerned with preventing evil men from outwitting or overcoming good men." Frederick Wyatt, in his "Some Observations on The Lone Ranger Radio Program" (Bulletin #27, Ohio State University, 1941,) further asserted that: "The Lone Ranger is the messenger who wanders around to help those in distress. While abiding by high moral standards, he acts in terms of his special insight, without regard to the local system of law and order." Examples of the juvenile adventure category include: *Red Ryder*, *Straight Arrow*, *Tom Mix*, *Bobby Benson*, and *Hopalong Cassidy*. Most of these series offered listeners a number of premiums (badges, rings, code books, western gear, etc.) in exchange for a small amount of cash and proof of purchase of the sponsor's product.

3. **Legend and Lore.** These programs were aimed at a young audience and were designed to inform and entertain listeners with nature stories of the frontier, legends of the West, and even tribal customs and songs. Most of these shows featured real or fictional Indians as host/narrator, i.e., *Lone Wolf Tribe*, *Red Goose Indian Tales* and *Chief Gray Wolf*. A few of these programs instead had an old cowboy or prospector as their host (*Cowboy Tom's Round-Up*, *Dr. Frackelton's Stories*) but they still included Indian material along with cowboy legends and frontier history.

4. **Adult Westerns.** Originating in the late 1940s, these programs reached their zenith in the mid–1950s. These programs portrayed the western frontier with all the gritty realism and historical background of that era. Most of the series' scripts were character-driven and accurately dramatized all the pain, injustice, and boredom of the Great Plains, while illustrating the courage and fortitude of the men and women who settled there. Most of these programs were a half-hour in length, and while some juveniles were listeners, the majority of the audience consisted of adults. Examples of this category include *Gunsmoke*, *Fort Laramie*, *The Six-Shooter*, and *Frontier Gentleman*.

5. **Soap Operas.** Despite the domination of soap operas in daytime radio, they were very seldom set in the West. Therefore western soap operas were the smallest of the five categories as few existed to be described in this book (*A Woman of America*, *Cactus Kate* and *Lone Journey*). Written to appeal primarily to women listeners, these serial stories featured strong women beset with continuing anxiety, pathos, discord, pain, humor, and love. These shows were usually sponsored by household products.

In structuring this book, the editors have used two formats in our summary of each series. Series with no known surviving audio copies and little print documentation are described in a single paragraph. For other series where audio copies and other source materials are available, each series entry begins with listings of alternate names of the show (if appropriate), its network or syndication format, duration of broadcast run, sponsor (if any), number of audio copies available, and where the scripts are archived (if known to be in existence) followed by a more detailed discussion of the series.

The series entries are arranged alphabetically, by the first word of the series' name. Series that had two or more names during its broadcast run are listed separately, with a "see" reference to the main listing. For example, the listing for *Songs of the B-Bar-B* is listed under "S" with the notation: "See *Bobby Benson*." In addition, to help identify the names of series included in the book, whenever a reference is made to the series, it is indicated in bold italic lettering.

By definition, the focus of the programs covered in this book, both those written for juvenile and adult audiences, dealt with the typical western issues of cowboys, Indians, bank robberies, life on the frontier, etc. But, interwoven into many of the individual episodes, whether by accident or design, listeners were also exposed to social and cultural messages that transcended the western experience — and which changed over time.

In his insightful analysis of juvenile western radio in *Don't Touch That Dial!* radio historian J. Fred MacDonald notes that many juvenile western programs, especially during the 1930s and early 1940s, presented a mixed picture of racial tolerance with Mexicans, East Asians, African Americans and Indians often, but not always, being portrayed as inferior to the programs' bold white heroes. This stereotyping began to change, however, during and after World War II when western programs, as well as other program genres, began to project a more positive image of non-white Americans and to stress racial and ethnic tolerance in their scripts and plot lines.

Mexicans, for example, were treated fairly on the *Cisco Kid*, but not in the Zorro type shows; and with few exceptions (*Lone Wolf Tribe*, *Lone Indian*, *Chief Gray Wolf*) Indians only played supporting roles until the debut of *Straight Arrow* in 1948. And, whereas Indians were often the enemy in the 1930s and early 1940s programs, by the 1950s both *Hopalong Cassidy* and *Luke Slaughter* featured episodes in which the heroes defended Indians when local townsfolk mistakenly accused them of misdeeds. L'il Beaver and Tonto, of course, were loyal sidekicks to their lead characters, Red Ryder and the Lone Ranger.

African Americans, when they did appear, which wasn't often, were in supporting roles and often used to provide comic relief, such as Wash on *Tom Mix*, Fireball in *Ranch House Jim* and Cookie in *Life on Red Horse Ranch*. And while the famed Buffalo Soldiers, the African American 10th Cavalry Regiment, weren't featured on *Fort Laramie*, they were prominent in an episode of the Armed Forces Radio & Television Service series *When the West Was Young*.

Other than the soap operas, e.g., *Cactus Kate* and *A Woman of America*, for the most part, women played minor roles in the programs, primarily as a love interest, or as schoolmarms, or victimized widows. One exception was *Light on the West* where a woman actually played the role of a law enforcement officer. It was only in the 1950s and the appearance of more sophisticated adult westerns that women came into their own, in part thanks to a woman script writer, Kathleen Hite. Kitty on *Gunsmoke* may have been the first strong, significant recurring woman's role in a western other than Sacajawea, the Indian woman who served as a guide for Lewis and Clark and who appeared in several western anthology programs. Other programs, such as **Frontier Gentleman**, highlighted the plight and progress of women in the West while an episode of **When the West Was Young** was a tribute to the strength of women on the frontier in terms of fighting for their rights of citizenship.

It should also be noted that with few exceptions, e.g., writers Kathleen Hite, Ruth Woodman, and director Mary Afflick, nearly all of the writers, directors, producers, sound personnel, musicians, announcers, advertising representatives, network executives — and even the ushers for live broadcasts — were men. Radio in that era was a white male dominated world.

Although most western radio dramas tended to follow a tried and true formula, and, by definition were set in the West, when America entered World War II, that didn't stop radio's western heroes from fighting Nazis and hunting for Axis spies as part of the nation's propaganda effort to build support for the war. Even the ever popular premiums associated with the programs took on a wartime focus: Kix, the sponsor of **The Lone Ranger**, offered a Lone Ranger Blackout Safety Belt, while **Tom Mix** in his programs and radio premiums was fighting Nazis and spies.

In selecting our contributors to this reference book, the editors invited only men and women who had a broad knowledge of U.S. broadcast history, coupled with a specialty in western radio drama. We wanted authors who were not only good writers, but those who were willing and able to put in long hours in research. Contributors were allowed to choose which series they would be responsible for; some of them, due to our time constraints, chose only one series. Others were able to research and write in depth about more than one program and still meet our deadline. Biographical information about the contributors is at the back of the book.

An explanation of some terms in radio history may be of value at this point.

Live: Many shows were done "live" in that the broadcast was aired at exactly the same time the performance was taking place. While this gave a sense of immediacy, any mistakes or miscues in the performance went out on the air, with no way to correct them. Because of the three-hour time difference between the East and West Coast, East Coast shows that were only done live, were frequently subject to repeats, in which the entire performance was done again, hours later for the West Coast.

Airchecks: Although theoretically there would be no recording surviving from a live show, there were exceptions. While the program was going out over the air, the studio engineer could record it in a process that resulted in an "aircheck," or a transcription of a live show. Sometimes the star of the show arranged for this; Rudy Vallee recorded most of his live shows and archived the copies. Also, the sponsors of a program could request an aircheck be made for them, usually to make sure the commercials were properly handled. Beginning in World War II, the Armed Forces Radio Service (AFRS) requested that airchecks be made of several popular programs that were only broadcast live. AFRS then made copies of those airchecks and played the programs to military personnel and dependents overseas. Several programs owe their survival to AFRS; for example, some of the existing episodes of **Bobby Benson** came from AFRS audio copies.

Syndication: Syndicated shows refer to those originally produced only on transcription disks, usually by the dozens of mostly small companies that specialized in this venue. The disks were rented or leased to the smaller stations, usually ones with no network affiliation. They were marketed in batches, normally a minimum of 39 episodes. Most of these programs consisted of 15-minute episodes, which contained about 12 minutes of dramatization, along with about 90 seconds of instrumental music at the beginning and the end, over which the local announcer would read the sponsor's commercial message. Few of the syndicated shows mentioned on their recordings the names of the actors, director, writers, or anyone else associated with its production, making research on them difficult, even if one has access to audio copies.

Transcriptions: While all syndicated shows were transcribed, not all transcriptions were syndicated. Many programs, including several westerns, were recorded on disk by a network for later playing on affiliate stations. (Disks would yield to tape after World War II.) This practice was common with the Mutual Broadcasting System in filling its time slots for its affiliates throughout the country. By the early 1950s, most of the CBS westerns, including **Gunsmoke**, **Fort Laramie**, and **Frontier Gentleman**, were all transcribed, thus contributing to the high survivability of these series.

Sustaining: Another term that may need explanation is "sustained." This refers to a series, usually on a network, which had no sponsor. This means that the network was responsible for all the costs of paying the cast, writers, producer, director and technical people, in addition to musicians. All marketing and advertising of the program would also be paid for by the network. A corollary of this was the amount of the salaries paid to all involved with the program; they received lower wages on a sustained show than they would if the show were sponsored. But the fact that a show could not attract a sponsor was no indication of the quality of the program; **Fort Laramie** and **The Six-Shooter**, two superior westerns, were sustained shows for most of their respective runs.

Throughout this book, sources are cited after each radio series or audition. Books are noted by the author's name, with the full citation shown in the Bibliography. If there is more than one book by the same author in the Bibliography, the first words of the book title appear in the citation. Similarly, the full citation for magazine articles is included in the Bibliography. When appropriate, newspaper citations include the city and state of the newspaper.

Old Time Radio researchers will readily admit that, despite their resolute and exhaustive efforts, it is not always possible to identify in depth every radio program pursued. So it is with the radio westerns, as we acknowledge in Appendix 1, which contains the titles of approximately five dozen programs for which we still have no audio copies and only scant documentation. It is hoped that this appendix will serve to encourage future researchers to continue the quest of documenting these programs.

THE PROGRAMS

THE ADVENTURES OF ANNIE OAKLEY AND TAGG

JACK FRENCH *and* DAVID S. SIEGEL

NETWORK: ABC
FORMAT: Half hour
DURATION OF RUN: Circa 1952, but may not have aired
AUDIO COPIES EXTANT: 1
SCRIPT ARCHIVED: Gene Autry Library & Research Services, Los Angeles, CA

In hearing the sole audio copy of *The Adventures of Annie Oakley and Tagg*, the discerning listener would probably be convinced that it was an actual ABC radio program from the early 1950s, heard every week on Thursdays. Announcer Charlie Lyon began with this introduction:

> "Yes, boys and girls, the American Broadcasting Company once again presents the transcribed Adventures of… (sound of gunshot and bullet hitting metal target) Annie Oakley, crack shot of the range country, and Tagg! A story of the West… a story of a young 17-year-old orphan girl named Annie and her 10-year-old brother, Tagg, who came West to find a home with their Uncle Luke McTavish, sheriff of the small mining and ranching town of Diablo."

After Annie and Uncle Luke solved their scripted radio mystery of the poisoning of Whispering Spring, Lyon concluded with: "Well, boys and girls, that sorta winds things up for this time, but Annie, Tagg, and the whole gang will be back next Thursday at this very same time and over this station for another thrill packed story of the West!"

This radio program contained no name credits, except for the announcer and Bill Burch, the director, both of whom filled those same jobs on *Gene Autry's Melody Ranch*. Uncle Luke is clearly the voice of Pat Buttram, longtime radio sidekick of Autry but the two youngsters' identities are not certain. Presumably they are Gail Davis and Billy Gray, who were originally cast in the television version of *Annie Oakley*. But despite Autry's apparent plans to produce a radio series as a companion piece to his proposed television series about Annie Oakley, the evidence suggests that only the video version reached the airwaves.

The real Annie Oakley (1860–1926) was born Phoebe Ann Mozee in Darke County, Ohio, the fifth of eight children of a poor woman who was twice widowed. "Annie" began shooting wild game at age 8 to provide food for her struggling family. The little girl became such an accurate shot that by the time she was a teenager, she was barred from local target competitions because she always won. At age 15, while visiting an older sister in Cincinnati, she was pitted in a target shooting contest against Frank Butler, a professional marksman with a touring stock company. She won that contest, the couple fell in love, and they were married a year later.

By 1882, she had adopted the professional name of "Annie Oakley" and she and Frank toured the country as a specialty act in various venues, including the Sells Brothers Circus. Oakley joined Buffalo Bill Cody's Wild West Show in April 1885, by which time

Frank had become her full-time manager. She quickly became that famed show's greatest attraction in both the U.S. and later on its European tours. Equally proficient with a pistol, rifle, and shotgun, she had no peers in any shooting arena. In 1888 at Gloucester NJ, a bet was made that she could not kill more than 40 live pigeons out of 50 rising at 30 yards. She downed 49. Her unerring skill with firearms lasted late into her life; at age 62, she broke 100 straight clay targets at 16 yards.

Her fame continued to flourish after her 1926 death. Barbara Stanwyck portrayed her in RKO's 1935 film, *Annie Oakley*, which bore some resemblance to her real life. A more accurate biography of her appeared on radio with the June 16, 1941, program of the *Cavalcade of America* series; Agnes Moorehead played the little sharp shooter. Irving Berlin brought the character of Oakley to the musical stage in 1946 with "Annie, Get Your Gun" featuring a brassy Ethel Merman in the Broadway lead.

A comic book series, which debuted in 1948, and newspaper strip portrayed Annie facetiously as a blonde sharpshooter in the Old West who romanced every cowboy she met. The comic book, produced by Atlas Division of Marvel Comics, would run until 1956. *Annie, Get Your Gun*, MGM's 1950 motion picture, starring Betty Hutton, was nominated for four Academy Awards and won for Best Music.

In January 1952, Gene Autry bought the radio, TV, and merchandizing rights to the newspaper comic strip "Annie Oakley" by Eli H. Leslie, which was then being syndicated to several dailies. *Variety* announced that Autry's Flying A Productions would begin filming 52 television episodes as soon as an 18-year-old girl could be found for the lead. Autry declared that he planned to hold auditions in several cities to find an unknown actress who could shoot and ride.

But this "star search" was all a sham. Autry already preferred Gail Davis for the lead, although he would not announce her selection until April 1952. Davis was born Betty Jeanne Grayson (1925–1997) in Arkansas and studied dance and theater at the University of Texas where she married Robert Davis. A 5-foot 2-inch blonde who sought her fortune in Hollywood, Davis was discovered by an MGM agent while working as a hatcheck girl. Since her name, Betty Davis, was too similar to screen star Bette Davis, she adopted the professional name of Gail Davis in 1947.

Davis got a lot of film work, mostly small roles in western and action motion pictures, gradually learning her craft. Gene Autry used her in fourteen of his B-movies and apparently became enamored with the pint-sized blonde. In this regard, *Variety* in its January 25, 1952, issue announced: "When Annie Oakley climbs off the comic page to gallop on Gene Autry's TV ranch, she will play it straight, without any romantic persiflage. The gal won't even kiss the boss."

This was probably an inside joke since the Hollywood cowboys knew that "Annie" was not only kissing the boss, she was also bedding him. In her 2007 biography of Autry, *Public Cowboy No. 1*, Holly George-Warren revealed that Gail Davis had an eight year intimate affair with Autry, who was nearly 20 years her senior. The fact that they were married to other people did not prevent their business relationship from moving into the bedroom, nor did it hinder the success of their respective careers.

The television version of *Annie Oakley* went through changes in cast and crew, including deleting Tagg from the title. Scriptwriter Dorothy Yost advanced the ages of brother and sister from the radio version; Annie went from 17 to mid–20s (Davis' actual age) and Tagg grew from a 10-year-old into a teenager. Billy Gray, originally cast as Tagg, was replaced by Jimmy Hawkins after the first few months of shooting. Then Norman Hall replaced Yost as the head writer.

Billboard reported in June 1952 that *Annie Oakley* was scheduled for both a radio and a television series in the coming months. To promote the series, Flying A Productions had ordered a run of 600,000 copies of the Annie comic book. Although the film company claimed that shooting had begun in April 1952 on a planned 52 TV episodes, only 23 episodes were completed by September 1953. By then Frank McDonald had replaced Wallace Fox as the director.

Apparently the radio series plans evaporated as Flying A Productions concentrated on the television version, which was finally released for syndication in January 1954, going on CBS-TV, sponsored by Canada Dry. Dubbed a show about "pigtails and pistols" by one source, *Annie Oakley* quickly became very popular with its young audience. *Variety* reported on March 17, 1954 that *Annie Oakley's* Nielsen ratings (17.7) surpassed those of Gene Autry's own television show, which came in at 11.8 for that period. *Annie Oakley* would go on to air a total of 81 syndicated episodes from 1954 to 1956; and then ABC-TV aired them as re-runs from 1959 to 1964.

Sources: Audio copy of *Adventures of Annie Oakley and Tagg* plus television episodes of *Annie Oakley*; Brooks; Carter; George-Warren; *Billboard*, June 14, 1952; *Broadcasting/ Telecasting*, April 23, 1952, May 26, 1952, and June 2, 1952; *Funk & Wagnalls New Encyclopedia*, Vol. 18, 2007; *Variety*, January 22, 25, 1952, April 7, 8 1952, May 8, 1952, September 14, 1953, and March 17, 1954; *www.lkwdpl.org/wihohio/oakl-ann.htm*; *www.imdb. com*; *www.encyclopediaofarkansas.net/encyclopedia*.

THE ADVENTURES OF CHAMPION

Jack French *and* David S. Siegel

NETWORK: Mutual
FORMAT: 15 minutes, Monday through Friday
DURATION OF RUN: June to November 1949
SPONSOR: Sustained
AUDIO COPIES EXTANT: 3
SCRIPTS ARCHIVED: American Radio Archives (1)

Orvon Gomer Autry, a Texas native born in 1907, began his singing career on radio in 1928 and later struck gold as a Hollywood cowboy. As Gene Autry he would go on to appear in 93 feature films, record over 600 songs, become a radio and television star, and ultimately attain multi-millionaire status. *The Adventures of Champion* would be little more than an asterisked entry on his resume.

The Adventures of Champion was not a spin-off of his popular radio show, **Melody Ranch**, even though both programs had the efforts of the same people. Just grasping the basic scenario of *The Adventures of Champion* required a substantial suspension of belief in what its juvenile listeners knew to be gospel. Champion was Autry's horse and had a major role in all of his movies, television programs, and personal appearances. The noble steed was as well-known as Roy Rogers' Trigger or Tom Mix's Tony. No one, except Autry, ever climbed in the saddle on Champion.

Although Autry's production company created *The Adventures of Champion*, Autry never appeared on the radio program. In the radio series, Champion was the leader of a herd of wild horses and the sole person who could ride him was little Ricky West, an orphan being raised by his Uncle Smoky on a prairie ranch. In addition to the skilled assistance that Champion provided Ricky, the young lad also had the services of a faithful German shepherd dog named Blaze. (His name was later changed to Rebel.)

Each Monday, Ricky and Uncle Smoky would be confronted by a new mystery, a sudden crime, the arrival of outlaws, or perhaps a natural disaster. By that Friday, with the help of Champion and Rebel, the elderly rancher and his young nephew had made everything right again — the stolen loot recovered, the evildoers behind bars, or the lost soul returned to safety. His mission over, Champion galloped back to his wild herd, but listeners soon realized he'd be back on Monday with Ricky in his saddle.

When the program debuted on June 20, 1949, it was preceded by a fanciful press release from Autry's production company stating that Gene's horse, Champion, would be auditioning for the title lead in the new series, *The Adventures of Champion*. Of course, this was an inside joke, since animal imitator and sound man, Dave Light, had already been hired to voice all the animals on that show, including Champion and the German shepherd. Light, in addition to portraying all the animals on **Gene Autry's Melody Ranch**, was also the cat and dog on the radio show, *Mayor of the Town* which starred Lionel Barrymore. William N. Burch, who was the producer/director of **Melody Ranch**, was chosen by Autry to fill the same role on *The Adventures of Champion*.

Mutual occasionally moved the time slot of *The Adventures of Champion*, but it was always aired around 5 P.M. (EST). Sometimes it was between **Bobby Benson and the B-Bar-B Riders** and *Curley Bradley Sings*. At other times, it preceded or followed *Ted Drake, Guardian of the Big Top*, but whenever it aired, it would be at the same time for the week, Monday through Friday.

Burch used substantially the same supporting cast members on *The Adventures of Champion* that he was using on **Melody Ranch**. However, one of most curious mysteries about this series was who played the leads of Ricky and Uncle Smoky; contemporary accounts of the program have been unsuccessful in unearthing their identities, and the vast Autry Library and Research Services in Los Angeles, CA, has no record of who the performers were. To date, only one script has survived; approximately 100 scripts were destroyed in an unfortunate accidental fire several years ago.

Although the radio series ended in November 1949, the series' concept was resurrected six years later on television with only minor changes. *The Adventures of Champion* debuted on CBS-TV on September 30, 1955, produced by Autry's company, Flying A Productions. Again, the horse and the dog helped Ricky and his uncle fight crime and solve mysteries. The two main characters had their names altered; Ricky West became Ricky North and Uncle Smoky West was renamed Uncle Sandy North. Ricky was played by a young Barry Curtis, while Uncle Sandy was portrayed by Jim Bannon. The latter was a former radio actor who coincidentally was starring as Red Ryder on the movie screen during the time *The Adventures of Champion* was on the radio.

The television show lasted only slightly longer than its radio counterpart; CBS-TV took it off the air in February 1956.

Sources: Audio copies of *Adventures of Champion*; Brooks; Katz; Mott; *Citizen Advertiser*, Auburn, NY, June 20, 1949; *Evening Observer*, Dunkirk, NY, June 4, 1949; *Leader Republican*, Gloversville and Johnstown, NY, October 7, 1949.

The Adventures of Red Ryder see **Red Ryder**

The Adventures of Rin Tin Tin see **Rin Tin Tin**

The Adventures of Tom Mix see **Tom Mix**

The Adventures of Zorro see **Zorro**

ALL-STAR WESTERN THEATRE

JACK FRENCH *and* DAVID S. SIEGEL

NETWORK: CBS (1946 to 1947); Mutual (1948)
FORMAT: Half hour, weekly
DURATION OF RUN: June 1946 to August 1948
SPONSOR: Weber's Bread
AUDIO COPIES EXTANT: 105
SCRIPTS ARCHIVED: Undetermined

This program was a spin-off from *The Hollywood Barn Dance*, a Los Angeles based country and western musical series that was created in 1943 by two established native Texas performers, Cottonseed Clark (real name, Clark Fulks) and Foy Willing (real name, Foy Willingham), as a replacement for **Gene Autry's Melody Ranch**, when Autry went on active military duty in the U.S. Army Air Corps during World War II. (When Autry returned home, *Hollywood Barn Dance* gave up the radio slot.) Clark was the master of ceremonies, writer, and talent scout for several western musical programs while Willing, a cowboy singer, had organized The Riders of the Purple Sage, borrowing the title from the Zane Grey novel. In addition to Willing, the musical group included Al Stoey, Kenny Driver, and Jimmy Dean.

For *All-Star Western Theatre*, Willing and Clark reworked the concept of *The Hollywood Barn Dance* and combined country and western music with a dramatic sketch. This new program, which debuted in June 1946, usually led off with about three songs, followed by a dramatization of 13 to 21 minutes, and then concluded with more songs. To increase audience appeal, the lead in the dramatic sketch was usually a well-known cowboy movie star, frequently from Republic Studios.

Some of the regulars were: Tim Holt, Johnny Mack Brown, "Smiley" Burnette, Alan "Rocky" Lane, Monte Hale, Ken Curtis, Donald "Red" Barry, and even Dale Evans, the wife of Roy Rogers. The supporting cast was filled out by The Riders of the Purple Sage and other radio actors, as necessary, especially to portray those in the women's roles.

Most of the plot lines involved standard western themes, akin to those of the B pictures that Republic Studios produced for juvenile audiences at the Saturday matinees in the hometown theaters. There were stories of cattle stampedes, stage coach holdups, disputes over water rights, nighttime rustling, bank robberies, and ranch mortgages being foreclosed. Most of the programs were written to ensure that the Republic Studios cowboy star would bring peace and justice to some part of the frontier.

In a typical story line, Donald "Red" Barry in "Bid for Election" is persuaded by friends to expose a crooked local sheriff by letting himself be arrested so he can observe in jail as if the sheriff has really captured a dangerous outlaw. Barry is successful in this endeavor and at the end of the drama he is allowed to step out of character and plug his newest motion picture.

But a few of these western adventures did not have a happy ending. In the program entitled "Little Hoof," an elderly miner and his old burro are about to retire on the gold they've accumulated when outlaws kill the burro in an ambush. Later the miner's pals help track down the outlaws and they kill or capture most of them. But a few escape, circle back to the miner's cabin, and steal all his gold. So the unfortunate miner ends up penniless, with his burro companion dead.

Not all of the guest actors were cowboy stars or their sidekicks; several other Hollywood actors and radio personalities were cast in leading roles, but usually in mysteries or comedies. Jackie Coogan starred in a ghost mystery entitled "The Bandit," Jerry Colona tickled the audience's ribs in "Why Did I Ever Leave Wyoming" and even Edgar Bergen appeared in a comedy episode.

Being a movie star does not necessarily mean than one is comfortable with a radio microphone and a few of the star leads were not convincing. While Ken Curtis seemed at ease, Monte Hale sounded a little stiff on the show and Donald "Red" Barry was barely adequate. Sound effects were realistic but kept to a minimum in all shows. Musical bridges were certainly acceptable. While Cottonseed Clark was usually the emcee, Terry O'Sullivan occasionally filled in for him.

Foy Willing did not restrict The Riders of the Purple Sage to only traditional cowboy songs and ballads, although most of their offerings were in this category; they also played and sang an occasional waltz, pop tune, or swing melody. Therefore songs like "Sweet Georgia Brown," "Managua, Nicaragua," and "Alexander's Ragtime Band" were played on various programs over the years.

Since the series was distributed on transcription disks, by both CBS and Mutual, an inordinately high percentage of the series' programs have survived to present day.

Sources: Audio copies of *All-Star Western Theatre*; Clark; Hickerson, *4th*; Hurst; http://www.radioarchives.com/All_Star_Western_Theatre.

THE AMERICAN TRAIL

JACK FRENCH *and* DAVID S. SIEGEL

NETWORK: Syndicated
FORMAT: 15 minutes, weekly
DURATION OF RUN: February to May, 1953
SPONSOR: None
AUDIO COPIES EXTANT: 13 (entire run)
SCRIPTS ARCHIVED: Undetermined

Each program in this series began with the voice of narrator Richard Janaver: "The American Trail... blazed in blood... defended in blood!" It was a startling opening for a radio series produced by the genteel women who comprised the Ladies Auxiliary to the Veterans of Foreign Wars and aimed at the youth of America.

In late 1952, the Ladies began the complex task of creating a radio series on American history, virtually from scratch. They located experienced advisors to guide them, hired a professional, talented production staff and accomplished actors, and then, through their local auxiliary units throughout the country, convinced over 300 radio stations to air the series on donated air time. In doing so, they reached an estimated 20 million students.

The total series consisted of 13 quarter hour chapters, each concentrating on a separate event or significant era in American history. Obviously the 15 minute format required judicious compression of the facts being dramatized so the scripts, written by John Fleming, had narration encompassing about 60 percent of each program, with dramatization filling the remaining time. Fleming brought a cosmopolitan background to his writing; he was born in London, lived in Australia, Egypt, and South Africa, and was a decorated Allied officer in World War II. When hired for *The American Trail*, he was primarily writing for U. S. television, although he had written and produced radio shows for the Scandinavian Broadcasting Operations during the war.

While the programs covered such topics as the adoption of the U.S. Constitution, the Northwest Ordinance, and even the Wright Brothers' first flight, nearly half of the shows involved historical events on the western frontier. Those six programs were:

Chapter #3: "The Louisiana Purchase," the great expansion of the U.S. borders west of the Mississippi River that vastly increased the size of our country.

Chapter #4: "Lewis and Clark Expedition," the dangerous and difficult exploration of this vast western region all the way to Oregon.

Chapter #6: "The Golden Ocean," how Cyrus McCormick's reaper transformed the western prairie into America's bread basket.

Chapter #8: "On to Monterey," how Frémont's soldiers led the way in the battle for the sovereignty of California.

Chapter #9: "The California Gold Rush," the impact the discovery of gold at Sutter's Mill had on the West Coast and all of America.

Chapter #10: "The Rich Desert," how the seemingly worthless land in the western desert was suddenly enriched by oil discoveries.

The series director, Walter Gorman, obtained the services of Charles Frederick Paul to handle all the musical duties. Both men had solid credentials in radio. Gorman was a graduate of Brown University and began as a writer in Hollywood. He then directed several radio series, among them, *Road of Life*, *The Kate Smith Hour*, and *Young Dr. Malone*. Paul conducted the New York Philharmonic Orchestra and provided the music for *Nora Drake*, *Old Gold Comedy Hour*, and *Martin Kane, Private Eye*. The series narrator, Richard Janaver, began as a stage actor but switched to radio, appearing regularly on *Thunder Over Paradise*, *The Avenger*, and the *Ave Maria* program. While doing *The American Trail*, he was also portraying "Myron" on *Stella Dallas* and "John Edwards" on *Lorenzo Jones*.

Gorman had assembled a strong supporting cast of experienced radio actors, including Bill Lipton, Evie Varden, Parker Fennelly, and in the juvenile roles, Butch Cavell. There was no shortage of prominent guest stars; President Dwight D. Eisenhower appeared on chapter #13, USAF General Jimmy Doolittle added a message on chapter #12, while Bing Crosby and son, Lindsay, introduced the events portrayed on chapter #9.

All of the programs were an excellent blend of skillful narration and crisp dramatization. The sound effects were executed well and enhanced the drama portions, as did the musical bridges. Of necessity, the historical events were covered in compact form, but this did not dilute the accuracy of the facts presented.

The series' emphasis on American heritage and unabashed patriotism resulted in widespread praise from several high ranking state and national officials, including the governors of over two dozen states. Senator Margaret Chase Smith of Maine read into the *Congressional Record* a statement lauding the series and thanking the Ladies Auxiliary to the Veterans of Foreign Wars for providing it.

In June 1953 the series won a first place award in a nationwide competition sponsored by the Ohio State Institute for Education by Radio & Television. Competing against dozens of other programs, mostly network shows, *The American Trail* took top honors in the category of best program for teenagers for out-of-school listening.

Sources: Audio recordings of *American Trail*; *National Bulletin of the Ladies Auxiliary to the Veterans of Foreign Wars*, Issues: November 1952, January 1953, February 1953, April 1953 and June 1953; *Putnam County Courier*, Carmel, NY, June 4, 1953; *Gazette*, Schenectady, NY, January 21, 1953.

THE ANDY DEVINE SHOW

JACK FRENCH *and* DAVID S. SIEGEL

NETWORK: Syndicated, circa 1947
FORMAT: Half hour, weekly
DURATION OF RUN: Probably never aired
SPONSOR: Was to be determined locally
AUDIO COPIES: 2
SCRIPTS ARCHIVED: Undetermined

This western program, which took its stories from historical American events in the late 1800s, featured Andy Devine as the narrator. It was produced by Teleways Radio Productions, a transcription company located at 8949 Sunset Boulevard, Hollywood, CA. Founded in 1946, the company specialized in producing and marketing 15 minute western music programs (*Sons of the Pioneers*, *Chuck Wagon Jamboree*, etc.) but also offered some 30 minute adventure shows, including *Strange Wills* and *Danger, Dr. Danfield.*

While the two surviving audio copies demonstrate the strengths of the scripts and acting, no evidence has yet been found that indicates that this program was ever aired. Possibly the appeal of Devine's personality and distinctive voice was not sufficient to convince any station owner to book the show. But more likely, and for whatever reason, only two shows were actually recorded. Since that is far fewer than the standard minimum 39 programs that were usually marketed, Teleways never finished this project and the company never advertised the series.

There is some conjecture involved in dating these transcriptions, but circa 1947 would appear to be a reasonable estimation. By this time, Teleways had been in business for a year and Devine (1905–1977) had progressed through 36 motion pictures, from walk-on parts to major supporting roles. His very recognizable, raspy voice was not heard often on radio, although he did do occasional spots on the *Jack Benny Show* and a few guest appearances on other programs.

Both of the surviving copies have the same introduction: announcer Charles Lyon would say "From way out West, it's the Andy Devine Show" and then Devine would invite the listeners, "C'mere, I've got a story for you." Devine introduced the drama and then would reappear at the microphone four more times in the next 30 minutes, with a last appearance to wrap up the drama at the very end. But he never appeared in the dramatizations.

The scripts appear to be solidly crafted, although some liberties were taken with historical facts. Both the acting and the sound effects were of high quality and demonstrated professionalism. One episode dealt with the relationship of Cochise, an Apache chief, and Thomas Jeffords, an Army scout and a stage coach driver. The two of them forged a peace treaty ending a bloody 12 year war in Arizona. The other recorded episode dramatizes a lesser known event: the early, and dangerous, exploration of the Colorado River through the Grand Canyon.

Both of these recordings contained the identities of the production staff: J. Clinton Stanley, director, Henry Russell, music, with Lou Fulton and Paul Pierce, writers, but the cast members were only named in the Cochise program. These actors included: Frank Graham, Joel Forte, Ken Christy, and Charlie Lung, all veteran radio performers. Graham was probably the most experienced; he had started out as a sports columnist, and then alternated between announcing and acting on network radio. He not only had the lead in *Romance of the Ranchos*, but he was also chosen as Jack Webb's replacement in the title role of *Jeff Regan, Investigator*.

Turning historical events into radio drama can result in errors, many of which may be attributed to dramatic license, carelessness, or deadlines. Jeffords, for example, was first an Army scout and much later, a stage coach driver, not the other way around as he was portrayed on the radio show. The correct name of the man who finally conquered the Colorado River was John Wesley Powell (1834–1902) not Wesley B. Powell, as he was repeatedly referred to in the recording. And while nerve damage to one arm, suffered in a Civil War battle, rendered the arm almost useless, Powell was not "a one-armed man." Incidentally, although none of the cast members in the Colorado episodes were identified in the recording; the actor who played Powell sounds very much like, and probably was, John Dehner.

Sources: Audio copies of the *Andy Devine Show*; Dunning, *On the Air*; Katz; *Sponsor*, October 1948, p. 71.

ARIZONA ADVENTURE

Karl Schadow *and* Jack French

This was a regional program from station KTAR in Phoenix which aired weekly from 1948 to 1954. The show's creator, writer and director was John McGreevey, an Indiana University graduate who settled in Arizona in 1944 and spent the rest of his career writing for radio and television. Each program in this series began with Wagner's "Overture to the Flying Dutchman," interrupted by a rifle shot and the announcer proclaiming "Arizona Adventure!" The programs dramatized famous persons and significant events in Arizona history; various programs featured the Earp brothers, Cochise, Sheriff John Slaughter, etc. While no audio copies have surfaced yet, over 250 original scripts are archived with the Arizona Historical Society in Tempe. Two scripts are also available in the Broadcast Arts Library.

Source: Personal correspondence with Norm Schickedanz, Tucson Old-Time Radio Club, February 2012.

Bill Cody, the Plainsman see *The Plainsman*

THE BLACK GHOST

JACK FRENCH *and* DAVID S. SIEGEL

NETWORK: Syndicated
FORMAT: 15 minutes, probably daily
DURATION OF RUN: Circa early 1930s
SPONSOR: Undetermined local sponsors
AUDIO COPIES EXTANT: 2, plus 2 in private collection
SCRIPTS ARCHIVED: Undetermined

The Black Ghost fits many of the characteristics of syndicated shows, including not identifying key members of the cast and production crew. And, as the musical introduction and conclusion of the four surviving episodes have been stripped from the recordings, nothing is known about the program's theme music. One of the few facts about the program that is known is that Barton Yarborough played the lead of Larry Brandin.

Using the name "Black Ghost" as a villain or hero was rather commonplace in the early years of show business. A stage drama, "The Black Ghost," played at the Chatham Theatre in New York City beginning in January 1845. *The Black Ghost Bandit*, a western melodrama featuring "Vivian Rich and an all-star cast," was a silent motion picture released in January 1915. But the production that may have given its name to the radio syndicated series was a popular 1932 RKO 12-chapter talking serial film which starred Lon Chaney, Jr. He played "The Black Ghost," a Zorro-like, masked hero who fought for justice in the West. Although the name of the serial was *The Last Frontier*, most fans referred to it as *The Black Ghost*. It seems possible that since this radio series was created about that same time, the transcription company borrowed the name of *The Black Ghost* and turned the hero into a villain.

This radio adventure begins when a cowpoke, Larry Brandin, drifts into Cameron City, a small western town run by Ace Cameron, who owns the bank, the saloon, and the hotel. Joe Haines, the local sheriff, has been unable for several months to capture a notorious robber, The Black Ghost. A ranger, Uncle Zack, is in town in an undercover capacity; he disguises himself by rubbing corn starch into his whiskers and wearing ragged clothing. Ace Cameron's beautiful daughter, Miss Sally, suspects Brandin might be a ranger also. Brandin, Zack, and Haines work secretly together to identify and capture The Black Ghost, who in the past has disappeared in a puff of smoke when pursued by a posse.

The script writing is fairly well done, especially for a syndicated series, many of which were churned out by hack writers under deadline. All of the main characters are interesting and well-drawn. With the exception of Miss Sally, they all speak in a colloquial, non-grammatical style. An example would be Brandin's first impressions of Cameron City: "She ain't a bad little town, but I knowed from what happened tonight that a peaceable gent like me ain't gonna get no repose. So I aim to locate in a place where there ain't no uncatched bandits."

Although the conversations are somewhat enjoyable, the sound effects were anything but. They were kept to a minimum and the few used were unrealistic. Hoofbeats, whether on gravel, a dirt trail, or a city street, all sounded the same and appeared to be elbows bumping on a wooden box. Rifle and pistol shots could not be told apart and were unconvincing; all of them resembled the noise created by slapping a piece of lathe on a leather cushion.

Most syndicated series of that era were produced and marketed in groups of 39 episodes so it's a safe assumption that *The Black Ghost* fell in that category. However, it's probable that most juvenile listeners gave up on this series at Episode #5, at which time the scripts ventured into chaste romance. In this episode, Brandin and Miss Sally get the whole program to themselves in a long trail ride that blossoms into mild flirting on the part of both. Brandin confesses "Sally is a right purdy name" and later admits, "I'd shore like to kiss you." Although he does not give her a smooch, the damage is already done, since most juvenile boys in the audience would have rolled their eyes in disgust and switched to another station. In that pre–World War II era, nothing was more discouraging to male youngsters than injecting romance into a western movie or radio show.

Barton Yarborough would go on to rise above this pedestrian syndicated series and would later win prominent roles on major network shows, including *One Man's Family*, *I Love a Mystery*, and *Dragnet*. It's even possible he may have left *The Black Ghost* off his resume.

Sources: Audio copies of *Black Ghost;* DeLong; *New York Dramatic Mirror*, December 30, 1914; *Journal Republican*, Lowville, NY, October 6, 1932; *New York Evening Mirror*, January 14, 1845.

BOB STERLING, AMERICAN RANGER

JACK FRENCH *and* DAVID S. SIEGEL

NETWORK: Syndicated
FORMAT: Half hour, weekly
DURATION OF RUN: Circa 1947, but may not have aired
SPONSOR: Sustaining
AUDIO COPIES EXTANT: 1 (audition)
SCRIPTS ARCHIVED: Undetermined

The grandiose introduction of this program by the announcer was a study in hyperbole:

"The early West of 1850 was a fabulous country where gold could be had for the taking, and men could become millionaires overnight. But it was also a lawless country where men lived by the rule of the gun. *[Sound of gunshot]* Against the forces of evil attracted by the easy wealth to be had, the defenders of law and order were almost helpless. *[Sound of gunshot]* The one bulwark standing between the settlers and the criminal element was a body of men who had dedicated their lives to the war against crime. These courageous men, who daily rode hand in hand with death, were the American Rangers. *[Sound of bugles]* And of all this group whose noble deeds became a tradition, the most outstanding was Bob Sterling. He could out-ride, out-rope and out-shoot *[sound of two gunshots]* any man west of the Rockies. But his life hung constantly by a hair for there was no western bad man who had not vowed to kill him at the first opportunity. But Bob Sterling seldom rode alone — his constant companions were fat, little Mexican, Pablo — as deadly with a knife as most men were with a gun *[sound of a swishing knife]* — and weather-beaten old Panhandle, who knew every trick of the gunfighter, including how to beat him to the draw by shooting through his holster. *[Sound of gunshot]*."

This single recording has confounded vintage radio researchers and collectors for many years, most of whom have cataloged it as a radio show recorded on March 19, 1935. Nearly every vintage radio dealer on the Internet offers it for sale using that date. But the recording contains three unusual elements indicating that it wasn't recorded in 1935 and that the true purpose of the recording was an audition for a kids' television cartoon.

(1) At its conclusion, the announcer says: "This telecast was produced by Eugene Conrad and directed by Charles B. Barrow."

(2) While many juvenile western radio programs incorporated a few stereotyped characters into the plot, *Bob Sterling, American Ranger* included every one in this category. They were: the deep-voiced hero, the grizzled old companion, the funny Mexican sidekick, the bumbling local sheriff, "the prettiest girl in town" who jilts the young deputy sheriff for the evil but suave banker, and a villain who is a headless horseman who leads a gang of ghostly klansmen.

(3) The outlandish derring-do of the hero and his two saddle buddies is more flamboyant that what even the juvenile listener would relate to on a radio show. Sterling and his two companions ride up to a ranch at the same time an eagle swoops down from the sky, grabs a baby from its crib, and soars aloft. From his galloping horse, the elderly sidekick kills the eagle with one shot, narrowly missing the baby. The infant tumbles swiftly from the sky as Sterling, standing in his saddle, rides toward the plummeting bundle. His arms are outstretched ("like a center fielder" the announcer tells listeners) and he adroitly catches the baby, saving it from certain death.

The cartoon series, *Bob Sterling, American Ranger*, began on local Chicago television in 1948, based on a presumed audition "telecast" that was produced in late 1947 or early 1948. Television station WBKB aired this half hour adventure cartoon on Sunday nights at 7:30 P.M. during the month of May. Whether the same actors that appeared in the audition recording were hired to voice the cartoon has not yet been determined. The only recognizable voice in the audition recording is that of Forrest Lewis portraying Pablo in much the same way he voiced Wash on the **Tom Mix** radio series.

A firm called American Television, Inc. at 5050 Broadway in Chicago, marketed *Bob Sterling, American Ranger*, as late as the summer of 1949, as a "video comic strip," which is what television cartoons were termed in that era. They advertised that thirteen half hour episodes were then ready and available for airing at an unstated "low cost."

Many sources claim that *Crusader Rabbit* was the first cartoon series aired on television since it was syndicated in 1949 and then aired on NBC-TV, beginning in August 1950. However it is clear that since *Bob Sterling, American Ranger* was airing in May 1948, it predated *Crusader Rabbit*.

Sources: Audio recording of *Bob Sterling, American Ranger*; Macdonnell, *Don't Touch*; *Broadcasting*, June 27 and 29, 1949; *Chicago Tribune*, May 2 and May 30, 1948.

BOBBY BENSON

JACK FRENCH

NAMES: *H-Bar-O Rangers, Bobby Benson's Adventures, Bobby Benson and Sunny Jim*
NETWORK: CBS
FORMAT: 15 minutes, 2–5 times weekly

DURATION OF RUN: September 26, 1932, to December 11, 1936
SPONSOR: Hecker H-O Cereals
AUDIO COPIES EXTANT: None
SCRIPTS ARCHIVED: Undetermined (but two in script anthologies: Dixon, *Radio Sketches* and Lawton)

NAME: *Bobby Benson and the B-Bar-B Riders*
NETWORK: Mutual
FORMAT: Half hour, 3–5 times weekly
DURATION OF RUN: June 21, 1949, to June 17, 1955
SPONSOR: Sustained for the run, except for January to June 1951 when sponsored by Kraft
AUDIO COPIES EXTANT: 20
SCRIPTS ARCHIVED: Private collection of Jim Shean family

NAME: *Songs of the B-Bar-B*
NETWORK: Mutual
FORMAT: 5 minutes, daily on weekdays
DURATION OF RUN: December 1951 to June 1952, and possibly in 1954
SPONSOR: Chiclets and Dentyne gum
AUDIO COPIES EXTANT: 5
SCRIPTS ARCHIVED: Undetermined

This 1932 western on CBS was one of the first juvenile shows on radio, predating *The Lone Ranger*, *Tom Mix*, and *Jack Armstrong*. When its second version on Mutual ended in 1955, it had virtually outlasted every other children's series, including *Superman*, *Captain Midnight*, **Sky King** and **Straight Arrow**, thus bookending the Golden Age of Radio.

The credit for creating this durable drama goes entirely to a British immigrant who had never been west of Detroit. Herbert C. Rice left his native England to seek his fortune in U.S. radio broadcasting in 1928 and found success in Buffalo, NY, as a director, writer, and actor. Prior to *Bobby Benson*, Rice had already created dozens of local radio drama series, including *Police Story*, *The Green Rose*, *Fearbound*, *The Cobra*, and *Cloud Trail*.

In the summer of 1932, the Hecker H-O Company of Buffalo approached Rice through its advertising agency, Erwin-Wasey, and offered to sponsor a kids' radio program to promote its cereal products. The "H-O" in their title suggested a cattle brand to Rice and he quickly drew up a story about an orphan named Bobby Benson under the guardianship of Sunny Jim. The latter character was the trade symbol for H-O cereals, a tall elderly man who resembled Ichabod Crane. In Rice's scenario, Bobby inherited a ranch in Texas called the H-Bar-O Ranch whose foreman was Buck Mason.

Hecker bought into the concept and Rice next convinced CBS to broadcast it nationally. He wrote several scripts and auditioned cast members in August 1932. An 11-year-old actor and son of a Buffalo attorney, Richard Wanamaker, won the lead. Rice, in addition to writing and directing the series, also voiced the roles of Buck Mason and Wong Lee, the Asian cook. Others in the cast were Fred Dampier and Lorraine Pankow, a local drama teacher and Rice's wife.

The series debuted on September 26, 1932, and its initial success was nothing short of phenomenal. Within a few months, the Hecker Company had to assign 12 women full-time to answer the fan mail and process the box tops of H-O Oats that arrived daily in exchange for premiums advertised on the show: Bobby Benson code books, cereal bowls, card games, and drinking tumblers. In addition to his microphone duties, the youthful Wanamaker, dressed up in cowboy attire, astride a pony named "Silver Spot," made personal appearances throughout the Buffalo area, all arranged by Herbert Rice. Bobby's nick-name was "The Cowboy Kid" and Rice promoted that also.

When the first season of 78 episodes ended in March 1933, CBS ordered the production moved to New York City, supposedly to ease technical problems in facilitating the national hook up. In addition, a second production with separate cast was organized in Los Angeles. The West Coast cast included George Breakstone (Bobby), Jean Darling (Polly), Lawrence Honeyman (Bart) and Muriel Reynolds (Aunt Lily).

The Manhattan cast was headed by 12-year-old Billy Halop, who not too much later, would achieve fame as the leader of the Dead End Kids on Broadway and in Hollywood. His younger sister, Florence, also an experienced juvenile actor, played Polly Armstead on the program. Buck Mason's name was changed to Tex Mason and he was voiced by Neil O'Malley. Lorraine Pankow was the only one from the Buffalo cast that made her way to New York City and she continued her role as Aunt Lily. Humor was provided by whoever was playing Windy Wales and Diogenes Dodwaddle.

Others in that cast were Eddie Wragge, Detmar Popper (who played Sunny Jim), Joe Wilton, John Shea, Jean Sothern, Craig McDonnell (who voiced Harka, an Indian) and Walter Tetley. An 18-year-old Bert Parks was also in the cast, as was David Dixon, the son of the head writer, Peter Dixon. Most of the actors would remain in the cast until the series was cancelled in 1936. Dixon wrote all of the episodes, with the exception of the 1934-1935 season when John Battle was the scriptwriter.

This was a modern western, in that although Bobby and his cowhands were on horseback a great deal, they also rode in automobiles and airplanes. In its promotional material the show was described as having "plenty of riding and fighting ... with Indians, Mexicans, and desperate outlaws." In the only two scripts that have been located, both in bound anthologies, the H-Bar-Rangers are preventing a jail escape in one episode and in the other, are in an airplane in a round-the-world race, with Bobby as the pilot.

Billy Halop received far more star treatment than Wanamaker did, in terms of publicity and personal appearances. Halop's photo was distributed as a radio premium and in summers he toured as Bobby Benson with the W. T. Johnson Circus Rodeo. In October 1935, he was one of the headliners in the World Championship Rodeo held in Madison Square Garden.

When Broadway beckoned, Halop left the radio show. He had won a role in "Dead End" playing a tough street kid; the rehearsals began in fall of 1935 so he gave up his Bobby Benson salary for one on the stage. Of course, the success of the dramatic play, which opened at the Belasco Theatre on October 28, 1935, kept it running until June of 1937. By that time, most of its cast, including Halop, was put under contract to make the movie version.

The departure of Halop from the leading role did not affect the popularity of *Bobby Benson* and it aired for another 16 months before it was cancelled in December 1936. Who played the lead for that last year and a half is still to be discovered.

It would be a little over a decade before *Bobby Benson* would be back on the air. But in the meantime, Hecker H-O Company continued the promotion of "The Cowboy Kid" through a series of comic strips and distribution of "Bobby Benson Money." Starting in

Florence Halop as Polly Armstead from *Bobby Benson and H-Bar-O Riders*, CBS 1934 (Jack French collection).

1937 and ongoing for at least two years, there were a series of comic strips (actually paid advertisements in that format) picturing Bobby in an adventure, each one ending with him finding a treasure, winning a valuable prize, or earning a large reward. In the comic strip, Bobby would then explain to the reader that he was giving this money back to anyone who bought Hecker's cereal, two and a half cents in Bobby Benson currency in every box, which was good in any store to buy candy, ice cream, etc. These "comic strip" advertisements appeared in newspapers throughout the Northeast.

Not until 1949 did "The Cowboy Kid" return to the airwaves for his second act. By that time Herbert Rice was a U.S. citizen working in New York City as a Vice President of the Mutual Network in charge of programming. Needing a half hour show for kids in Mutual's afternoon slot, he brought back Bobby Benson to the microphone. Unable at first to obtain a sponsor, Rice changed the name of the ranch to the B-Bar-B and trimmed down the cast to only five regulars, played by four actors. The production would use the studios of station WOR.

The versatile Craig McDonnell was again in the cast, playing both Harka and Irish with completely different voice characterizations. Ivan Cury, a talented 12-year-old with two years in the business, became the new Bobby Benson. The Tex Mason role was given to veteran performer Charles Irving. Rounding out the cast was Don Knotts, then in his mid–20s, who portrayed the old geezer, Walter Wellington "Windy" Wales. Knotts would go on later to become an Emmy Award winning actor on television.

The supporting cast had several of the best radio voices in Manhattan: Bill Zuckert, Earl George, Ross Martin, Gil Mack, Jim Boles, and his wife, Athena Lord, who played the cook, Tia Maria. In the summer of 1951, Bob Haag took over the role of Tex from Charles Irving.

A 31-year-old director, Bob Novak, was in charge, and Peter Dixon returned to write the scripts. But age and illness prevented him from keeping pace with the series and his son, David, was brought in to help. However the problem was not solved until Jim Shean arrived. A young man and military veteran, he took over the bulk of the script writing duties, and within a year, was the sole writer.

Sound effects were handled by Jim Goode, with occasional assistance from Barney Beck. One of Barney's duties was to scour Manhattan's produce district in order to obtain free crates and boxes to be later crushed to replicate the sound of a smashed door, broken fence, and shattered chair. There were plenty of gun shots on the show, so blank pistols were not practicable. WOR had provided a firing mechanism, a small metal box holding a number of blank cartridges, which could be fired electronically in sequence.

Animal sounds (horses, cows, dogs, mountain lions, etc.) were all voiced by Frank Milano. He had started doing animal sounds on stage with USO troupes and later found success in Hollywood voicing cartoons, including that of *Mighty Mouse*. Milano soon became one of the best in the business, doing both humorous characterizations, i.e. "Pepito Mosquito" and the very realistic animals sounds on the *B-Bar-B Ranch*. There he voiced Bobby's horse, Amigo, his dog, Hero, and Windy's pet skunk, Honeysuckle, in addition to cows, chickens, wolves, and an occasional cougar.

The announcers varied over the years: first Bob Emerick, then Bucky Cosgrove, and finally, and the longest one, "Cactus" Carl Warren. John Gart was the musical director and the program's theme song was "Westward Ho," a composition by Hugo Reisenfeld, written for the 1923 silent film, *The Covered Wagon*. The music was played different ways over the years as Mutual gradually clamped down on the budget. At first three live musicians were used, then merely an organist (either John Gart or Ernestine Holmes) and finally, just a transcription disk.

The series was successful and Mutual alternated it with a West Coast show, **Straight Arrow**, in the same time slot every other weekday. In an attempt to find a sponsor for the show, Rice sent Ivan Cury out to several personal appearances, including large department stores who were selling B-Bar-B merchandise, various festivals, and even the Macy's

Craig McDonnell dressed as Harka in a publicity shot for *Bobby Benson and the H-Bar-O Riders,* CBS, 1934 (Jack French collection).

Day Parade. But when Rice tried to send Ivan overseas (the show was very popular on Armed Forces Radio Service) his mother refused.

Rice then corralled a juvenile singer, Robert J. McKnight, put him in B-Bar-B attire, and sent him on a 10 day tour of NATO countries. Thereafter McKnight handled most of the personal appearances of "Bobby Benson" in the U.S. while Ivan continued to handle all the radio duties.

In early 1951, Ivan left the B-Bar-B for a better paying job on *Portia Faces Life* and more freelance work on network radio. McKnight was pressed into service in the WOR studio as the next Bobby Benson. While a good singer, he lacked radio experience, and soon, as his voice started to squeak into maturity, another replacement was sought.

Rice looked no farther than next door in Stamford, CT, where his nephew and niece lived with their parents; their father was Rice's brother who had followed him to the U.S. the prior year. Clive Rice, 10-years-old, was a fine singer, and after some diction lessons to "Americanize" his accent, he auditioned for the role under the professional name that Rice gave him, "Clyde Campbell." He got the job and became the new "Cowboy Kid."

Clive and his parents did not object to the personal appearances so Rice extended the range to include state fairs and related events in Florida, Iowa, South

Clive Rice (professional name Clyde Campbell) in 1952 publicity shot as *Bobby Benson* (Jack French collection).

Dakota, and Indiana. Sometimes Clive would be accompanied by Don Knotts as Windy and a country singer, Tex Fletcher who would portray Tex Mason. But whether or not they came on the tour, Clive was always chaperoned by Rice's executive assistant, Mary Jane Williams, who was disguised as his "tutor" in press releases.

This radio series was sponsored by Kraft Foods, usually promoting its candy, for the first six months of 1951. This turned out to be bad news for Clive since he was almost always expected to ride a horse at these promotional events and parades. The sponsor routinely passed out samples of its Kraft caramels to the kids so the mischievous juvenile attendees would throw the caramels at Clive's horse, frequently startling the animal and making it difficult for Clive to control him.

Some of the more serious moments for Clive and Mary Jane were their visits to schools, churches and hospitals. At one Midwestern hospital, one of the young patients was immobile in his bed and his eyes glistened with wonder as he talked to his hero. "Can I hold your pistol?" he asked earnestly. When Mary Jane nodded assent, Clive took his toy pistol out of its holster and extended it to the patient, whose frail fingers closed around it. The two boys chatted briefly and it was time to go to the next personal appearance so Mary Jane slowly extracted the six-gun from the patient's hand and put it back in Clive's holster as they departed. A nurse caught up with them and whispered to Mary Jane, "That's the first time he's executed any physical motion since he came to this hospital months ago."

Jim Shean continued to write the scripts and filled them with exciting tales of robberies, prairie fires, escaped convicts, wild horses, cattle rustling and border smuggling. For a change of pace, Shean asked Novak, the director, if he could write occasional humorous episodes, and after some discussion, they agreed that Shean could write every third

Bobby Benson Reunion at SPERDVAC circa 1994, from left: Don Knotts (Windy Wales); Bob Novak, director; Ivan Cury (Bobby Benson); and Jim Shean, head writer (Jack French collection).

program as a comedy. While the shows still had excitement and danger, they were funny. Usually the comedy episodes featured Windy Wales and his misadventures included getting the lead in a stage play of "Cyrano," being mistaken by a gang for a fugitive killer, and having an unwelcome suitor track him to the B-Bar-B when a lonely hearts club mixed up the mail.

Live radio always held the potential for accidents, which had to be quickly fixed. One such incident occurred when Clive's younger sister had come to attend the rehearsal and the live show. Just as the On the Air sign lit up, Clive developed a sudden nose bleed and when he held his head up, he couldn't see his script. His sister grabbed his script and joined the cast at the microphone. She delivered all his lines without a mistake until his nose bleed was contained and he could resume the role. Since her voice sounded so much like his, no one in the radio audience noticed the switch.

In December 1951 the makers of Dentyne and Chiclets approached the *Bobby Benson* team and asked about sponsorship. They said that while they could not afford to sponsor a full half hour show; they could do so only if the program was very short. Rice accepted their offer and a spinoff was created called *Songs of the B-Bar-B* which was only 5 minutes in length, including commercials.

Jim McMenney was in charge of producing these programs, including writing and directing. Most of them were done in his studio on transcription disks, usually recording up to a dozen in the same session. Each consisted of one western song from Clive and another by Tex Fletcher, with a "tall tale" by Don Knotts as Windy between the two songs. The duration of the run of this mini-series is not confirmed but it appears that it aired for several months in 1951 to 1952 with perhaps limited re-runs in 1954.

In addition to the various merchandizing items related to *Bobby Benson and the B-Bar-B Riders*, there were 20 issues of a Bobby Benson comic book published from 1951 to 1953. Both Ivan and Clive as "Bobby Benson" were the subjects of many articles in entertainment periodicals, including appearances on the respective covers. In 1954 *Air Trails Magazine*, promoted a contest to build the best model of the B-Bar-B ranch house, with the first prize winner getting a gold mine claim and a one month trip to Deadwood, SD. Even though the majority of entrants were young boys, it was a 12-year-old girl, Nancy Nibler, who was the first place winner.

In 1953, the Australian company, Grace Gibson Productions, recorded one audition episode of *Bobby Benson* entitled "The Ghost Rustlers" with an all-Australian cast. This episode begins with a brief retelling of the "origin story" of Bobby Benson and follows with mysterious rustlers who make herds of cattle disappear. The attempt to market *Bobby Benson* "down under" was unsuccessful, however, and the series never aired.

Sources: Audio copies of *Bobby Benson and the B-Bar-B Riders;* Dixon; Dunning, *On the Air*; Hickerson, *4th Revised*; Personal scrapbook of Richard Wanamaker; Personal scrapbook of Clive Rice; *Radiogram*, January 2007; *Sponsor*, May 22, 1950; *Courier*, Chatham, NY, February 1, 1951; *Brooklyn Daily Eagle*, September 26, 1932; *Los Angeles Times*, October 7, 1933; *Patriot*, Fulton, NY, April 7, 1938; *Variety*, June 29, 1949.

BOOTS AND SADDLES

KARL SCHADOW *and* JACK FRENCH

Based on novels and stories written by Edward Beverly Mann (1902–1989), this was a 15 minute syndicated program, marketed to be aired three times a week. Produced by Sam Hammer Radio Productions, New York, NY, the program was pitched primarily towards children, but this syndication firm also considered it suitable for family listening. Thus far, no contemporary evidence has been uncovered to establish that the program was actually aired by any stations.

Source: *Radio Daily*, May 23, 1940.

BUFFALO BILLY BATES

KARL SCHADOW *and* JACK FRENCH

The radio adaptation of stories which appeared in *Popular Western Magazine*, the program featured Buffalo Billy, a stock western-type character with appeal for both children and adults. The syndicated 30 minute program usually aired three times week and was produced by Cruger Radio Productions of Hollywood, CA. This transcribed program is known to have been broadcast in 1945.

Source: *Radio Daily*, July 26, 1945, p. 55.

CACTUS KATE

JACK FRENCH *and* DAVID S. SIEGEL

A 1937 quarter hour program that aired five days a week, this was a soap opera featuring a western heroine. In the leading role was Ethel Owen portraying Kate, as listeners might imagine Calamity Jane or Annie Oakley speaking like a typical cowboy. The series was a product of the Blackett-Sample-Hummert script factory and Midwesterners listened to this program courtesy of the General Mills company via WGN in Chicago. Supporting cast included Ray Jones, Margaret Shanna and Vic Smith. Since this was a soap opera, not a western adventure drama, long conversations tended to dominate short portions of action.

Source: *Variety*, March 24, 1937, p. 39.

CALIFORNIA CARAVAN

JACK FRENCH *and* DAVID S. SIEGEL

NETWORK: Don Lee Mutual, ABC
FORMAT: 15 minutes, weekly (1947); half hour, weekly (1948 to 1952)
DURATION OF RUN: 1947 to 1952
SPONSOR: California Physicians Service
AUDIO COPIES EXTANT: 3, plus 2 more in private collection
SCRIPTS ARCHIVED: Undetermined

Beginning June 19, 1947, this series was produced by station KHJ in Los Angeles, CA for the Don Lee-Mutual Network and broadcast only on the West Coast. This may have been built into the original contract since the primary sponsor, a health insurance company, was only interested in reaching potential customers in California. Although it is not known exactly when the company dropped its sponsorship, the show's final months were carried on ABC on a sustaining basis.

The sponsorship may also have dictated the subject matter of the scripts which had to be grounded in California. While it may not have been true for the entire run, the surviving five audio copies indicate the scripts involved real California based historical figures or were adapted from short stories set in California.

(1) "How Santa Claus Came to Simpson's Bar," how the discouraged residents of an isolated town brightened Christmas for a sick boy by bringing him unexpected toys. (Script by Beth Barnes, based upon a short story of the same name by Bret Harte.)

(2) "The Saga of Charlie Parkhurst," the true story of Charlotte Parkhurst who passed herself off for many years as a "rough and tough" male driver of a California stage coach. (Script by Karl Schlicter.)

(3) "The Poet of Oakland," a fictionalized version of the life of Edwin Markham who achieved fame through his 1899 poem, "The Man with the Hoe" and later fought for child labor laws. (Script by Richard Hill Wilkinson.)

(4) "The Outcasts of Poker Flat," a slightly sanitized version of an original story that told the tale of four immoral people who were banished into a California snow storm. (Script by Karl Schlicter, based upon a short story of the same name by Bret Harte.)

(5) "The Death of the Don," the story of a young girl who delivered the announcement of the death of the last California Don. (Script by Beth Barnes.)

Other early scripts related the story of the rainmaker who actually caused a flood and the unsuccessful attempt to introduce camels to the California desert. In addition to the writers above, Lee Roddy contributed several scripts to this series. Producer/director Lou Holzer had no difficulty in finding talented radio performers to fill out his cast, and many of his regulars went on to become prominent network actors. These included: John

Dehner, Virginia Gregg, Harry Bartell, Paul Frees, Irene Tedrow, Ken Christy, and Bob Purcell.

The original scripts and the adaptations were solid and well-paced. The program's musical theme and interior bridges consisted of the organ work of Milton Charles, who did an excellent job. The sound effects were kept to a minimum, but when utilized, were both realistic and appropriate.

The series holds the unique distinction of being the first radio program sponsored by physicians, since doctors were prohibited by ethical standards from promoting themselves through commercial advertising. However, in this case, the sponsor was an insurance company, organized and managed by the state medical association. So the announcer could introduce each program by saying: "The California Medical Association and your family doctor present... California Caravan!"

Sources: Audio Copies of *California Caravan*; Dunning, *On the Air*; Hart; *Old California Gazette*, May/June 2006.

CHIEF GRAY WOLF

Jack French *and* David S. Siegel

NETWORK: Syndicated, New England region
FORMAT: 15 minutes, varied days
DURATION OF RUN: Unknown, circa 1940
SPONSOR: Undetermined
AUDIO COPIES EXTANT: 2
SCRIPTS ARCHIVED: Undetermined

Comparatively little is documented about this series, and what is known about it can primarily be gleaned from an examination of the two audio copies in circulation. This was a 15 minute show produced by the Imperial Broadcasting Company apparently for syndication in the New England area. In one of the two shows, the announcer, Bill Cavanaugh, states that the broadcasting station is "The Voice of Central New England." Later, he identifies the station as what sounds like "WTHV" (the call letters are somewhat blurred in the transcription).

In that era, WTHV and sound-alike station WTHB were both located in the deep South, not New England. However there was a radio station WTHT in Hartford, CT, in that period, so the odds would seem to favor it as the broadcasting station.

The format of this program, featuring an actor known as Chief Gray Wolf, consisted of an Indian song (in tribal tongue), a story of Indian lore in English, and ending with an Indian song or prayer, in either English or a tribal tongue. While the actor was probably an Indian, his scriptwriter was a little careless with facts about Indian history and tribal locations. The beginning of each program, after the sound of drums and a coyote cry, had this introduction: "Here comes Chief Gray Wolf of the Chippewa Nation who brings the past to life with salutations from the Plains Indians." In actuality, the Chippewas, usually called Ojibway, occupied the north woods around the Great Lakes. They fished, hunted, and traveled in birch bark canoes. However, the Sioux or Lakota tribes roamed the Great Plains on horseback and hunted primarily buffalo.

Chief Gray Wolf addressed his juvenile audience as "my little braves and maidens" and taught his listeners Indian songs and prayers. But the majority of the 15 minutes was devoted to him telling a story, in which a few other actors would join in what became a dramatization. In one program, the spirit of the missing buffalo, voiced by an actor, speaks to an elderly Indian brave and neither of these two appears to be "doubled" by Chief Gray Wolf. In another episode, a young Indian boy named Red Plume is engaged in a question and answer session with the chief around the campfire which moves the story along.

The known subjects of three of the programs (the third is announced at the end of the second program) are: "Why the Buffalo Disappeared," "How the Pinto Pony Got His Spots," and "How the Chipmunk Got His Stripes." From these titles one might assume that the scriptwriter may have been leaning upon the *Just So Stories* of Rudyard Kipling (1865–1936.) These tales, first published in 1902, contained such stories as: "How the Leopard Got His Spots," "How the Tiger Got His Stripes," and "How the Camel Got His Hump."

It is apparent that either the scriptwriter, or Chief Gray Wolf, was attempting to mention almost every Indian tribe, in song, prayer, or story. In the two surviving audio copies, the chief mentions seven tribes: Hopi, Sioux, Navaho, Cheyenne, Chippewa, Omaha, and Arapaho. The dramatizations have little in the way of sound effects, mostly just a drum and an organ. A coyote howls at the beginning of the program but no other animal sounds appear in the two existing shows.

Possibly to test audience response, some offers were made to the juvenile listeners on behalf of the chief. His announcer said that Chief Gray Wolf would send you "your own Indian name" and the words to an Indian song if you would write him a card or letter in care of the radio station. A second free offer told listeners that responders would receive a picture of the chief and "his sister."

With the exception of Chief Gray Wolf and announcer Bill Cavanaugh, none of the cast or production crew is identified by name on either of the two recordings. However it is likely that Chief Gray Wolf is the same Indian who, in the 1941 to 1942 period, was making stage appearances at New York schools. An Albany, NY newspaper reported in October 1941 that the upcoming season of the Children's Theatre at Albany High School would include two performances by Chief Gray Wolf and his wife, Morning Star. They were scheduled to present an evening of songs, stories, and dances of the Sioux Indians on March 14 and 28, 1942.

In the summer of 1951, New York newspapers announced that two American Indians in full tribal regalia would greet the young campers at Camp Northwoods in Remsen, NY. The two, named as "Chief Gray Wolf and Princess Morning Star, television and radio performers," would be directors of Indian lore at the camp for the summer. It's possible that one of the teenaged camp counselors might have said to the chief, "I can remember listening to you on the radio."

Sources: Audio copies of *Chief Gray Wolf*; Harvey; *Daily Press*, Utica, NY, June 30, 1951; *Knickerbocker News*, Albany, NY, October 6, 1941; *Observer-Dispatch*, Utica, NY, July 2, 1951.

CIMARRON TAVERN

BOB BURNHAM

NETWORK: CBS
FORMAT: 15 minutes, five times weekly

DURATION OF RUN: April 1945 to September 1946
SPONSOR: Sustaining
AUDIO COPIES EXTANT: 2
SCRIPTS ARCHIVED: Undetermined

Cimarron Tavern was a juvenile western adventure serial heard daily on weekdays over the CBS radio network, usually in a time slot around 5 P.M. It featured four central characters: Morning Star Travis, a Federal scout; Randy Martin, a young orphan; and Pa and Ma Buford, who owned and operated the tavern. The action was located in Cimarron County, Oklahoma, and set in the late 1800s.

John Dietz directed the series. He was no stranger to CBS, having directed other network shows, including *Suspense*. The producer was Bob Shayon; prior to his duties with *Cimarron Tavern*, he had spent years at New York's radio station WOR, producing and writing shows for both Mutual and CBS. Shayon is perhaps best known for his later work with Edward R. Murrow.

Felix Holt wrote the scripts; he had started in Detroit at radio station WXYZ as a contributing writer to both **The Lone Ranger** and *Challenge of the Yukon*.

Despite the apparent incongruity of having a grown man and a young boy, unrelated to him, as partners in adventure and fighting crime, this scenario was not unusual in the radio world of juvenile western programming. There were several shows that utilized this premise, including **Tom Mix**, **Bobby Benson and the B-Bar-B Riders**, **Red Ryder**, **Rin-Tin-Tin**, and **The Adventures of Champion**. CBS scheduled *Cimarron Tavern* in the time slot next to its *The Sparrow and the Hawk*, an aviation adventure program pairing an experienced male pilot with a young boy.

Randy, whose parents were killed by Indians, naturally had a dislike for them, but Travis convinced him that there are good Indians and bad Indians, just like any other race. As in most juvenile westerns, the character's horses get a lot of attention. The scout's horse is a black stallion, Raven, named in honor of Sam Houston. It's a historical fact that having spent most of his youth living with the Cherokee, Houston was called "The Raven" by his Indian companions. The other horse of note in the series is Chief who belongs to Randy; Pa and Randy tamed this former wild mustang.

Paul Conrad played Morning Star Travis while Ron Liss was the voice of the youthful Randy. Others in the supporting cast were Ethel Everett, Stephen Courtleigh and Chester Stratton. The usual announcer was Bob Hite.

While it is not known who handled the sound effects on this program, they were done well, particularly the horses' whinnies and hoofbeats. All of the music, both main theme and scene bridges, was the work of one organist, and the results were quite satisfactory.

The fact that only two audio copies have survived and the scripts have not yet been located prevents knowing how the series progressed during its 18 month run on the air.

Sources: Audio copies of *Cimarron Tavern*; Dunning, *On the Air*; Hickerson, *4th Revised*; Swartz.

THE CISCO KID

WILLIAM NADEL

NAME: *The Cisco Kid* (Series 1)
NETWORK: Mutual (East Coast WOR origination)

FORMAT: Half hour, weekly
DURATION OF RUN: Intermittently from October 1942 to February 1945
SPONSOR: Unknown
AUDIO COPIES EXTANT: 329
SCRIPTS ARCHIVED: Undetermined

NAME: *The Cisco Kid* (Series 2)
NETWORK: Ziv Syndication, and Mutual Don Lee
FORMAT: Half hour, sometimes several shows a week
DURATION OF RUN: Approximately fall 1947 to about 1959
SPONSOR: Local sponsors
AUDIO COPIES EXTANT: Over 400 of approximately 800 recorded programs
SCRIPTS ARCHIVED: Voice of America Museum; Collections of Media Heritage, Inc., Cincinnati OH; American Heritage Center

William S. Porter, writing under the name O. Henry, was one of the greatest American authors of the first decade of the 20th century. Among his creations were: Jimmy Valentine, the Cisco Kid, the eternal American Christmas tale, "The Gift of the Magi," and hundreds of other stories with his classic twist at the end. But Porter was also an alcoholic, a consumptive, an ex-convict, an embezzler, and probably a drug addict. He relied on alcohol and other substances to ease the growing pain in his lungs. On many occasions his family members tried to "dry him out," but to no avail. Born in North Carolina in 1862 into a family plagued with tuberculosis, Porter became a licensed pharmacist at the age of 19.

Moving to Texas to live in a better climate, the young William became a cowboy on a sheep and cattle ranch. In Austin, he met and married his first wife. Soon he got a job in an Austin bank, while writing and publishing his own satiric newspaper. When his accounts at the bank showed a shortage, his wife's father offered to make good on the missing money, but the case was referred to a federal grand jury. While the jury did not indict him, pressure from the people he had offended forced an eventual trial and Porter was found guilty and imprisoned. He was also found guilty of taking money from his accounts on a day when he wasn't even at the bank. Although probably guilty of stealing some money, Porter took the blame for most of the other thefts that had occurred.

During the roughly three years he was in jail, Porter honed his writing skills and functioned as a prison pharmacist. By 1902 Porter started using the name O. Henry and moved to New York City, what he called his "Bagdad on the subway." Although he tried to hide his identity, his family members knew who he was, and with mixed feelings they followed his success. In 1910, O. Henry died in poverty, a victim of tuberculosis, drugs, alcohol, and diabetes. His funeral was at New York's Little Church Around the Corner in the author's favorite neighborhood. A plaque honoring him is on its inner wall. O. Henry died with the fond wish that his tales would live on long after him.

The Cisco Kid made his first appearance in "The Caballero's Way," one of a series of tales in the book *The Heart of the West* published in 1907. An adventurer and gunslinger who "could shoot five-sixths of a second sooner than any sheriff or ranger in the service," the Kid made his home along the Texas-Mexican border. He was an American named Goodall who looked younger than his age and loved a Mexican woman who would betray him. The tale was so successful that it eventually spawned no fewer than 28 films, 156 half hour TV shows, and about 900 radio adventures. And somehow the Cisco Kid turned into a Mexican hero. The movies presented him as a version of a Latin lover, passionate and adventurous in the persons of Warner Baxter, Cesar Romero, Gilbert Roland, and Duncan Renaldo. Renaldo took the character into television in the 1950s, and Jimmy Smits later took him into the made-for-TV movie world.

In 1942 *The Cisco Kid* came to radio in the person of Jackson Beck. Beck had been in the broadcasting medium since 1931; he also played the voice of Bluto in Popeye animated cartoons. In fact, his Cisco Kid was a kinder version of Bluto with a Mexican accent, but there was still an edge in his portrayal. (Beck worked steadily in radio and voiceovers until just before his death in 2004 at the age of 92.)

In a typical adventure, Cisco is lured into a trap by a woman posing as his sister, while his sidekick Pancho is "fleeced" by a con man working a shell game. This episode, airing from New York on the Mutual Network, had Louis Soring as Pancho; and John Sinn was the writer. The director was Jock Macgregor; the show aired December 12, 1942. From October 1942 until February 1945 nearly 100 adventures were presented from New York. Among the other directors for the series were Alvin Flanagan and Jeanne Harrison; Ralph Rosenberg, Jr. also contributed some of the scripts. One of the most risqué juvenile programs ever broadcast, the Cisco Kid romanced every charming woman, although often it was the woman who threw herself at the Kid.

The program resurfaced on the West Coast in 1947. Another Jack, Jack Mather, was selected to play the O. Henry-derived character. Mather entered radio in the 1920s, after having joined a circus as a youth. Born on a farm outside Chicago, the actor kept running away from home and tried football, auto racing, wrestling, and construction. He even worked as a trader in the Chicago stock exchange. In 1929 he was at NBC. A cast member of the *First Nighter* show, he went to Los Angeles when the show moved to California. He also appeared in many TV shows and such classic films as *The Bravados* and *Some Like It Hot.* Few knew that Jack was of Crow Indian descent, even though he played in western TV shows. Mather became the perfect Cisco on the airwaves, channeling the warmth of Duncan Renaldo from the films with his own unique warmth. The shows were fun to hear and this Cisco was an adventurer, friend, avenger of wrongs perpetrated by the greedy or wicked on the helpless and unsuspecting, and the ideal hero for women looking for that valiant, exciting man. Many shows featured the Kid's superb marksmanship and prowess at beating up the evildoers. Mather died on August 15, 1966, at the age of 58, after acting in about 800 *Cisco Kid* episodes.

Aiding Mather in his exploits was the talented Harry Lang as Pancho. Lang had been a bit actor on radio since 1936. He appeared on the screen in *Bad Boy* and was a regular on the Jack Haley and Joe Penner radio shows. For more than seven years he was the faithful "compañero" to Cisco. And in one of the most ironic occurrences ever, both Lang and Mather died of heart attacks at the age of 58. Lang was heard in about 600 episodes. His replacement was none other than the vocal comic Mel Blanc, who by the 1950s was one of the most familiar of all voices, due to his work with Jack Benny and the characters he played in many Warner Bros. cartoons. Blanc was first heard as a comic relative of Pancho during Lang's initial illness; then he slipped into the role of Pancho. Sometimes he was very effective, but often he became more of a squeaky cartoon-like version of Pancho, which was jarring when heard with the other actors in dramatic situations.

Syndicated by Fred Ziv, about 400 of the 800 or more West Coast episodes are known to survive. These shows exist mainly as Ziv syndication or as Armed Forces Radio Service disks. With Mather on his trusty steed Diablo and Lang on Loco, Cisco and Pancho rode fictionally throughout the airwaves of the last 30 years of the 19th century — on the radio!

Very few cowboy programs of that era dealt with mental illness, but on at least one episode (program #52) from about 1948, Herb Butterfield as Mr. Davis has a mental breakdown after a leg injury and vows to kill Cisco and Pancho, who were his friends. The poor man is so far out of touch with reality that he begins to shoot the sheriff and his other friend Neil, portrayed by Barton Yarborough. Eventually he stalks Pancho and captures him, thinking that Cisco's amigo is the man who shot him in the leg. Cisco, taking pity on the disturbed man, prevents the sheriff from killing him, rescues Pancho, and, as the Kid puts it: "A wound on the body can cause a wound of the mind."

Herb Butterfield was frequently on the program, appearing as Mr. Morris, a gullible purchaser of worthless land in Dixon Flats, in "Pancho and the Parrot" (program #49). When the land turns out to have a vein of gold on it, its original owner goes to great lengths to reclaim its deed. Fortunately, a parrot sees, hears, and mimics the thieves' efforts, thereby informing Cisco of the truth. Butterfield returned as the gullible Chicago-based Professor Carlson in "Mummy in the Desert" (program #78). This time, Butterfield buys a mummy that has been buried in the West by two con men. When jewels are found in the mummy case, the con men do their best to get the gems. Butterfield became Marshal Adams in "Blazing Guns at Lone Bend" (program #96), asking Cisco to stop a fight between nesters and cattlemen. In the same episode, Tony Barrett, as Bud Cushman, is intent on creating trouble, only to be thwarted by the valiant duo. In "The British Come to Brimstone" (program #215), Cisco and Pancho have their hands full with an uppity Englishwoman and Butterfield plays the sheriff; at the end of the ordeal, Cisco wants a kiss from the elitist English lady.

Herbert Rawlinson, another familiar face from the movies, also frequently appeared on the program matching wits with Cisco. In "The British Come to Brimstone" he played the greedy Rex Parker who wants to conceal his cattle thievery as well as get the ranch, while as Tom Caine, a traveler to Cottonwood Center in "Deputy Marshal" (program #335), he robs a stagecoach while en route to claim his legacy from his dead brother.

Barton Yarborough was another of those great radio actors who appeared on the program. In "Masquerade" (program #130) Yarborough played Jolly Dukes who, with his partner Tom, has the perfect plan for robbing stagecoaches. They will impersonate Cisco and Pancho during their robberies, placing the blame for the thefts and murders on the heroic duo. In the end, the Kid and his compañero catch Jolly with the fake costumes and stolen loot. As Blaze Keller in "The Ace of Hearts" (program #250), Yarborough sends playing cards to those he plans to kill — Sheriff Dixon's family, including Peggy Webber as Ruth. He almost succeeds with his crazy plan of vengeance. Tragically, Yarborough died in December 1951, half-way through *The Cisco Kid* series.

Another one of radio's talented voices also died during that month — veteran actor Wally Maher. This fact helps date the numbered Ziv disks. Maher appeared in "Hoodoo Driver" (program #100) as Blake Lee. Blake wants Cisco dead in this tale of Bull Whip Martin, a stage driver who is cursed with bad luck. Maher returned for a final farewell in "Messenger of Doom" (program #331) recorded shortly before his death. As Logan in this exploit, Maher is an accomplice to Cora and Monk Gamill in their scheme to rustle cattle from the Barstows. Cisco likes Barbara Barstow, and at night, after the cattle are saved, Cisco and Barbara smooch.

No one was more adept at playing slimy villains on the series than Lou Krugman. In "The Duel" (program #94), Krugman played Duke, a bank robber and killer. When George Wayne, an innocent man, is tricked into accompanying Duke during a bank robbery, George finds himself accused of the crime and is about to be hanged when Cisco and Pancho make it their business to find Duke. A master with the rapier, and with thievery, Duke challenges anyone who crosses his path to a duel and Cisco abandons his guns for a sword fight with the villain. Cisco wins (of course) while Pancho finds the stolen bank bonds that will save George from the hangman's noose. Krugman also played Richie, a gunslinger out to kill the Kid when he and his partner catch up with Cisco in Adobe City in "Tin Horn Killer" (program #217). And, as Reed Larson, an escapee from the Arizona Territorial Penitentiary in "The Manhunt" (program #274), Krugman's character wants to help his friend Scarp get the man who arrested him — Cisco. In still another episode, "The Handsome Bandit" (program #419), Krugman portrays an ugly thief named Squint Dane "who accompanies another scoundrel as handsome as he is wicked."

Willis "Bill" Bouchey was a popular actor who is best remembered for his many appearances as a judge on the *Perry Mason* TV show. He lent his talents to three wonderful Cisco exploits. When Prudence Carey refuses to sell her land to thug Sol Benson (played by Bouchey) in "Devil Town" (program #98), Benson decides to do all he can to throw her off her land; but for the presence of Cisco and Pancho he would have been successful. In "Outlaw Trail" (program #216), Bouchey, as Al Montana, covets the gold strike of George Hammond. His attempt to enrich himself and his partner is thwarted by the western duo, but Al vows to knife Cisco. Into this chaos steps the sheriff (played by Francis X. Bushman) who nearly gets Cisco and Pancho killed by Al and his cohort. Bouchey was also the cattle rustler Jack Downes in "Pueblo Justice" (program #420) who wants Cisco and Pancho to join his gang; of course Cisco refuses and helps trap the crooks.

Jay Novello, diminutive on the screen, specialized in playing effete foreigners. In "Murder Wagon" (program #260), he played Pierre Du Lac, an arsonist thief who loves to steal rings and other items and then destroy all the evidence of his crimes as he and his accomplice ride away; Cisco gets into the fray when Pierre tries to steal the rings of a waitress. In "The Gunslinger" (program #279), Novello is the gunslinger Hub Barris out to kill Cisco and beats him in a gunfight. The gunman is out to find the murderer of a man called Vin. Only the murderer is quicker than the Novello character, but not smart enough to outwit the Mexican hero! As Jerry the blacksmith in "Dead Man's Gold" (program #322), Novello was out for vengeance on Cisco and vows to kill him with a red-hot iron.

During the Ziv years, Cisco evolved from the Latin lover to a western knight, sometimes taking on the role of a criminal to join with and eventually bring crooks to justice. But even in this guise Cisco is always honorable and actually on the side of law and order. Always the defender of the weak and the oppressed, Cisco stands up for a traveling band of gypsies when many of their number are gunned down by racist cowboys ("The Law of the Dead," program #323). Cisco even puts his life on the line with the gypsies, when he fights one of them in order to gain a fair trial for one of those racist cowboys. The romantic kissing was toned down during the Ziv years, but Pancho was often finding himself chased by some woman. His main girlfriend was Big Maria, and she is referred to in many shows. A close call for Pancho comes in "Pancho Escapes" (program #282) when he almost winds up marrying Maria. But Pancho gets away, just in time!

There are few other re-occurring characters in the adventures. The most interesting of these is Morbid Jones. Jones is a gloomy, thin man married to a heavy, bossy wife. They are always arguing and their problems seem to ensnare Cisco and Pancho. Portrayed by Herb Vigran, Morbid Jones occurs in at least five exploits, starting with "The Saga of Morbid Jones" (program #95). Today, Vigran is best remembered as a villain in the *Superman* TV show. Vigran had previously appeared in "The Feud" (program #60) as Doc Moran, a crook who plans to derail a train and steal its gold cargo; and in "Fire in the Night" (program #76) where he played Slade Cummings, a victim of a coercive scheme to steal his home and property.

Every so often the series would present a show that was unique for its title and plot. "3-7-77" (program #97) was one such tale. The title represents the dimensions of a grave. A man named Gus Benz hands his victims little tin pieces with those numbers on them. They are a talisman for those members of a jury who convicted Benz of murder. Benz murders the sheriff of the town of Lucifer and plans to kill all surviving jury members, and also Cisco. Peggy Webber plays Ann Lincoln, the daughter of a jury member and the valiant defender of her crippled father.

On other occasions a stellar cast would make the exploit memorable. "Prophet of Boot Hill" (program #101), for example, featured Frank Lovejoy, Junius Matthews, Howard McNear and Sam Edwards. The plot deals with bank robbers hiding their cache of gold in an old prospector's cabin. The prospector can predict the future and predicts his own death, at the hands of the bank robbers.

Howard McNear, best remembered as Doc on *Gunsmoke*, made several guest appearances with Cisco and Pancho. As Sheriff Nolan, he keeps arresting the duo in "Passport to Death" (program #334), and in "A Killer Quits" (program #418), McNear, as Rance Higgins, mistakenly goes after the pair for revenge. In the first adventure, Cisco sums up his feelings about Americans: "No one hombre or group of hombres can ever set themselves up to rule over another. That is what the people of these United States believe and that is what they will fight for."

The most familiar "cowboy" actor to appear on the show was John Dehner. He was the lead in two other western series: *Frontier Gentleman* and *Have Gun — Will Travel*. However, on *The Cisco Kid* program he was Ted Grindle in "The Double" (program #135), impersonating Cisco, whom he resembles. As Neil in "Gold in the Conestoga" (program #288) Dehner impersonates another character named Will Dunbar. "The Battle of the Lost Mine" (program #330) has the actor trying to wrest control of a gold mine from its rightful heirs. Dehner also appeared as Pecos in "The Marshal of Goldfield" (program #478) in which Cisco and Pancho had the unenviable task of taming the town.

Significant changes occurred in the show between 1953 and 1957. The ailing Harry Lang was replaced by Mel Blanc, and eventually, Jack Mather took over the role of announcing the program, greeting the listeners with "Hola amigos! This is the Cisco Kid!" Mather would then go on to narrate the current exploit. Canned musical bridges using the show's themes replaced the familiar organ interludes. The program also became a venue during its last couple of years for Hollywood newcomers. One of these performers was the very beautiful and talented Joanna Moore, who appeared in several episodes in 1956. In "Border Justice" Moore is Molly Barton, an undercover government agent functioning as a mole in El Paso in a smuggler's gang that Cisco and Pancho are investigating. In the very strange biblical parable "Uncle Noah's Ark," Moore is the daughter of Uncle Noah, who spends his time outside the lawless town of Woodland, California building an ark for the time of the flood, which actually comes at the end of the adventure.

Toward the end of the show's run, scripts were reused with slightly changed titles and minor alterations. Thus "The Hook Murders" (program #496) with Barney Phillips as a greedy sheriff killing off the members of his family with a sharpened hoof pick in order to clear his way to an inheritance later became "The Hoof Pick Killer" during Mel Blanc's years portraying Pancho.

Commercial network radio breathed its last gasps towards the end of the 1950s, as did Cisco and Pancho, but one of the final exploits is worth noting. In San Antonio, the cowboy duo runs into an early plastic surgeon who has transformed the faces of a couple of wanted criminals in "Two Faces of Death," a western adventure that rivals any horror tale.

During its many years on the air, several things changed about this series, but its popular signature sign-off remained consistent: the finale which featured the duo joking around and chuckling as they exclaimed, "Oh, Pancho!" ... "Oh, Cisco!"

Sources: Audio copies of *Cisco Kid*; Barbour; Hart; Hickerson, *4th Revised*; Nivens, *Films of the Cisco Kid*; Nivens, *Cisco Kid*.

COLORADO COWBOYS

KARL SCHADOW *and* JACK FRENCH

Initially without sponsor, this 1931 program on Denver station KOA later obtained the sponsorship of Morey Mercantile Company. Its general format was a fairly standard mix of western music intertwined with a thinly plotted dramatization. The mythical location for this series was the Flying M Ranch and most of the action occurred in the bunkhouse. To their credit, the cast of five performers managed to sound like 10 different characters. Overall, the action was very limited. In a typical episode, the cowboys had fun at the expense of a newly arrived tenderfoot by pretending that he will have to participate in the hunt for a nonexistent wild animal.

Source: *Variety*, September 15, 1931, p. 58.

COVERED WAGON DAYS

KARL SCHADOW *and* JACK FRENCH

Author Bob Redd wrote the original scripts for this program, which originated in 1931 on station KEX-KGW in Portland, OR. The plot line of this western followed a fictional group of pioneers who left the Midwest to settle in Oregon territory in 1850, experiencing the frontier hardships of that period. When Redd left the program, he was replaced as scriptwriter by Dave Drummond, who in turn was succeeded by Fred White. While each episode related a complete story, the same four protagonists appeared throughout the five years. The cast included Mark Daniels, Joe Hallock, Francis Herrick, Harry Davis, Ted O'Hara, Lawrence Keating, Dorothy Folger, Isabel Errington and preschooler Cora May Christopher. Playing the romantic lead was Chet Huntley, later to achieve fame as a newscaster on TV's *Huntley and Brinkley*. The program was sponsored for part of its long run by Gevurtz Furniture Company in Portland and its regular announcer was Phil Irwin. Fan mail indicated that *Covered Wagon Days* had one of the largest audiences of any program aired in the Northwest and it aired through 1936. Approximately 30 of its scripts are currently archived at the Library of Congress but no audio copies have surfaced.

Source: Kramer.

COVERED WAGON DAYS

JACK FRENCH

A second series with the same name, this *Covered Wagon Days* was a syndicated program that Fran Striker, Sr., created and wrote from his home in Buffalo, NY, beginning about 1930. The leading character, a happy-go-lucky cowboy, would become the precursor of *The Lone Ranger* produced at WXYZ in Detroit. The original hero laughed and sang through his western adventures and used silver-tipped arrows. Another character in this series was a half-breed named Gobo.

Source: Osgood.

COWBOY TOM'S ROUND-UP

JACK FRENCH

A juvenile western sponsored by Remington Rand, the program aired weekdays 1933 to 1936 in the late afternoon over station WINS in New York and later on NBC. It was a variety program of music, western tales, and comedy. Playing the title role was George Martin as an elderly prairie philosopher who related stories about the Old West. Tex Ritter sang cowboy songs on the program and played the romantic lead, if the script called for such. Two unknown actors portrayed a couple of Indians, respectively, "Chief Shunatona" and "Shookum." Despite the rather simplistic content, it was very popular with its northeastern audience. It even generated a publication that eager young buyers put out a hard-earned 50 cents to purchase. *Cowboy Tom's Round-Up Book* contained music and words to many songs, plus instructions for playing the harmonica and the ukulele, Pawnee words with English translation, how to spin a rope (instructions by "Cheyenne" Al Macdowell), and cowboy terms and phrases explained by Tex Ritter.

Source: O'Neal.

Curley Bradley, the Singing Marshal see **The Singing Marshal**

DARROW OF THE DIAMOND X

JACK FRENCH *and* DAVID S. SIEGEL

NETWORK: NBC (West Coast)
FORMAT: Half hour, weekly
DURATION OF RUN: 1950 to April 1951
SPONSOR: Sustaining
AUDIO COPIES EXTANT: 2
SCRIPTS ARCHIVED: Undetermined

This series, from station KPO in San Francisco, arrived in 1950 which was a little too late for a routine western to secure a lengthy run on network radio. It had some strengths, including the talents of the NBC Players, who could perform a variety of needed accents skillfully. Another valuable linchpin to the series was one of the best sound men in the Bay area, William "Bill" Brownell. Tony Freeman handled all the musical duties and Phil Walker was the announcer.

The scripts of the two existing audio episodes were a little weak. Nearly every exciting event on the program appeared "off stage," that is, one character would tell another later what had transpired. Example: the villain fell off a steep cliff to his likely death but was miraculously snagged by a tree. Since the others on the cliff above could not see him, the villain broke off a limb and sent it crashing into the gully. Hearing that sound, his pursuers concluded his lifeless body was at the bottom of the gorge. The villain then clambered to safety unseen. But the radio audience was not privy to this until the villain later described the event.

Another exciting bit of action was not performed by the actors, but merely recited by one of the participants later. The villain was about to begin a forced march while Darrow and his sidekick ride their horses behind him. But before the journey began, the villain spooked the sidekick's horse, and then leapt into the empty saddle, and galloped away with Darrow in pursuit on his own horse. Again, the network listeners heard nothing of this excitement as it transpired; they merely heard the sidekick talk about it later to the other cowpokes.

Samuel Dickson, who wrote and directed this series, was responsible for the snail's pace at which each program dragged along. In the first 10 minutes of one surviving episode, Darrow and companion, William Shakespeare Hawkins, were on a mountain awaiting the arrival of Snowden, the villain. For 5 minutes, Darrow, with drawn six-guns, boasted to Hawkins how he will kill Snowden. Hawkins keeps interrupting with Elizabethan phraseology while Darrow repeatedly tells him to shut up so he rambles on with his threats.

Snowden finally made the summit and another 5 minutes elapsed while Darrow spouted lengthy insults against the unflappable Snowden. "Yore a snake; yore the lowest life, an ill-begotten blasted piece of slimy crawling flesh that ever crept from under a log and messed up a purdy good world." So one third of the script was used up in lengthy conversation that barely advanced the plot.

This was certainly not typical of Dickson's work. He had started as a staff writer for KYA in San Francisco in the 1920s and by the 1950s was the second most popular and productive radio writer in that area (topped only by Carlton E. Morse.) Dickson wrote several lengthy and respected series including, *Hawthorne House, This is Your Home*, and *The California Story*.

Another interesting scene is only described, not dramatized. Mary, the ranch owner's daughter, tells of how her invalid father tried again to walk but his legs could not support him and he crumpled to the floor. Mary rushed to cradle him in her arms. From this scene, it was apparent that Dickson was recycling plots from his **Saunders of the Circle X** which he'd written a decade earlier. This identical scene appeared in that 1941 series, except that the ranch owner fell into his daughter's arms because he was temporarily blind, not because of an infirmity in his legs.

Dickson obviously liked to insert unusual characters into his ranch life westerns. In the *Saunders* series, the leading character is Singapore Bill, who after a lifetime on the high seas, spoke with nautical phraseology that confused most of the cowhands. For the Darrow series, Dickson created William Shakespeare Hawkins (the voice of John Grover) who emoted only in Elizabethan English, quoted and misquoted the Bard of Avon, and generally befuddled all of his fellow ranch hands.

This device further slowed up every scene Hawkins was in, since after every fanciful statement, he was asked for a translation. He replied with an equally obtuse declaration and then was requested to restate it in plain talk. Hawkins then provided an equally convoluted explanation so that some of his listeners were still scratching their respective heads.

Since the *Darrow* series was produced in the same period and same station as *Candy Matson, YU 2-8209*, it was inevitable that there was significant overlap in the cast and production crews. Henry Leff, who portrayed Candy's love interest, Lt. Mallard, also played Snowden, the villain, in this western series. The facile tongue of Lu Tobin was utilized for a variety of unusual accents in both series; on Darrow, he played both Larimore and Wong Lee, the Chinese cook. Bill Brownell, either by himself or with an assistant, produced all the sound effects on both series.

Jack Grover, who played Hawkins, was also the backup announcer on Candy Matson. Other actors who appeared in both series were: Jack Cahill, Jerry Walter, Mary Barnett, and Kurt Martell. Barnett voiced the rancher's daughter while Martell had the title lead.

Documentation is lacking on the date that *Darrow* began airing, although there were at least sixteen weekly episodes aired. NBC cancelled it, along with other low-rated San Francisco shows, according to *Variety* in April 1951.

Sources: Audio copies of *Darrow of the Diamond X*; French, *Private Eyelashes*; Hickerson, *4th Revised*; *Radiogram*, March 1992; *Variety*, April 4, 1951.

DEATH VALLEY DAYS

Stan Claussen

NAMES: *Death Valley Days, Death Valley Sheriff, The Sheriff*
NETWORK: NBC Blue; NBC; CBS; ABC
FORMAT: Half hour, weekly
DURATION OF RUN: *Death Valley Days*: September 30, 1930, to August 3, 1944; *Death Valley Sheriff*: August 10, 1944, to June 23, 1945; *The Sheriff*: June 29, 1945, to September 14, 1951
SPONSOR: Pacific Coast Borax Company
AUDIO COPIES EXTANT: 4
SCRIPTS ARCHIVED: Special Collections Library, University of Oregon at Eugene; Broadcast Arts Library

Death Valley Days, an anthology show which told stories about pioneer life in the Old West, was one of network radio's earliest and longest lasting programs (1930 to 1945). The series was created by Ruth Woodman née Cornwall (1894–1970) who took great pains to find and interview actual participants in the settlement of the western frontier. The series was sponsored throughout its entire run by the Pacific Coast Borax Company and its 20-Mule Team products Borax and Boraxo. After its radio run, the program was syndicated on television from the 1950s to the 1970s, making it one of the longest western programs in broadcast history.

Originally broadcast from San Francisco on the Blue Network of NBC, in 1941 the program moved to CBS; and in 1944 was retitled *Death Valley Sheriff* until 1945. Thereafter, it was simply *The Sheriff* with story lines more suitable to post World War II America; the sponsor decided that horses would be replaced by cars and trucks. From 1945 to 1951, the program was heard on ABC, formerly the Blue Network of NBC. And in 1951, two new sponsors replaced Borax: Proctor & Gamble and the American Chicle Company.

When *Death Valley Days* moved to CBS in July of 1941, it was touted as a "Program Premiere" for the "oldest dramatic half hour program on the networks." Since its first network broadcast in 1930, *Death Valley Days* had presented 600 "true stories of the old and new West," ranging in plots from fast-moving melodrama to simple human comedy with "every one based on fact, diligently traced to its sources and carefully checked." CBS asserted that because of its reputation for accuracy in broadcasting the dramatic history of the development of the West, *Death Valley Days* was recommended by teachers to their students wherever it was heard to supplement their studies at school.

The character who narrated *Death Valley Days* was "The Old Ranger," an ageless, traditional but fictional prospector, who was born in a prairie schooner and drove one of the 20-mule teams owned by the Borax company. He hobnobbed with desert rats, desperadoes, and dance-hall girls, and he knew the country he talked about and the people who inhabited it.

Over the years, the narrator was played by Jack MacBryde, Tim Daniel Frawley, George Rand, and Harry Humphrey. Two other characters, the Lonesome Cowboy and the Old Prospector, were played respectively by John White and Harvey Hays. Walter Scanlan and Florence Ortman directed, and the producer was Dorothy McCann. Ruth Woodman created the series and wrote the scripts; she was later assisted by Ruth Adams Knight. Sound effects were the work of Bob Prescott and Keene Crockett. The bugle call at the opening was performed by Harry Glantz and the music was supplied by Joseph Bonime. The announcers were Dresser Dahlstead, George Hicks, and John Reed.

In *The Sheriff*, Sheriff Mark Chase of Canyon County, CA, was played in turn by Robert Haag, Don Briggs and Bob Warren. Olyn Landrick, a male, played Cassandra "Cassie" Drinkwater, the sheriff's female cousin — a character added for comedy relief. Professor Barnabas Thackery was played by William Podmore, and the sheriff's daughter, Jan Thackery, was played by Helen Claire. Milton Lieberthal joined Ruth Woodman in writing these scripts. John Reed King was the announcer. John Wilkinson was added to the directorial team of Walter Scanlan and Florence Ortman. The bugle call by Harry Glantz and the music of Joseph Bonime survived from the original *Death Valley Days*.

It would be difficult to imagine a less likely candidate to create and write a western anthology than Ruth Woodman. Born Ruth Pond Cornwall in Brooklyn, NY, she received a degree from Vassar College in 1916 where she won her Phi Beta Kappa key. She began her career as a bank secretary in Rye, NY, but in 1920 she went to Turkey as an instructor for the YMCA Service. From Turkey she made side trips to Egypt, India and China, before relocating to New York City in 1921 where she was hired as a copy writer by the H. H. McCann advertising agency whose officials had seen her writings about Turkey in the *New York Times*. She married William Ezra Woodman in 1925 and three years later, Ruth began writing scripts for her agency's radio clients, including *Dr. Christian*, *Believe It or Not* and *Cavalcade of America*.

In 1930 McCann merged with the Erickson Agency to become McCann Erickson and Woodman began writing a new series, *Death Valley Days*, as no one else at the agency was interested in the assignment and she was one of the few employees writing for radio. As the sponsor specified that the series writer had to have firsthand knowledge of Death Valley, for the next 14 years, Woodman made long trips out West; even though she had traveled overseas, she told the press she found the American West to be "the most fascinating place of all." She may have inherited this admiration for the West; before she was born, her father, George R. Cornwall, was a miner and rancher near Gunnison, CO in the late 1880s, when the famous Wyatt Earp lived there.

Beginning in 1930 Woodman spent several months each year in the Death Valley region of California and Nevada, interviewing old prospectors, visiting ghost towns and museums, going through newspaper files, and tracking down leads suggested by others. As she had no idea of what awaited her on her first visit to the vast, hot and desolate portions of the West, she picked an experienced guide, Washington W. Cahill, a picturesque old-time westerner and Borax employee, who was an expert on the desert. She gathered enough material each trip for a year's worth of stories, and began writing scripts about six weeks in advance of each broadcast so she could verify the accounts she had collected from persons still living.

"I imagine that a person either loves the desert or hates it," Woodman observed, "I happen to love it." Cahill's job was to find fellow old-timers she could talk to with as small an audience as possible, so she could encourage "those with fascinating yarns to spin" to tell them to her. One woman told her, "I don't want my life used as an evening's entertainment." Woodman was pleased to find that the people she interviewed on her trips were unique, "singular souls who had very little, yet faced much" throughout their lives. "One is particularly impressed," she wrote, "by their good humor and their hospitality." When Woodman knocked on their doors, they never said: "What do you want?" but always simply, "Come in, my dear."

One 70-year-old woman who had worked on the 20-Mule Team borax wagons went so far as to suggest that Ruth stay "right there in her hut for a spell." In all her years of gathering material for *Death Valley Days* stories, Woodman never found it necessary to carry credentials or present a calling card.

Besides her writing career, Woodman managed a household as the wife of a banker and mother of two children. She told Shirley Gordon of *Radio Life* that she was pleased her son Billy hoped to take over the writing chores on *Death Valley Days*, but mildly disappointed that her daughter Winthrop was a fan of *The Aldrich Family* in the same time slot. When asked why she didn't listen to her mother's program, Winthrop complained that her mother's program "gave her nightmares."

"The stories I like best," Woodman told Gordon, "are the simple home-spun ones: like the one about the woman who lived her whole life on the desert." Woodman was referring to the September 26, 1935, broadcast of "Cynthia Ann Parker" (also known as "Cynthia's Dream Dress") in which the woman's fondest dream is that someday she would have a new dress. As a new bride, Cynthia waits patiently and ages painfully while her husband loses money in his first two gold strikes. Her boredom and despair end when she finally gets her silk dress after her husband's third strike.

In a similar story a prospector almost loses his wife because of the hard life of the desolate West. In "Sego Lilies" (March 26, 1942), a Mormon pioneer named David Cannon brings his Boston wife Wilhelmina to settle down in St. George, UT. She is not happy and asks David "to show her one thing of beauty" in the area. She is about to pack up and leave when David breaks his leg trying to pick Sego lilies for her on a dangerous cliff. She decides to remain in the West.

The most popular stories among *Death Valley Days* listeners were those that dealt with lost mines and buried treasures. As many of these shows were aired in the depths of the Great Depression, listeners might be forgiven if, after the broadcast, the radio stations received a deluge of letters requesting maps and diagrams so that they too could search for hidden wealth. After "Hidden Hills of Gold" was aired, a listener sent a letter stating that he was due to go on vacation and would appreciate getting all the available information concerning this area so that he could go in search of the gold. Woodman replied "Believe me, sir, if I had the slightest idea concerning the whereabouts of these hills of gold, I assure you I would not be sitting here in my New York office, but I'd be standing right on top of the biggest hill, digging like mad." But, it didn't always help to know where the strike was. In "The Lost Pegleg Mine" (July 29, 1938), an unrepentant horse thief stumbles on a rich vein of gold and makes a map of its location; then spends the rest of his life looking for it in vain.

Woodman's stories centered mostly on the men who searched, often in vain, for that one big gold or silver strike, and the strong women who supported them or realized they had to make their own lives without their husbands. Nothing was ever simple in the plots she wove from the stories she had gathered and many of them involved unusual complications and surprise endings. The strength of her scripts was one of the reasons for the long-term success of the series.

Early in *Death Valley Days* Woodman dramatized the story of the Pacific Coast Borax Company. The discovery of borax at Furnace Creek was featured in the third episode, "She Burns Green" (October 14, 1930). Aaron Winter's wife leaves him when he cannot find gold. On her return she finds out he has found a borax deposit instead. In the tenth episode, "Philander Lee, The Squaw Man" (December 2, 1930), Lee discovers the Monte Blanco borates deposit that ensures the prosperity of the Pacific Coast Borax Company. He sells the claim for $4,000. The seventh episode of *Death Valley Days* (November 11, 1930) describes the first trip taken by a 20-mule team borax wagon. The culture of the 20-mule teams, actually 18 mules and two horses, was an important theme in such early programs as "The 20-Mule Team Songfest" (April 7, 1931), the tale of "The Mule Team and the Mute" (June 30, 1931) and the story of "The 20-Mule Teamsters Foundling" (September 7, 1931). "The Last of the 20-Mule Teams" (December 7, 1931) told the story of their demise.

In 1933 Pacific Coast Borax began offering a radio premium to listeners which they could obtain by sending in a box top from 20-Mule Team Borax. It was a large 9 × 12 booklet entitled "Old Ranger's Yarns of Death Valley" and it fully illustrated the text of four radio shows, told in short-story format. It also contained advertisements for Borax products: 20-Mule Team Borax Soap Chips, 20-Mule Team Borax (a water softener) and 20-Mule Team Boric Acid. The booklet featured a full page advertisement for the Furnace Creek Inn, a resort in Death Valley, that claimed to offer golf, swimming, riding, and tennis, but only from November 1 to May 1 of each year.

Pacific Coast Borax's founder, Francis Marion Smith, replaced the 20 mule teams with railroad tracks in 1905, both to process borax and transport it to market. From its main connection to the Atchison, Topeka and Santa Fe Railroad at Ludlow, CA, the Tidewater and Tonopah Railroad (T & T) wandered northward through Death Valley and the Amargosa Valley to the mining towns of Tonopah and Goldfield, NV. Narrow gauge branch lines connected several mining operations in the nearby hills to the T & T. One of these mining hamlets was Bullfrog, where an attractive waitress named Mamie was courted by all the local boys in "The Little Bullfrog Nugget" (November 18, 1930). Nellie ultimately picks the one of the fellows who is able to supply her with fresh eggs every day.

When the tracks came to Rhyolite, NV ("The Iron Horse Reaches Rhyolite," April 21, 1931), the small town built near the Montgomery Shoshone mine attracted the attention of eastern investor Charles M. Schwab. After he purchased the mine in 1906, Rhyolite became a boom town with electric lights, water mains, telephones, newspapers, a school and a hospital by 1907. From this era *Death Valley Days* told the stories of "Tiger Lil of Rhyolite " (December 30, 1930), "The Ornery and Worthless Men's Club of Rhyolite" (February 21, 1935), and "The Three R's in Rhyolite" (March 14,1935). "Claim Jumpin' Jennie of Rhyolite" (April 14, 1931) featured a "Stella Dallas type" of single mother who labored in hard-rock mining to keep her unappreciative daughter in an eastern finishing school.

Woodman discovered some characters lived in Death Valley because they needed to hide out for a while. She described the best known of these when she told "The Story of Death Valley Scotty" on March 24, 1931. Scotty was working in Buffalo Bill's Wild West Show in 1905 when he met New York businessman Albert Johnson, who was told he was terminally ill. When Scotty helped him recover his health, Johnson gratefully invested for the first time in one of Scotty's Death Valley gold mine stock schemes. After many complaints from the victims of his swindles, Scotty was fired by Buffalo Bill; only to continue his stock schemes after his four-car "Scott Special" train caused a sensation when it broke the speed record between Los Angeles and Chicago in "Death Valley Scotty's Gold Mine" (June 2, 1931). Scotty's on-again, off-again patron, Albert Johnson, began construction in 1906 on a vacation home in Death Valley, which Scotty claimed was his "castle." To keep the home out of Scotty's hands when his company went bankrupt, Johnson donated it to a religious cult with the proviso that Scotty could live in the castle until he died.

Another well-known scoundrel was Black Bart whose late-in-life crime spree was described on the episode of November 9, 1931. Bart's real name was Charles E. Boles and he was a 60-year-old high school teacher who began holding up stagecoaches as a practical joke. When he impersonated a highwayman and robbed a coach of $2,000 in gold dust and coins, he realized that it was more than he could earn in two years of teaching. So he continued robbing coaches and was successful enough to move to San Francisco, where he befriended two Wells Fargo detectives who had been trying to catch him. They ultimately got him when they traced a laundry mark on a shirt cuff he left at the scene of a robbery. Bart often left poetic notes in empty strongboxes to taunt the lawmen who were after him. Because of his age at conviction, Black Bart only had to serve four years in the California State Penitentiary.

One of Woodman's most moving scripts told the story of a western outlaw who was regarded by some as a Robin Hood. "Not so," claimed the Old Ranger, "at least no more than any other train robber and killer." Sam Bass and the Joe Collins gang held up the Union Pacific train in Big Springs, TX, on September 18, 1877. As recounted in "Sam

Bass" on September 18, 1936, Bass forced the station agent to open the express car where the robbers found boxes of twenty-dollar gold pieces worth $60,000. The masked bandits left one bandana behind, however, and the storekeeper who sold it took it upon himself to track them down. He reported their location to the authorities after he watched them divide the spoils.

Three members of the gang were arrested, but Sam Bass got away and hid out in his home town. His only mistake at that point was to be seen at the local saloon where he attracted the attention of the singer, Annie. Jim Murphy, the station agent at Big Springs, was recruited by the Texas Rangers to befriend Bass so they could storm the saloon. One evening, as Annie sang "Sam Bass, a kinder-hearted fellow you'll never see," the local marshal confronted the outlaw, and Bass shot him dead. When the Texas Rangers arrived a gunfight ensued and Bass was mortally wounded. He dragged himself to a live oak grove outside of town where he died. At his funeral Annie sang her "Sam Bass" song.

Another theme that Woodman dealt with was racial prejudice. In "The Story of Swamper Ike" from December 9, 1930, a white man raised by Indians falls in love with a white girl, but she will not marry him because he is a tribesman. When his "red mother" dies, she leaves him a locket with his picture and a message that he can find out who his parents were by looking for "the rock by the wagon wheel." The man takes a job as a swamper on a 20-mule team wagon to search for the rock. When he finds it, writing on the rock reveals that he was the child of two white pioneers who died on a wagon train.

In "Sequoia" (November 4, 1938), a noble Indian despises whites, but admires them because they read and write. Disabled in an accident he decides to make a written language for his tribe. Using berries for ink, a twig for a pen and birchbark for paper he creates an alphabet with 86 signs. His accomplishments were recognized years later when the great redwood trees in the Sierra Nevada were named for him.

"Ishi, Last of the Yahis" (July 3, 1941), told the remarkable story of Ishi, the lone survivor of an Indian tribe of 20,000, which was decimated by massacres and disease. Ishi had no name when he walked out of the wilderness into Oroville, CA in 1911. When he was taken in by two anthropologists, A. L. Kroeber and Thomas Waterman, they gave him the name Ishi, which meant "Man" in the Yahi dialect. Ishi helped them transcribe his dialect as he had a fervent wish that his language live on. He was a wise and gentle man who spent his last years working at various tasks at the University of California, San Francisco medical school and anthropological museum.

When *Death Valley Days* went to television in 1952, the Old Ranger, played by Stanley Andrews, was its narrator. When he retired, Ronald Reagan took his place until he was elected governor of California. His fellow Hollywood star, Robert Taylor, became the new narrator and later Dale Robertson held the job. Woodman wrote all of the scripts for the first five years, and thereafter served as story editor. The show would run for 558 television episodes, mostly in syndication, through 1975, breaking all records for longevity for a western broadcast.

The impact that *Death Valley Days* had on Americans who followed it faithfully on network radio and syndicated television for years is profound. Its chief writer, Ruth Woodman, was given the task of creating an anthology of western drama and character studies which would not reflect the attitudes of a well-educated eastern advertising agency copy writer. That she succeeded far beyond any expectations is without question. Woodman was hailed in her own lifetime as one of the foremost authorities on Death Valley history and folklore. She won many awards, one for "The Land of the Free," on radio on September 17, 1934, and on television, May 26, 1953, which won the Freedoms Foundation Award in 1953; and a second for "The Great Lounsberry Scoop," which won the Western Heritage Award for the Best Factual Television Show at the end of her writing career in 1961. Among the other awards the show garnered was the Award of Honor in 1960 from the Southern California Historical Society for 30 years of truthful portrayal of the early days of the Golden West.

Sources: Audio copies of *Death Valley Days*; Dunning, *On the Air*; *Radio Life*; *Old Ranger's Yarns of Death Valley*, Pacific Coast Borax Company publication; CBS Press Release, June 23, 1941; http://library.uoregon.edu/tools/blogs/scua/check-out-ruth-corn-wall-woodman-papers.

THE DESERT KID

JACK FRENCH

Originating from NBC in Chicago, this 15 minute show was the story of an eastern lad, portrayed by Burton Eisner, who was found in the desert by three cowboys, Jack Ross, Curley Bradley, and Shorty Carson. They were the Ranch Boys Trio, and while they sang some songs on the show, most of it was a dramatization of their exciting adventures in the southwest desert region. This series ran three times a week from November 1934 through the summer of 1935, usually at 6:15 P.M. (EST.) The Ranch Boys would become part of the **Tom Mix** radio show and Bradley would eventually get the title lead.

Source: *New York Sun*, March 30, 1935.

DESTINY TRAILS

JACK FRENCH *and* DAVID S. SIEGEL

NETWORK: NBC syndicated
FORMAT: 15 minute show, three times weekly
DURATION OF RUN: 1945 to 1948
SPONSOR: Various regional ones, including Lady Betty Bread and West's Firestone Store
AUDIO COPIES EXTANT: 30, of run of 156 episodes
SCRIPTS ARCHIVED: Undetermined

This 15 minute NBC syndicated series, produced in New York, eventually totaled 156 episodes, making it one of the longest radio syndicated series. It was based upon the five Leather-Stocking novels of James Fenimore Cooper (1789–1851). Only those episodes drawn from *The Prairie* qualify for this book since this is the sole novel that takes place west of the Mississippi River.

The frontier hero of all five novels and the lead in this radio series was Natty Bumppo, who in *The Prairie* is nearly 90 years old, but spry and active as ever. The scriptwriters of this series stuck closely to the original novel and incorporated all the strangely-named characters that Cooper had associated with Bumppo, including Ishmael Bush, Abiram White, Dr. Obed Battins, Duncan Uncas Middletown, and Chief Hard Heart. The only significant change from the novel to the radio adaptation involved Bumppo. In the novel, he is always referred to as "the old trapper" or "Leather-Stocking," but in *Destiny Trails* he is called Natty Bumppo in virtually every scene.

Cooper was born in New Jersey but raised in the New York village his father founded, Cooperstown. (In 1939, the village would become the home of the National Baseball Hall of Fame and Museum.) Dismissed from Yale University in 1806, Cooper spent the next five years as a midshipman in the navy. He embarked on a literary career at age 30 to prove to his wife he could write a better novel than the British one he was then reading. His third novel, *The Pioneers* (1823) began his series called "Leather-Stocking Tales" based upon fictional frontier scout, Natty Bumppo. This was followed by *The Last of the Mohicans* (1826) and *The Prairie* (1827). A decade later, he completed the series of five novels with *The Pathfinder* (1840) and *The Deerslayer* (1841). A very prolific writer, his published volumes totaled over 50 novels, histories, social criticisms, biographies, and other works.

Production planning for the *Destiny Trails* series began as early as the fall of 1944 when William R. Seth, promotional director of the NBC Radio Recording Division, contacted the Cooperstown Chamber of Commerce and obtained background information on Cooper and his frontier novels. By March of 1945, the first section of *Destiny Trails*, based upon *The Deerslayer* had aired throughout the U.S. and the second section, *The Last of the Mohicans* had begun. The dramatization of these two novels comprised the first 76 episodes.

By the end of 1945, NBC was offering the full 156 episodes to radio stations through advertisements in broadcast magazines. The latter half of this series contained episodes based upon *The Pioneers*, *The Pathfinder* and *The Prairie*. NBC promoted the series to all radio stations in the standard radio trade magazines and reached out to juvenile listeners with advertisements in *Classic Comic Books*.

Unlike many syndicated shows produced by commercial companies who hired second-tier talent at the microphone, NBC's *Destiny Trails* employed some of New York's finest radio actors. The cast was headed by announcer/narrator Jackson Beck, and joined by Lesley Woods, Frank Lovejoy, Grace Matthews, Jean Gillespie, Stacy Harris, and Kay Loring. Beck's distinctive baritone voice was familiar to radio youngsters as the announcer/narrator of *The Adventures of Superman*, which aired in the same 5 to 6 P.M. time slot as *Destiny Trails*. Beck's voice was also well-known to adults as the narrator of *Pathe* news reels.

Despite the past success of Cooper's frontier novels in the 1800s, his cumbersome, convoluted stories did not translate easily to the airwaves. His contemporary American critics, including Mark Twain, found his novels full of poor plotting, glaring inconsistencies, innumerable clichés, and cardboard characterizations. The poet James Russell Lowell wrote of Cooper: "The women he draws from one model don't vary: all sappy as maples and as flat as a prairie." So transposing the dusty pages of Cooper's Leather-Stocking novels to exciting radio drama must have been difficult for the scriptwriters.

To help keep the radio listeners on track, each episode began, much like a soap opera, with a lengthy summary of the past few weeks of each ensuing story. How well this technique worked for the juvenile radio audience members in that post World War II era can be evaluated by examining a typical verbatim opening, read by Jackson Beck:

Now ... Chapter 19! You'll recall that the leader of the wagon train, Ishmael Bush, had joined with the Sioux Indians to capture every member of Leather-Stocking's party. He had promised the Sioux chief, Mahtoree, a great prize: young Chief Hard Heart, leader of a Pawnee war party, and now a close friend of Natty's. But returning to the Dakota camp, Mahtoree had demanded Obed and the two girls, Ellen and Inez, in addition to Hard Heart. Natty, taking advantage of this rift among his enemies, and of the redskins' superstitious belief in Obed's magic powers, had contrived to set the young Pawnee chief free. Now in doing this, he knew very well that Chief Mahtoree would demand the death of both of them, but he also knew that Ishmael would not give up his own plans for revenge for the killing of his son. Thus, when Mahtoree refused to part with the mutually hated captive, Natty Bumppo, Ishmael had become very angry. There had been a brief fight, and even though many of the braves were hunting for Hard Heart, the Sioux had driven Ishmael back unto the prairie, where he is now awaiting another chance. There is still another reason for growing tension in both camps and as dawn comes up over the plains, the two men who caused all this trouble, sit calmly in one of the Dakota teepees, discussing it....

While radio historians have not yet unearthed the identity of the production staff, including the director, producer, scriptwriters, sound effects personnel, and musicians, all of them appeared to be quite competent, as one might expect from an NBC show of that era. *Destiny Trails* was one of several series syndicated by NBC, which included the half hour shows, *Weird Circle* and *The Haunting Hour*, the 15 minute *Betty and Bob* soap opera, and *Five Minute Mysteries*.

In September 1945, NBC announced what they termed "sweeping reductions in prices" on most of their syndicated shows. *The Haunting Hour* was reduced from $150 per show to $100, *Destiny Trails* was lowered from $50 a show to $30, and the soap opera, *Modern Romances*, went from $5 to only $3.50 per airing. Whether these lower rates or the residual popularity of James Fenimore Cooper kept *Destiny Trails* on the air is not known, but there is some indication that some stations were still carrying it in 1948.

Sources: Audio copies of *Destiny Trails*; Hart; *Funk & Wagnalls New Encyclopedia*, 1972; *Knickerbocker News*, Albany, NY, March 29, 1945; *Otsego Farmer*, Cooperstown, NY, October 20, 1944, and January 12, 1945; *Radio Daily*, March 15, 1945, September 6, 1945, and June 27, 1946; http://www.radiogoldindex.com.

Double M Ranch see *Gene Autry's Melody Ranch*

DR. FRACKELTON'S STORIES OF CHEYENNE & CROW INDIANS

KARL SCHADOW

Also called *Sagebrush Dentist*, this radio show was written by the program's creator and host, Dr. Will Frackelton, a frontier dentist who practiced in Sheridan, WY from 1893 until his death in 1943. He began his series of evening, 15 minute programs on KWYO in 1939 and they apparently continued through 1941. Each of his radio programs began with "Veagafange pfance duac ishira" or "People come to camp" in the Crow language, followed by his stories of the adventures of prominent pioneers, missionaries and local ranchers. There were also tales related to other Indian tribes, in addition to the Cheyenne and Crow. The dentist was an honorary member of the Crow tribe and claimed he had many famous patients, including Buffalo Bill Cody and Calamity Jane. Some scripts of this show are archived at the Sheridan County/Fulmer, Wyoming Public Library.

Source: *Variety Radio Directory*, 1940-41 Annual Edition.

DR. SIXGUN

STAN CLAUSSEN

NETWORK: NBC
FORMAT: Half hour, weekly
DURATION OF RUN: September 2, 1954, to October 13, 1955
SPONSOR: Sustaining
AUDIO COPIES EXTANT: 25
SCRIPTS ARCHIVED: Ernest Kinoy Papers, Wisconsin Historical Society, Madison, WI

An half hour adult western that appeared on NBC, *Dr. Sixgun* premiered on September 2, 1954, but ran for only one season, going off the air on October 13, 1955. It was a transcribed series that was heard first on Thursdays, 8:30 P.M., then at Saturdays, 8:00 P.M. It starred Karl Weber as Dr. Grey Matson and Bill Griffis as his sidekick, Pablo, who also narrated the stories. Pablo, a jolly Gypsy peddler, was occasionally tipsy and had a trained pet raven, Midnight, who was so vocal he could be considered a third regular in the cast. It is not known who voiced Midnight (probably one of the uncredited sound effects personnel) but William Keene played O'Shea, the proprietor of the Bull Run Saloon, who also appeared in enough episodes to be the fourth regular on the series.

Fred Collins and Bill Rippe were the announcers. Despite its short run, the series went through three directors: Fred Weihe, Harry Frazee and Daniel Sutter. The live music on each program was composed and conducted by Art Ryerson. The scripts were by two of the most prolific writers in radio's Golden Age, George Lefferts and Ernest Kinoy.

"Across the rugged Indian Territory rides a tall young man on a mission of mercy, his medical bag strapped on one hip and his six-shooter to the other. This is Dr. Sixgun, Grey Matson, MD, the gun-toting frontier doctor who roamed the length and breadth of the Indian Territory, friend and physician to white man and Indian alike, the symbol of justice and mercy in the lawless west of the 1870s." This introduction, a version of which introduced each episode of *Dr. Sixgun*, was slightly reminiscent of another adult-oriented western that just preceded it on NBC: *The Six Shooter* with James Stewart as Britt Ponsett. It is probable that NBC, with these two shows, was trying to replicate the successful *Gunsmoke* on CBS.

There were obvious differences between NBC's two westerns. *Dr. Sixgun* was set in the Montana Territory of the post–Civil War 1870s while Ponsett roamed the entire western frontier. Doc Matson had a constant "muse" in Pablo, unlike the loner cowboy in the Stewart series. Pablo spent much of his time in the Bull Run Saloon describing the exploits of Matson to residents of Frenchman's Ford, sort of a reverse Holmes and Watson, where this time the hero is the doctor, not the chronicler.

The hero, Dr. Sixgun, or more commonly called, Doc Matson, was typical of leads in adult westerns of the 1950s, influenced by the prevailing "neo-realism" of serious radio drama. Doc was brave, flexible but flawed in judgment when human emotions were concerned. Like Sherlock Holmes, he seems to have fallen in love only once, and was rebuffed by the woman he chose. He accepted the constitutional right to bear arms reluctantly, packing a six-gun in his holster and a Derringer in his medical bag. He was not fond of capital punishment, but when he was truly convinced a man should hang for murder, it sometimes turned out the accused was innocent.

This medical man was never fooled by a con artist, although O'Shea the bartender often was. Pablo was mirthful and had good common sense derived from his experiences as a Gypsy peddler. While this was an adult series in almost every respect, one factor kept it from being so: Midnight the raven possessed attributes far beyond those bestowed upon any trained bird. He spoke and understood English, sang, prompted Pablo when the peddler occasionally forgot something, and best of all, could be counted upon to rescue Matson and Pablo when they were in dire straits.

In one episode, Pablo is rambling on to the radio audience, when Midnight interrupts with the word "stage" which reminds Pablo of the program's adventure of the evening (a stagecoach robbery) so he switches subjects. During another scene, Midnight is observing the two chums play chess, and when the Doc makes his final victorious move, Midnight calls out "Checkmate" demonstrating his understanding of the game. The big black bird also understands an alternative meaning for "Checkmate" because he calls it out again upon hearing that the posse has captured the outlaws.

But his most outlandish accomplishment is featured in an episode where Matson and Pablo are captured by Apache Indians and tied to a giant cactus with wet rawhide strips which, when they dry out, will shrink, pulling the two victims into the deadly needles of the plant. But they are saved… by Midnight. The helpful bird sees their plight and flies to their aid. Pablo instructs Midnight to untie them and miraculously he does exactly that. While being saved by the hero's horse or his dog was commonplace in most juvenile westerns, being rescued by a raven would seem inappropriate for an adult western.

The only other characteristic that does not ring true in this series is the strange language the scriptwriters frequently put in the mouths of the American Indian. Rather than just using pidgin-English as most westerns did in their scripts, the Indians in *Dr. Sixgun* frequently speak in a form of English straight from the King James Bible: "Who art thou?" or "Dost thee not know" etc. While this must have been disconcerting to the listeners, it became even stranger when Matson would slip into this vernacular when speaking to his red brothers, as if he were speaking their native tongue.

But even with these two reservations, there is not a doubt that *Dr. Sixgun* was an adult program and dealt with rather bold themes like bigotry, prejudice against Indians and immigrants, as well as religious and ethnic discrimination. Several times *Dr. Sixgun* demonstrated a slightly feminist outlook, at least by the standards of the 1950s. In several of his adventures, he is battling intolerance and injustice while trying to thwart evildoers.

In the premiere episode (September 2, 1954) Pablo tells the story of a sick Indian boy left behind by Rev. Gaunt's wagon train and taken by Pablo to his friend, Doc Matson, the region's only physician. Doc recognizes the boy as the son of the Apache chief. The boy tells Matson that many tribal members were very ill and that Grey Fox, the medicine man, wants to take them to the mountains to recover. Doc knows the boy has measles and is getting better; so he thinks the Apaches should stay in their village. Meanwhile Gaunt, the leader of the wagon train, covets the rich farmland that would be left behind when the tribe moves to the mountains. When Doc is able to get Chief Tall Horse to stay, Gaunt poisons the chief's son. The boy appears to be dead, but Doc Matson revives the boy with ammonia, and when he revives, the boy tells his father that it was Gaunt who tried to kill him.

One of the major difficulties in writing an adult western is the research involved in being accurate about customs, weapons, phraseology, and habits of that era on the frontier.

While mistakes by the writer would not be noticed by juvenile listeners, most mature people see the errors. In the above episode, nothing could be more unlikely than the Apaches being accorded rich farmland for their reservation. During this period in American history, the federal government invariably confined the Indians to the poorest land that no white men would want.

This episode also demonstrates the difficulty of being too accurate historically and thus confusing the radio audience. Gaunt steals a bottle from Matson that is marked "prussic acid" on the label and tells his henchman he will poison the Chief's son with it. Listeners may have been surprised when the lad is not only poisoned, but apparently dies after ingesting the prussic acid. What few in the radio audience knew was that prussic acid was an archaic term for hydrogen cyanide (more simply, cyanide) an extremely deadly poison. So while it was called prussic acid in the 1870s, few radio listeners in the 1950s would realize that. Gaunt was also unaware of the fact that Matson had filled an empty prussic acid bottle with morphine. Thus the Indian boy merely went into a coma from the morphine and Matson was able to revive him.

The Armed Forces Radio and Television Service (AFRTS) maintained transcriptions of *Dr. Sixgun* and played them abroad to military personnel and their dependents from 1954 through 1958. From these disks several programs from 1955 survived that would not have been preserved otherwise, including one entitled "Baseball at Frenchman's Ford." When Harvey Braithwaite from Princeton arrives in town, he finds Pablo at the Bull Run who introduces him to "another university man," Doc Matson. Harvey tells the assembled patrons that his father wanted to buy out all the ranches in the territory, if Harvey thinks it's a good idea. Harvey starts drinking with Randy Stewart; and they wake up the next morning realizing that Stewart has bet Harvey $1,000 he can organize a baseball game in Frenchman's Ford on the next Saturday. Harvey will act as umpire. Stewart finds eighteen men, so "The Pintos" and "The Wranglers" play ball until an inevitable brawl breaks out. Gunshots end all efforts to continue and Harvey is horrified to discover that one team was paid money to participate. In a fit of pique, Harvey takes the next stagecoach out and vows there'll be no ranch buy-outs in Montana Territory.

A baseball game on the frontier of the 1870s would seem to be an unlikely event, perhaps historically impossible. But it certainly could have happened. Baseball began in New York in the early 1800s and its popularity soon assured its presence throughout New England. As early as 1867, there were over 100 so-called "baseball clubs" playing throughout the country, with clubs as far south as Louisiana and as far west as San Francisco. So this script can be accepted as reasonable.

Scriptwriters Lefferts and Kinoy were expansive in their choices of plots, and while many of them involved similar devices of the standard western, the *Dr. Sixgun* stories presented them with more realism and emphasis on human behavior than the average radio western drama. In "Land Development Program" (September 9, 1954) a convoluted land swindle that, despite Matson's best efforts, leaves O'Shea with worthless $1,000 bills. The episode that could have been a routine gambling story, "Belle and the Baby" (September 16, 1954), instead becomes a tale of generosity overcoming greed and grief. The plot involves Belle Porter, a wealthy casino owner who assists a starving couple and their daughter and who donates her casino to the community to convert it into a much-needed school.

Two sensitive themes are woven into the program called "Colonel Crown Is a Madman" (September 30, 1954). The episode deals with the brutality of a military officer toward enlisted men and then later delves into the possibility of cavalry troopers being ordered by an arrogant officer to attack a peaceful Indian village. Another episode, "Duel on Yom Kippur" (September 23, 1954), focused around a character who was Jewish; while Jews were not uncommon on the frontier, few radio westerns ever mentioned them in any way. In this episode, the central figure is Colonel Turow, a Jewish man who formerly was a plantation owner. Turow explains to Matson and Pablo that Yom Kippur is a day when members of his faith consider their consciences carefully and often repent for past mistakes. When a drunken cowboy challenges Turow to a gunfight, the Colonel must choose between defending his honor and fighting on Yom Kippur, his religion's most sacred day.

Vigilantism is prevalent in "Fred Garth Jailed for Murder" (October 7, 1954) when an innocent man is jailed for a robbery he did not commit and a circuit judge sentences him the next day. Matson wants to get the governor to intercede but a lynch mob confronts the doctor. Fortunately Pablo arrives with information that proves a member of the lynch mob is the real robber. Even more sinister vigilantism is present in "The Immigrant Settler" (October 21, 1954). In this program, immigrant settlers in the region are confronted with hooded "Nightriders," akin to the Ku Klux Klan, who terrorize immigrants by brutal beatings. The thugs on horseback next target Pablo since he is a Gypsy but Matson and an honest sheriff are able to identify and arrest the vigilantes.

Occasionally one of the scriptwriters would make an obvious mistake, perhaps because of deadlines, and the director failed to catch it. Many of the episodes make it clear that Matson always carries a holstered six-gun and a Derringer in his medical bag. In "Stage Robber Saved" (November 28, 1954), for example, an outlaw confronts Matson, gets his six-gun, and then orders him to throw away the Derringer in his bag, "that everybody knows you have there." However, in another program, the outlaws do not know about the concealed weapon when they confront him. Matson pulls the Derringer out and with two shots, shoots the rifle out of the leader's hands. He then keeps his weapon on them while he lectures them and then rides away unimpeded.

The Derringer, a single shot pistol, was favored for concealment by people with evil intent. John Wilkes Booth murdered President Abraham Lincoln with one. In 1866 Remington came out with a double barrel Derringer that accommodated two .41 caliber rimfire cartridges and it quickly became the Derringer of choice in most regions, including the frontier. But no Derringer ever had the capacity to fire more than two rounds without reloading, so Doc Matson basically held off the highway bandits with an empty weapon, which they should have known.

Mature subject matter prevailed in most of the scripts. "Old Man's Atonement" (November 7, 1954), dealt with the serious consequences of alcoholism, including death. In the program "Captain Langdon's Honor," the residual pain of the Confederate "dual of honor code" is explored. The episode "Mark Corning's Mail Order Bride" discussed a problem common on the frontier: the lack of women to marry. Some historians have claimed that Wyoming, the first state to give women the right to vote, did so in part so it would attract more eligible women to that state.

Only rarely would one of the scriptwriters borrow a real personality in history upon which to build a fictional story. One of the few obvious examples of this was "Male Teacher Trouble" (December 5, 1954) in which Mr. Ferris is hired as the new school teacher in Frenchman's Ford. Ferris likes to walk alone at night and some locals fear that these night walks might pose a danger to him, especially from a recent robber in town who wears a black slicker and has robbed and hurt several citizens, including Mr. Ferris. Eventually the man in the slicker gets wounded and Doc finds out Ferris is the thief. Before he dies, Mr. Ferris tells Doc that he couldn't live on a teacher's salary. This script is a re-telling of the life of the West Coast bandit "Black Bart" (Charles Earl Boles, 1829–1889) who was a teacher, and after posing as a highwayman, found that he could make two years' salary with just one stage-coach robbery.

Other episodes concentrated on actual, historical problems of the average frontier region, some of which Matson could alleviate, with the help of Pablo and Midnight, but others that did not have a happy ending. The practicality of a town banning all firearms was dealt with in "No Guns Ordinance" (October 31, 1954) when Matson and Pablo find themselves in the village of Rail End. By the end of the program, Doc concludes that the Second Amendment protection for citizens who bear arms "might be worth sewing up a few bullet holes." Pablo's zest for liquor and Doc's attempts to modify this condition work their way into the plot of "Willie Wyman and His Land Grant" (December 12, 1954). The title refers to a voided document which is passed off as a valid land grant for the total ownership of everything in Frenchman's Ford. Justice does not prevail in an episode called "Eddie Baker Had It Coming." When Matt Wilder is murdered and his daughter Alice is beaten to death, the Sheriff and Doc Matson both assume that Eddie Baker killed them. Baker is jailed, tried and sentenced to hang. After Baker is hanged, it is revealed that renegade Apaches actually committed both crimes. Doc is devastated and he leaves town to contemplate his mistake in the wilderness.

Swindle by medical quackery was the basis of "Oberdorfer Electric Belt," an episode in which Professor James Case comes to town with an electric belt which supposedly will cure most major diseases. By the end of the program, Matson has tricked Case into admitting his belt is a total fraud. Kindness toward the Indians is stressed in the "Old Man Hastings." Matson joins a cattle drive to tend to an old man with a heart condition. When an armed Comanche challenges the cowhands on the drive, they determine he wants only one cow to feed his family so the old man gives him a fine steer. Both races celebrate the generous gift, but the old man dies a few days later before they reach the trail head.

The entire series had the services of some excellent, but uncredited sound effects personnel. This was typical of the networks, and only in the 1950s did one network, CBS, start giving name credits for "sound patterns." On *Dr. Sixgun* the standard sounds (hoof-beats, gunshots, doors opening, etc.) were done well but the crowd scenes and outdoor background patterns were excellent. When a scene took place in a wagon train encampment, people talking in the background could be heard, but also chickens clucking and an occasional rooster crowing added to the realism. Outdoors on the main street of Frenchman's Ford, it was common to hear in the background: wagon wheels, a horse's whinny, and a dog barking down the street, all of which made the scene more realistic.

First tier, East Coast actors appeared in *Dr. Sixgun*. Karl Weber, who played Grey Matson, MD, was well known for his voiceovers for both President Lyndon Johnson and Nelson Rockefeller. A trained Shakespearean thespian from the University of Iowa drama program, he was a regular on radio soap operas, including: *Woman in White*, **Lone Journey** and *The Romance of Helen Trent*.

Both Bill Griffis as Pablo and William Keene as O'Shea supported Weber in almost every episode, as well as doubling in other roles. Griffis had broad experience before the radio microphone and had been in the supporting cast of dozens of series, *Crime of Peter Chambers*, *Dimension X*, *The Road of Life*, *Adventures of Father Brown*, *Lights Out*, etc. Occasionally he was the announcer, a role he filled on the program *Believe It or Not*. However, *Dr. Sixgun* was apparently his first western and his first co-lead role in a series.

Many skilled actors got regular work on this series in a variety of parts: Ken Williams, Cameron Prud'Homme, John Tomin, Peter Capell, Kermit Murdock, Richard Saunders, Donald Buka, Luis Van Rooten, Betty Garde, Virginia Payne, Denise Alexander, Ralph Bell, Santos Ortega, Bill Adams, Kenny Delmar, Joe De Santis, Wendell Holmes, John Gibson, Bryna Raeburn, Bill Lipton, Bob Hastings, William Redfield, Peggy Loughran, Leon Janney, and Terri Keane.

Young fans of **Bobby Benson and the B-Bar-B Riders** must have recognized the voice of Chief Tall Horse in the premier episode. He was portrayed by veteran actor Craig McDonnell, who had been playing the Indian, Harka, on that juvenile western since 1949 on Mutual. McDonnell had a wide variety of accents he could utilize on radio; on **Bobby Benson**, he doubled as Irish in a Gaelic brogue. He also voiced Elmer the bull in Borden's commercials and in his regular voice, was Police Captain Drake, the lead in *Under Arrest*, also on Mutual.

Dr. Sixgun was a sustained series, designed by NBC to be sold as a syndicated package, not just to their affiliates, but also to independent stations. It had all the linchpins of a cost-effective production: pre-recorded music, gritty adult scenes, with added gun battles characteristic of the western genre. The scripts generally were first-rate and the New York actors were all experienced with extensive radio, theatrical and television experience. But NBC didn't give the series the chance it deserved and without that support, it was no match for the adult westerns that came out of CBS: **Gunsmoke**, **Frontier Gentleman**, **Have Gun — Will Travel** and **Fort Laramie**.

Sources: Audio copies of *Dr. Sixgun*; Beller; DeLong; Menke; Newark; Hogg; Dunning, *On the Air*; www.factmonster.com/encyclopedia/science/hydrogen-cyanide.html; *Program logs*: http://www.digitaldeliftp.com/DigitalDeliToo/dd2jb-Dr-Sixgun.html.

DUDE RANCH

Karl Schadow *and* Jack French

This weekly one hour program was broadcast from 1938 to 1939 on station KGVO, Missoula, MT, in the heart of actual ranch territory. The program contained a mix of storytelling, music, western poetry, and good humored bantering, originating from the Circle D Dude Ranch, which was a real ranch owned by a KGVO staffer. The scripts featured a large cast of ranch regulars including: the ranch's owner Myra, played by Loretta Matthieson; the lovable Old Timer, the ranch foreman played by Verne Sawyer; Arizona, the Old Timer's assistant and the program's storyteller played by Marion Dixon; Nora, the ranch's Irish cook played by Evelyn Henry; and ranch guests Mrs. Smythe-Smythe played by Lucille Davis, Lord Chumley, played by Bill Marquis and Virginia Calhoun played by Ernestine Flannery. The series was written by Jimmy Barber who also doubled as the production manager for KGVO. The traditional western music was provided by the Ranch-House Gang.

Source: *Radio Guide*, June 18, 1938.

EAGLE WING, THE NAVAHO

KARL SCHADOW *and* JACK FRENCH

This 15 minute juvenile western program was broadcast Tuesdays and Thursdays at 5:15 P.M. from radio station KFRC in San Francisco beginning in 1933. The series, which incorporated Indian legends into its script, was written and directed by Mrs. John Cuddy. The cast included Baldwin McGaw, Dorothy Scott, and Frank Provo. KFRC was part of the Don Lee Network.

Source: *Broadcast Weekly*, March 26–April 1, 1933.

THE EMPIRE BUILDERS

JACK FRENCH *and* DAVID S. SIEGEL

NETWORK: NBC Blue
FORMAT: Half hour, weekly
DURATION OF RUN: January 14, 1929, to June 22, 1931
SPONSOR: The Great Northern Railroad
AUDIO COPIES EXTANT: 9
SCRIPTS ARCHIVED: http://www.genericradio.com; Broadcast Arts Library

This may have been the first western drama on radio; it certainly was one of the most unique. It managed to combine romance and music in one program, along with gritty adventure and occasional bitter violence. The scripts used much stronger language than would be permitted on network radio only a few years later. Finally, it alternated real historical figures with fictional ones and often made no effort to differentiate between them.

As an anthology series, it moved from one era to another, placing a show in the mid–1700s one week and jumping to the Great Depression of the 1930s in its next program. But the scripts tried to stay within the geographic realm of the sponsor's primary rail lines so most of the action occurred in Montana, Idaho, Oregon, Washington state, and California.

The music on the series was excellent since it usually had a full orchestra under a skilled conductor. The musical bridges were lush and the accompaniment to the singers was supportive without pulling focus. However the sound effects, as one might expect from a series beginning prior to 1930, were primitive and unrealistic. Footsteps were usually eliminated, although hoofbeats were adequate. Gunshots were flat and unconvincing, probably because they were created by slapping a wooden lathe on a leather pillow.

The shows were produced live, first at station WJZ in Manhattan, usually beginning at 10:30 P.M. Mondays, so the Midwest listeners heard it at 9:30 P.M. while the West Coast audience received it at 7:30 P.M. At least on one occasion (February 11, 1929) the show aired from Portland, OR, where the services of the Portland Symphony Orchestra were utilized. The original cast starred Virginia Gardner and Bob McGimsey, a three-part harmony whistler. There were also occasional guest stars that appeared under their own name. Vachel Lindsay, who ranked among the greatest of the American poets of that era, read one of his best known works on a June 1929 program.

In September 1930 the production was moved to Chicago, where it would remain for the rest of the run. Don Ameche, Bernadine Flynn, and Harvey Hayes (or Hays) held

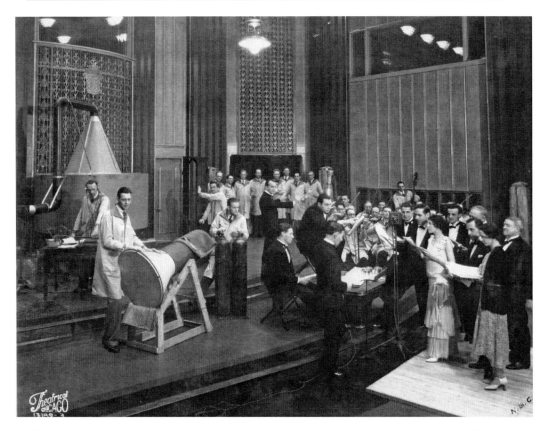

Chicago NBC sound effects personnel and equipment together with orchestra led by Josef Koestner. The cast of *Empire Builders* is at far right. Circa 1930 (courtesy Milwaukee Area Radio Enthusiasts).

the leading roles in the programs from Chicago. Don Bernard directed the series, Josef Koestner conducted the orchestra and Ted Pearson was the announcer. A country singer, Obed "Dad" Pickard, was also in the cast. The identity of the scriptwriter(s) has yet to be discovered. Thus far, a total of nine airchecks has surfaced, mostly from the period December 1930 to February 1931, and they constitute the total extant copies today.

The name of the series was deeply engrained in both its sponsoring railroad and that railroad's founder. James J. Hill (1838–1916), a native of Canada, started as a St. Paul, Minnesota, shipping clerk, got into the railroad business, and eventually became very successful in that transportation industry. By 1889, his Great Northern Railroad spanned over 2000 miles from Chicago to the Pacific Northwest and it was the only major railroad in the United States which was built without any government subsidies.

Eventually Hill's economic power, generosity, and vision earned him the nickname of "The Empire Builder." Though primarily a freight transporter, the Great Northern also operated several passenger trains and its premier one was called "The Empire Builder." It followed a northern route, from the Midwest to the Pacific Ocean, and traveled through many picturesque areas, including Glacier National Park. Today, under Amtrak, the Empire Builder is still carrying passengers to the West Coast and it still goes through Glacier National Park.

Chicago cast of *Empire Builders*, circa 1930. Fourth from left is Don Ameche, the two women are Lucille Husting (blonde) and Bernadine Flynn (brunette), and guitarist at far right is Obed "Dad" Pickard. Man in center kneeling with dog is Harvey Hays, who played The Old Timer (courtesy Milwaukee Area Radio Enthusiasts).

The Great Northern Railroad did not overstep its bounds as the sole sponsor. It had a short commercial message at the beginning, usually suggesting listeners patronize its rail service in their transportation plans. The drama would then commence, with the Old Timer introducing the story, which would go uninterrupted until the closing minutes. Another "soft-sell" commercial would end the program.

Each program, despite the wide range of time periods available for its plot, had certain parameters. Each began with the Old Timer, portrayed by Harvey Hayes, who served as narrator and would assist the announcer with the commercial messages. He also might briefly interact with some cast members. Virtually every episode contained music and frequently one, two or more songs, woven into the plot. Don Ameche was the leading male in the cast and regularly played either the brave hero or the arch villain, depending on who had the most lines.

Backing up Ameche and Bernadine Flynn, were a group of talented Chicago actors, including Lucille Husting, Betty White (no relation to the TV actress), John Daly (no relation to the TV commentator), and Bob White. Many of the programs were biographical. In fact, its first three shows portrayed the life and career of Great Northern's founder, James J. Hill, demonstrating him to be a great railroad builder, a philanthropist, and modern conservationist. In later programs, frontier explorers were featured in the scripts, including Pierce de la Verendrye, who traversed the Mississippi River in 1738.

There were other programs that detailed the history of certain regions or cities and among these were Glacier National Park and the city of Seattle. Some of the episodes were based upon holidays; the December 22, 1930, program was a Christmas romance involving an accident victim in a hospital who meets a young woman there. The following week, Don Ameche played a young man searching for his wife (played by Lucille Husting) on New Year's Eve. When he finds her singing in a night club, the husband and his wife harmonize "Body and Soul" at midnight as the program ended.

Historical accuracy was not required of all the programs that involved actual frontier persons. Joaquin Murrieta, the notorious Mexican bandit during the 1850s California Gold Rush, was the central character in the January 26, 1931, episode. He has to choose between two singers, one beautiful but treacherous, the other unattractive but faithful. In the process, all three characters sing love songs. When Murrieta is called "a dirty greaser" by one American, another American quickly comes to Murrieta's defense.

There is also plenty of music in another episode, which aired February 16, 1931, in which a frontier saloon singer, Jenny, is in love with outlaw Buck Brewster. She uses salty language, "You know damn well what" when talking to her boss Spike, the cruel saloon owner who won't let her leave with Buck. "You go to hell" he threatens her. In the final showdown, she tries to scratch Spike's face, but he shoots and kills her. Buck lunges at him and Spike kills him also. The enraged saloon patrons, appalled at Spike's violence, grab him and put a noose around his neck. He's soon dead, at the end of a rope, hanging from a rafter in his own saloon.

Harvey Hayes, as the Old Timer, became such a popular figure with the radio audience that the Great Northern Railroad began a series of vacation tours to and from Glacier National Park in which the Old Timer was the tour leader. Interested listeners were directed to send their reservation requests to: "The Great Northern Railroad, 113 N. Clark Street, Chicago, Illinois." Each tour was capped at 40 people and the railroad had no trouble selling out several of these.

Sources: Audio copies of *Empire Builders*; Hickerson, *4th Revised*; Swartz; *Daily News*, Geneva, NY, June 17, 1929; *Brooklyn Daily Eagle*, January 28, 1929; *Los Angeles Times*, June 22, 1931; *Oakland Tribune*, February 11, 1929, and March 25, 1929; *Gazette*, Billings, MT, September 16, 1930.

The Flying Horse Ranch see *Life on Red Horse Ranch*

FORT LARAMIE

JACK FRENCH

NETWORK: CBS
FORMAT: Half hour, weekly
DURATION OF RUN: January 22, 1956, to October 28, 1956
SPONSOR: Sustaining
AUDIO COPIES EXTANT: 40 (complete run)

SCRIPTS ARCHIVED: American University Library, Washington, DC; American Radio Archives; John Dunkel Papers, University of California, Los Angeles; SPERDVAC

Although public interest and advertising dollars in the 1950s were switching to television, CBS created, in succession, four superb radio series about the western frontier: *Gunsmoke* (1952 to 1961), *Fort Laramie* (1956), **Frontier Gentleman** (1958) and **Have Gun — Will Travel** (1958 to 1960). Despite the fact it had the shortest run of these four, *Fort Laramie* was certainly the equal of the others in terms of excellent production values and historical accuracy, plus brilliant writing and acting.

Fort Laramie was a very close relative of **Gunsmoke** since the two series had the same producer/director, writers, sound effects men, and many of the same actors. **Gunsmoke** had been running for almost four years when Norman Macdonnell created *Fort Laramie* and brought it to the CBS microphones. The latter had the same gritty realism, attention to detail, and integrity that audiences had long admired in **Gunsmoke**.

Both Dodge City, KS, and Fort Laramie, WY, were real, and significant, locations in the history of the Western Expansion. The original Fort Laramie, located on the eastern Wyoming prairie (about 100 miles from where the city of Laramie is now located) was an important civilian fur trading post from 1834 to 1849; between 1841 to 1849 the fur trade in that area continued to decline, but the fort was a major stopover for wagon trains of settlers heading west, en route to Oregon.

The U.S. government bought the site of Fort Laramie in 1849 to house a military force which would protect this part of the Oregon Trail from hostile Indians and for the next 40 years it would be a U.S. Army post. Located near the North Platte and Laramie Rivers, the military post was in the homeland of the Sioux, Cheyenne, and Arapaho Indians. The fort served as a station for the Overland Stage, the short-lived Pony Express, and as a supply depot for the lengthy military campaigns against the Sioux and the Cheyenne under Sitting Bull in the 1870s.

The earliest paintings of the fort, dating back to 1837, show it to be a log stockade with high walls and raised blockhouses. However, by the time it became a military outpost in the 1840s, the original structure had disappeared and, because Congress refused to appropriate the money for a new and larger stockade, over the

A CBS publicity photo of Raymond Burr, who played the lead role in *Fort Laramie* (courtesy American Radio Archives at Thousand Oaks Library, Thousand Oaks, California).

two decades that the Army occupied Fort Laramie, the fort just consisted of several military buildings arranged about a parade ground on the flat prairie. Regardless of how radio listeners imagined it in 1956, it was not enclosed by walled fortifications.

When Norman Macdonnell began the creation of *Fort Laramie* in late 1955, he insisted upon historical accuracy to preserve the integrity of the series. Correct geographic names, authentic Indian practices, military terminology, and actual names of the original buildings of the real fort were required. So when the radio characters referred to the sutler's store (which is what the trading post was called in that era), the surgeon's quarters, "Old Bedlam" (the officers' quarters) or the old bakery, they were naming actual structures in the original fort.

Although Macdonnell used the same writers, soundmen, and supporting actors in *Fort Laramie* who had been so successful in **Gunsmoke**, he naturally picked different actors for the lead roles. Heading up the cast was Raymond Burr, a 39-year-old Canadian-born actor with a long history in broadcasting and the movies. Burr had begun his career in 1939, alternating between the stage and radio. He then turned to Hollywood, and from 1946 until he got the part of Captain Lee Quince in *Fort Laramie* in 1956, he had appeared in 37 films. A few were excellent (*Rear Window*, *The Blue Gardenia*), some were average (*Walk a Crooked Mile*, *A Place in the Sun*), but a few were dreadful (*Bride of Vengeance*, *Red Light* and *Abandoned*).

With Burr in the lead, Macdonnell selected three supporting players: Vic Perrin as Sergeant Gorce, Jack Moyles as Major Daggett, the commanding officer of the post, and Harry Bartell as Lieutenant Siberts. Macdonnell knew the original Fort Laramie usually had a Lieutenant Colonel as the C.O. but he probably preferred a shorter military title. Perrin, a 40-year-old veteran radio actor had been in countless productions, but had achieved name recognition only on **The Zane Grey Show** where he played the lead, Tex Thorne. Jack Moyles was also a busy radio actor, having started in 1935 in *Hawthorne House*, with later major roles in *Romance*, *Twelve Players*, *Night Editor*, as well as the lead in *A Man Called Jordan*. From 1947 to 1948 he was a regular on *The Adventures of Philip Marlowe* which Macdonnell also directed.

Born in New Orleans, Bartell was raised in Houston, TX,

A CBS publicity photo of Vic Perrin, who appeared on *Fort Laramie* as Sgt. Gorce (courtesy American Radio Archives at Thousand Oaks Library, Thousand Oaks, California).

where he got his first radio job there on station KRPC. In the 1940s, he relocated to Los Angeles and found regular employment as an actor on *Lux Radio Theater, Suspense,* and *The Saint*; he also had multiple roles in Norman Corwin's V-E Day special, "On a Note of Triumph." Bartell was on the first *Gunsmoke* radio program in 1952 and became a member of its repertory company. With Vic Perrin, he co-wrote two *Gunsmoke* episodes in its final year.

Bartell, who in 1956 was 42 years of age, and older than both Perrin and Burr, had doubts about being able to project the voice of a young, junior officer. However, anyone who has heard Bartell in this role will be convinced his fears were groundless. His voice clearly portrayed that of a youthful, inexperienced, but earnest military college graduate. The Siberts character has the central role in the March 4, 1956, episode, "Shavetail." The title was based upon the nickname that enlisted men in the U.S. Cavalry in the 1800s gave to new officers fresh out of West Point. The term originated from a custom of shaving or docking the tail of an untrained horse so the troopers would be wary of such a mount.

To back up the four main military characters, a large number of skilled actors were called upon. While there were many other officers, enlisted men, scouts, and civilians at Fort Laramie, most of the actors who played them appeared in only one or two separate episodes. In addition to Howard McNear, who played Doc on *Gunsmoke*, and had a reoccurring role as the sutler Pliny, Sam Edwards appeared in several programs as Trooper Harrison. Parley Baer, who portrayed Chester on the long running *Gunsmoke*, was only on *Fort Laramie* for one episode, "Nature Boy" July 27, 1956). Other supporting actors included John Dehner who had leads in other series, Virginia Gregg, Barney Phillips, Larry Dobkin, Ben Wright, and Jeanette Nolan, all of whom were also working regularly on *Gunsmoke*. *Fort Laramie* also utilized the versatile voices of Bob Sweeney, Virginia Christine, Lou Krugman, Howard Culver, Helen Kleeb, and Jack Kruschen.

By the mid–1950s when *Fort Laramie* began, many of the actors on the West Coast were doing some television and movie work during the daytime so this radio series was rehearsed and taped for transcription during the evening. Once a week the cast and crew gathered at CBS Studio One in Hollywood to tape the show; this was the last radio production stu-

A CBS publicity photo of Raymond Burr, left, and Vic Perrin in *Fort Laramie* (courtesy American Radio Archives at Thousand Oaks Library, Thousand Oaks, California).

dio in use in California. *Fort Laramie* debuted on January 22, 1956, with an episode entitled "Playing Indian."

The scripts were honest, accurate to the period, and character-driven. Military expressions of the late 1800s were used appropriately. When officers ordered their troopers to "pin-
graze" their mounts, they were referring to a picket pin, which every cavalry soldier packed,
which they would shove into the ground and tie the horses reins to it. Troopers on the
show frequently complained about their pay, 50 cents a day, their salary in 1870. Officers
did not object to their income; in that era a captain made $2,000 a year, or over $5 daily.

Like its counterpart *Gunsmoke*, this military adventure show had strong women's
roles, realistic and sympathetic portrayals of Indians, and an emphasis on the ordinary
struggles of the prairie frontier. *Fort Laramie* was an honest reflection of the difficulties,
danger, and boredom of life on an isolated Army post in the early 1880s.

Just four writers produced nearly all of the scripts for this series, the same quartet
that did most of the writing on *Gunsmoke*: John Meston, Les Crutchfield, (Mary) Kathleen Hite and John Dunkel. Hite was praised by her contemporaries as "one helluva
writer" and certainly was responsible for some of the best episodes in this remarkable
series. Although there was little room for humor in this gritty, poignant western program,
Hite could manage to fit some into her scripts, both realistically and logically. Her stories
provided little bursts of zest and humanity mixed with somber themes of betrayal, death,
remorse, and in one episode, rape.

Hite, a 1938 graduate of the University of Wichita, became the first woman staff
writer at CBS during World War II. She not only wrote nine of the first 20 scripts of *Fort
Laramie*, she also wrote the last 19. Moreover, her script for "Woman of Horse Creek"
was the only one to be given the honor of a second production during the run of *Fort
Laramie*, airing on both February 12 and September 23, 1956. In addition, a number of
her *Fort Laramie* scripts were also used on *Gunsmoke*: her "Woman of Horse Creek" and
"Hattie Pelfrey" aired on *Gunsmoke* under the titles "Solomon River" and "Nettie Sitton."

But regardless of who was writing the script, the story line of each episode accurately
reflected military life at the original Fort Laramie. The February 1, 1956, program, "Boredom," dealt with the threat of scurvy, the March 3, 1956, show, "The Coward," described
the residual pain of the Civil War, and the February 5, 1956, episode, "Squaw Man,"
chronicled the tragedy of the disappearing buffalo. One of the more unusual scripts in the
series was the only one written by William N. Robson. He took the title, "Never the Twain,"
from Kipling and portions of the plot from actual history, creating the star-crossed lovers:
Lieutenant Siberts and Ah-ho-appa, daughter of Spotted Tail, a tribal chief.

Spotted Tail, a chief of the Brules Sioux, brought his daughter to Fort Laramie
several times. She liked the men in uniform and dreamed of marrying an officer, although
there was no evidence of any actual romance. At age 18, Ah-ho-appa, dying of tuberculosis,
made her father promise to bury her at Fort Laramie and make peace with the U.S. Army.
When she died, he brought her corpse on a travois to the fort and got permission for her
to be buried there. The funeral took place on March 8, 1866, and the post chaplain, with
Spotted Tail's permission, conducted a Christian burial service, which the fort interpreter
translated for her family.

Another actual incident from the history of the West was dramatized in the August
5, 1956, episode, "The Massacre," in which John Dehner played a religious zealot, Major
Petrie, who leads his troopers into slaughtering a large group of peaceful and unsuspecting

Indians. This particular episode closely parallels the historical facts of the Sand Creek Massacre of November 1864 when Colonel J.M. Chivington (a former Methodist preacher) and his Colorado volunteers attacked a placid group of reservation Cheyenne and murdered 150 of them, mostly women and children.

The soundmen, Ray Kemper and Bill James, who were assisted by Tom Hanley, were simply second to none in this department. Just as they were doing on *Gunsmoke*, they created the most convincing and imaginative sound effects which even a critical listener could appreciate. Every crack of a rifle, creak of the McClellan saddle (official Cavalry issue in the mid–1800s), and footsteps going across the dirt parade ground, over the gravel path, and up the wooden steps, were all done with authentic precision. Each time a character got up from a table, listeners heard the chair legs scrape against the wooden floor before the footsteps started.

Some of the best examples of their sound artistry are found in the complex realism of their battle scenes. Very impressive are the compelling sound patterns of the combat between the troopers and several dozen renegade Sioux in the January 29, 1956, episode of "Boatman's Story." Another example of the convincing sound patterns of a group of people is the wagon train leaving the fort in the February 5, program "Squaw Man." Kemper, James, and Hanley never missed a chance to shade the texture of a scene with the perfect sounds, whether they created them manually or mixed them with their reservoir of audio disks.

The talented musical director on this series was Amerigo Marino; he had risen from the orchestra ranks as a first-rate violinist eventually to become the conductor of the CBS Orchestra, a position he held until 1964. For the main theme of *Fort Laramie*, Marino chose "Garry-Owen" the unofficial marching song of the 7th Cavalry, which was derived from an 18th century Irish folk tune.

Fort Laramie lasted for only 10 months but most of the cast regulars got to be good friends, if they were not already before. Late in 1956 Burr announced that he just won the title role in a new television series, *Perry Mason*, and he promised them all jobs. Unfortunately, Burr overestimated the power of the leading man in a television series to get work for his friends, and although *Perry Mason* ran for nine years in prime time, Bartell only received one day's work on the series while Perrin and Moyles got none.

The final broadcast of *Fort Laramie*, the 40th episode, "Army Wife," was aired on October 28, 1956. Thereafter, many of the cast regulars continued to see each other, both in a social and professional vein. Vic Perrin and Ben Wright were both close personal friends of Harry Bartell and their camaraderie was undiminished after *Fort Laramie* ended. Dramatic radio was nearly gone as television ascended quickly. *Frontier Gentleman* (with John Dehner in the lead) lasted 41 episodes in 1958 and *Gunsmoke* hung on until the summer of 1961 and many of the former cast members of *Fort Laramie* found work on these shows, among others. But the bugle was clearly sounding "retreat" for network radio drama. Too soon, it was over.

Most of the *Fort Laramie* regulars, including the writers, moved into the emerging television industry. Hite was very successful writing for television and she regularly wrote scripts for *The Waltons, Guns of Will Sonnet, Falcon Crest, Wagon Train*, and *Crown Theater*. Jack Moyles only lived to 1973, dying at the age of 60. Hite died in February 1989, the same year as Vic Perrin. Burr and Bartell lived longer; Burr died in September 1993 at the age of 76 while Bartell was 90 when he passed away in February, 2004.

Fortunately, every episode of *Fort Laramie* was transcribed and audio copies of all of them are available today. It must be very comforting for the few remaining cast and crew members of that esteemed series to know that the series will continue to be enjoyed by generations to come, including future visitors to the Fort Laramie historic site.

NOTE: Fort Laramie, the military post, was abandoned in 1890 and allowed to fall into decay; no significant restoration was attempted for nearly a half century. In 1937 the state of Wyoming purchased the site of some 200 acres and later deeded it over to the National Park Service, who partially restored several of the buildings. The area is currently administered as the Fort Laramie National Historical Site under the Department of Interior and is open year-round. Approximately 57,000 tourists visit this famous military post annually. A virtual tour of today's Fort Laramie is available on the internet by going to: www.nps.gov/fola/index.htm.

Sources: Audio copies of *Fort Laramie*; Dunning, *On the Air*; Urwin; *Fort Laramie Official National Park Handbook*, Department of the Interior, 1983; *Fort Laramie Official Map and Guide*, Department of the Interior, 1996; *Return With Us Now*, January/February 2012; *Smithsonian Magazine*, April 1996.

FRONTIER FIGHTERS

JACK FRENCH *and* DAVID S. SIEGEL

NETWORK: Syndicated

FORMAT: 15 minutes, broadcast intervals determined by local stations, but usually aired weekly

DURATION OF RUN: Circa 1935 to 1943

SPONSORS: Various regional sponsors, including Dairylea Milk, Peak-Hagedon Funeral Homes, etc.

AUDIO COPIES EXTANT: 39

SCRIPTS ARCHIVED: A single script in *One Hundred Non-Royalty Plays* edited by William Kozlenko.

This quarter hour western, concentrating on people and events of the American frontier, was produced and syndicated by Radio Transcription Company of America, Ltd., usually called "Transco." It was located in Hollywood, had its own studio on Cosmo Street, and also rented other studios when business was very good. Lindsay McHarrie, formerly a production manager at station KHJ, supervised many of Transco's transcribed series, frequently using both performers and production personnel from KHJ.

From 1930 to 1938, Transco turned out a steady stream of modestly priced radio series; some would encompass as few as 13 episodes or as many as 52, each of them 15 minutes in length. The standard episode would consist of 12 minutes of drama or comedy, with a minute and a half of recorded music at both the beginning and the end. This enabled the local stations, when they found a paying sponsor, to have one of their staff announcers do three minutes of voiceover commercials.

Many of Transco's series are long forgotten, including *Police Headquarters*, *Comedy Capers*, and *Hollywood Spotlight*, but one of them was the holiday classic *The Cinnamon Bear*, which can still be heard on a few stations today. Although Transco went out of business in 1938, many of its recordings were obtained by Bruce Eells Productions in the early 1940s, who then kept some of the more profitable programs in circulation for another decade.

While the complete history of *The Cinnamon Bear* and the personnel involved are common knowledge, radio historians know virtually nothing about other individual Transco series, in terms of the identity of directors, writers, and performers. That certainly applies to *Frontier Fighters*. With the exception of the recognizable voice of Hanley Stafford in a number of episodes, none of the others performers have been positively identified. But for the most part, all of them were competent actors.

The premise of each individual program was relatively simple in design; a significant historical figure or event in U.S. frontier history would be chosen and the writer would script a concise summary of that person (Kit Carson) or military action (Custer's Last Stand.) While most of the people portrayed were famous (Lewis & Clark, Brigham Young, Buffalo Bill Cody) several were then, or are now, unknown to most Americans (Jebediah Strong Smith, the Reverend Thomas Starr King, Ira Burton Perrine).

Although one of the variations of the standard introduction to each episode was: "Frontier Fighters: The stirring tales of the men and women who have pushed the frontier of North American ever westward," women were not represented well in the series' 39 episodes. Only two women, Annie D. Tallant and Eliza Ann Brooks, got their own episode while Sacagawea had a significant role in the Lewis and Clark drama. Tallant and her husband had joined a group of gold seekers who slipped into the North Dakota Territory in violation of the 1868 Treaty of Ft. Laramie and were later escorted back to Iowa by the U.S. Cavalry, a fact ignored in the radio drama. But never the less, Tallant achieved the distinction of being the first white woman to enter the Black Hills.

Brooks, in order to join her husband in California, took her six children in a covered wagon across the vast prairie. While she had a hired driver for the first part of her continental journey from Michigan, she and the youngsters faced the trail dangers alone for most of the 2,000 mile trek. Her courageous adventure was dramatized on radio twice; in addition to *Frontier Fighters*, she was also portrayed by Agnes Moorehead in a half hour *Cavalcade of America* program that aired April 3, 1939.

The quality of the 39 episodes of *Frontier Fighters* varied significantly in terms of the script writing and the sound effects. Gunshots could be very realistic in one episode but flat and unconvincing in another. Crowd and fight scenes were uniformly well done, while specific actions were sometimes off the mark. When Sacagawea's husband was whipping her with a leather strap, it sounded like wet yarn hitting a pillow.

In the scripts, the depictions of Indians involved descriptions that may have been part of the 1800s vernacular but surely would have caused some discomfort to American radio audiences of the 1930s and 1940s, such as "Let's kill those painted savage devils." In addition, hackneyed expressions abounded: "I'll thrash you within an inch of your life," "You're lower than a skunk," and "They died with their boots on."

Probably the most confusing aspect of the series was: what type of radio audience was it designed to attract? The majority of the programs had adult themes, but mature listeners were seldom interested in 15 minute adventure shows. Female audience members would find little to capture their attention. Some stations were apparently aiming for the youngsters since they broadcast the show in the 5 P.M. to 6 P.M. time slot, along with *Tom Mix*, *Captain Midnight*, and *Superman*.

This scheduling may have been a mistake since many of the programs featured brutality, suffering, and violence that would disturb the average child listener. Station WHEC in Rochester, NY ran this promotional advertisement in November 1938: "Boys and girls will thrill to the story of the Donner Party (on *Frontier Fighters*)." Youngsters who accepted this invitation heard a brutal retelling of this tragic event where two thirds of a wagon train of 87 men, women, and children starved or froze to death, trapped by 20 feet of snow in the Sierra Nevada Mountains in the winter of 1846-47. As the narrator described it: "Brave rescuers split up, leaving some to die with the Donner party. Draft animals gone, the starving victims ate their moccasins, harness leather, the strings from their snow shoes, the boots in which they stood." The only fact the scriptwriter left out was the cannibalism that also occurred, but even this script of *Frontier Fighters* guaranteed nightmares for many a young listener.

Almost as terrifying to juvenile followers of this series must have been the episode, "The Massacre at Taos." This was a dramatization of a bloody revolt in New Mexico in January 1847 where American fathers were killed or scalped in the presence of their wives and children. The invaders of their homes were Mexican renegades and Pueblo Indians, determined to destroy the territorial government. Some women and children narrowly escaped capture by burrowing through an adobe wall.

But these types of fearful dramatizations were the exception since most of the episodes contained nothing scarier that youngsters would have heard on their favorite juvenile adventure series. Moreover, some of these programs, which were factual presentations about significant, but relatively unknown explorers, missionaries, and civic leaders, would have supplemented the listeners' knowledge of American history.

Sources: Audio copies of *Frontier Fighters*; French, *Private Eyelashes*; Hickerson, *4th Revised*; *Rochester Democrat & Chronicle*, November 17, 1938, and January 26, 1939; *Chicago Tribune*, February 28, 1942, and August 7, 1942.

FRONTIER GENTLEMAN

Stewart Wright

NETWORK: CBS
FORMAT: Half hour, weekly
DURATION OF RUN: February 2, 1958, to November 16, 1958
SPONSORS: Mainly sustaining with occasional sponsors, including Chrysler Corporation (Dodge and Plymouth), Kent Cigarettes, Studebaker Lark, and Tums Anti-Acid
AUDIO COPIES EXTANT: 41 (total run), plus 2 audition copies
SCRIPTS ARCHIVED: American Radio Archives; Chuck Schaden Collection, Library of American Broadcasting; SPERDVAC

One of the best original radio westerns was also one of the last to hit the network radio waves: *Frontier Gentleman*. The series was unusual in many aspects, including the fact that its central character was not a lawman, rancher, cowboy, or other typical denizen of the Old West, but rather a foreign correspondent with some unfamiliar credentials. The basic premise of the series was explained in its opening: "Herewith an Englishman's account of life and death in the West. As a reporter for the *London Times*, he writes his colorful and unusual accounts. But as a man with a gun, he lives and becomes a part of the violent years in the new territories."

A CBS press release supplies additional elaboration and some incorrect information on *Frontier Gentleman* which premiered on Sunday, February 2, 1958, "Antony Ellis, who created the show, will also write, produce and direct the series. Featured in the leading role of J. B. Kendall, a quiet-spoken freelance correspondent for a London newspaper and a veteran of a long service with the British army in India will be the versatile radio and TV actor Ben Wright, who has appeared in many of CBS Radio's most popular dramatic programs...." This release incorrectly listed Ben Wright and not John Dehner in the Kendall role. "Tony" Ellis, one of the Golden Age's finest writers, directors, and producers, was an Englishman who became a naturalized American citizen.

As a reporter, Kendall was a keen observer of the people, places, and things around him. Through his encounters with the various people he met, the audience learned a great deal about the J. B. Kendall character. He had a wry sense of humor and could appreciate a good joke even when it was at his own expense. Generally an easy-going man, he could be pushed, but only so far. Kendall had a strong sense of justice and was not afraid to stand up and be counted. In the episode "Lost Mine," the listeners learned Kendall's full name; he mentioned that J. B. stood for "Jeremy Brian."

Kendall was a "remittance man," a son who was banished from England by his family and paid to stay away. The reason for the banishment was he been cashiered out of the Army as a result of his refusal to testify at the court martial of a brother officer whom he believed to be innocent. He supplemented the remittance from his family with the money he earned as a reporter for the *London Times*. By the end of the series, it is vaguely implied that his family had forgiven him and wanted him to return to England.

While J. B. Kendall was new to the West; the man was not a true dude or tenderfoot. As a British Army veteran with much combat experience, he was accustomed to a primitive and often dangerous living environment. Kendall was proficient in the usual soldierly skills, including weaponry such as rifles, hand guns, and knives; in hand-to-hand combat; and most importantly, survival. His military skills made him a formidable opponent in the Old West as several men learned to their bitter regret.

This 1958 adult western series was interestingly and well written; it was clearly aimed at a mature audience. Ellis was a student of the history of the Old West and his scripts were packed with remarkable characters and unusual story lines. Ellis incorporated period authentic slang and terms into his dialog such as "hucky dummy," a baking powder bread with raisins while "gut-warmer" and "wild mare's milk" were just a couple of the myriad of slang terms used for frontier whiskey. In the episode "Gentle Virtue," Kendall learns the game of poker and wins a most unusual pot: a Chinese slave girl. In "The Trial," the Englishman acts as the lawyer for a man accused of murder when a defendant comes to court heavily armed. Several of the more seemingly typical story lines included such topics as cowboys at the end of a cattle drive, prospecting and gold fever, Indian fighting, and cattlemen versus homesteaders. But even these episodes were filled with wonderful characters and unexpected plot line twists.

While quite a few historical figures are mentioned in various episodes, Kendall also had personal interaction with several. He was robbed by outlaw Jesse James and in the twice produced episode "Aces and Eights," Kendall was present at the poker table when Wild Bill Hickok drew his deadly hand. Particularly noteworthy were Kendall's encounters with Madame Verdi, an alias of former Confederate spy Belle Siddons, who ran a traveling gambling establishment. These meetings provided the story lines for four episodes: "Gambling Lady," "Belle Siddons' Encore," "Belle Siddons Strikes Back," and "Last of Belle Siddons." Kendall first meets Siddons in Cheyenne and later in Deadwood and Ellis's dialog between Kendall and Madame Verdi, played by Jeanne Bates Lansworth, rings true as between two adults who have become good friends and understand each other very well.

The series accurately relates the plights of minorities and women of the period. A vignette from the twice produced episode, "Random Notes," provides a representative example. It relates the story of a Chinese storekeeper who is duped into buying a "salted" placer gold claim and the townspeople find the Chinaman's plight quite funny until he sells the worthless claim for even a greater profit and goes home to China. Several episodes dealt with the hard life women faced on the frontier. Some of the women in Ellis's stories suffered significant losses, but did not give up trying to build a better life.

Antony Ellis was a multi-talented man. During the waning years of the Golden Age of radio, Ellis was much in demand because he could write, direct, produce and even narrate. He started in Hollywood as an actor and soon began writing and adapting scripts for *Pursuit, Escape, Romance, Suspense,* and *O'Hara*; all series on which he

John Dehner had the leading role in two CBS western series, *Frontier Gentleman* and *Have Gun — Will Travel*, and was frequently in the supporting casts of *Gunsmoke* and *Fort Laramie* (courtesy American Radio Archives at Thousand Oaks Library, Thousand Oaks, California).

would later become the director/producer. The first script he wrote for **Gunsmoke**, "The Ride Back," was later used as the basis for the motion picture of the same name with Ellis penning the screenplay. In early 1950 Ellis got his initial directing experience on the series *Pursuit*. By late 1952, Ellis's directing career started in earnest; he took over *Escape*. Ellis later added the prestigious *CBS Radio Workshop* and finally, *Frontier Gentleman* to his directorial resume. Incidentally, Ellis directed two John Dehner-written scripts: "The Man with the Steel Teeth" on *Escape* and "Lily and The Colonel" on *Suspense*. Starting in the early 1950s, Ellis was also writing scripts for television and would continue to do so until his untimely death from cancer at the early age of 47 in 1967.

During the last 15 years of the Golden Age of Radio John Dehner was one of the busiest actors in Hollywood. The talented Dehner could play an incredibly wide range of roles on radio: romantic leads, pillars of the community, policeman and judges, crooks, and down-and-outers. However, he is probably best remembered for his appearances in a single genre that composed a very small portion of his entire body of work: the western. In those he played rustlers, saddle bums, con men, cowards, gunmen, and killers; he also played honest cowboys, lawmen, ministers, judges, army officers, ranchers, and merchants.

There was a common denominator in all four CBS radio adult western series, **Gunsmoke, Fort Laramie,** *Frontier Gentleman,* and **Have Gun — Will Travel.** One actor auditioned for the lead roles in all four series, was offered the lead role in the first series, but turned it down and won the starring roles in the latter two series. John Dehner was that actor. Dehner turned down the role of Matt Dillon in **Gunsmoke** because he thought he might get typecast as an actor who specialized in playing western roles. Yet he went on to appear in nearly half of the 480 **Gunsmoke** episodes; more than any other guest star. Out of the 667 combined network episodes in these four CBS radio series, John Dehner either starred or made guest appearances in an incredible 394 episodes which was nearly 60 percent of the episodes of these four series.

Dehner also had great success in television and motion pictures; he appeared in approximately 150 series on the small screen and in more than 125 movies. It is not surprising that he played the same role in both the radio and television versions of three episodes of **Gunsmoke**: Nate Springer in "Crack-Up," Nip Cullers in "Tap Day for Kitty," and Wayne Russell in "Daddy-O." John Dehner would out live his good friend, Antony Ellis, by nearly twenty-five years, dying in 1992 at age 76.

Talented cast members ably supported Dehner. While some actors now worked on television exclusively, the performers on *Frontier Gentleman*, despite their television roles, also found time for radio work. These performers were not only skilled but also enjoyed acting on radio. Network mainstays such as Jack Moyles, Jack Kruschen, Harry Bartell, Virginia Gregg, Vic Perrin, Stacy Harris, Lawrence Dobkin, Joseph Kearns, Eddie Firestone, Jeanette Nolan, Charles Seel, Jeanne Bates (also credited as Jeanne Lansworth), Barney Phillips, Paula Winslowe, and Ben Wright, plied their craft on this series. Three familiar voices with unfamiliar names also appeared on *Frontier Gentleman*: Richard Perkins, Ray Woods, and Waldo Epperson. (Actually, these familiar strangers were Vic Perrin, Ralph Moody, and Parley Baer respectively using pseudonyms.)

As Kendall was the only continuing character in the series, the supporting cast had to carry more of the load so Ellis gave these actors numerous interesting roles to play and lines to speak. Virginia Gregg got to play many roles including the Chinese slave girl, Gentle Virtue, a rancher's wife portraying Desdemona in "Othello" as well as frontier legend Calamity Jane. Several of the most colorful characters encountered by Kendall were ably played by veteran actor Joseph Kearns. Both Lawrence Dobkin and John McIntire played the doomed Wild Bill Hickok. Dobkin also appeared as Jesse James. Vic Perrin played an actual frontier outlaw, Archie McLaughlin.

Composer Jerry Goldsmith wrote the main theme for *Frontier Gentleman*. The trumpet version was used for each episode's closing. The theme's haunting melody was almost like a slightly premature "Taps" for the American Golden Age of Radio. Wilbur Hatch and others wrote much of the episode-specific music.

Veteran sound pattern artists Tom Hanley and Bill James did most of the sound effects for *Frontier Gentleman*. Their skills had been honed on other CBS series like **Gunsmoke** and **Fort Laramie** and added realism and authenticity to the Ellis productions. Their use of exaggerated sound patterns to replace dialog or narration with appropriate sounds for common activities, such as a person leaving a building and crossing a street, was quite effective.

Use of this aforementioned technique is nowhere more compelling than in the episode "Justice of the Peace" when sound patterns alone are used to tell the end result of a lynch mob who has a bound victim with a rope around his neck mounted on a horse. The audience hears in rapid succession: a slap, a clatter of horse hoof beats that rapidly slow to a stop, a very short silence, then the ominous sound of twisting of a creaking rope and finally the faint clucking of undisturbed chickens nearby. The imagination of the listener needs nothing more to visualize the dead man slowly swinging in direct view of the now-silent mob.

Frontier Gentleman came to the airwaves at a time when network radio dramatic programming was reaching its end. Advertising money was moving to television, which ironically radio revenues had helped to start. Limited time slots were now available for new network radio shows since the networks were turning over more air time to their affiliate stations for local programming. New shows had to attract sponsors quickly or be cancelled. *Frontier Gentleman* failed to obtain sufficient sponsorship, so it was replaced by the radio version of a popular television series, ***Have Gun — Will Travel***. On the radio, this television transfer would also star John Dehner. *Frontier Gentleman* deserved a better fate than being just a late footnote to the Golden Age of Radio.

Sources: Audio copies of *Frontier Gentleman*; French, *Frontier Gentleman*; Hickerson, *4th Revised*; Wright; Interview of John Dehner by John Dunning, February 19, 1984; 1958 program listings in: *Bridgeport Sunday Post*, *Independent Star-News*, *New York Times*, and *Los Angeles Times*; *The Old Radio Times*, March 2006; *Radio Recall*, Volume 28, August and October 2011; *Return With Us Now*, Volume 30, Number 11, November 2005; *Program logs*: Salomonson; Wright, *O'Hara* and *Pursuit*.

FRONTIER TOWN

STAN CLAUSSEN

NETWORK: Syndicated, CBS
FORMAT: Half hour, weekly
DURATION OF RUN: March 5, 1949, to March 26, 1953 (with breaks)
SPONSOR: Various (Broadcasters Program Syndicate)
AUDIO COPIES EXTANT: 47
SCRIPTS ARCHIVED: Undetermined

Frontier Town started out with a reformist point of view. Its protagonist, Chad Remington, was a young lawyer who wanted to replace the disorder of his home town with a legal justice system; however, as the syndicated program evolved it came to be more of a traditional "shoot-'em-up" juvenile western. It was created in the twilight zone of the late 1940s, running first on San Francisco local station KQW, March 5 to April 9, 1949. CBS changed its call letters to KCBS, where the series aired April 16 to August 8, 1949. *Frontier Town* returned on the CBS network May 6, 1952, and aired until March 26, 1953.

The fictional Chad Remington was called home to Dos Rios, TX to find out who murdered his father. In his quest to bring law and order to the wild frontier in 47 episodes, Remington used both persuasion and quick gun play. Jeff Chandler (born Ira Grossel) played Chad Remington both in the KQW/KCBS series and in the first 23 episodes of the CBS series. Bill Foreman was the announcer and he always identified Jeff Chandler as "Tex Chandler."

Remington's saddle partner was Cherokee O'Bannon, played by Wade Crosby, using a W.C. Fields-like voice and bar room humor. O'Bannon, a former traveling medicine man, still promoted and consumed "Cherokee Indian Rattlesnake Oil," guaranteed to be 90 proof. Remington, who ran his father's ranch, also maintained his law office over the town's livery stable, which was operated by O'Bannon.

Paul Franklin directed and wrote the scripts with Joel Murcott. Franklin who also wrote for **Red Ryder** and **The Zane Grey Theater**; while Franklin's scripts emphasized Chad's persuasive side, Murcott usually wrote the "shoot-'em-ups." The main theme and all musical bridges were supplied by a lone organist, either Ivan Ditmars or Bob Mitchell. Bruce Eells produced and distributed the series for the Broadcasters Program Syndicate, whose 127 member stations were both network affiliates and independents. The syndicated program was delivered with organ interludes for local commercials and bundled with two other shows at a total cost of $25 per episode for all three.

No programs exist from the KQW/KCBS series. All 47 shows that do survive come from the syndicated CBS programs, with Jeff Chandler in the title role for 23 episodes, Reed Hadley taking over for the remaining 24 episodes and Wade Crosby in the role of Cherokee O'Bannon in all the shows.

The relative strengths and the weaknesses of the syndicated show are well defined in two episodes. In "Return to Dos Rios" September 26, 1952, the first show of the CBS series, Remington has the sad chore of settling his father's affairs when the old man is murdered with an Indian arrow. The local marshal assumes a former Indian employee is responsible and allows a lynch mob to hang the alleged killer. But Chad regards the old Indian as a member of the family and believes he was too frail to pull a bow and arrow. In addition, the Indian's main accusers, the Kincaid brothers next door, grab off a big piece of his father's ranch. When Chad asks to see the deed for the land sale, he realizes that his father's signature has been forged.

Later Chad and Cherokee search the Kincaid residence and find Indian arrows and a bow, plus the paperwork for the actual land sale agreed to by Chad's father. They show the evidence to the marshal, who has Chad's father's six-guns and belt. Chad straps them on and he and Cherokee go to the saloon to confront the Kincaids. Only a few shots are fired before the marshal arrests the Kincaids. Chad tells his woman friend Libby that Dos Rios probably needs him more than any big city law firm.

Just three months later in "The Guns of Wrath" (December 26, 1952), Remington has established his law practice in Dos Rios, and routinely dines with Libby and her father, a judge. They are interrupted by news that the Cheever gang is robbing the Wells Fargo agency. Chad, Cherokee, the judge and a deputy chase the culprits into a box canyon which contains the headwaters of both the Red and White Rivers (thus Dos Rios).

Both rivers have check dams regulating the water flow to the town. The crooks control the White River dam and Chad and the law officers control the Red River dam. What ensues is that both groups begin to use the dams and the rivers like pawns in a chess game. The crooks next kidnap Helga Peterson and send word that if Chad and the law officers don't let the Cheever gang go, the crooks will blow the White River dam and flood the town. Chad refuses; the dam blows, but only a small amount of water inundates Dos Rios. The Cheever gang follows the flood waters into town and starts to steal everything that's not nailed down. So Chad retaliates by threatening to blow the Red River dam; but instead he sneaks into the slightly-flooded town with a large posse. All the evildoers are captured.

The series was produced in Hollywood and had the services of good sound effects personnel. They handled the manual and transcribed sounds of cattle, horses, footsteps, and even furniture scraping on wooden floors. The many gunshots on each show were realistic and included ricocheting rifle reports.

Jeff Chandler was forceful and melodramatic in the role of Chad Remington despite the fact that persuasion was often offset by blazing six shooters. When Reed Hadley took over the part, the contrast between them was evident but it had little effect on the continuity of the show. Some thought that Hadley was "lighter, kinder and more humorous" in the role.

Chandler got his first radio job with Dick Powell and was cast in Powell's movie *Johnny O'Clock*. His best known radio parts were as Michael Shayne and Eve Arden's faculty boyfriend in *Our Miss Brooks*. He was also portraying movie Indians, long after actual Indians were making films. Reed Hadley became well known for his voicing of **Red Ryder** on radio; he had a big following among young listeners in the early 1940s. He was also popular on television in *Racket Squad* and *Public Defender* and most recognizable as the watch commander in the TV version of *Dragnet*.

Sources: Audio copies of *Frontier Town*; Dunning, *On the Air*; Katz; Swartz.

GENE AUTRY'S MELODY RANCH

Bobb Lynes

NAMES: *Gene Autry's Melody Ranch, Double M Ranch, Sergeant Gene Autry, The Gene Autry Show*

NETWORK: Columbia Broadcasting System

FORMAT: Western songs and adventure

DURATION OF RUN: January 7, 1940, to August 1, 1943, and September 23, 1945, to May 16, 1956

AUDIO COPIES EXTANT: 97

SCRIPTS ARCHIVED: Gene Autry Library & Research Services; American Radio Archives; Dudley Dean McGaughey (McGaughy) Papers, American Heritage Center; J. Walter Thompson Archives, Duke University, Durham, NC; Chuck Schaden Collection, Library of American Broadcasting; SPERDVAC.

One of the most prominent Hollywood cowboy singers didn't get his own show on network radio until 1940 by which time he already had a very successful career in western B-movies and the recording industry.

Popular myth has it that while Orvon Grover Autry was working in Oklahoma for a railroad company, Will Rogers heard him strumming his guitar and advised him to get more experience by going on the radio. Whether the story is true or not, in 1928 Gene started appearing on Tulsa's KVOO and, after changing his name, began what was soon to become a budding recording career.

Shortly after his Tulsa debut, Gene became one of the major stars of Chicago's *WLS Barn Dance*. The job didn't pay much, but WLS's in-house artists' agency allowed its cast members such as Autry, Bradley Kincaid, Lulu Belle & Scotty and Little Georgie Gobel to supplement their salaries by touring in packaged stage shows during their off-air days. This further increased these performers' popularity since fans could see the stars they heard on their radios every Saturday night.

Gene continued writing and singing his songs, aided by the Marvin Brothers, Johnny and Frankie, eventually recording his first big hit "That Silver-Haired Daddy of Mine." This success, combined with his radio fame as "Oklahoma's Singing Cowboy" on *WLS Barn Dance*, led Gene to Hollywood in 1934 where, together with his fellow WLSer Lester "Smiley" Burnette, he made his film debut in *In Old Santa Fe*, a Ken Maynard feature western for Nat Levine's Mascot Pictures. Next, Gene and Burnette had bit parts in Maynard's Mascot serial *Mystery Mountain* which had no singing. When Maynard balked at starring in the Mascot serial *The Phantom Empire*, Levine asked Gene to substitute. This leading role resulted in some initial fame for Autry.

In 1934 and 1935, Mascot, Monogram and other small independent studios were brought together, merging into Republic Studios, under the control of Herbert J. Yates. Under this new arrangement, both Gene (Mascot) and John Wayne (Lone Star/Monogram) became the first Republic stars and from 1934 to 1939 Gene was so busy making singing cowboy westerns for Republic, together with personal appearances in theaters and rodeos, he literally didn't have much time for radio, with the exception of some guest appearances on *WLS Barn Dance*.

During the 1930s, Gene also continued to make records, many of which were songs written by him and Smiley and featured in their movies, and his recording activities (for Columbia and later, RCA Victor) helped keep his name alive on the radio. Disk jockeys, as they became known, were the linchpins in popularizing the hillbilly, folk and country/western music of the 1930s and radio was the keystone of that popularity. Small stations couldn't afford to pay the big stars to appear on their airwaves, but they could certainly play their 78 rpm records — and they did. Gene rode this crest of popularity during the late 1930s with several hit records.

In 1939 Philip Wrigley, on behalf of Wrigley's Doublemint Gum, agreed to sponsor Gene Autry on a weekly radio show and a 15 minute audition broadcast on New Year's Eve, December 31, 1939, was set up as part of a special show on the Columbia Broadcasting System. On the show, which was aimed at a family audience, Gene sang a few songs, dramatized a western adventure, and bantered with co-stars and guests. The audition was a success and the series premiered on CBS, Sunday, January 7, 1940, at 6:30 P.M. (EST). Gene and cast did the show live from the new studios at CBS Columbia Square in Hollywood.

Originally, the show was called *Double M Ranch* for Wrigley's Doublemint Gum. Although Wrigley's was also marketing both Spearmint and Juicy Fruit during that era, only Doublemint was ever mentioned on the show. The regular cast included singer "Miss Nancy" Mason and character actor Horace Murphy as Shorty Long. Murphy had appeared in Gene's movies and was a popular sidekick to another cowboy singer, Tex Ritter. Murphy would eventually move over to the **Red Ryder** show and play Buckskin on that very popular Mutual series. Wendell Niles announced and sold the gum on *Double M Ranch*, Johnny Marvin and Lou Bring led the band and Gene was backed up by The Texas Rangers. Gene later replaced the Rangers with a group from Oklahoma called the Jimmy Wakely Trio which featured Johnny Bond, a young song writer who would figure in Gene's later career. During the early months of 1940, the show was renamed *Gene Autry's Melody Ranch* which was also the title of one of Gene's Republic Studios western films.

Melody Ranch would have continued to be aired had it not been for the Japanese attack on Pearl Harbor on December 7, 1941. As a novice civilian pilot, Gene immediately wanted to join in the United States war effort but he agreed to finish a few more westerns for Republic before joining the Army. When the time came to enlist, Gene made his oath-taking a very special occasion; he did it during the July 26, 1942, broadcast of *Melody Ranch*.

As Sergeant Gene Autry, Gene was allowed to continue his radio show each week

Gene Autry, cowboy star of motion pictures, television and radio (courtesy the Library of American Broadcasting, University of Maryland, College Park).

on CBS, but he wasn't paid his former salary. As a member of the active duty military, Gene received about $114, an Army Sergeant's monthly wage, and the money he would have earned from Wrigley was put into a trust fund to be paid when he returned to civilian life at war's end.

Initially, the Army used Gene and his show for public relations purposes and recruitment. The plan was well received, with Gene doing *Sergeant Gene Autry* (as the show was re-titled) on tours of various Army posts and bases. But Gene wanted to get into the actual combat of the war; after all, he wanted to be trained as a pilot and enlisted to do just that. But, since he was too old to qualify as an air cadet, he took enough flying lessons to be transferred from Army Special Services to the Army Air Force Ferrying Services.

Serving overseas in the China/Burma Theater of war, ferrying planes through highly dangerous areas, meant no more radio shows for Sergeant Autry for the next few years. When the war was over, he was honorably discharged from the U.S. Army Air Force on June 17, 1945, and just ten days later he headed up a USO troupe which entertained troops in the South Pacific.

Gene Autry's Melody Ranch, again sponsored by Wrigley's Doublemint, returned to the CBS schedule on Sunday, September 23, 1945, in a 15 minute time slot with a revised format and a different cast. Joining Gene in song were The Pinafores (also called The

Three Kettle Sisters) and The Cass County Boys with Lou Crosby doing the Wrigley's commercials. These folks also backed up Gene on his continued recording career. Having toured with him during the war years, it was natural that Gene asked Johnny Bond to be on this new series. The 15 minute show expanded to 30 minutes on June 16, 1946, and continued on CBS's Sunday schedule in various time-slots; 5:30 or 7:00 P.M. (EST), moving to Saturday nights at 8:00 P.M. from 1949 to 1953. From 1953 to 1956, it was back on Sundays at 6:00 P.M. The director was William "Bill" Burch.

In 1946 Gene welcomed young vocalist Colleen Summers as a new cast member who would later (as Mary Ford) team up with Les Paul in a duo that went on to enjoy great success with many hits. Also during the 1946-1947 season, Gene's old WLS/Republic sidekick, "Smiley" Burnette guested on the show periodically.

The post war format of *Melody Ranch* featured Johnny Bond's guitar strumming leading into the theme song "Back in the Saddle Again" and Gene singing a couple of songs to start off the show. The songs were frequently, but not always, cowboy songs. Gene also sang love ballads, popular tunes, and old favorites. His songs were seasonal also; in December he always sang both "Here Comes Santa Claus" and "Rudolph the Red-Nosed Reindeer." By 1948 Gene enjoyed the assistance of two sidekicks on the show, Johnny Bond and another WLS alumnus, Maxwell Emmet "Pat" Buttram.

After the middle commercial for Doublemint by Gene, there would be some comedy bits with Bond and Buttram. This was followed by a short dramatization of approximately 10 minutes in which Gene would narrate and star. Some of the plots were little morality plays, showing that honesty and truth were the best behavior, while others were western mysteries involving illegal activity or unsolved crimes which Gene would unravel. The stories were modern westerns, taking place on ranches, at rodeos, circuses and cattle drives, etc. A live orchestra provided the musical bridges and talented sound personnel provided realistic hoofbeats, clanging tools, chair legs moving on wooden floors, footsteps, and other sounds as needed.

Many of Hollywood's veteran radio actors appeared in the dramatic sections of *Melody Ranch* over the years: Jeff Chandler, Howard McNear, Tyler McVey, Bea Benadaret, Ken Christy, Earle Ross, Joe DuVal, Harry Lang, Shirley Mitchell, Jerry Hausner and others. Although most programs were produced in Hollywood, when Gene was on personal appearance tours, including his Rodeo Championship annually held in Madison Square Garden, the show would be performed in the closest CBS studio. During one Manhattan production, Parker Fennelly guest starred as Caleb Hooten and appeared in the drama portion of the program. After the dramatizations, there was just enough time for Gene and his associates to sing another song, finish with a final commercial about Doublemint and then ride off signing "Back in the Saddle Again" again. Kids growing up during the 1940s and 1950s could go to a picture show at a Saturday matinee and see Gene Autry sing and round up the bad guys on the big screen and then return home just in time to hear him do it on the radio that same evening.

There was a spin-off western radio show from this series; Gene Autry was not in it, but his horse, Champion, was. It was called ***The Adventures of Champion*** and it ran from June to November in 1949. Bill Burch also directed this show. Like *Melody Ranch*, it eventually became a television series, but with a different cast than the one on radio.

The final *Gene Autry's Melody Ranch* was heard on radio on May 13, 1956, although Gene wasn't on it. Johnny Bond and Pat Buttram said "adios" for their boss man. Of course, by 1956, Gene had already moved on to his successful CBS-TV series. For 16 years, with time off during World War II, Gene Autry rode the radio range on CBS for only one sponsor, Wrigley's Doublemint Gum, and for most of those shows, he did the gum commercials himself.

Sources: Audio copies of *Gene Autry's Melody Ranch*; Dunning, *On the Air* and *Tune In*; George-Warren; Summers.

GOLD RUSH

KARL SCHADOW *and* JACK FRENCH

A 1933 sustaining program on NBC's Blue Network, each episode told a gold rush tale that was heavy on excitement and adventure but light on character development. The tales, which purportedly came from actual events that had taken place, primarily in America, tended to focus on two human themes: one friend sacrificing to help another, and the double cross. Featured in the cast were Horace Sinclair, Jack MacBryde, Richard Gordon and Joseph Grant. Given each episode's changing locale, the cast was adept at offering listeners a variety of seemingly authentic dialects.

Source: *Variety*, June 27, 1933, p. 40.

GRAPEVINE RANCHO

JACK FRENCH

This was a 30 minute western variety program that was broadcast on CBS from 1943 to 1944 and sponsored by Roma Wines of Fresno, CA. Ransom Sherman hosted and played a ranch owner where the music and dramatizations took place. The cast included Leo Carrillo, Carlos Ramirez, Lionel Stander, and Anne O'Neill. The program usually aired on Thursday evenings and featured the music of Lud Gluskins. It was very successful in attracting top guest stars who took part in the dramatizations, including Basil Rathbone, Charles Ruggles, Alan Hale, Jimmie Gleason, Bert Lahr, and Tommy Riggs.

Source: Swartz.

GUNSMOKE

STEWART WRIGHT

NETWORK: CBS
FORMAT: Half hour, weekly
DURATION OF RUN: April 26, 1952, to June 18, 1961.
SPONSOR: Post Toasties, Chesterfield, Liggett & Myers, and multiple sponsors
AUDIO COPIES EXTANT: 474 of 480 episodes, plus 3 audition disks
SCRIPTS ARCHIVED: Huntington Library, San Marino, CA; American Radio Archives; Katherine Hite collection, Wichita State University Library; http://www.genericradio. com; Broadcast Arts Library

While some might debate if *Gunsmoke* was the first adult radio western series; there is no doubt it was the most successful. The series became the model for the western radio programs that followed it and an entire generation of television westerns. It was a series to which an incredibly talented group of people contributed their skills in writing, acting,

Norman Macdonnell, left, and John Dehner in a 1958 CBS photograph discussing a script. Macdonnell was the producer/director of *Gunsmoke* and Dehner appeared in its supporting cast more than any other actor (courtesy American Radio Archives at Thousand Oaks Library, Thousand Oaks, California).

directing and producing, music, and sound effects. Their efforts made *Gunsmoke* one of the most memorable and popular series at the end of the Golden Age of Radio.

Gunsmoke was the combined result of the vision and persistence of two men: director-producer Norman Macdonnell and writer John Meston. Together, they were committed to destroying the long-held network radio tradition that westerns were for kids, by bringing a new type of radio show to the airwaves: an authentic, realistic western for an adult audience. Macdonnell was one of radio's best directors, and equally important, he was quite adept at picking the right people for cast and crew. Meston was an excellent writer, well-versed in the lore and history of the Old West as he had grown up in Colorado where he had worked as a cowboy on the family ranch.

As director/producer Macdonnell steadfastly believed that when selecting his actors it was more important to get actors who worked well together, rather than it was to get those who worked well individually. To gain familiarity with actors, Macdonnell sat in the control booth with nearly every Hollywood-based director in CBS radio and watched actors work, as individuals and groups. This activity gave him extensive knowledge of actors and their skills that later paid enormous dividends with *Gunsmoke*.

In a 1959 article written by Charles Mercer, *Gunsmoke* co-creator John Meston said that when the series began, "We were determined to try to avoid every cliché or rule of the B movie westerns. We tried to do the opposite in everything — plot, language, and character.... (I) tried to avoid making Dillon a typical western hero. My aim is to make him a fallible human being."

Meston and Macdonnell had initially experimented with their adult western concept on *Escape* with "Wild Jack Rhett" in December, 1950. The episode featured a John Meston adaptation of an Ernest Haycox story. The characters were realistic and dialog was blunt and terse; long-winded speeches were not Meston's style. The duo enhanced the production with a new technique for using sound patterns.

They refined their concept with "Pagosa" on *Romance* in early August 1951, which featured a Meston-written script. One only has to listen to that *Romance* production to hear the similarities between Jeff Spain and Matt Dillon, both played by William Conrad, as well as Teal Travis and Kitty Russell, both played by Georgia Ellis.

By mid–April 1952, Macdonnell was a highly influential and respected radio director/producer for CBS. He had a solid reputation for his work on *Escape*, *Doorway to Life*, *The Adventures of Philip Marlowe*, *Romance*, and *Suspense*. So, when a gap unexpectedly occurred in the CBS prime time line-up (the spy series *Operation Underground* was abruptly cancelled and an earlier Harry Ackerman adult western project failed to make it to the network airwaves) CBS gave Macdonnell and Meston a week to get their adult western on the air, including assembling a cast and crew plus getting a script and composing music. The series would use the title of the unsuccessful Ackerman project: *Gunsmoke*. Many actors were auditioned for the Matt Dillon role; some CBS executives wanted Robert Stack, but Macdonnell and Meston wanted Bill Conrad for their lead. The CBS executives finally acquiesced and Conrad was cast as Matt Dillon.

Bill Conrad played the lead role in *Gunsmoke* (courtesy American Radio Archives at Thousand Oaks Library, Thousand Oaks, California).

Gunsmoke's central character, U.S. Marshal Matt Dillon, was unlike any of his radio western predecessors. Dillon was a complex, flawed man who did the best he could in an extremely difficult job under incredibly trying conditions. He often failed, but he never gave up. Matt tried to walk away from the job in the twice produced episode "Bloody Hands" but his commitment to establishing law and order drew him back.

A roughly eight minute audio fragment

of the missing second episode, "Ben Thompson" (May 3, 1952), is in circulation. It includes a narration by Matt after he is forced to kill Lassiter, a gunfighter who was once his friend. This narration provides significant insight into the character of Matt Dillon:

> I couldn't tell anyone, but the bitterness icing my stomach made me sick as I remembered Lassiter as a friend ... now dead by my gun. Then I got over it ... I always got over it. The frontier code was a harsh one ... and I knew my job was one that had to be done if the West was ever to see peace. As long as killers like Lassiter lived, I would carry a gun ... and use it. It was the way it had to be. Sometimes a man's dying was the end of it ... sometimes the beginning of something worse.

Initially, Macdonnell and Meston thought that the only continuing character in their series would be the marshal. But once they got the go ahead from CBS, they realized that Matt needed recurring characters with whom he could react, so the Chester Proudfoot and Doc Adams characters played by Parley Baer and Howard McNear, respectively, were continued. The Kitty Russell character, played by Georgia Ellis, eventually became a regular and started receiving featured billing with Baer and McNear in the 17th episode, "The Lynching."

The development of the four main characters was an ongoing, collaborative effort. Meston worked very closely with Macdonnell and the actors and was usually in the radio studio during the first years of the series. Meston remembered that, "After the shows, Conrad, Norm, Parley, and I and whoever else was around, would sit around and discuss the show. We were all interested. We would discuss characters; why they should not do this or that; how they should behave. It was kind of a joint effort."

Much has been made of Norman Macdonnell's radio "stock company" of highly talented and versatile actors. This stock company was a result of Macdonnell's philosophy of hiring actors who could work well together and by the fact that during most of the 1950s he was extremely busy directing and producing many CBS radio series, and for several years, was also the producer for the television version of *Gunsmoke*. Without auditions, he knew the actors he wanted and could get them. His stock company reached its epitome during the run of *Gunsmoke*.

This core group of 29 guest actors accounted for nearly 90 percent of the supporting cast appearances on *Gunsmoke*: John Dehner, Vic Perrin, Lawrence Dobkin, Harry Bartell, Sam Edwards, Ralph Moody, James Nusser, Barney Phillips, Joseph Kearns, Virginia Christine, Virginia Gregg, Jeanne Bates, Paul Dubov, Dick Beals, Jack Moyles, Helen Kleeb, Lou Krugman, Vivi Janiss, Ben Wright, Jack Kruschen, Jeanette Nolan, Joe Du Val, Lynn Allen, Lillian Buyeff, Tom Tully, Frank Cady, Joe Cranston, Michael Ann Barrett, and Don Diamond. The announcers over the years were George Walsh, Roy Rowan, Ken Peters, and others.

During a 1998 interview Harry Bartell, who had 182 appearances on *Gunsmoke*, talked in general about Macdonnell's stock company of actors and specifically about its use on that series.

> *Gunsmoke* was unique.... It was an experience different from any other show I did. There was a sense of camaraderie, a great warmth, and respect. No matter how much kidding around there was at rehearsal, once that thing started, it became very, very professional. There was a sense of reliance of one actor on another and through experience being able to anticipate timing, being able to anticipate any changes in line reading from the person with whom you were working. Part of it was the group that worked the show was comparatively limited.

Norman Macdonnell got screamed at for having a "stock company." I was just very happy to be part of it.

Gunsmoke scripts possessed consistent characteristics. The story lines were character driven rather than plot driven and the dialog was lean and terse with few, if any, long speeches or narrations. Music and sound patterns played important parts in helping to tell each story. Series co-creator John Meston provided editorial supervision that ensured all scripts were realistic, historically accurate, and reflected his and Macdonnell's concept of the series and the characters.

Three writers wrote the vast majority of scripts for the series. Meston penned scripts for nearly half of the radio episodes. Les Crutchfield and Marian Clark wrote 95 and 76 scripts respectively, mainly after Meston became heavily involved in the television version of the series in the Fall, 1956. Macdonnell, John Dunkel, Antony Ellis, Kathleen Hite, and Herb Purdum also made major script contributions. Crew and cast members such as sound pattern artists Tom Hanley and Ray Kemper and actors William Conrad, Vic Perrin, and Harry Bartell also wrote occasional scripts.

During its first year on the air, 10 writers produced 53 scripts for *Gunsmoke*. Meston wrote 16 of those scripts, but spent most of his time editing the rest. Macdonnell remembered that, "After about a year, John said, he didn't quite know why he was working this hard and not having the fun of writing them himself. So he left CBS, left an extraordinarily good job with a great deal of promise on what was really a gamble, because who knew how long *Gunsmoke* would go." From May 1953 through August 1956, Meston wrote all but 20 *Gunsmoke* radio scripts. Recurring themes that ran through many of Meston's scripts were: the dignity of man, man's inhumanity to man, the inescapability of life and problems, and the difficult position of women on the western frontier. These themes were also frequently incorporated into scripts by other writers for the series.

On the 1976 *Gunsmoke* radio documentary, frequent guest performer John Dehner reminisced about the series:

> You didn't have so much plot as you had characters, interesting people to listen to.... It was a novelty. We were all so used to "Hi-Ho Silver Away" that this was a total departure into the serious examination of people and their problems. When you get that kind of writing and that kind of concept, it's a glorious thing for actors because this is the very thing that an actor wants; to play a person, a human being.

Over its run, 59 *Gunsmoke* scripts were reworked and formed the basis for new episodes and seven scripts served as the basis for two new episodes each. These new programs included one or more the following difference from their original productions: changes in time slot length, dialog, plot line, character's names, and most frequently, cast and crew members.

The radio *Gunsmoke* scripts obviously worked well when adapted for television. During the first four seasons of the television version of *Gunsmoke* (September 1955 to June 1959) 156 episodes were aired on the small screen; over 90 percent were adapted from radio scripts.

Rex Koury was responsible for the music used on *Gunsmoke*. His initial meeting with Norman Macdonnell gave the composer the background he needed relating to the series concept and the Matt Dillon character. He wrote the now famous theme for the series, "Old Trail," in a matter of minutes. Koury's job was more than to just write musical transitions between scenes and acts; his ongoing assignment from director/producer Macdonnell was to compose music that played an important role in establishing the moods of situations and helped define the complex character of Matt Dillon. The music played an important part in helping to tell each story.

In "Wild Jack Rhett" and "Pagosa" Macdonnell and his sound effects artists experimented with, what was then called, "exaggerated" sound patterns. These patterns weren't really exaggerated; rather, they would sometimes replace dialog and play a more important part in telling the story. For example, if a character was leaving a building and crossing the street, the listener would hear the door close, and, as he came down the steps, the sound effects would also indicate that he was crossing the sidewalk and the street. With such skilled artists, primarily Tom Hanley, Bill James, and Ray Kemper, these sound patterns were very effective in replacing some narrative dialog, adding authenticity, and keeping *Gunsmoke* listeners appraised of what was happening. Others occasionally assisting this trio were Cliff Thorsness, Gus Bayz, and Clark Casey. Kemper and Hanley also solved a long time sound effects problem of network radio: consistently producing realistic sounding gun shots. When experiments in a sound studio failed to produce adequate results, the sound patterns artists spent two days firing hand guns and rifles in a local canyon and recording the gunshots on tape. Their results became the industry standard and further enhanced the realism of sound effects on *Gunsmoke*.

Gunsmoke episodes were devoid of stereotype characters; its characters were real people with individual faults and strengths. No race or sex was totally virtuous or evil. The series attempted to accurately reflect the difficult and dangerous life on the frontier in the 1870s; numerous episodes ended tragically. Many episodes dealt with the treatment of Indians. John Meston remembered, "As I recall, we were about the first show that treated Indians as human beings, not just 'red skins' or 'the only good Indians are dead ones.' We did a number of shows about that, and about intermarriage, and of course, the buffalo."

Matt Dillon understood the situation of the Indians he encountered and respected them. In return, he was trusted and respected by most of them. Matt sometimes went to extraordinary lengths to keep the peace. In the missing "The Dodge City Killer" episode Dillon finds justice for the daughter of a Comanche warrior chief who killed a man while he was trying to rape her. The episode "Cheyennes" focuses on Matt's efforts to avert a full-scale war by stopping gunrunners who are supplying rifles to a small band of renegades. In the two productions of "No Indians" Matt and Chester place themselves in harm's way to stop a gang of horse thieves that are massacring settlers and placing the blame on the Pawnees.

The plight of women on the frontier was a frequent theme on *Gunsmoke*, especially in the scripts written by Marian Clark and Kathleen Hite. The rugged life and harsh conditions on the frontier, combined with very limited opportunities for women, often made them bitter and old before their time. "The Cabin," "The Old Lady," and "The Piano" are three fine examples which illustrate this central theme and how its realities impacted each of the primary female characters.

Minorities were sometimes the focus in *Gunsmoke* episodes. In the first episode of the series, "Billy the Kid." Matt protects an innocent immigrant from a lynch mob. The episode "The Queue" deals with perceptions of racial stereotypes while it tells the tragic story of the treatment of Chen Wong, a man from China.

By the end of November, 1960, *Gunsmoke* was the last CBS prime time radio drama series originating from Hollywood; production of *Yours Truly, Johnny Dollar* had moved to New York and the radio version of **Have Gun — Will Travel** had left the radio airwaves. The end for *Gunsmoke* was not far off. On Saturday, April 29, 1961, the *Gunsmoke* radio cast and crew gathered for the last time to record episodes for the series. At the time, they did not know that *Gunsmoke* was being cancelled. On Sunday, June 18, 1961, just after the credits were read for "Letter of the Law," announcer George Walsh simply stated, "This broadcast concludes the current *Gunsmoke* series." With that brief statement, the most successful and influential radio western of the last decade of the Golden Age of Radio departed the network airwaves.

Syndicated columnist Hal Humphrey astutely wrote about *Gunsmoke* shortly after its demise, "Probably no program in the annals of broadcasting ever had more influence on the entertainment we've witnessed during the past five years.... Many *Gunsmoke* episodes are minor classics and did as much for the real Old West as Paddy Chayefsky did for New York's Lower East Side."

An exceptional, five hour radio documentary, "The Story of *Gunsmoke*," was produced by John Hickman and Norman Macdonnell and first aired in April, 1976. It featured many contributors to the success of the series including Macdonnell, Meston, Conrad, Baer, Ellis, Koury, and Walsh. The making of the documentary was the last get- together for some of the *Gunsmoke* radio family. The co-creators of *Gunsmoke* both died in 1979; John Meston in March of a cerebral hemorrhage at 64 years of age and Norman Macdonnell of kidney failure at 63 in November.

Sources: Audio copies of *Gunsmoke* and *The Story of Gunsmoke*, WAMU, Washington D. C., April 26, 1976, produced by John Hickman; Barabas; Wright; Hickerson, *New Ultimate*; Interview of Harry Bartell by Stewart Wright; *Kerrville Times*, July 9, 1961; *Los Angeles Times*, March 15, 1959; Daily radio programming listings (numerous major dailies) 1952–1961; *New York Herald*, December 25, 1960; *New York Times*, August 11, 1954; *Radio and Television Life*, May 6, 1953; *Return With Us Now*, May 8, 1949; *Radiogram*, December, 2005; *Variety*, May 7, 1954; http://forums.oldradio.net/forum13.html.

GUNSMOKE LAW

JACK FRENCH *and* DAVID S. SIEGEL

NETWORK: NBC Blue
FORMAT: Half hour, weekly
DURATION OF RUN: 1937–?
AUDIO COPIES EXTANT: 1
SCRIPTS ARCHIVED: Library of Congress

This was the fourth frontier radio series written by Wilbur Hall, a native son of the West, born in Montana in August 1883. By the time he was a teenager, his family had moved to California where he would spend the rest of his life as an author.

Gunsmoke Law, which began in August 1937, had been preceded by Hall's 1931 *Colonel Kibbe's Round-Ups*, his 1933 **The Winning the West**, and his 1935 **Six Gun Justice**. In addition, Hall penned a series of occasional programs which involved railroad stories of the West, all broadcast from station KPO in San Francisco.

Although the unnamed announcer on *Gunsmoke Law* introduced the program as "a fast moving thriller," the sole surviving audio copy shows no evidence of either thrills or fast moving elements. The entire half hour was taken up by long scenes of incessant conversation, with no action sequences to break up the constant chatter. The basic scenario evolved around a young cowboy, Dave Service, who just reported to the T & L Greenback Ranch to check up on its owner's suspicions of theft of yearlings, as well as loss of a mine payroll.

Sound effects were primitive and minimalist: occasional hoofbeats and a dinner bell that was rung once. Musical bridges transitioned the scenes with a cowboy singing snatches of a western ballad. Despite the fact that one of the cowhands declared "I don't like gabby cowboys," apparently scriptwriter Hall did and he filled every scene with chit-chat. Sample dialogue: "You ain't made of the stuff that rides away from trouble." In the closing scene of the surviving episode, Service attempts to flirt with Harriet Adair, the new school teacher, by telling her, "Yore mighty easy to look at."

The overall scenario of the program may have suggested a setting of the late 1800s, with everyone on horseback, worries of cattle and sheep rustling, and the musical bridges of cowboy folk songs. However, it is clear that Hall actually placed the series in the late 1920s or early 1930s as he had one character announce that the rustlers "used two trucks" to transport the stolen animals.

The cast included: Lawson Gerbe, Jack MacBryde, Milton Herman, Fred Lewis, Len Sterling, Nan Dorland (as Harriet) and Jack Negley. Supporting cast also included three people who would become prominent in network radio: Jay Jostyn (the lead in *Mr. District Attorney*), Anne Elstner (the lead in *Stella Dallas*), and Milton J. Cross (an announcer for many programs). W.S. Roberts produced this series, George Cross was the organist, and Keene Crockett handled sound effects.

It's possible that *Gunsmoke Law* was not representative of Hall's best work since he was very successful in many other writing endeavors. In 1926 he was chosen by the widow of Luther Burbank, the famous horticulturist, to write Burbank's biography, *Harvest of the Years* which was released in 1927. He also wrote and staged a number of historical pageants in California, as well as radio adaptations of famous novels. In 1933 he wrote several dramas for a Bible series on station KPO.

Hall's writing successes were financially lucrative and he bought a large ranch in Sonoma County, CA, where he enjoyed a very comfortable retirement. He died at age 65 in June 1948.

Sources: Audio copy of *Gunsmoke Law*; NBC Collections, Recorded South Retention Center, Library of Congress; *Oakland Tribune*, June 9, 1931, and May 6, 1935.

HASHKNIFE HARTLEY

Stan Claussen

Network: Mutual Don Lee
Format: Half hour, weekly
Duration of Run: July 2, 1950, to December 30, 1951
Sponsor: Sustaining
Audio Copies Extant: 2
Scripts Archived: Undetermined

Hashknife Hartley featured two wandering cowpokes in a western series broadcast Sunday afternoons on the Mutual Don Lee network from July 2, 1950, to Dec. 30, 1951.

The only two surviving episodes were preserved by the Armed Forces Radio Service and that organization routinely cut openings and closings of their shows and substituted their own music. Hashknife Hartley was played by Frank Martin and Sleepy Stevens was played by Barton Yarborough. Tragically, Yarborough died Dec. 22, 1951, which may have contributed to the end of this series. At the time of his death he was also portraying Ben Romero, Joe Friday's new sidekick, on *Dragnet*. The role was taken over by Ben Alexander.

The scripts were adapted by Fred Luke and Burt Kennedy from stories by prolific western author W. C. Tuttle. Wilbur Coleman Tuttle (1883–1969) was born and raised in the cattle county of Montana and correctly surmised few readers of adventure stories would seek stories by a writer named "Wilbur." So he always used just his initials in the mountain of fiction he produced: about 1,000 articles for pulp magazines, over 30 western novels, and about 50 screen plays. While he did not write the radio scripts of this series, he was its narrator, delivering his lines in a rapid manner. The music was composed by Harry Zimmerman and the producer/director was Tom Hargis.

This radio series had an interesting back story. The term "hashknife" was used in the Old West to describe two related items: a cooking implement and a cattle brand. The brand was designed to make it difficult for cattle rustlers to superimpose another brand on the animal. The knife it was named for was designed by camp cooks to slice beef cubes for corned beef hash. The rough and tumble lifestyle celebrated in the series was based on the reminiscences of the Vandevert family that invented the cattle brand. Bill Vandevert and his wife Sadie had moved to Holbrook, AZ in 1884 to work for the Aztec Land and Cattle Company.

"The Hashknife Outfit," as it came to be known, distributed Texas cattle along the new Atlantic and Pacific (Santa Fe) railroad between New Mexico and Flagstaff, AZ. Zane Grey immortalized the rough cattle ranching life of northern Arizona in *The Hashknife Outfit* published in 1933. But Tuttle's first Hashknife novel was published in 1920 and he would go on to write 17 more books starring Hashknife and Sleepy.

In Tuttle's Hashknife novels the two saddle buddies were usually range detectives, solving criminal mysteries and facilitating the apprehension of the guilty. The radio scripts followed that theme. In one of the surviving audio copies, the two are confronted with the murder of Ed Harmon on the main street of Arroyo City and they begin their search for the unknown killer. An outlaw nicknamed The Pinto Bandit, because of the horse he rides, is one of their suspects and a trigger-happy cowboy, Jimmy, who wants to marry Harmon's daughter, is the other suspect. Hashknife and Sleepy eventually determine the pinto is a white horse splotched with dark mud and the real murderer is the deputy sheriff.

The other surviving audio copy deals with the mysterious rustling of cattle, first from a modest homesteader, and then from a wealthy ranch owner. Both of the victims suspect each other and only the calming influence of Hashknife and Sleepy prevents bloodshed. The range detectives conduct their investigation and conclude that two of the wealthy rancher's hands are the cattle rustlers. A trap is sprung and the outlaw duo is taken into custody to be turned over to the local law officers.

Throughout their adventures and crime solving, Hashknife and Sleepy make a good pair and their strengths complement each other. Although Hashknife chides Sleepy as being "more brawn than brains" he appreciates his saddle partner's quick draw and deadly aim. Script writers Luke and Kennedy copied Tuttle's folksy, humorous writing style. One character, commenting on an angry expression of a villain, says: "Did you see the look on his face? You could bottle it and use it for paint remover."

Good sound effects are important to every western and this series was no exception. Nearly all of the sound effects, either manual or transcribed, appeared realistic and timely. That included hoof beats, sounds of cattle, horse whinnies, and gun shots. The live music used in the bridges was appropriate and judicious.

The series was well done with the usual supporting cast members from the Hollywood "Radio Row" pool that were also heard on *Red Ryder* in the 1940s, and the more adult westerns that would soon appear on CBS in the 1950s. Mutual Don Lee Network served a purpose in that era, not only opening the airwaves to some new programming, but also holding up the traditional format of the better known westerns.

Sources: Audio copies of *Hashknife Hartley*; Carlock; Dunning, *On the Air*; Lesser; Swartz.

HAVE GUN — WILL TRAVEL

MARTIN GRAMS, JR.

NETWORK: CBS
FORMAT: Half hour, weekly
DURATION OF RUN: November 23, 1958, to November 27, 1960
SPONSORS: Multiple sponsors
AUDIO COPIES EXTANT: 106 shows (complete run), plus audition voice tracks
SCRIPTS ARCHIVED: American Radio Archives; John Dunkel Collection, University of California, Los Angles; Broadcast Arts Library

Have Gun — Will Travel began as a television western over CBS-TV in 1957, starring Richard Boone as Paladin (first name unknown), a gun-for-hire who, on occasion, found himself fighting against his employer to seek justice or a personal vendetta. Paladin resided in a luxury suite at the Hotel Carlton in San Francisco. His business card read "Have Gun — Will Travel, Wire Paladin." His clients ranged from marshals and sheriffs, ranch owners, sheep herders and anyone who could afford his price. Paladin sometimes went off to hunt and apprehend a criminal with a price on his head, but never shot to kill unless he found it necessary. The series was an immediate success and one year later, a radio program of the same name, featuring the same character, premiered on CBS Radio.

The story behind how the program came to radio and why the initial radio scripts were reworked television scripts is a combination of CBS' efforts to assuage the feelings of one of its leading directors as well as the economics of broadcasting. When CBS took **Gunsmoke** to television, Norman Macdonnell, the director/producer of the radio version, wanted to be involved in the new venture but network executives chose other people. To "calm down" a disappointed Macdonnell, the network suggested that he do a radio version of the popular *Have Gun — Will Travel* television program and Macdonnell, in turn, decided to show the network that his radio version could be better than its television version.

According to John Dehner, who played Paladin on the radio, "Dick Boone was doing it on television and while he was doing it, we also were doing the radio version. They thought it would be a good idea — whoever the 'they' are — but they thought it would be a good idea to take the scripts that were being used on television, convert them to radio

Ben Wright, left, and John Dehner in *Have Gun — Will Travel* (courtesy American Radio Archives at Thousand Oaks Library, Thousand Oaks, California).

and *violà*, you have a radio show, not having to pay any money for a new script." And Ben Wright, who played Hey Boy on the radio, remembers that "there were definite ill feelings between Norm and the television crew responsible for **Gunsmoke**. They took that [radio] show away from him. He had no say in who or what went on the [television] air. He later became a producer for the [television] program and that settled a little. I think Norm came up with the idea for doing the radio version of *Have Gun*, possibly to show them that 'Hey, look what I can do with your program and I did it even better.' But don't take my word for it. I wouldn't be surprised if Norm originated the idea of doing the radio version."

On November 8, 1958, Macdonnell conducted three voice tests for the Paladin role, with Harry Bartell, Vic Perrin and John Dehner reading lines from the opening scenes of "Strange Vendetta." "We three were called in for those tests," Harry Bartell recalled. "I don't know if it was Norm Macdonnell who suggested us or not. I know we were the only three to do those voice tests." None of the four primary actors on radio's **Gunsmoke** were tested for the role.

John Dehner ultimately won the role, ironic when you consider that Dehner was among the actors offered the role of Matt Dillon in early 1952 but turned it down because he didn't want to be typecast in a western. Dehner chose to play the role of Paladin his own way, without attempting to reproduce the television counterpart. "I didn't pay any attention to him [Boone] at all. It was whatever came out of me. I knew that it would be deadly if I were to imitate him or do anything that was even vaguely similar to him. His Paladin was strictly Dick Boone. And I am not about to imitate. So I just did it the way I felt it."

The first 30 plus radio scripts were adaptations of television dramas, all from the first or second season of the television program. The scriptwriters who wrote the teleplays were never paid any residuals for the reuse of their scripts or plots, which at times were dramatized on radio word-for-word. "We were given a huge stack of television scripts and asked by Norm to try and make radio scripts from them," writer John Dawson recalled. "We had to shorten the 26 to 30 page scripts into short 22 page radio dramas. We kind of divided the scripts, Frank Michael and Ann Doud and I... I was in admiration of Gene Roddenberry's work, so I grabbed all of his scripts. We were allowed to use any dialogue from the scripts, but I found I had to re-word some of it so descriptive actions could be portrayed."

Ray Kemper, sound technician, had also turned writer by the time *Have Gun* premiered in 1958. "I do recall an incident on the very first show. John was really trying hard to do the Paladin character just right. At one point I stopped the rehearsal and asked Norm in a loud voice if he wanted 'Big Dome' (referring to Paladin) to wear spurs. Dehner looked stricken and asked, 'Big Dome?' In the booth, Norm was laughing like crazy — he hit the talkback and said, 'John, you just shrank about a foot.' Of course, Dehner laughed too."

After more than 20 episodes, Macdonnell realized that the show was not a success for radio as it was for television. Perhaps it was because the television audience had a strong impres-

Ben Wright and Virginia Gregg rehearsing 1958 *Have Gun — Will Travel* script. Both portrayed Asians on this series; he was Hey Boy and she played Missy Wong (courtesy American Radio Archives at Thousand Oaks Library, Thousand Oaks, California).

Virginia Gregg with Vic Perrin in background during 1958 CBS rehearsal of *Have Gun — Will Travel.* Perrin played Sgt. Gorce in *Fort Laramie* and Gregg played leading lady roles on many western dramas (courtesy American Radio Archives at Thousand Oaks Library, Thousand Oaks, California).

sion of what the Paladin character should look — and act — like, courtesy of Richard Boone's treatment for the small screen. More importantly, adapting television scripts into an audio medium was egregious at best. "Well, it turned out they were totally inappropriate for radio, and they were forced to write new and original radio shows which is really what happened," Dehner recalled. "But they were simultaneously on the air, one on television and one on radio."

In "The Hanging Cross," Paladin attempts to thwart a lynching on Christmas Eve, and make peace between the Sioux Indians and the white men on Nathaniel Beecher's ranch. The television version concludes with Paladin taking down some of the boards from the homemade gallows, and riding off observing the shadow on the ground, from the gallows, depicting a cross. This kind of imagery could not have been captured in an audio medium.

Of the first 39 radio episodes, 35 were adaptations of television scripts. Beginning with episode 40, the series consisted completely of original radio plots. Sound man Ray

From left, John Dehner, Frank Paris, and Virginia Gregg discuss a 1958 *Have Gun — Will Travel* script. Dehner played the lead, Gregg was Missy Wong and Paris was its producer/director (courtesy American Radio Archives at Thousand Oaks Library, Thousand Oaks, California).

Kemper would ultimately script a total of nine episodes, and the majority of his submissions are now considered some of the best episodes of the radio series. Reference guides continue to state inaccurately that Gene Roddenberry was a scriptwriter for five *Have Gun — Will Travel* radio broadcasts. The correction should be noted: John Dawson adapted all five of those episodes from Roddenberry's television scripts and Roddenberry himself had no personal involvement with the radio program.

Paladin never had a sidekick, but the beginning and closing of almost every episode featured a discussion between the hired gun and Hey Boy, the bellhop of the Hotel Carlton. The role of Hey Boy was played by Ben Wright, a talented radio actor who was actually British, not an Asian which he portrayed on the program. A few months after the radio series premiered, actress Virginia Gregg began playing the role of Missy Wong, another Asian. Later the television show introduced a similar character, Hey Girl, played by Lisa Lu, but not until after the radio program concluded in 1960.

After 36 episodes, Macdonnell left the series to pursue other ventures and his associate producer, Frank Paris, took over the production and direction beginning with episode 37 and remained with the program until the series concluded in 1960. Under Paris' guidance, original scripts were written for the series — a vast improvement compared with prior productions.

The final episode of the radio series, "From Here to Boston" (November 27, 1960), is regarded by fans of *Have Gun — Will Travel* as a landmark in the series. Paladin receives a fat envelope from attorneys in Boston, alerting him to the recent death of his Aunt Grace. Paladin has inherited $100,000 and must travel East to collect. Meanwhile, the gunman is unaware that his latest romantic fling, Louvenia Todd Hunter, was responsible for the death of his Aunt and that she plans, with Myles Todd Hunter, to murder Paladin and make it look like an accident. They stand to gain the inheritance after Paladin is found dead. However, Paladin outsmarts the woman, a struggle occurs with a gun, and Myles is shot by accident. The episode closes with Hey Boy riding to the train station with Paladin. Hey Boy asks when the man in black will return. "At least until I can settle my Aunt's estate," he explains. "Who knows? I might take a liking there and decide to settle down personally." Paladin suggests a future marriage for Hey Boy and Missy Wong, asking to be notified in advance so he can return for the wedding. Instead of riding horseback into the sunset (West), he boards a train into the sunrise (East).

The radio program faded away with no mention in the trade columns. "There was no feedback, really," recalled John Dehner. "And there would have been no way of our getting feedback really, in terms of fan letters and audio response. It dwindled away to nothing — like a dead leaf in the wind. And that was it. We as actors were aghast at the brutality of the networks. I don't want to sound too dramatic about this, but after all, it was an industry and an important industry and a very big industry. But all of a sudden the powers that were in charge of the industry just said 'The hell with it. We don't need you. Good-bye and go home.' And they closed the doors and it was that fast. It was a shock to all of us."

Sources: Audio copies of *Have Gun–Will Travel*; Scripts; Grams; *New York Times*: November 23, 1958, May 3, October 4, and December 20, 1959, November 27 December 4, 1960; Recording labels on tape masters at Audio Classics Archive in Howell, Michigan.

HAWK LARABEE

Donald Ramlow

NAMES: *Hawk Durango, Hawk Larabee*
NETWORK: CBS
FORMAT: Half hour, weekly, various days and times
DURATION OF RUN: July 4, 1946, to August 9, 1946 (Durango); October 3, 1946, to February 7, 1948 (Larabee)
SPONSOR: Sustaining
AUDIO COPIES EXTANT: 9
SCRIPTS ARCHIVED: Undetermined

Prior to 1946, the majority of western radio programs were targeted at younger audiences. Shows like **The Lone Ranger**, **The Cisco Kid**, **Tom Mix** and **Red Ryder** were all popular, and while adults also listened to them, their primary audience was younger people. A few western radio programs featuring adult themes did appear on radio but usually as productions on anthology shows such as *Lux Radio Theater*.

This all changed when the Columbia Broadcasting System decided to premier a new program entitled *Hawk Durango* as a summer replacement program for *The Adventures of Maisie* which starred Ann Sothern. This western first appeared on July 4, 1946, and aired for six weeks until Sothern returned to the airwaves on August 16, 1946. *Hawk Durango* was an adult western featuring Elliott Lewis (1917–1990) as Jim Carter, a young man who lived in the East. Carter's father, Hawk Durango, had been living in the town of Sundown Wells, a typical desert town, when he was killed. Carter traveled to Sundown when he learned of his father's death and he eventually avenged his father's killing. At this point, Jim decided to stay in Sundown Wells, and, taking the name of his father, he purchased a hotel/gambling establishment called the Gold Bar House. This debut episode also included Frank Lovejoy (1912–1962) one of the premier radio, stage and film actors of the 1940s, 1950s and 1960s.

Hawk Durango was produced by William N. Robson (1906–1995), who also was one of the directors for the series. Robson was a respected producer and director for CBS and worked on many key programs during his career at the network, including the popular *Suspense* and *Escape*.

Only the fifth episode of the *Hawk Durango* series, dated August 2, 1946, is currently in circulation. It tells the story of a woman who has traveled from the East to get married. Somewhat disappointed in her fiancé, she becomes attracted to a gunslinger, Brazos John, played by Barton Yarborough (1900–1951). Eventually the woman and her fiancé leave to travel to his ranch and are attacked by bandits while on the trail. Hawk and Brazos, having heard about the impending attack, travel out to help them, where they succeed in protecting the woman and her companions from harm. The woman, still enamored of Brazos, thanks him for saving her. However, Brazos intentionally gives all the credit to Hawk, telling the woman that he himself was one of the bandits, thus breaking the attraction that the woman had for him.

Barton Yarborough, a leading actor in several radio series, including westerns (courtesy Library of American Broadcasting, University of Maryland, College Park).

Elliott Lewis is considered a renaissance man in the Golden Age of Radio, with success as a director, producer, scriptwriter and actor. While perhaps best known for playing the comedic role of Remley on *The Phil Harris–Alice Faye Show*, he also starred in *Suspense*, *On-Stage* and *The Voyage of the Scarlet Queen*, among other programs. Barton Yarborough also had a long history of working in radio and was associated with three very popular programs: he played Cliff Barbour on *One Man's Family*, Doc Long on *I Love a Mystery*, and Ben Romero in early episodes of *Dragnet*.

Hawk Durango ended its run in August, but only a short while later it was announced that it would be returning to the airways on October 3, 1946. Fans of the earlier series were most likely surprised when they listened to the first episode, because *Hawk Durango* was now titled *Hawk Larabee* and the title lead was now played by Barton Yarborough. (Elliott Lewis was no longer on the series.) The reason for the name change is unclear since CBS was promoting the show's return to the airwaves as *Hawk Durango* in early September, just five weeks prior to its return.

Brazos John was no longer mentioned and Barney Phillips (1913–1982) was added to the series as the recurring character Somber Jones in the May 22, 1947, episode "The Great Giveaway." In that program, Larabee drifts into a frontier mining camp and finds an innocent man, Lucius, charged with murder and confined in the jail of the town marshal, Somber Jones. The latter got his nickname from his mournful attitude about life. By the end of the program, Jones has turned in his badge and he becomes Larabee's sidekick following him across the plains.

Later the scripts had story lines away from Sundown Wells, with Hawk traveling from one location to another, encountering adventure along the way. In one episode, Hawk confides to his radio audience that some folks consider him a "fiddle-foot" which is apparently true, as he explains that he "left my old stampin' grounds at Sundown Wells and hit the trail." For most of the rest of the series, the two drifters wandered the frontier, and each week, found a different site that provided them troubles to resolve.

The announcer's opening over the years did not remain the same. In mid–1947 Jack McCoy gave this introduction: "It's *Hawk Larabee*, starring Barton Yarborough, with his exciting stories of the timeless West... stories of men and women, famous and infamous, who loved and hated, lived and died, in the colorful drama of the American West."

The program's music was also modified. For most of the series, live music was used in both the theme and the scene bridges, which complemented the production values. Whereas the initial series featured fairly generic orchestral music, the new series utilized a theme song opening and music written in a western style. The music was initially performed by an orchestra, but eventually featured vocal groups handling most of the musical renderings. The early episodes featured the western group The Texas Rangers, consisting of Roderick "Dave" May, Fran Mahaney, Bob Crawford and Edward "Tookie" Cronenbold and, from time to time, additional musicians, including a fiddle player named Gomer Cool. (Cool later became a successful radio scriptwriter, penning at least one script for *Hawk Larabee*.) The Rangers appeared in several radio programs in the 1940s, in addition to western films, some featuring singing cowboy movie star Gene Autry. Later episodes featured Andy Parker and the Plainsmen. The Plainsmen were well known within the western music industry and they appeared in many film productions during their years together. In 1946, the group consisted of Andy Parker, Charlie Morgan, Hank Caldwell, Joaquin Murphy, Harry Simms and George Bamby.

While none of the closing credits identify the sound effects personnel, their efforts enhanced the series with realistic and appropriate sounds that helped the dramatization. There were plenty of hoofbeats, crowd scenes, gun shots, door openings and closings, footsteps, and even an occasional runaway wagon; and all of them were handled very well.

The earliest circulating episode of *Hawk Larabee*, November 7, 1946, featured Hawk taking on the role of an assistant preacher to carry out the last wishes of the preacher, while the last known episode told the story of a man wanting to build a new church in town. Parley Baer appeared in this episode, as did William Conrad. Baer and Conrad were part of the elite group of radio actors that appeared on many CBS radio programs throughout the 1940s and 1950s. This early pairing of the two actors predated their appearing together regularly in the classic adult western **Gunsmoke**, which debuted in 1952 and had Conrad playing Matt Dillon while Baer played Chester.

In September 1947, Elliott Lewis returned to the series as Hawk Larabee and Barton

Yarborough again portrayed the role of Brazos John with no explanation publicly given for the casting change. The standard opening of the show also changed, adding the whistle of a hawk, followed by galloping hoofbeats.

William N. Robson continued in his role of producer of the series and directed from time to time. Richard Sanville directed most of the programs in its last year. The primary announcer for the program remained Jack McCoy (1918–1991). McCoy was the announcer for many radio and television programs, including *The Adventures of Maisie*, *The Steve Allen Show* and *The Dinah Shore Show*.

Despite its relatively short run, this western series had at least five different scriptwriters. They included Dean Owen, a pseudonym of Dudley Dean McGaughy (1909–1986) whose specialty was westerns and who wrote many stories and radio scripts under a variety of names; Gomer Cool (1908–2012), a professional musician who eventually became a professional writer; E. Jack Neuman (1921–1998), a prolific writer who contributed scripts to radio and television; William N. Robson, who wrote many scripts for radio including *Suspense* and *Escape*; and Kenneth Perkins (1890–1951), who wrote many radio and television scripts, most of them as western stories.

The series ended on February 7, 1948, but it was a genuine harbinger of the great adult westerns that CBS would launch within the next few years: **Gunsmoke**, **Frontier Gentleman**, **Fort Laramie**, and **Have Gun — Will Travel**.

Sources: Audio copies of *Hawk Durango* and *Hawk Larabee*; Dunning, *Tune In*; *Radio Recall*, February 2011; http://www.westernmusic.com; http://www.b-westerns.com; http://www.mysteryfile.com/DOwen/Bibliography.html.

HISTORICAL SOUTHERN CALIFORNIA

Karl Schadow *and* Jack French

This twice weekly early radio historical drama series was written for two target audiences: tourists contemplating visits to southern California sites and California natives interested in learning more about their state's history. The program, aired on station KHJ, Los Angeles, in 1932, was sponsored by the Pacific Electric Street Car Company and its motor transit subsidiaries. Some of the history covered included the battles between early settlers and Mexicans, the exploration of California, and the gold rush era.

Source: *Variety*, May 17, 1932.

HOOFBEATS

J. David Goldin

NETWORK: Syndicated
FORMAT: 15 minutes, daily or weekly
DURATION OF RUN: Circa 1936 to 1937
SPONSOR: Post Grape:Nuts Flakes
AUDIO COPIES EXTANT: 10
SCRIPTS ARCHIVED: Undetermined

Hoofbeats is significant for several reasons. It featured a major film star, Buck Jones, and was sponsored by Post Grape:Nuts Flakes, a major brand advertising on radio at the time. The show was sold by a major advertising agency, Young and Rubicam, and was produced by Raymond R. Morgan and Company, which was also known for *Chandu the Magician*, and later, *Queen for a Day*. That popular cereal was spelled Grape:Nuts Flakes in the mid–1930s, not Grape-Nuts Flakes as it is today.

The real Buck Jones was Charles Frederick Gebhart, who was born in Indiana in 1891. His birth date is disputed, because he lied about his age to get into the Army — twice. He was a tinsmith; worked as a test driver for the Marmon automobile company; a cowboy in a Wild West show; a Hollywood stuntman; and finally, a movie star. He made his first silent film in 1913, and made more than 160 movies over the years. His fame as a movie cowboy made him one of the richest movie stars in Hollywood, making $25,000 per picture in 1935 and $50,000 per picture by 1937. His Buck Jones Rangers Club boasted an incredible three million members, but this was an exaggeration. He was said to be receiving more fan mail than any actor in the world. A poll from the *Motion Picture Herald* named him the Number One Western star in Hollywood.

By 1935 Buck had become somewhat vulnerable to the new breed of singing cowboy that had evolved and featured Gene Autry, Roy Rogers, Dick Foran, Bob Baker, Tex Ritter, and Fred Scott. He started his own Wild West show, not too successfully, organized his own film production company, and dabbled a bit in radio.

Jones had appeared on radio several times before the *Hoofbeats* series. On June 5, 1933, he was heard on an NBC network program titled *Hollywood Is on the Air* (not to be confused with the long-running series of syndicated movie air-trailers of the same title.) On this show, Buck urged members of his movie fan club to help "lick the Depression." On January 17, 1937, he appeared on Jack Benny's program, possibly as a link to the series of five radio satires Jack had done previously about a western character named "Buck Benny." On November 17, 1937, Buck again appeared on radio in a comic western skit, this time with George Jessel and Norma Talmadge, on their Mutual network program, *Thirty Minutes in Hollywood*. And on July 29, 1938, Buck appeared on a special NBC broadcast with Bing Crosby and Dorothy Lamour. The event was the opening of the racetrack in Del Mar, CA.

The origin of *Hoofbeats* is unclear. It is possible that around 1935 Raymond Morgan was offered a script, or a concept, and he in turn offered it to Young and Rubicam, Post's long-time advertising agency. After the Post Cereal division signed off on the idea, the agency then shopped for a lead, and selected Buck Jones. It is equally unclear how many episodes of *Hoofbeats* were recorded, but 39 was the traditional number for a new syndicated series. Nor has the starting date of the initial airing been confirmed, although an original disk of episode #5 bears the date of March 3, 1937. This date was written by hand in the manner of radio engineers who dated and initialed transcriptions after playing the disk on the air. The recording date was not printed on the disk label.

There is a presumption that *Hoofbeats* was only syndicated on the West Coast, because many of the Raymond R. Morgan series were regional, not national, at least until he invented *Queen for a Day*. There was an experienced crew to record *Hoofbeats* at Recordings, Inc. in Hollywood. The theme music on the series sounds recorded; the sound effects are adequate but minimal. The amount of time needed to produce the transcriptions would be from six to eight weeks. Instantaneous acetate transcription, invented in 1935, was used. Selling the series to radio stations, writing cue sheets for announcers, and shipping the disks to the radio stations would round out the process. With syndicated shows, any station could start the series whenever it wanted; but on this set of disks, backing up the dates takes us back to the end of 1936. This time frame could have been shortened somewhat if the programs had been produced and recorded as they were broadcast, live-on-the-air. The February 5, 1937, issue of *Variety* mentions that production of the program was about to begin. This coincides nicely with the March 3, 1937, air date on episode #5. However, those types of notices in *Variety* were often generated by press releases, and unless it was big news, would be printed when and if there was space available.

Cherry Wilson was the scriptwriter for the series. "Cherry" was actually Robert Lee Wilson; his wife was named Cherry Wilson. Robert had written of the West before and had used "Cherry" as a pen name. Later in 1937, Wilson's wife said that she wrote 39 episodes of the story. So it is possible that the Wilsons, writing as a team named Cherry Wilson, wrote the 39 episodes.

There's another reason to link the program with late 1936 or early 1937; and that reason is "premiums." The Post Grape:Nuts Flakes commercials on the show said very little about what a great cereal Buck loved to eat, but the sponsor did try very hard to get the young listeners to join the Buck Jones Club. To be a "member" of Buck's Club, you wrote in to the radio station, sending in one Post Grape:Nuts Flakes box-top, agreeing as you did so to believe in "outdoor exercise; clean living; and sticking up for the underdog." In return for this pledge you received a membership card, a red and gold metallic Buck Jones pin, and a booklet with "lots of prizes" that were available to Club members at no cost. There were in fact 41 prizes, among them, a cowboy hat, a cowboy shirt, chaps, a camera, and many more. To get a "Buck Jones Shirt" for free, you simply sent in 24 box-tops. To receive a "Buck Jones Lariat" you needed to send in 18 box-tops. A "Buck Jones Cowboy Hat" would set you back 72 box-tops; and "Buck Jones Chaps" required 103 box-tops! Then you could save up for the 37 other great prizes; and all of this had to be done before December 31, 1937, the prize catalog's expiration date that was printed in small letters on the box-tops. Juvenile listeners must have had to shovel in that famous cereal all day long for months to get those box-tops.

The 10 extant episodes tell a typical B-western story. Buck rides up to a bunch of cowboys herding cattle to market. He's on his beloved horse Silver. Yes, his horse was named Silver long before **The Lone Ranger** debuted on the air. The cowboys are mostly hostile to Buck, except for Red River, the owner of the herd. Buck makes instant friends with Red River, and instant enemies with his foreman, whose name is Gore. The Dagger Hilt Gang had killed Buck's father and two brothers, and Buck is out for an eye-for-an-eye revenge. His dying brother told Buck that one of the killers had the tattoo of a dagger hilt on his shoulder, another was left-handed and "his eyes don't track." In later episodes other characters appear in the story. There's little Bud, an orphan who owns a cow named Sue that he rides; Piney, who's been shot by Gore, and Piney's beautiful daughter Glory, who instantly falls for Buck.

As the story line progresses, Buck discovers that Gore has a dagger hilt tattoo on his shoulder, just as the herd stampedes, killing one gang member and breaking Red River's leg. After the stampede, Gore escapes from Buck, and despite Glory's imploring him "not to ride this dark trail," Buck starts tracking Gore, leaving Red River's cattle drive. Before leaving, Buck tells Glory how the Dagger Hilt Gang killed his family. As episode #6 ends Buck promises Glory, "We'll meet again when the trail gets dark." This episode is noteworthy for having the only commercial spokesman other than the "Old Wrangler" and

Buck himself. He's a ten-year-old lad named Tim, who just loves Post Grape:Nuts Flakes and whose voice sounds similar to Bobby Breen.

In later episodes, Duke, who owns a gambling saloon, meets up with Gore, who has been running from Buck. Duke offers to buy Buck's horse, Silver. Buck declines to sell his horse, and then chooses not to have a drink with Duke, which provokes Duke somewhat. Duke later pays a visit to Buck's hotel room and offers once again to buy Silver. He even hints at hiring Buck as a gunman. By now members of the Buck Jones Club are beginning to suspect that Duke might be the third member of the Dagger Hilt Gang. Buck captures two of Duke's men after a saloon fight that pits ten bad guys against Buck and Sheriff Brant — fair odds for this kind of western. Buck turns down Brant's offer of a deputy's badge. He can't accept the badge because he plans on taking justice into his own hands with the Dagger Hilt Gang. As Chapter 10 ends, Duke decides that if he can't fight Buck or pay him off, he will use the services of Carmella to vamp the stalwart Buck. What happens following this will not be known until more audio copies, or the scripts, are discovered. Perhaps Buck's supporting cast will also be identified. There is still a lot to be learned about this syndicated series, including how much Buck Jones was paid for it.

After *Hoofbeats*, there would be little radio work for Buck, but his movie career continued past his 50th birthday, until that horrendous fire on the night of November 30, 1942. During a tour to promote his films in the Northeast, he spent the evening at Boston's Cocoanut Grove nightclub. After the tragic fire was extinguished, the body of Buck Jones was discovered near his table; he had died from smoke inhalation, burned lungs, and second and third degree burns of the face and neck.

Sources: Audio copies of *Hoofbeats*; Barbour; Katz; *Variety*, February 5, 1937.

HOPALONG CASSIDY

WILLIAM NADEL

NETWORK: Syndicated, 1949; Mutual, 1950; CBS, Fall 1950 to 1952
FORMAT: Half hour, weekly
DURATION OF RUN: 1949 to 1952
SPONSOR: Various, then General Foods (Post Cereals) on Mutual and CBS
AUDIO COPIES EXTANT: 104 (complete run)
SCRIPTS ARCHIVED: Dudley Dean McGaughey (McGaughy) Papers and William Boyd Papers, American Heritage Center

In 1950 it seemed as though *Hopalong Cassidy* was everywhere: on television with his old movies, on watch dials, on lunch boxes — and on the radio. He was even on the back of milk cartons. The hero jumped off the printed page into just about all of the media, and everywhere he looked like William Boyd, the actor who portrayed him. Boyd, who had been an up-and-coming actor in Cecil B. DeMille's silent films, had made it into talkies, but suffered a severe case of career setback when another performer, also named William Boyd, got into trouble with the law. But, after a chance opportunity to play a much sanitized version of Clarence E. Mulford's craggy, crude, but wonderful Hopalong Cassidy creation in a film, Boyd went on to make another 65 *Hopalong* features. Recognizing that it was his fate to be Hopalong Cassidy for the rest of his entertainment career, Boyd spent all the money he had to buy the rights to the films and the character, which forced him to negotiate on several occasions with Mulford. Eventually, his gamble paid off—handsomely.

The unique aspect of *Hopalong Cassidy* was that the character on radio (as well as television and the movies) bore no similarity to the original created by western author Mulford (1883–1956). In the pulp magazines and in the early novels, Cassidy was a scruffy, cussing, tobacco-chewing cripple. But Hollywood, and William Boyd, transformed this cowpuncher into an elegant gentleman with pure speech, abstaining from tobacco and alcohol, with nary a physical deformity.

In 1941 an attempt to bring Cassidy to radio did not succeed, but by the end of 1949, with the films on television, a new market had opened. With the cooperation of Mulford and Boyd, Walter W. White, Jr., and his Commodore Productions began to record and market a series of half hour radio programs recounting exploits of the movie hero. From January through December 1948, 26 episodes were prepared, with the remaining shows recorded from 1949 through the summer of 1951. Finally a total of 104 adventures were produced and all survive today.

Along with Cassidy there was his old sidekick California Carlson, superbly played

by movie veteran Andy Clyde. Clyde had been a member of Mack Sennett's "fun factory" in the 1920s and is best remembered as appearing with Billy Bevan on the screen. Their classics, *Whispering Whiskers*, and *Railroad Stowaways*, are regarded as two of the gems of silent films. Clyde would appear in half of the *Cassidy* features as California as well. The third, and younger, character of Lucky from the *Hopalong* films was eliminated from the radio version.

The Carlson character had been a replacement in films for George "Gabby" Hayes, who was an irascible, yet concerned, elder sidekick. When Gabby left the movies, scriptwriter Norton Parker created California as an older, lovable, comic teller of tall tales, afraid of just about everything but who also could be counted upon in a time of great trouble to rise to the occasion. On radio, without a younger hero (Lucky) to balance the cowboy

William Boyd in his traditional role of Hopalong Cassidy, which he played in movies, on television and radio (courtesy American Radio Archives at Thousand Oaks Library, Thousand Oaks, California).

team, it was just the middle-aged, fatherly Hoppy and the elder partner. Radio scriptwriters made Carlson a more heroic older cowboy who was always hungry, and also more of a balance to Cassidy. On the air he was dependable and reliable, and somewhat less comic than on the screen, as he had absorbed many of the traits of Lucky.

Each radio adventure cost between $2,000 and $3,000 to produce. Pressed on 16 inch transcription disks, the series was syndicated to various radio stations around the country, before being bought by the Mutual Broadcasting Company for airing in 1950. General Foods then picked up the cost of the series. In the fall of 1950 the show left Mutual's afternoon juvenile time slot to move to CBS and an evening adult slot. One of the most intriguing puzzles concerning the show was the temporary departure of Andy Clyde after the first 26 programs. Did he leave for monetary or health reasons? Joe DuVal, a supporting actor in some of the first 26 shows, replaced Clyde as California, but DuVal had difficulty in his characterization. His portrayal varied widely until his last few performances, after which Clyde returned to the program.

Production people, credited in each show, were Walter White, director, Albert Glaser, musical composer, and the scriptwriter for that particular episode. Over the years scripts were accepted from 20 different authors. Neither one of the announcers, James Matthews nor Charles Lyon, was identified on any program. The sound effects on the program were well crafted and realistic, but never intrusive. Musical bridges, including those signaling the three commercial breaks in each show, were created by Glaser, the composer of the main theme.

One of the most unique episodes was "The Sundown Kid" (program #27), because Hoppy solves a complex problem alone. Recorded on January 25, 1949, the adventure finally reached the Mutual airwaves on July 2, 1950. The cowboy meets a man suffering from sunstroke and the effects of a bullet wound. Is the delirious man actually the notorious outlaw, or innocent of the crime of murdering his wife? At a pivotal moment at the end of the episode, it isn't Hoppy who fires a bullet to save the Sundown Kid, but actually a determined young woman who is fond of the Kid.

Producers of the radio series turned to some of the last motion pictures made by Boyd, and five episodes are wonderful as abridged audio versions of those movies. The first cinema exploit to be adapted for the listener was *The Marauders*, a tale of Hoppy and California trapped in a church, which stands in a nearly deserted ghost town. There the cowboys encounter a widow, her daughter, and those anxious to dismantle the religious edifice, ostensibly for its wood. What they really want are the oil deposits under the town. Recorded on February 4, 1948, as "The Coltsville Terror (program #3) the finished disk was one of the shows used to sell the series to prospective radio stations, and was heard on Mutual on January 15, 1950.

In the film *The Unexpected Guest*, Hoppy and California explored the world of "Old Dark House" mysteries. On radio it became "The Voice of the Dead," (program #9, recorded August 24, 1948; aired February 26, 1950). It featured Wally Maher as Ralph and Phineas with Lurene Tuttle as both Matilda Hackett and Ruth. California and Cassidy visit the Box O Ranch to hear the reading of Carlson's cousin's will. The holdings are to be divided among all of them who survive. There's no money left, but they can sell the ranch. Suddenly, the heirs begin to die off.

Scriptwriter Harold Swanton transformed the movie *Silent Conflict* into the radio adventure "The Medicine Man" (program #25, recorded November 30, 1948, and broadcast on June 18, 1950). In the film, the entire plot revolves around Lucky and his gambling debt, and is further complicated by his involvement with a traveling medicine man who drugs and hypnotizes his victims to commit crimes. When the con man gets Lucky to steal the money that Hoppy, California, and Lucky are transporting from the sale of a joint cattle herd, the ranchers fear that Cassidy has become a crook. In the radio version, Swanton solved the dilemma of Lucky not being a member of the radio team by renaming the Lucky character "Marty Brett" but keeping the plot intact. The great radio actor Frank Lovejoy played Brett and Joe DuVal was Pete in this hypnotic tale.

A similar Lucky logistical problem befell Tom Shirley when he reworked *Borrowed Trouble* for the air. At a crucial point, California is left to teach school in place of the kidnapped schoolmarm who has been offended by a saloon being located next to the school house. Cassidy and Lucky go to free the disgruntled teacher from her captors. However, on the radio version, "Hoppy and the Schoolmarm," (program #29, recorded February 1, 1949; aired July 16, 1950), Hoppy's assistant becomes older student Jimmy who assists Hoppy in the rescue of the educator.

The last official audio version of a Hoppy film was "Hoppy and the Iron Horse" (program #39, recorded, March 29, 1949, and aired, September 24, 1950), based on *Sinister Journey*. The ex-con husband of the daughter of a railroad executive is suspected of killing his father-in-law, but the cowboy reveals that the rejected suitor of the wife is the real culprit. Although this weak story had great scenes on the screen, its radio version actually reveals the real culprit early in the adventure. It was also the last Cassidy exploit heard on Sunday afternoons on the Mutual network.

Astride his white horse Topper, Cassidy was the 19th century embodiment of the medieval knight, righting wrongs and fighting for truth and justice, and yet the cowboy was every bit a detective as his 20th century counterpart, Philip Marlowe. So close were the two, that when Hoppy took a vacation from the CBS Sunday night 8:30 P.M. time slot, it was Marlowe who replaced him for the summer of 1951. Given a prime time adult position, the network hoped that Hoppy's appeal would continue to reach all age groups, not just juveniles. Unlike other western heroes, he did not hide his age or features behind a mask, and although he was usually dressed in all black, he exudes fairness, honor, and loyalty.

An examination of the programs indicates the care and attention the star and his producer put into the series. In "A Jailer Named Satan" (program #75, recorded on September 27, 1950, and aired on June 9, 1951), both Carlson and Cassidy are incensed by the actions of sheriff/town boss Satan Blue. The episode is set in the town of Paradise, NM, a desert village where those passing through are imprisoned and forced to labor at building channels for water to make the place rich and fertile. The land is owned by Satan and his partner. Veteran character actor Vic Rodman voiced the evil Satan. Rodman was a master at playing old codgers on the air. However, the best characterization is by the great, though lesser-known radio star Wally Maher, whose portrayal of the rowdy convict Brian Gahagan is compelling.

One of the most impressive of all the West Coast supporting actors on the *Cassidy* show was Harry Bartell, a performer who made the actors with him all seem better. Harry's best role in the series was as Fred Oakes in "Right Rope... Wrong Neck" (program #101, recorded April 2, 1951; aired on February 23, 1952). Hoppy obtains a release pardon for a prisoner condemned to death, only to find that the prisoner killed a guard while escaping. But he wasn't the only prisoner to escape. There actually was a spate of escapees and Jack Moyles plays Warden Davis in this strange tale of crooked guards and murder.

Bartell could also play despicable villains. In "Run Sheep Run" (program #77, recorded October 2, 1950; aired on June 23, 1951), he is Slagle, a sheep man who buys land and its water rights, keeping the water from the cattle ranchers. Slagle wants to make an obscene profit from the cattlemen. Aiding and abetting Slagle in his crime is Lou Krugman, as Sime. After Hoppy confronts Slagle, the crook orders Sime to kill the cowboy.

A cold dark Dakota winter is the setting for another great Bartell performance. When a jealous sister-in-law conspires with the town marshal to frame a man for the murder of his wife, only Hoppy can prevent the bewildered husband's lynching and solve the murder. Bartell is Luke, the husband as well as his best friend, with Jeanette Nolan as Myra, the sister-in-law, and Vic Perrin as Marshal Kingman, in "Cold Country" (program #60, recorded February 28, 1950, aired on February 25, 1951).

As ranch boss of the Bar 20, Cassidy's main job was to see that the cattle got to market, and to manage the ranch. Although the Bar 20 was actually located in Texas, several movies place it in Arizona, and many radio adventures are vague as to its location. However, in "Bayou Drums Mean Death" (program #84, recorded December 13, 1950, aired on October 27, 1951), Cassidy and California are bringing horses to the Louisiana plantation of Blanche and her cousin Philippe Lavaseur. Betty Lou Gerson plays Blanche, who finds California "her type of man." Howard McNear schemes as Philippe, while Hoppy and Carlson fight off a deadly snake, a voodoo witch, and the plantation workers who follow her. They finally reveal the secret of the Lavaseurs' Death Ruby.

It was not unusual for the Bar 20 duo to find itself facing corrupt officials in a western town. Sheriff Fancher, portrayed by Jack Moyles, and the mayor of Cherokee have a great racket. They and their thugs terrify and get money from ranchers who buy the town's prized cattle. Those who don't pay never leave alive with their herd. Cassidy helps the townspeople reclaim their village in "Border of Nowhere" (program #24, recorded November 22, 1948, aired on June 11, 1950).

There was excitement at the Bar 20 when Senator Hiram Sprague came for a visit in "Kidnapper's Trail" (program #70, recorded April 3, 1950, aired on May 5, 1951). There was only one problem. Sprague's daughter has been kidnapped, just before the stagecoach arrives. Buck Peters, the ranch owner (played by Ralph Moody) would do anything to get Cathy Sprague back, and there's a $50,000 ransom to be paid. Sam Fuller (portrayed by Vic Rodman) is invited to the ranch to meet Sprague. All signs seem to point to the neighboring owner Ward McCauley as the kidnapper. Cassidy then investigates, finding that the solution lies with Fuller's greed.

Few of Hoppy's adventures are specifically dated. One of the best of them is "Letter from the Grave" (program #22, recorded November 15, 1948, aired on May 28, 1950). When Cassidy receives a letter asking for help from his old friend Jack Bannock, which was dated 1873, but delivered in 1888, he decides to track down his old pal in Montana. Of course, Bannock has been murdered, and the cowboy solves the crime. But the important facts revealed in the episode show that Cassidy has worked at the Bar 20 Ranch since the early 1870s.

Another of the unique dated episodes is from 1886, "The Failure" (program #13, recorded September 10, 1948, aired on March 26, 1950). A young man out West has been unable to make a success of his ranch and has just sold it. The man, Ted, helps Hoppy solve the murder of the former sheriff, eventually returning to New York, and then deciding to run for mayor. At the conclusion, Ted is revealed to be President Theodore "Teddy" Roosevelt.

Sympathetic to the plight of minorities in the country, Cassidy is not quick to blame them for any crimes seemingly perpetrated by Hispanics or Indians. In "Stagecoach West" (program #68, recorded March 29, 1950, aired on April 21, 1951), Apaches apparently have burned and destroyed coach change stations, killing the station folk. Hoppy defends the Indians and helps prove that an outlaw band of whites disguised as Indians were the actual culprits. Heard in this unique episode are Barton Yarborough as Johnny, and Earle Ross as the Colonel.

Likewise, Hoppy helped former criminals who are trying to rehabilitate themselves. When one gets a job at the Bar 20 and is later accused of a stagecoach robbery and murder, in "Hoppy Takes a Chance" (program #8, recorded August 17, 1948, aired on February 19, 1950), the cowboy saves the unfortunate fellow from a lynch mob and gets help from another former criminal, who just happens to be Mexican. Harry Bartell is hilarious as the Mexican former pickpocket, forger, and convict, Mike DeSico. Earle Ross was the sheriff and Howard McNear was both Red Conroy and Sam Wellman in this touching episode.

On August 10, 1951, William Boyd, Andy Clyde, and Harry Bartell (as Wayne) stood at the microphones to record the last *Hopalong Cassidy* radio show. After more than three years, the show would become a part of history. The efforts of Ted Bliss (director), James Matthews and Charles Lyon (announcers), Albert Glaser (musical director), and David Light (sound effects expert) to bring the West of the 1880s to the airwaves was now at its conclusion. That last recorded show, "Cowtown Troubleshooters," reached the CBS airwaves on March 8, 1952. But this tale of rival cow companies and murder was not the final show to be aired. The actual final CBS episode, "The Santa Claus Rustlers," was heard a week later. It was recorded in 1950 and had been pre-empted at its originally planned air date during Christmas week 1951. The Christmas episode was syndicated for many years as part of an old radio Christmas package that was aired on many stations from the late 1970s on. It was a staple of station WABC in New York, and aired for years on Christmas day.

Sources: Audio copies of *Hopalong Cassidy*; Drew; *Jingles*; Drew; *Hopalong*; Nivens.

HORIZONS WEST

STEWART WRIGHT *and* JACK FRENCH

NETWORK: Armed Forces Radio & Television Service (AFRTS)
FORMAT: Half hour, weekly
DURATION OF RUN: Early 1960s
SPONSOR: None
AUDIO COPIES EXTANT: 13 (complete run)
SCRIPTS ARCHIVED: Undetermined

This remarkable series, a retelling of the Lewis and Clark Expedition, had everything that radio audiences could hope for: strong scripts, great acting, realistic sound effects, and the highest of production standards. Moreover, it was a transcribed series and all audio copies have survived so anyone can enjoy this program today as much as its original overseas audience did in the 1960s.

Although we know the programs were originally recorded in either 1962 or 1963, the air dates have not been firmly documented. It was produced in Studio B of Capitol Records in Hollywood, CA for the express purpose of broadcasting only over the AFRTS stations in Europe and Asia between 1965 and 1967. It remains a compelling illustration of an AFRTS commissioned and produced series, specifically intended for the U.S. military, the U.N. Armed Forces, and their families.

Summarizing the story of an 8,000 mile expedition that encompassed two years and four months into only 13 half hour programs was a daunting challenge but scriptwriters Karl and William Tunberg were up to the task. They researched the historical details of the expedition, from President Thomas Jefferson initiating the project with Captains William Clark and Meriwether Lewis to the triumphant return of the explorers years later.

The Turnbergs managed to dramatize most of the significant events of the expedition as well as include the true names of many of the relatively unknown 45 military men and boat handlers (John Colter, Patrick Glass, George Shannon, John Ordway, Pierre Cruzatte, the Fields Brothers, et. al.). Even York, the African slave whom Clark had inherited from his father, and who made the entire journey to the Pacific and back, figures prominently, and accurately, in several episodes.

Director William "Bill" Lally had little trouble casting the leads and supporting cast members. Harry Bartell, a veteran radio actor who had significant roles on *Fort Laramie*, *Gunsmoke*, and many others, got the role of Meriwether Lewis. The choice for William Clark was a good one, although the actor selected had virtually no radio experience. John Anderson, primarily a stage and television actor portrayed Clark and did an excellent job. His voice resembled John Dehner's, which may have been one of the reasons he was chosen.

Backing up the leads was a strong supporting cast of over two dozen actors with substantial network experience. Some of the more well-known ones were: Herb Ellis, Ben Cooper, Howard Culver, Sam and Jack Edwards, Jack Kruschen, Tyler McVey, Karl Swenson, Les Tremayne and Ben Wright. Other skilled performers were: Dan Barton, Steven Bell, Jim Boles, John Cedar, Gary Collins, Paul Conrad, Don Diamond, Stan Farrar, Eddie Firestone, Frank Gerstle, Clark Gordon, Bill Irwin, Bill Keene, Don Messick, Jay Novello, Richard Peel, Bill Quinn, Dan Randolph, Don Spruance, and John Stephenson.

British-born Sebastian Cabot, primarily a movie and television performer, was cast as the Frenchman, Toussaint Charbonneau, the husband of Sacagawea, portrayed by Helen Gerald. Cabot would later achieve television fame as Mr. French in *Family Affair* (1966–1971).

York was played by Cliff Holland, the announcer was Michael Rye (also known as Rye Billsbury) and the Newfoundland dog owned by Lewis was voiced by Dal McKennon, who also played other small roles in the series. The sound effects, which were both convincing and compelling, were the work of Gene Twombly.

All 13 chapters began in this identical manner. The announcer opened with "The American West! Once it could have been the British, Spanish, or even the Russian West. It became American primarily because of the explorations of two, young Army officers,

Meriwether Lewis and William Clark. Their pioneering journey stands as one of the great achievements in the history of the United States." This was followed by a short dramatic scene, less than two minutes, which set the scene for the chapter. The announcer returned to the microphone and provided the series title and individual chapter name and then the drama began.

The scripts were not only faithful to historical fact; they also included all the highs and lows of the lengthy expedition. Their successes, discoveries, and joys were set forth but also the back-breaking work of portages, the serious accidents and illnesses, and even the boredom of the lack of progress on a difficult section of the trail.

The various Indian tribes which the expedition encountered were given a fair and accurate treatment in the scripts. Some of the tribes were friendly and generous, some were arrogant and suspicious, and a few were aggressive and warlike. Sacajawea, the Shoshone woman who served as both interpreter and guide to the expedition, contributed an additional benefit that the scripts made clear. Since she and her baby boy were part of the expeditionary forces, the tribes they encountered believed Lewis and Clark came in peace since no war party would have a woman and infant within its ranks.

The program's broad appeal reached a large audience in the U. S. military community as it was enjoyed by both the active duty adults and their young dependents that were stationed abroad with them. While the series was primarily aimed at mature listeners, juvenile audience members found it equally enjoyable. Probably without realizing it, they were learning American history in the easiest and most pleasant educational process.

Sources: Audio copies of *Horizons West*; Brooks; Howard; Interviews with Harry Bartell by Stewart Wright; *Program log*: http://www.old-time.com/otrlogs2/hw_sw.log.txt; http://www.lewisclark.net; http://www.lewisandclarktrail.com/sacajawea.htm.

Indian Stories see *The Lone Indian*

Indian Trails see *The Lone Indian*

Indian Village see *The Lone Indian*

JUSTICE RIDES THE RANGE

JACK FRENCH *and* KARL SCHADOW

Falstaff Brewing Corporation of St. Louis sponsored this prairie adventure series which aired as a transcribed program, principally in the Midwest. It was a quarter hour program, broadcast Monday through Friday, usually in the late evening, from 1941 to 1942. This was a Frank Hummert production, the bulk of whose output in radio was soap operas, and this western didn't stray too far from that concept. Each episode began with a summary of "what had happened before" and ended with broad hints as to how the plot would evolve. In addition, like a soap opera, conversation dominated over action. The cast included Don MacLaughlin, Joan Thompkins, and Robert Shayne, with Bill Adams announcing. A single script for the program is included in the book *Best Broadcasts of 1940–41*.

Source: Wylie.

Ken Maynard Show see Roundup Trail

LAW WEST OF THE PECOS

JACK FRENCH *and* DAVID S. SIEGEL

NETWORK: Not aired
FORMAT: Half hour
DURATION OF RUN: Not aired
SPONSOR: None
AUDIO COPIES EXTANT: 1 audition disk
SCRIPTS: Undetermined

Based on an audition recording, the only available audio for this "would be" program, the series had the potential of becoming a successful show as it was produced with skilled actors, had realistic sound effects and impressive music, and was held together by an interesting script. But, for reasons now lost in time, the series appears never to have been picked up by any network.

Radio historians have dated the audition recording as having been made in 1946 based on the fact that the announcer, Fort Pearson, reminds listeners to attend the current movies of the program's two stars, Walter Brennan in *Centennial Summer* and Andy Devine in *Canyon Passage*, both of which were released in 1946.

The series was based on an actual historical figure, the self-appointed Judge Roy Bean whose saloon/courtroom followed the railroad expansion across Texas, ultimately setting up shop in a saloon he called "The Jersey Lilly" in the town of Langtry near the Pecos River. However, the radio program was more focused upon the fictionalized version of Bean in the 1940 motion picture, *The Westerner*, which featured Gary Cooper and Walter Brennan, portraying Bean, a role that earned him an Academy Award for Best Supporting Actor and, at that time, the first actor in history to win three Oscars. Perhaps the producers of *Law West of the Pecos* hoped Brennan's popularity would propel the program onto a network slot. But that was not to be.

Set in a tent saloon in the fictional village of Vinegarroon, mostly a construction site and home to 8,000 railroad workers, the show opened with a vibrant theme of music by Wilbur Hatch and his orchestra. Brennan introduced the program with: "That's me, Judge Roy Bean, of Vinegarroon. I hold high court in my own saloon, for killin', thievin' and other such fracas. For I'm the law, out west of the Pecos."

The program's only weakness (and perhaps the reason why it was never broadcast) became evident very quickly; Judge Roy Bean lost his place in the spotlight to the Pecos Kid. The unknown scriptwriter, probably unwilling to keep all the action in a saloon/court room, introduced a mysterious Robin Hood of the range called the Pecos Kid and while Bean had threatened to "hang him from a cottonwood tree," the irascible judge could not apprehend, or even identify, the Kid. So Bean only got the first and last five minutes of his program while the adventures of the masked avenger took up the other 20 minutes.

In the audition recording, Jim Grant (voiced by Lou Crosby) a likable cowpoke disguises himself to be the Pecos Kid and his secret identity is known only to Buck Taylor (the scratchy voice of oversized Andy Devine). This duo then get most of the action in the program, including stopping a stampede and uncovering the plot of rustlers but Grant has time to pursue the hand of a comely daughter of a local "nester." The program ends back in Bean's courtroom where he vows again to capture the Pecos Kid, who confronts the judge from a saloon window before disappearing from sight.

Brennan and Devine, despite their obvious talent, were never a significant part of radio but both would go on to continued success in the movies and television. Brennan (1894–1974) was a lumberjack, bank clerk and vaudeville performer before he went into military service in World War I. In 1923, he broke into movies as a stuntman and extra but was soon getting major roles, usually playing elderly characters when he was barely into middle-age. Andrew Vabre Devine (1905–1977) grew up in Arizona and after high school, was a college football star. He came to Hollywood where his raspy voice (the result of a childhood accident) and his boundless personality won him a variety of sidekick roles in both television and motion pictures.

Unlike Brennan and Devine, who had little broadcasting experience, Crosby and Pearson were widely known on network radio; Pearson was the announcer on *Beat the Band*, *Attorney at Law*, *The Guiding Light* and *Quiz Kids*, in addition to being a sports announcer, and Crosby was usually an announcer (*Lum & Abner*, **Melody Ranch**, and the *Rise Stevens Show*) but he also produced the quiz show, *Double or Nothing*. The music was provided by Wilbur Hatch and his orchestra who were also heard regularly on *Broadway Is My Beat*, *Meet Corliss Archer*, *Escape*, and *Gateway to Hollywood*.

Sources: Audio copy of *Law West of the Pecos*; Dunning, *On the Air*; Katz; McDaniel.

LIFE ON RED HORSE RANCH

RYAN ELLETT

NAMES: *Life on Red Horse Ranch*, *Red Horse Ranch*, *The Flying Horse Ranch*
NETWORK: Syndicated
FORMAT: 15 minutes, daily for 13 weeks
DURATION OF RUN: May 1935 to mid–1936 on various midwestern stations
SPONSORS: Primarily Socony-Vacuum but other local sponsors, including Mrs. Wagner's
     Pies (Chicago)
AUDIO COPIES EXTANT: 64 (of run of 65)
SCRIPTS ARCHIVED: University of Missouri-Kansas City, Kansas City, MO; Iowa State
     University, Ames, IA

Life on Red Horse Ranch may be the most widely remembered radio work of the western musical act, The Texas Rangers. Despite the growing awareness now of this song-laden serial, it was a relatively minor production in the overall career of the Texas Rangers band which stretched nearly 20 years from 1932 to 1950. Historical circumstances being what they are, *Life on Red Horse Ranch* has left an impressive document trail for fans and historians to study, while other much more prominent works by the Texas Rangers have left far less evidence of their existence.

The series is best understood within the larger context of the history of the Texas Rangers, a band which emerged from Kansas City in the early 1930s, flirted with stardom in Hollywood during the early 1940s, and was still entertaining radio station KMBC listeners as late as 1950. The exact origins of the band are hazy and surviving records and personal memories are not sufficient to paint a clear picture. Briefly, the Rangers were an eight-piece band that was created from a quartet of singers (billed on and off separately as The Midwesterners) who were all on staff at Kansas City's KMBC, the city's small CBS affiliate, and four musicians who were also on the station's payroll. It's not known who first had the idea of forming this octet but the detail is moot; the Texas Rangers were a commercial property entirely owned and controlled by Arthur B. Church, owner of KMBC. No matter what each of the Rangers invested creatively and emotionally in the group, they were individually never more than hired performers as far as any contract was concerned. While Church was certainly fond of his musicians and thought highly of their work, over the years he was not slow to remind them of exactly where they stood in the employee-employer relationship.

Several of the individual members of the Texas Rangers were working for KMBC as early as 1927 and therefore had several years of radio performing experience as writers, announcers, and musicians before they were merged into a group which found itself sustained on the CBS network by November, 1932. The traditional eight-man line-up was solidified within a year: Paul Sells (accordion), Carl Hays (bass), Herb Kratoska (guitar), Gomer Cool (fiddle), Duane Swalley (lead tenor), Bob Crawford (baritone), Rodney May (2nd tenor), and Edward "Tookie" Cronenbold (bass). The musicians would change over the years but Arthur Church never deviated from an octet format. Ironically, none of the eight had considered themselves country or western musicians; Cool had even studied violin at the Kansas City Conservatory of Music for a time.

Surviving records don't indicate exactly what inspired Arthur Church to invest in the *Life on Red Horse Ranch* transcription series, a mix of songs and dramatic storyline. The Texas Rangers were a musical outfit which earned their salaries performing live over KMBC and in person throughout the surrounding Kansas and Missouri counties. They were not actors nor were the musicians known to be involved with the original dramatic programming produced over the station. They did, however, appear in a series of song dramas broadcast locally during the summer of 1934.

Beginning with a traditional western song such as "Sam Bass" or "Old Chisholm Trail," an unknown author crafted a 15 minute program that interspersed a story with several musical performances by the Texas Rangers who presumably played the dramatic roles as well. One possibility is that local response to the show was positive enough that Church began to consider new musical drama outlets for his group.

During this same period the Rangers began entering the recording studio, thus possibly preparing for entirely new avenues of promotion. They laid down eight tracks during the summer of 1934, the most famous of which was "Cattle Call," a tune penned by Tex Owens. Owens, incidentally, had an interesting relationship with the band; known as The Original Texas Ranger while performing on KMBC, his use of the Texas Ranger moniker predated that of the band. He performed regularly with the group over the radio yet was never considered an actual member of the band. Owens' connection with the Texas Rangers lasted through most of the 1930s but documents suggest—without revealing specific details—that he and the band members were not on good terms with each other by the time Owens left KMBC for other prospects.

Following the summer recording session the group returned to the World Broadcasting studios in Chicago on August 27, 1934, for further recordings with Tex Owens. Studio records show that Jim and Marian Jordan, who would achieve stardom as Fibber McGee and Molly, recorded at the same studio just two weeks later. Before the year was out Arthur Church's salesmen were attempting to sell the Texas Rangers as a transcription feature.

Perhaps it was the success of the previously mentioned series of drama songs and the two recording sessions that convinced Church to assign fiddler and aspiring writer Gomer Cool the task of creating a series of scripts entitled *The Flying Horse Ranch*. The resulting 65 scripts were for a weekday serial which combined a dramatic story set on a western ranch with numerous songs by the Texas Rangers. We do not know when the original scripts were penned; one set of existing scripts is hand dated as being checked on March 27, 1935, so they were all completed at least by then.

How the Texas Rangers came to the attention of the J. Stirling Getchell advertising agency is not known but on March 30, 1935, the agency signed a contract with Church's Midland Broadcasting Company to use the *Flying Horse Ranch* series for their client Socony-Vacuum. In honor of the company's famous red Pegasus logo the program was promptly renamed *Life on the Red Horse Ranch*, though generally referred to simply as *Red Horse Ranch* in company documents. Twelve performers are listed on the contract although 14 appear in a photograph identified as having been taken during the *Red Horse* recording sessions. All but one of the contractual dozen were KMBC employees: Gomer Cool, Doie Henlasey (Tex) Owens, Duane Swalley, Edward Cronenbold, Roderick May, Robert Crawford, Ruth Barth, Paul Sells, Herbert Kratoska (frequently referred to as "Herbie"), Eddie Edwards, and Marion Fonville. John Preston, the final performer, was a western film actor credited with a number of B-pictures. Of the extra two pictured in the photograph, one is Clarence Hartman who took over for Carl Hays on bass around this time. The fourteenth person in the *Red Horse Ranch* photograph remains unidentified but may be Fran Heyser who served as the producer and/or director for numerous KMBC productions including those which were recorded outside of Kansas City.

No definitive documentation has been discovered to identify firmly each character in the program, but most of the parts can be pinned down with some certainty. Robert Crawford and Tex Owens surely played Bob and Tex respectively, the only two characters named for their players. The other roles played by the Rangers are well established and were consistent over the years: Gomer Cool was Tenderfoot, Edward Cronenbold was Tuscon, Herb Kratoska was Arizona, Paul Sells was Montana or Monty, and Clarence Hartman was Idaho.

Ruth Barth was a KMBC employee who later married Paul Henning, another KMBC man, who eventually made a name for himself on the West Coast writing for radio and television. *Red Horse Ranch* only has one female character across its run, thus "Rose" is easily identified as Barth. Eddie Edwards, a jack-of-all-trades performer for the station, specialized in blackface characters, most notably one named George Washington White. He is the most likely candidate for the part of "Cookie," a slow, African American cook who only appears sporadically in a part which makes the modern listener cringe. The Alabama-born announcer Marion Fonville joined the station in early 1932 and served as emcee for a number of Texas Rangers broadcasts at the station. Separate Rangers scripts point to Fonville as Alabam, an appropriate nickname considering his home state.

The final three primary characters of the series can be identified with less certainty. Rod May or Duane Swalley very likely portrayed Cheyenne, based on the Rangers' habit of adopting western nicknames. Sam Carter, the patriarch of the *Red Horse Ranch*, very likely was played by John Preston, star of numerous B-western films during the 1930s. When the idea of recording further *Red Horse Ranch* episodes was discussed in later years, the role of Sam Carter was to be omitted. While no reason was given, since Preston was not known ever to be a KMBC employee, it makes sense to assume he was not available to resume the part. The final unidentified role, the series villain Steve Bradford must then be either May or Swalley, whoever was not cast as Cheyenne.

With the Socony contract signed on March 30, 1935, the KMBC staff had two weeks to deliver the first 26 episodes; Socony wanted to send them out to participating stations by April 15. A total of 65 episodes were written, recorded, and aired. Additional episodes were written and two undated scripts numbered 97 and 100 still exist but there is no evidence that further episodes were ever broadcast, even locally. Church wasted no time and had the cast in the World Broadcasting Studios on April 2. The entire series — all 65 episodes — were recorded in four days, indicating a hectic pace of 16 episodes per day. Such a schedule could not have allowed for many retakes or rehearsals.

In addition to the $50 each actor earned for each day's work on *Red Horse Ranch*, the members of the Texas Rangers stayed an extra day and on April 6 recorded eight songs that afternoon. Immediately after completing the set they recorded an extra three songs as the "Happy Hollow Hoodlums," named after KMBC's rural sketch show *Happy Hollow* which had been on the air since 1929.

Throughout 1935 *Life on Red Horse Ranch* was distributed to over three dozen stations throughout the Midwest and West, from large markets such as Chicago (WGN) and Detroit (WWJ) to modest outlets such as Lamar, CO (KIDW) and Wolf Point, MT (KGCX). The series appears to have circulated about a year before station interest waned entirely. One review from a Chicago newspaper may hint at its relatively short commercial shelf life: "It's a bad show from all angles. And the commercial plug is even worse, and to top the general aura of poorness there was an announcer who stumbled, stuttered and stammered."

Set on a ranch in an unidentified state, *Life on Red Horse Ranch* followed the exploits of the hired help of *Red Horse Ranch* as well as Sam Carter, owner of the ranch, and his daughter, Rose. During the first half of the series a stranger, Steve Bradford, moves into the area and sets his sights on buying the Red Horse Ranch. Unable to determine the reason for Bradford's dogged pursuit of purchasing the ranch, the ranch hands (played by the Texas Rangers but never referred to by that name) investigate mysterious gunshots and rustled cattle. Bradford is on his way to acquiring the ranch through Sam Carter's misfortune — as well as to winning Rose's affection — before Carter's herd is tracked down. The sale of the herd allows Carter to avoid selling the Red Horse Ranch to Bradford who, Alabam has discovered, is aware of potential oil strikes on the land.

After the series' first major story arc wound down, *Life on Red Horse Ranch* began to meander with short multi-part stories concerning the "adoption" of Dewey Dawson, son of a slain outlaw gang leader, by the ranch family, and a rodeo competition in which Steve Bradford reappeared. The final storyline, running approximately the last dozen episodes, focused on a locket given to Dewey by his father. In it, he and the Red Horse gang discover a map to Dawson's hidden treasure. Outwitting former members of Dawson's gang, the Rangers manage to track down the loot which is subsequently turned over to the local sheriff. The series ended somewhat abruptly. Though the mystery of Dawson's hidden treasure was solved, other threads, including the oil discovered on Carter's land, were left up in the air. Clearly Cool wrote the original 65 episodes with future stories in mind, as illustrated by the final lines of script 65:

CARTER: The oil company's already moved on to the Red Horse Ranch and they're ready to start drillin'.

CHEYENNE: Man, listen to that. Things sure have taken a turn to the good on this Red Horse Ranch.

CARTER: Yes, boys, thanks to you. Go on, play your music. I hope you never stop!

MUSIC   "WAIT TILL THE SUN SHINES NELLIE"   QUARTET

YELLS

THEME

ANNCR   We found a happy gang on Red Horse Ranch today, didn't we? We wonder if he feels that everything will go so smooth when the oil company begins its drilling operations.

What further problems Cool anticipated for the Red Horse Ranch are forever forgotten, neither having been recorded nor left in unproduced script form. Few listeners, apparently, cared enough to request that their local station acquire more adventures.

It is primarily through the music of the Texas Rangers that the series engages modern listeners. The storyline is thin with only mild elements of suspense and the characters populating the series are rarely more than one dimensional figures. Only the fact that the Rangers regularly refer to each other by nickname allows the listener to know which Ranger is which. They are, for the most part, interchangeable as far as the story is concerned, with few traits or personality quirks to distinguish one from another.

By virtue of being the bad guy Steve Bradford is easily discernible as is Sam Carter, the patriarch of the Ranch, who has a gruffer, distinctive voice and a bit of personality which sets him apart from the ranch hands. Rose Carter, being the only female in the series, is memorable though her part is unspectacular, serving primarily as the love interest of Alabam and, briefly, Bradford. Rose is passive, swept along by the events impacting Red Horse Ranch; it is the men, specifically the Rangers, who are the decisive actors resisting and counteracting the tide that would rip the ranch from its loving owner, Sam Carter.

Cookie, the Red Horse Ranch cook, is one of the most unique characters of the series but for all the wrong reasons. Edwards portrays the African American cook as "lazy but lovable," a dim witted buffoon written in solely for comedic affect who is comparable to the character of "Lightning" on the far more popular *Amos 'n Andy* program. Like many (but not all) black film and radio characters of the era, Cookie regularly causes the contemporary listener to cringe with such utterances as "Mistuh Alabam, Mistah Bob — Is dey after me? Is dey followin' me? Oh lawsee.'" Cool does provide a drop of humanity to Cookie in episode 26 during which Cookie and Arizona spend a few minutes reminiscing about lost loves. The mood is melancholy and the listener realizes, if only briefly, that Cookie is human and capable of love and inner reflection, a man who suffers like any other. The moment is all too brief compared to the countless "yas suhs" sprinkled liberally through the 65 other episodes.

The responsibility for the mediocre scripts does not belong entirely to Cool; many obstacles were placed in his way. A cast of more than a dozen characters is far too many for a 65 episode series, especially when each broadcast only ran 15 minutes. To make matters more difficult, Cool generally only had four to five minutes per episode to develop the story, the rest of the time being dedicated to Texas Rangers music. There is no doubt that Cool had writing talent; he eventually was hired by CBS in the 1940s to write radio and television programming. But in 1935, at the relatively young age of 27 and without the benefit of any formal writing training, Cool was not yet ready to produce a timeless radio epic that would hold up over succeeding decades.

Though not an overwhelming success, Arthur Church was satisfied enough with the results to have his staff look into the logistics of creating a second 65 episode series in the spring of 1936. Cool thought it was definitely possible and could be successful if they took their time with the recordings. He was positive that with extra time Church would "note a great improvement — in script, music, and production" over the initial run of episodes. Beyond perhaps some sample scripts such as those labeled 97 and 100 mentioned above, the project was not developed any further.

As late as 1939 staff at KMBC was still suggesting that *Life on Red Horse Ranch* had viable commercial prospects. Not directly contradicting such pronouncements, Cool was quick to point out the difficulties of doing so. The program was not an action show and station salesmen could not be expected to promote it as such. It was a bit dishonest and would disappoint any sponsor which thought it was acquiring an action or adventure program. The disks in KMBC's possession were deteriorating by then as well and they had few quality samples to share.

Interest in *Life on Red Horse Ranch* faded within the station's ranks and it was eventually consigned to the company's dusty storage shelves. Meanwhile, the Texas Rangers continued on radio until 1950, both via an extensive transcription library of cowboy, gospel, and traditional tunes and network series such as **Gene Autry's Melody Ranch**, *Life on the Circle G Ranch*, and **Hawk Larabee**. Though not representing the Rangers at their performing best, *Red Horse Ranch* provides a good insight, not only to the earlier sound and style of the band, but also to the production qualities of that era's small, independent radio transcription companies.

Sources: Audio copies of *Life on the Red Horse Ranch*; Arthur Church Collection, Iowa State University; Arthur B. Church — KMBC Radio Collection, University of Missouri-Kansas City; KMBC Collection, Union Station, Kansas City, MO; Recollections of the families of Gomer Cool, Robert Crawford, and Ozie Waters, as compiled by the author.

LIGHT ON THE WEST

KARL SCHADOW *and* STEWART WRIGHT

Sponsored by the Public Service Company, the electric and gas utility of Denver, CO, this series aired over station KOA beginning in December 1935 and would air until 1939. It was written and produced by Derby Sproul until 1937 when Sproul went back East and Roscoe Stockton took over. C. Scheuerman conducted a 12 piece orchestra on the program. The half hour dramatizations involved ranchers, miners, explorers, railroaders, etc. and were set in various time periods from the 1850s to the 1930s, almost always in the Colorado region. One of the principal actors on this series was James Herrick. Typical plot lines included murder, robbery, horse theft, cattle rustling, and claim jumping, but romance was not avoided. Nearly all of the shows featured fictional characters although real-life con-man Jefferson "Soapy" Smith was portrayed on one program. Women played major roles in many episodes, including the portrayal of law enforcement officers. Sproul and Stockton captioned each episode with an interesting title, i.e. "Buckskin Breeze," "Ghost Corral," "Shorty Hagen's Kid," and "Lady Law." Because KOA was a powerful

50,000 watt station, this series was heard in several neighboring states. Years later, Sproul recycled some of these scripts for use in **Under Western Skies**, a series he produced in Pittsburgh.

Source: Archives of Western History Division of the Denver, CO Public Library.

LIGHTNING JIM

CHARLIE *and* KATHERINE SUMMERS

NAMES: *Lightning Jim, The Meadow Gold Round-Up*
NETWORK: WGN Mutual, NBC Blue, Syndicated
FORMAT: Half hour, twice weekly
DURATION OF RUN: October 18, 1938, to November 1939; syndicated through the late 1940s
SPONSOR: Meadow Gold Dairy Products, various others
AUDIO COPIES EXTANT: 42
SCRIPTS ARCHIVED: Undetermined

Lightning Jim was a relatively routine western program originally performed and broadcast locally in Chicago; yet it was eventually heard around the country in syndication. It was produced and aired on radio station WGN in Chicago, and premiered Tuesday, October 18, 1938, with the episode "Indian War Drums" which detailed a dangerous Indian uprising while the heroes dealt with a band of outlaws, according to a press release in the *Chicago Daily Tribune*, parent company of WGN. The series starred former matinee idol Francis X. Bushman as Lightning Jim Whipple while Chicago radio character actor Henry Hoople portrayed his sidekick, Deputy Whitey Larsen. The program was scheduled as a twice weekly half hour, every Tuesday and Thursday evening at 7:30 P.M. (CT). Various newspaper advertisements of the period show the program was sponsored by the Beatrice Creamery Company, manufacturers of Meadow Gold Dairy Products. The show was referenced locally in radio advertisements as *The Meadow Gold Round-Up*.

Francis Xavier Bushman was born on January 10, 1883. His father wanted him to be a doctor, but he chose instead to be an actor. He started working in various Baltimore stock companies, achieving little more than walk-on roles. After winning a local strongman's contest, he became a sculptor's model. He then attended Maryland's Ammendale College, finally launching his professional acting career. In 1911, he was invited to make films with the Essanay company and had to sign a contract saying that his wife and children were not to be publicized so his perceived availability as a leading man wouldn't be questioned. His silent films include the 1916 *Romeo and Juliet*, 1925's *Ben-Hur*, and 1927's *The Thirteenth Juror*.

In the great financial crash of 1929, Bushman's reported $6 million fortune was decimated, forcing him to start over, working in small stock companies and radio programs. On the front page of Ogdensburg, NY's *Republican-Journal* for March 13, 1931, is a bizarre feature photo of Bushman, possibly from a wire service, with a crafted "For Sale" sign around his neck, headlined, "Just A Prospective Gigolo," suggesting the penniless Bushman was offering himself in marriage to any wealthy woman making the offer.

Bushman's radio career, stretching to some 2,500 programs, included soap operas like *Masquarede* and *Stepmother*, comedies like *The Opie Cates Show*, and even a stint as Rex Stout's *Nero Wolfe*. In later years he appeared in popular television programs like

Peter Gunn, *Perry Mason*, and *Batman*. Bushman died August 23, 1966, of a heart rupture after an accident in his home outside Los Angeles, CA.

Naming the central character of this particular radio play was surprisingly simple. In a January 1939 article, the *Chicago Tribune* discussed the problems radio producers were having with lawsuits brought by people with the same name as characters in radio plays. The article pointed out that the producer of *Lightning Jim* solved the problem neatly and admirably by simply giving the character Jim Whipple his own name. It would be almost impossible for anyone else to claim this character was meant to defame them.

One of the series' writers, Sol Saks, a New York City native who grew up in Chicago, went on to write for radio's *Duffy's Tavern*, and in the 1960s created the beloved television series *Bewitched* starring Elizabeth Montgomery. He lived to be 100 and died in 2011.

The WGN run of *Lightning Jim* continued twice weekly until the beginning of November 1939 when the program left the airwaves. It appears that transcriptions of the WGN-produced program were then broadcast on the NBC Blue network, at least to the Pacific coast, beginning in 1942. Articles in *Billboard* in August 1942 originating from Hollywood, and September 1942 originating from Chicago, both mention the NBC Blue network airing the transcriptions as a juvenile western show, with the Chicago article specifically pointing to it airing on the Pacific coast only.

The program was eventually purchased by the Fredrick W. Ziv Co., a syndicator better known for its later string of television programs including *Sea Hunt*, *Highway Patrol*, *The Cisco Kid*, and *Ripcord*. Ziv had a large stable of radio programs available for syndication over the years, shows like *Bold Venture* and *Boston Blackie*, so purchasing *Lightning Jim* was a natural. Ziv advertised in April 1947 that the company had 104 episodes available for syndication, a reasonable number since the original broadcasts lasted a bit over a year. It is from Ziv transcription disks that the 42 episodes in general circulation are apparently from; each episode has a long musical bed at the beginning, middle, and end to accommodate local commercial inserts at the purchasing station. There are conventional numbers contemporarily used for the episodes, but they seem to have very little to do with the original WOR production order.

Lightning Jim was a rather average western radio program, well before the period of *Gunsmoke* and the other adult westerns by CBS where mature situations and historical realism were the rule; the program leaned more toward the Saturday matinee juvenile model that featured a brave U.S. Marshal and a frequently comic relief sidekick battling the outlaws and hostile Indian tribes of the Old West. Astride his great black horse Thunder, Jim got along well with most Indians, although renegade tribal members were often a problem for the marshal. More frequently, outlaws were Jim's focus, and of course his lightning-fast quick draw was feared by most and challenged by the few.

Henry Hoople, putting on a Swedish accent as thick as an old woolen trail poncho, played Lighting Jim's loyal sidekick, Deputy Whitey Larsen. His gun always ready, Whitey sometimes questions Jim's methods, but neither of them have questionable motives; they are the "good guys" of a bygone era. Most episodes follow the traditional formula: outlaw plots of criminality, our heroes intervene and spoil the evil plans at the last moment, leaving only time for an amusing anti-climax, usually involving Whitey, before the final commercial. The stories are entertaining but not particularly memorable.

Jim and Whitey seem to run into much more than their fair share of Old West celebrities, at least in the existing episodes. Jesse James, Wild Bill Hickok, Calamity Jane,

Belle Starr, and even Deadwood Dick all make appearances on the program, making radio's Wild West seem a little crowded with the famous lawmen and infamous outlaws. The encounter with Jesse James and the James Gang is somewhat unique in frontier fiction since Jesse actually helps the marshal, and for a brief moment is on the side of law and order.

Because of the generational loss from the 1938 original production through the Blue Network and on to the Ziv syndicated disks from which the existing shows likely came, this series is frequently a bit difficult to understand clearly. Even the best examples suffer from transfer cross talk (where another episode is heard quietly beneath the main episode), transcription disk pops and noise, skips, and other audio problems. Still, the existing 42 episodes are easily found on the Internet for those willing to exert a little aural effort to hear stories of a simplistic western frontier, where heroes are always courageous, villains are always brought to justice, and women wistfully watch the heroes ride out of town into the sunset.

Sources: Audio copies of *Lightning Jim*; Dunning, *On the Air*; Katz; Hickerson, *4th Revised*; *Billboard*, August 22, 1942; *Billboard*, September 12, p. 7; *Chicago Daily Tribune*, October 16, 1938, p. SW6 and January 29, 1939, p. SW6; *Chicago Magazine*, April 22, 2011; *New York Times*; *Ogdensburg (NY) Republican-Journal*, March 13, 1931; http://www.britannica.com; http://www.imdb.com/name/nm0124279/bio.

LITTLE HUNTER

JACK FRENCH

This was a Saturday morning kids' western written, directed and produced by Francel Hudson Cooper for station KVOR, Colorado Springs, CO in 1949-1950. It revolved around an Indian boy who was told stories of western history and Indian lore by his grandfather at their campfire. The series was sponsored by Vorhes Shoe Company.

Source: *Reminisce*, February/March 2011.

THE LONE INDIAN

DOUG HOPKINSON

NAMES: *The Lone Indian* (1932 to 1934), *Indian Village* (1930, 1937), *Indian Stories* (1931 to 1932), *Santa Fe Trail* (1935), *Indian Trails* (1937, 1939)
NETWORK: Syndicated
FORMAT: 15 minutes, usually daily
DURATION OF RUN: October 1930 to July 1939
SPONSOR: Walker's Department Store (1931 to 1933)
AUDIO COPIES EXTANT: *Lone Indian* 15, *Indian Trails* 21, *Santa Fe Trail* 9
SCRIPTS ARCHIVED: Undetermined

This series, produced and marketed under a variety of names in different years, was the creation of Robert E. Callahan, who wrote and directed them all. In many programs, he was also the narrator. Considered to be a recognized expert on North American Indians, he worked tirelessly to create interest in and sympathy for the plight of the Indians.

Whatever its title, this was a radio show for the family but intended for children. It had equal elements of action, dramatic history, philosophy and spiritualism. Most of the scripts were short stories rooted in the late 1800s, about pioneers making their way west and the adventures they encountered along the way. While some of the adventures involved only Indians, some Indians were central in every episode.

Callahan left no tribe unmentioned: Apache, Shoshone, Sioux, Iroquois, Cheyenne, Blackfoot, Cherokee, Shawnee, Pawnee, Hopi, Delaware, etc. Most programs featured Indian songs and chants and usually the announcer at the beginning of the show would claim that "real Indians appear on every broadcast." Some of the surviving shows have Callahan as the narrator and some have an actor playing the role of the Old Trapper. The titles of the broadcasts include: "The Butterfly Dance," "The Bear Dance," "Who Killed Luke Berry?" "The Original Mud Bath," and "The Apache Kid."

Most broadcasts were designed to educate the listener about some aspect of the American Indian and his culture. Callahan wanted especially children to listen to his shows as he felt they were the future and the key to acceptance of the American Indian as equal citizens of the United States. *The Lone Indian* radio program was endorsed by California's public schools because of its educational value.

Although nearly all tribes throughout North America were eventually mentioned on this series, it tended to concentrate on Indians living in the valleys, canyons and forests of the Southwest. Many broadcasts covered Indian philosophies of peace, nature, health and simplicity. It was common for shows to begin and end with Callahan speaking, sometimes with an almost evangelistic fervor.

Callahan had no problem speaking out against, or writing about, the injustices done to the American Indian by the greed and power of the white man and the United States government. He was convinced that the American Indian was misunderstood and unappreciated by the American public so he emphasized what he saw as the gentle nature and loyalty of the Indian tribes. Occasionally he even recited Indian prayers, or he would end a program by saying: "Yo-ho means farewell, how-ko-la means friendship and no-ta-ba means love, so yo-ho, how-ko-la, no-ta-ba to you."

Callahan's broadcasting career began in 1930 and lasted well into 1939. In 1930, Callahan debuted on California airwaves with his radio program titled *Indian Village*. It was broadcast afternoons, Monday through Sunday on radio station KTM in 15 minute slots while a Sunday version featured KTM's ranch boys doing concerts for 30 minutes. The program was on the air from mid–October through the end of December, 1930.

In mid–August 1931 Callahan moved to radio station KFWB, owned by Warner Bros. Pictures Inc., where he produced a program titled *Indian Stories* three afternoons a week. He also picked up a sponsor in Walker's Department Store and they would remain a sponsor for at least the next two years. Early in 1932 *Indian Stories* began to be listed in local radio guides as *Indian Stories—The Lone Indian*. By May 1932 it was only listed as *The Lone Indian* and remained as such until May 1934.

Over these three years *The Lone Indian* was broadcast afternoons, up to six days a week, and for a period it was also on twice a week in evening slots. In the spring of 1932 it was cut back to just twice a week, Mondays and Fridays until that fall when it was switched to an evening slot and once again was on six days a week. By 1933 *The Lone Indian* had slowly been reduced to five, and then to only four, evenings a week. In 1934 it was down to only two evenings a week and in May of that year it disappeared from the local radio listings entirely.

From August 1931 through May 1934 it was a 15 minute show. There were occasions that it was listed in a time slot of 30 minutes, 45 minutes and once for an hour. However, this could be attributed easily to anomalies or inaccuracies of newspaper radio listings of that era.

In the spring of 1935, Callahan began broadcasting his radio program from the airwaves of KFAC. This program was sporadically listed as *Lone Indian Theater, Indian Theater, Indian Theater — Santa Fe Trail* or just *Santa Fe Trail*. In any event, this only lasted for three months (March to June). There are extant audio copies of Callahan's *Santa Fe Trail* which again bear similarities to *The Lone Indian*, such as the program beginning with Indian whoops and Callahan narrating and speaking an Indian language. The extant audio again has pioneer caravans moving west with an old trapper type character explaining to fellow travelers who are bent on shooting some "redskins" that the Indian is misunderstood. Callahan's introduction to this new series certainly describes *The Lone Indian*. All the same ingredients are present and even some familiar lines from earlier *Lone Indian* programs.

One last reiteration of the same *Lone Indian* theme was Callahan's *Indian Trails*, broadcast in 1937 on radio station KMTR two evenings per week from May until November. An interesting fact is that during the period it was on the air in 1937, it was alternately listed as *Indian Village* in the local radio listings. This establishes that there was very little difference in Callahan's programs despite their different titles.

Indian Trails had a brief resurgence on radio station KMTR in 1939 when it suddenly reappeared in a morning slot on weekdays and Saturdays from April to July. Comparisons of the extant audio copies of *The Lone Indian* and *Indian Trails* demonstrate the similarities of both programs. In each program, an announcer introduced either Callahan or the Old Trapper. Callahan always appeared as himself in both of these shows, always as a host, sometimes a narrator, occasionally both. He was an excellent speaker, with good timing and command of the English language. He would usually close with a spiritual message, or an Indian prayer, or to talk about his next broadcast.

Both of these shows varied in format between being fully narrated but augmented with Indian chants, pioneer fiddle, banjo music and sound effects or being narrated and fully dramatized with a cast of actors. *The Lone Indian* program concentrated on attempting to educate and familiarize the listener with more abstract concepts like bigotry, fairness, appreciation of nature and respect for other cultures. *Indian Trails* was more refined in its production and more focused on specific objects of Indian life and culture while still exuding the message to appreciate and respect.

The Lone Indian scripts set the action in the Southwest. *The Indian Trails* stories were not limited to the Southwest but also took place in Ohio, North Carolina and Mexico among other locations. The Old Trapper became a more personal character in *Indian Trails* when two youngsters were brought on. A young boy, Danny, appeared with him on the show. Danny would alternate with a niece, Nancy, who called the Old Trapper Uncle Luke. *Indian Trails* had another improvement over *The Lone Indian* since it produced shows which took place in the present time rather than only the past.

Based upon research and extant audio evidence, it seems clear that Callahan really only had one radio show, although it slowly changed and evolved over the years. Each title change corresponded with a change in radio stations. Whether this was Callahan's idea or the preference of the individual stations has not been determined. What is known is that while Callahan's program moved up and down the Los Angeles radio dial for nine years, his purpose of sharing the character and culture of the Indian with the listening audience never faltered.

Sources: Audio copies of *Lone Indian, Indian Trails,* and *Santa Fe Trail;* Callahan; *Los Angeles Times,* September 26, 1930, p. 2, December 13, 1933, p. 11, and December 20, 1933, p. 4; *Los Angeles Times* radio listings of October 19, 1930-December 28, 1930, February 6, 1932, and May 16, 1932.

LONE JOURNEY

DAVID S. SIEGEL

NETWORK: NBC Red, CBS, ABC
FORMAT: 15 minutes, weekdays
DURATION OF RUN: May 27, 1940, to June 25, 1943, NBC; April 1, 1946, to September 30, 1946, NBC; October 1, 1946, to September 26, 1947, CBS; and July 2, 1951, to June 27, 1952, ABC
SPONSOR: Dreft, Carnation Company (Friskies Dog Food), Lever Brothers
AUDIO COPIES EXTANT: 5
SCRIPTS ARCHIVED: Library of American Broadcasting; Wylie (1)

This modern day soap opera was set on the real Double Spear-T (sometimes referred to as the Double Spear-T) Ranch near the real mining town of Lewistown, MT, population, 5,358 in the 1940s. For most of its run, the show was written by Sandra Michael (neé Michelsen in Denmark) and her brother Peter. The siblings actually lived in Montana for three years when they were growing up. And although both lived in the East as adults, newspaper and magazine articles noted that she and Peter had purchased the real Spear-T Ranch before setting out to write their new program.

One of radio's highly regarded writers who believed that daytime serials need not be "mindless," Sandra Michael is best known for *Against the Storm,* which had three runs between 1939 and 1952, and which was the only soap opera to ever win a Peabody Award (in 1942). In 1943, together with Doria Folliott (who also wrote the soap, *A Woman in America*) she wrote the short lived *The Open Door,* another higher quality daytime serial about the life of a dean of a fictional Vermont university.

While some critics praised the quality of Michael's writing and her focus of character development over standard soap plot lines, her scripts were often criticizes for being too "high-brow." And, when their content dealt with truths that the "powers-that-be" were not comfortable with, it was not uncommon for scripts to be censored, something that was allowed under her contract. When a *Lone Journey* script stated that "Negro blood is just the same as ours," NBC censored the line, lest the network offend southern segregationists.

Unlike *A Woman in America* which dealt with the trials and tribulations of life on the frontier, *Lone Journey* dealt with the everyday lives of real people who lived in the modern West, with a focus on the personal life of Wolfe Bennett, an architect who left Chicago to create a new life for himself and his wife Nita in the wide open West. Wolfe's love of the West was evident in a 1940-41 script: The announcer begins by explaining that Wolfe is returning home to Lewiston by train. "And even there in the coach, breathing its stale, dusty ancient air, he knew what the Montana morning smelled like, felt like, tasted like out there in the open." The next speaker is Wolfe who shares his enthusiasm at being home with his listeners: "Hello Montana. Hello, Home! ... Ah, it's good to be back! Good to look out on a world of peace and order and reason... far as you can see, you look on something that's sound and real and right, to the core. Would to heaven the rest of the world could find its way back to sanity like this... and soon... soon!"

But *Lone Journey* was a soap, and so in lieu of bank robberies and Indian ambushes, the plot lines focused on "ones man's search for happiness in a lone journey through life." For example, the opening of the March 17, 1943, episode included a reference to the fact that Wolfe's wife wasn't happy in the West and had left her husband. And a magazine article about the series asked: "Can a woman like Sydney live a lie — convince a man (Wolfe) she loves him when in reality she loves another man (Lance) — her missing husband presumed dead in the war?

Because of the program's on-again, off-again history, there were several cast changes during its three broadcast cycles. Four actors played Wolfe Bennett: Lester (Les) Damon, Staats Cotsworth (1946 to 1957 and 1951 to 1952), Henry Hunter and Reese Taylor, while Warren Mills played Wolfe in childhood flashbacks. The love interests, Nita, Wolfe's first wife, was played by Claudia Morgan, Eloise Kummer, Betty Winkler and Betty Ruth Smith, while Laurette Fillbrandt and Charlotte Holland played Sydney Sherwood Mackenzie, the music teacher who falls in love with Wolfe.

Supporting characters include Henry Newman, a bachelor sheep rancher, philosopher and good neighbor played by Cliff Soubier, Mrs. King, played by Bess McCammon, and her daughter-in-law Jessie King, played by Geraldine Kay who live on a nearby ranch, Wylie Adams and DeWitt McBride played Mel Tanner, the ranch foreman before he joined the army, and Cameron Andrews and Bob Jellison who played Enor, a ranch hand.

Other actors appearing in the show included: Nancy Osgood, John Larkin, Genelle Gibbs, Frank Dane, Oliver Cliff, Joan Alexander, Grace Valentine, and Eileen Palmer. The show's announcers were Durward Kirby, Nelson Case, Richard Stark and Charles Woods.

The show was originally produced in Chicago but later moved to New York. Although some references credit Frank and Anne Hummert as the producers, several *Variety* articles have John Gibbs, Michael's business manager and husband, as the producer. The program was directed at various times by Ted McMurray, Fred Weihe, Bill Hamilton, and Martin Magner. Sometime during the program's run, the Michaels turned the writing over to other people but eventually returned to the series. Always a 15 minute program, the time slots changed over time and during the mid–1940s, the program was heard on both the NBC and CBS networks.

Sources: Audio copies of *Lone Journey*; Dunning, *On the Air*; Hickerson, *4th Revised*; Siegel, *Remembering Radio*; Wylie; French, "Story behind"; scrapbook of clippings about the program.

THE LONE RANGER

TERRY SALOMONSON

NETWORK: Michigan Radio Network, Mutual, Blue Network, ABC, NBC
FORMAT: Half hour
DURATION OF RUN: January 31, 1933, to September 3, 1954; September 6, 1954, to September 2, 1955, transcribed re-broadcasts ABC, 52 weeks, three times a week for 156

broadcasts; May 30, 1955, to May 18, 1956, transcribed re-broadcasts NBC, 52 weeks, five times a week for 253 broadcasts

SPONSORS: Multiple sponsors, including General Mills

AUDIO COPIES EXTANT: Over 2,300

SCRIPTS ARCHIVED: Library of Congress; Brace Beemer Papers and Raymond Meurer Papers, Detroit Public Library; American Radio Archives; Chuck Schaden Collection, Library of American Broadcasting; SPERDVAC; Francis Hamilton Striker Papers, University of Buffalo; http://www.genericradio.com

Out of the thousands of radio programs over nine decades of broadcast history, one of the juggernauts of American popular culture is *The Lone Ranger*. The program's hold on the listening audience from the very beginning was challenged only once for a short period of time during a network change. Within a few weeks of the beginning of its twenty-one and a half years of live original broadcasts, the production had a permanent grip on tens of thousands of listeners that very quickly developed into millions of devoted followers. In the process, it saved a radio station from financial ruin and helped to develop, and many believe was hugely responsible for the success of, a new national network, Mutual.

The origin of this radio series began with sound being introduced in the late 1920s into theaters across the country at a huge expense to theater owners. Many owners were going into bankruptcy when they couldn't afford the conversion. George W. Trendle decided that the next best investment would be radio. Armed with the recent sale of the Kunsky chain of theaters, which gave Trendle and John Kunsky's partnership a reported $4 to $6 million net worth, they went shopping for their next investment. They had just missed out on the purchase of a radio station they wanted when George Harrison Phelps sold station WGHP to George B. Storer the day before they knew it was available. However, on April 25, 1930, they purchased station WGHP from Storer for $250,000 giving Storer a large profit over his original investment. Trendle and Kunsky also acquired a new junior partner, Howard Pierce.

Their purchase was originally licensed on June 2, 1925, and first took to the air waves on October 10, 1925, as a 500 watt station. By June 30, 1926, they were at 1,500 watts with only one other station in the Detroit area, WJR, at 5,000 watts. In January of 1927 CBS picked WGHP as its Detroit outlet and the station moved to the fifteenth floor of the Maccabees Building. On September 18, 1927, it was one of 16 stations to begin airing CBS network broadcasts.

By July 1, 1930, Trendle was successful in getting the call letters changed from WGHP to WXYZ and under the control of the Kunsky-Trendle Broadcasting Corporation. Although Trendle believed that the station had great potential to make money, he was unable to interest local sponsors in advertising because of the station's affiliation to CBS. CBS was scheduling all the best hours of the broadcast day and evening and under its contract with WXYZ, and the network would not allow any tampering with their broadcast day. It soon became very apparent to Trendle that if he wanted his station to become profitable he would have to become independent, with his own productions and ability to sell time to sponsors. At the end of 1931 he simply did not renew the contract with CBS.

With the loss of the CBS schedule, programming became a major issue and headache. No transcribed programs were available and all drama and musical broadcasts were live. It was a big programming hole to fill. This was the period when Harold True suggested that James Jewell contact Fran Striker of Buffalo, NY to supply six half hour scripts a week. On the telephone Striker agreed to a deal of $4 per half hour script, giving WXYZ first performance rights in the Detroit area. He started providing three different series.

Harold True, James Jewel and George Trendle wanted a western theme for an original program and turned to Fran Striker, already on the payroll, to provide this new idea. The first of a series of letters that were exchanged started with a letter from James Jewell dated December 28, 1932. Striker, who was supplying scripts to other stations around the country on a syndication basis, was happy to take on this new responsibility. He dusted off a script from a previously written series entitled *Covered Wagon Days*, re-wrote script #10 and submitted it to the Detroit station on January 6, 1933, with a letter requesting their comments on this first *Lone Ranger* script. There were some additional adjustments and the possibility of an unscheduled test broadcast on January 20, 1933.

Another letter from Jewell to Striker on January 21, 1933, states: "I'm going to start *The Lone Ranger* series Monday the 30th." A follow-up letter dated January 26, 1933, to Striker, corrects the premier of the series: "*The Lone Ranger* goes on the air Tuesday instead of Monday, so hope you'll be listening."

The first regularly scheduled broadcasts began on January 31, 1933, and were carried over the entire Michigan Radio Network made up of WXYZ in Detroit, WIBM in Jackson, WKZO in Kalamazoo, WJIM in Lansing, WBCM in Bay City, WFDF in Flint, both WASH and WOOD in Grand Rapids and WELL in Battle Creek. The first newspaper listing of the series was on February 9, 1933. The first 63 programs aired locally in Detroit at 9:00 P.M. on Tuesday, Thursday and Saturday. Later, the broadcast time was changed to 8:30 P.M. until the last Saturday show on November 25, 1933.

During this time period, four different actors appeared as the Lone Ranger. From January 31, 1933, to May 9, 1933, the first 43 broadcasts, George Stenius played the title role. After leaving the series, Stenius moved to Hollywood where, under the name George Seaton, he began a career as a director in the film industry. The May 11, 1933, broadcast had Lee Trent, using the name "Jack Deeds," at the microphone. While Trent had appeared in some of the previous WXYZ productions, he wasn't up to the task of the lead role under the directorship of James Jewell. Totally intimidated, Trent only played the part of the Lone Ranger once.

For the May 13, 1933, broadcast, director James Jewel performed the lead role while the station looked for and found a new lead. Two things happened starting with May 16, 1933, broadcast #46: Earle W. Graser, an actor at WXYZ for a year, and a Wayne State University law student, took over the role of the Lone Ranger and, in order to judge the program's popularity as well as the size of its audience, a special announcement was added to the script. At the end of broadcast, the Lone Ranger made the following announcement:

> Did you hear those six shots, boys and girls? Those came from the genuine Lone Ranger six-shooters and I have three hundred of these guns to give away this evening ... three hundred genuine Lone Ranger guns which shoot straight and true. Of course, they don't shoot bullets of silver, but then they are not just paper affairs or pop-guns with a cork, but real Lone Ranger guns. The revolver is 14 inches in length, and looks just exactly like my guns. However, they are quite harmless, but I am sure every one of you would like to have one. Now, I repeat, I only have three hundred to give away tonight, so here's how you may be able to get one for your very own. The first three hundred letters received at the studio tomorrow morning, or in the first mail, will entitle the writer of the letter to a genuine Lone Ranger gun.

So, sit down right away and write your letter to the Lone Ranger in care of station WXYZ, Detroit. Remember, the first three hundred letters reaching here will entitle the writer to a Lone Ranger six-shooter. Address your letter to the Lone Ranger — station WXYZ, Detroit. Hi-yo, Silver, away!

To say the response was overwhelming would be an understatement. In their premier issue of the *WXYZ Michigan Radio Network* newspaper, this event made the headline and front page story. The article was accompanied by a large photograph showing thousands of letters with the caption "Mayor Frank Couzens of Detroit and Postmaster Roscoe B. Huston, examining the record breaking mail response ... received from one announcement on the Michigan Radio Network, immediately following the half hour broadcast of an episode of *The Lone Ranger* adventure series."

Immediately following the receipt of the first 10,000 letters, announcements were aired informing children listeners that the supply of Lone Ranger toy six-shooters, promised to the writers of the first three hundred letters, had been exhausted. But letters kept pouring in from all parts of the Detroit region. The total of letters received ultimately reached 24,905, all the result of a radio announcement delivered at 9:30 P.M. at the end of *The Lone Ranger* program. It conclusively demonstrated the tremendous drawing power of the Masked Rider of the Plains, and WXYZ knew it had an absolute hit.

July 30, 1933, was the first public appearance of the Lone Ranger, with station announcer Brace Beemer, not Earle Graser, masked and suited up for the occasion. The event took place at the very popular Detroit park, Belle Isle. Trendle had chosen Beemer over Graser because the announcer was taller and huskier. Park officials didn't expect a large crowd, but were overwhelmed by more than 10,000 people.

Starting on Wednesday, November 29, 1933, the series changed to the much remembered Monday, Wednesday, Friday night broadcasts, and with broadcast #130, the series was also picked up by a sponsorship with Gordon Baking Co., producers of Silvercup Bread. Another major milestone on this same night was that the show was now being heard over two additional outlets, WGN in Chicago and WOR in New York.

As of January 17, 1934, *The Lone Ranger* program was carried by the following stations: WXYZ in Detroit, Michigan (including the full Michigan Radio Network); WOR in Newark NJ; WGN in Chicago; and WLW in Cincinnati. This combination was originally called the Quality Network and one of its most popular programs was *The Lone Ranger*.

Francis H. Striker sold "all manuscripts of which I am the author ... entitled *Lone Ranger, Manhunters*, and *Thrills of the Secret Service*" to the management of WXYZ in a bill of sale executed on May 22, 1934. Scripts soon started to be copyrighted.

Since all the stations shared the network and connection costs, the Quality Network changed its name to the Mutual Broadcasting System when it was established on September 29, 1934. Mutual incorporated on October 29, 1934. The network started looking for a West Coast outlet, thus going coast-to-coast. They found it in the seriously distressed Don Lee Network that had just lost its CBS connection. The official startup date was December 29, 1936.

On January 1, 1936, the program picked up a large sponsorship from General Baking, producers of Bond Bread. Sixteen days later, with broadcast #776, the series began to be transcribed. The Don Lee Network started airing *The Lone Ranger* program on the West Coast on January 18, 1937, with Gingham Bread as sponsor for that regional area. The Mutual/Don Lee stations were: KJH in Los Angeles, KGB in San Diego, KXO in El

Centro, KDB in Santa Barbara, KPMC in Bakersfield, KVOE in Santa Ana and KFXN in San Bernardino.

The adventures of the Masked Rider of the Plains and his Indian companion were not complicated. They had no fixed location and they traversed the western frontier, encountering injustice, knavery, and assorted thefts and swindles of innocent folk. In each episode, the duo would inject themselves into the situation and defeat evil, without expecting thanks or reward. Often the beneficiaries of their efforts were unaware of who had saved them until they found a silver bullet left behind, the signature card of the Lone Ranger. Up to that time, some of them thought he might be an outlaw, since he always wore a mask.

Striker was primarily responsible for originating the silver bullets carried by the Ranger and the silver horseshoes worn by his trusty steed. However the term "Kemo Sabe," with which Tonto addressed his saddle companion, came from James Jewell. Tradition held that it meant "faithful friend" in Tonto's tribal tongue. However Jewell eventually admitted he merely borrowed the term from a summer camp his father-in-law formerly operated in Michigan; it was called Ke-Mo-Sah-Bee.

A new advertiser, American Bakeries (Merita Bread) located in Atlanta GA, started sponsoring the program for the South on September 19, 1939. Like the prior mentioned sponsors, the company began featuring the *Lone Ranger* in its print ads.

After Earle W. Graser was killed in an automobile accident on April 8, 1941, the next five broadcasts, usually referred to as "the transition series," had the Lone Ranger ill and being taken care of by Tonto. The voice of the Lone Ranger then became Brace Beemer, who had been the program's announcer. To soften the transition, Beemer was only heard whispering until the April 18, 1941, broadcast.

May 1, 1942, marked the end of *The Lone Ranger* broadcasts on Mutual when the program moved to the NBC Blue Network (soon to be ABC). At that time, **Red Ryder**, mostly a West Coast favorite, was also heard on the East Coast via the Mutual Network. But when *The Lone Ranger* moved to the Blue Network, Mutual programmed **Red Ryder** in direct competition with *The Lone Ranger* and it briefly pulled in better Hooper ratings. But it failed to hold on to the lead, since it was regionally sponsored, unlike *The Lone Ranger*'s national audience.

In late 1943 WXYZ purchased a three story structure to be called "The Mansion," formerly known as the Mendelssohn Mansion, in Detroit's Indian Village area, at East Jefferson Avenue and Iroquois Street. A large sign over the main entrance simply stated "WXYZ Radio Studio." The station began broadcasting from its new studios in February 1944 after leaving the Maccabees Building.

The Lone Ranger had begun as a solo character but it was soon realized that a companion was necessary. Tonto was added starting with the twelfth script, since the Lone Ranger needed someone to talk to, other than his horse, to help the audience follow the action. Over the years, Tonto was played by Rollon Parker, Bob Kidder and lastly and longest by John Todd (the stage name of an actor born Fred McCarthy).

Until WXYZ controlled the property, Fran Striker also sold scripts to other stations and they created their own broadcast productions of *The Lone Ranger*. John Barrett played the Ranger at WEBR in Buffalo, NY. Other stations airing their own versions included WOR in Omaha, KOIL in Oklahoma City, and WOR in New York. At one point, silent film star Francis X. Bushman auditioned for the Ranger at WGN in Chicago.

There were several different "origin stories" over the early years, but the one most cited was of the Butch Cavendish Gang's ambush and killing of the Texas Rangers at Bryant's Gap. Reid, whose first name was never given in the original radio scripts and early books, was the only Ranger to survive the attack. His brother, Dan Reid, was killed along with the rest of the Texas Rangers. Tonto discovered the ambush scene and also that one Ranger was still alive. In addition to helping the surviving Ranger return to health, Tonto buried the five dead Rangers with an additional sixth grave creating a belief that all the Rangers were indeed killed in the attack.

While Striker wrote nearly all of the early scripts of this series, others contributed over the years under his watchful eye. These other scriptwriters included: Bob Green, Dan Beattie, Felix Holt, Leo Boulette, Tom Dougall, and even a woman, Betty Joyce. Most of the writers also contributed to the two other popular WXYZ shows: *Challenge of the Yukon* and *The Green Hornet*.

Most of the supporting cast members of *The Lone Ranger* were also used on *Challenge of the Yukon* and *The Green Hornet*, among them, Paul Hughes, Ernie Winstanley, Jay Michael, Ted Johnstone, Beatrice Leiblee, Frank Russell, Bertha Forman, Mel Palmer, Jack McCarthy, Ruth Dean Rickaby, as well as Dick Beals, who played juvenile roles.

The sound effects on *The Lone Ranger*, both manual and transcribed, were done skillfully and imaginatively by various members of a crew that combined youth with experienced personnel. Handling the sound effects were: Bert Djerkiss, Fred Flowerday, Ted Robertson, Jim Fletcher, and Fred Fry. Dewey Cole specialized in replicating animal sounds, including dogs, horses, cattle, and other creatures.

The Lone Ranger's horse was originally a chestnut mare called Dusty. This was mentioned in a special anniversary broadcast on December 9, 1938. But that name didn't last long as it was soon changed to Silver. Silver later sired Victor, the horse ridden by Dan Reid, the Lone Ranger's nephew. In Dave Holland's book, *From Out of the Past*, a reference was made to a horse by the name of Nellie. But that name was in conjunction with a seven-part Silvercup promotional giveaway in 1936 and was not actually part of any broadcast.

Tonto, who originally rode a jackass named Sago that was mentioned in the July 16, 1934 (episode #228), and October 24, 1934 (episode #271), broadcasts, finally got a horse, White Feller, in episode #416 broadcast on September 30, 1935. For roughly the next three years, until the broadcast of July 25, 1938 (episode #857), Tonto continued to ride White Feller, but on the September 2, 1938 (episode #874), broadcast, Tonto named his horse Scout.

The program was pre-empted only twice in its entire history, on July 13, 1945, for the death of President Franklin D. Roosevelt and on V-J Day, August 15, 1945. Of the 3,377 live original broadcasts, 2,602 were recorded, including at least two broadcasts in 1937, one on September 24, 1937, and the other on December 17, 1937. Although there was a sponsor booth in the studio, there was never an audience to witness the productions.

The musical themes and bridges were classical pieces that were in the public domain so no royalties were ever paid, with the primary compositions being the "William Tell Overture" by Gioachino Rossini (1792–1868) and "Les Preludes" by Franz Liszt (1811–1886).

Some characters in the scripts reappeared from time to time, such as Mustang Mag, The Padre, and on a rare occasion, Jim Blaine, who worked the Lone Ranger's silver mine.

Over the years the program was broadcast, millions of youngsters across the joined Lone Ranger Safety Clubs and millions more attended live appearances by Brace Beemer at rodeos and special shows around the country.

Fred Foy became the permanent announcer for the series on July 2, 1948, and continued in that role until the end of the live broadcasts. Foy was also Brace Beemer's understudy for the program, stepping into the role only once, on March 29, 1954 ("Burly Scott's Sacrifice"), when Beemer arrived at the station with laryngitis.

About three months later, on July 2, 1954, all of the actors and staff were gathered at The Mansion and told that *The Lone Ranger* would start re-broadcasts via transcribed shows for 52 weeks beginning in September. The live original broadcasts would continue only until the first week of September when the transcribed shows began on ABC. The actors were also informed that those who were selected to appear on the re-broadcasts would be paid half salary; there would be no compensation for the others. So, on September 3, 1954, with the broadcast of "Cold Spring Showdown," (episode #3,377), the live series ended.

Through 3,377 broadcasts in twenty-one-and-a-half years, the Lone Ranger never shot to kill, but only to wound. He never drank, smoked or used bad language. He always used perfect grammar and pronunciation. There was no love interest in the Lone Ranger's life. Only a few ever saw his unmasked face in fewer than half a dozen episodes.

Beyond the horizons of the radio shows, Grosset and Dunlap, Whitman, and Big Little Books published books featuring the Lone Ranger that fascinated countless readers. There were also comic books, newspaper comic strips, two cliffhanger movie serials, three feature movies, 221 television episodes, hundreds of radio and television premiums, and collectibles of every kind.

Sources: Audio copies and original scripts of *Lone Ranger*; interviews of Richard "Dick" Osgood, David Parker, Fred and Fran Foy, Barbara Beemer Daniels, George W. Trendle, Jr., Leonore "Lee" Allman, Fred Flowerday, Tony Caminita, Ernie Winstanley, Michael Winstanley, Richard Beals, Clayton Moore, Ralph Jewell, William Jewell, Patrick Jewell, Janet M. (Mrs. Fran) Striker, Janet E. Striker, and Fran Striker, Jr. by Terry Salomonson; Dunning, *On the Air*; Holland; Osgood; *Program log*: Salomonson.

LONE WOLF TRIBE

WILLIAM HARPER

One of the earliest juvenile westerns on radio, this 15 minute show originated as a local program in Chicago in 1931 and began on the CBS network in January 1932, running until June 1933. Sponsored by Wrigley's Gum, it aired Monday, Wednesday and Friday usually in a 5:45 P.M. (EST) time slot. Two fictional characters, Chief Wolf Paw and Chief Whirling Thunder, narrated the dramatized stories of Indian lore and adventure. Since no audio copies or scripts have yet surfaced for this program, much of what is known about it is derived from the many premiums that were offered to juvenile listeners by the sponsor in exchange for "wampum" (Wrigley's Gum wrappers.) These items included: a drum, arrowhead, ring, bracelet, tie clip, photographs, and a 32 page booklet about Indian sign language and picture writing. When the show went off the air in the summer of 1933, fans with pending requests for premiums instead received this sad news on a post card: "Chief Wolf Paw's Helpers Have Left. Therefore, No More Lone Wolf Articles Will Be Distributed in Exchange for Gum Wrappers."

Sources: Swartz; Hake.

LUKE SLAUGHTER OF TOMBSTONE

BARBARA WATKINS

NETWORK: CBS
FORMAT: Half hour, weekly
DURATION OF RUN: February 23, 1958, to June 15, 1958
SPONSOR: Sustaining (May 4, 1958, broadcast had commercials for O'Brien Paints)
AUDIO COPIES EXTANT: 16 shows (complete run)
SCRIPTS ARCHIVED: SPERDVAC

Each show opened with Sam Buffington in the title lead saying, "Slaughter's my name, Luke Slaughter. Cattle's my business. It's a tough business. It's big business. I've got a big stake in it and there's no man west of the Rio Grande big enough to take it from me." Announcer Dan Cubberley next informed listeners just who Luke Slaughter was: "Civil war cavalry man turned Arizona cattleman. Across the territory from Yuma to Fort Defiance, from Flagstaff to the Huachucas, and below the border through Chihuahua and Sonora, his name was respected, or feared, depending on which side of the law you were on. Man of vision, man of legend, Luke Slaughter of Tombstone."

Thus began sixteen weeks of this exciting western adventure that shared the 2 to 3 P.M. slot on Sundays with **Frontier Gentleman**. *Luke Slaughter* was reminiscent of another CBS series, **Gunsmoke**, which had been airing since 1952. Both series dealt with the people and problems of life in the frontier towns of the late 1800s. While **Gunsmoke**'s Matt Dillon had the authority of a U.S. Marshal bringing law and order to Dodge City, Slaughter fought his battles in and around the rough town of Tombstone as a representative of the Cattlemen's Association.

Luke Slaughter had many parallels with **Gunsmoke** since it was an adult western, well written, with perhaps less violence but still gritty, with good music and sound effects well used. And like Matt Dillon, Luke Slaughter was not only tough but intelligent and a good judge of character. The lead actors in both series were cast well. William Conrad had the commanding voice needed for Dillon, capable of delivering the toughness of a no-nonsense lawman, and at times the weariness that would overcome him and, on rare occasions, tenderness.

Sam Buffington was an ideal choice for the role of Slaughter. His voice carried the respect and authority needed to back up his boast of toughness. Buffington was a relative stranger to radio listeners when he stepped into Slaughter's boots at the age of 26. He was an easterner, born in Swansea, MA on October 12, 1931. In his early 20s, he had qualified for Actors Equity based upon his stage work on the East Coast, which included many glowing reviews. Then in Hollywood, his roles were primarily in television with appearances in several network shows, including *Tales of Wells Fargo*, *Maverick*, *Sugarfoot*, and *Cheyenne*. A balding, chunky fellow with a big mustache, he had the physicality of a much older man and was frequently cast as a doctor, sheriff, and bartender.

In the debut episode, Luke Slaughter is in Laredo, Texas to convince a rancher that his cattle in Mexico should be driven west to Tombstone where there is a good market for beef. He declares he is the man to do it, that he can get them there safely, despite the Indians, the banditos and the rustlers. He proves that the man who was scheduled to drive the cattle was dishonest in his previous drive by selling 43 head of "lost" cattle and pocketing the money himself. Slaughter hires men to help in the drive, and defend against the attack by the outfit he replaced. One man hired on was Wichita, a nervous geezer, who would become a regular cast member and Luke's sidekick. During the drive Slaughter sets one young man's life on the right path.

In Tombstone, a wild town filled with a mix of dangerous drifters and peaceable folk, Slaughter was a man to be reckoned with. When the rights of cattlemen needed defending or when outlaws and crooks preyed upon the innocent, Slaughter was there to step in and defend the weak and bring the bad guys to justice. Slaughter was asked to run for sheriff against an incumbent of dubious character, but he declined, preferring the life of a cattleman. When his money from the cattle drive is stolen, he finds that the sheriff is involved in robbery and murder.

Variety gave this series mixed reviews, rating it below **Gunsmoke** but above **Frontier Gentleman**. The reviewer called the program "intense and low-keyed" although some scripts made Slaughter seem mean and cheap. It "suffered seriously in comparison to the highly original, most always authentic, *Gunsmoke*." However, the reviewer concluded, it was "still more creditable than the effete Englishman in *Frontier Gentleman*."

Each week Slaughter confronts trouble: dealing with a crooked sheriff, defending an old army buddy accused of rustling, turning the tables on a crooked politician who sold a salted mine, or proving land grant deeds fraudulent. He even successfully defends himself against a charge of horse stealing and cattle rustling.

By the sixth episode Slaughter decides that there would be more profit in raising cattle of his own instead of driving other men's herds up from Mexico. So, he buys a ranch with several hundred acres of grazing land and a good healthy herd. This, of course, leads to serious trouble when the previous owners hide the money they were paid and two drifters who want the money brutally kill the owner's wife.

Slaughter also learns something about tolerance when he allows an Apache chief and a few of his braves to try their hand at cattle raising on his spread. Some townsfolk fear they will be massacred, but Slaughter has faith that the Apaches will be peaceful. The trouble starts when a tenderfoot from the East comes to paint the West. He paints a portrait of the Chief with his permission but when a young buck sees the picture the painter is attacked. The Apaches and the townsfolk are about to go to war but Slaughter sees the problem and resolves the conflict.

The series used the talents of some of the busiest and best personnel working in radio. It was produced and directed by William N. Robson (who was concurrently producing and directing *Suspense*). The staff of writers included Robert Stanley, Alan Botzer, Don Clark, Fran Van Hartesveldt, and Paul Pierce, all under the editorial supervision by Tom Hanley. The latter was also part of the talented CBS trio of sound artists, along with Ray Kemper and Bill James. Music was composed and conducted by Wilbur Hatch and/or Amerigo Moreno.

Junius Matthews played Slaughter's elderly sidekick, Wichita. Other cast members included Ed Marr, Herb Vigran, Lillian Buyeff, Sam Edwards, Vic Perrin, Jack Moyles, Lawrence Dobkin, Frank Gerstle, Barney Phillips, Howard McNear, Lou Merrill, Chester Stratton, Joseph Kearns, John McIntire, Irene Tedrow, Don Diamond, Karl Swenson, Jack Kruschen, Luis Van Rooten, Norma Jean Nilsson, and Jack Edwards. Most of them also appeared regularly on **Gunsmoke**, **Fort Laramie** and **Frontier Gentleman**.

Although this series would be Buffington's only radio series, he had roles in over 40 network TV shows in his brief career in Hollywood, which came to an end after only four years. Buffington had worked his way up to co-starring with Audie Murphy in NBC-TV's *Whispering Smith*. But half way through the production run, Buffington, who was only 28 years old, took his own life on May 15, 1960.

Sources: Audio copies of *Luke Slaughter of Tombstone*; Dunning, *On the Air*; *Variety*, February 16, 1958; http://www.imdb.com/name/nm0119383; http://archive.org/details/LukeSlaughterOfTombstone_826; http://www.digitaldeliftp.com/DigitalDeliToo/dd2jb-Luke-Slaughter.html.

MAVERICK JIM

KARL SCHADOW *and* JACK FRENCH

This rough and tumble half hour western melodrama aired on station WOR in New York City (1933 to 1934). The title lead was played by Artells Dickson, who would later be radio's first *Tom Mix*. In this series, scripts were written by Stuart Sterling, who kept the action flowing and the guns blazing from 7:00 to 7:30 P.M. on Wednesdays and Fridays. Its cast of characters included Amy, Sackfull Wilkes, Sam, and Aunt Sarah Hardy. The program was sponsored by Runkle's Chocolate and Cocoa. The intensity of the action left little time for meaningful dialogue and akin to the pulp magazines of that era, Mexican villains were referred to as "greasers."

Source: *Variety*, December. 19, 1933, p. 40.

The Meadow Gold Round-Up see *Lightning Jim*

Melody Ranch see *Gene Autry's Melody Ranch*

THE NIGHT HAWK RIDES

JACK FRENCH *and* DAVID S. SIEGEL

NETWORK: Syndicated
FORMAT: 15 minutes, Monday to Friday
DURATION OF RUN: Circa 1935
SPONSOR: Unknown
AUDIO COPIES EXTANT: 2
SCRIPTS ARCHIVED: Undetermined

The concept of a reckless, masked champion of justice, combined with a secret identity, debuted in a 1903 stage play in London. Its hero, the Scarlet Pimpernel, was created by a British novelist and playwright, Baroness Emmuska Orczy (1865–1947) who was a native of Hungary. The phenomenal success of the play and a subsequent novel inspired countless imitations in popular culture. Much like *Zorro* and *The Lone Ranger*, the title lead in *The Night Hawk Rides* was another in a long line of masked crime fighters, albeit of much less significance.

Although only the first two episodes of *The Night Hawk Rides* have survived to present day, it is safe to assume there were a total of 39 episodes in the series, as 39 was the minimum industry standard for syndicated radio transcriptions. Each of these two existing audio copies runs just under 13 minutes, with one minute of organ theme music at both the beginning and the end. Local announcers would read the sponsor's commercials over this music when the station played the disk, thus making it fill a 15 minute time slot.

None of the cast or production crew has yet been identified, but the performers seem to be competent radio actors who do their best, despite mediocre scripts. The sound effects are well done and a skilled organist not only plays the prelude and postlude of each episode, but also all the musical bridges within the drama.

The plot is set in motion by the announcer, also unnamed, who tells the listeners about the Circle E Ranch in Forgotten Valley in the shadow of the Cascade Mountains. The ranch residents are old, crippled Fred Evans, his mid–20s daughter, Dorothy, and their faithful foreman, Pete Steele. Most syndicated shows, for the purposes of economy, kept the number of main characters to a few. But *The Night Hawk Rides* had no such restrictions; in the first two episodes nine characters appear, all with a substantial number of lines.

In addition to the three characters at the Circle E Ranch, the story includes: Shirley, who is Dorothy's school chum from back east; the Night Hawk, a mysterious and terrible character according to the announcer but someone Shirley thinks is a romantic bandit; Sam Blackmun, supposedly an old friend of Fred, but really a sinister character who holds the mortgage on all of the Evans' property, including the lost mine; Ruby, the goodhearted owner of the saloon and gambling house in the nearby town of Nine Mile; Bill Martin, a likable drifter who's enamored of Ruby's charms; and Mr. Masterpiece, a mysterious gambler, dressed all in black, who lives in the town's hotel, wins every night in Ruby's gambling house, but never spends any money.

Another important character is talked about in these two episodes but does not appear, at least under his family identity. He is the unnamed son of Michael Grogan, who, after the attack that killed his father and crippled Fred years ago, disappeared from the region and supposedly never returned. While the juvenile listeners to this series were probably unaware of the connection, it was apparent to most of the other listeners that because of the obvious clues in the script, Grogan's missing son is not only Mr. Masterpiece, but also the Night Hawk.

The Night Hawk Rides shared at least three characteristics with the soap operas of that era. First, it utilized organ music for the main theme at the beginning and end of every episode, as well as all musical bridges and underscoring of dramatic scenes. Second, the announcer began every program by telling the listeners what they had missed in prior episodes. Third, each show ended with the announcer posing dramatic questions, hoping to entice the audience to tune in to the next installment of the story, such as:

(1) "But is he (the Night Hawk) really Dorothy Evans' friend?" (2) "Or is he trying to get the mining property for himself?" (3) "Will Blackmun foreclose on the mortgage?" (4) "Is there a lost mine?"

In the absence of the other 37 remaining audio episodes and the still missing scripts, the answers to these questions may never be known.

Sources: Audio copies of *The Night Hawk Rides*; Hickerson, *4th Revised*; Harvey.

OLD DODGE DRAMAS

Karl Schadow

In conjunction with the celebration of the movie premiere of *Dodge City* in April 1939, station KGNO produced an eight episode series entitled *Old Dodge Dramas*. These programs aired at 6:45 P.M., Mondays from March 13 through May 1. Each 15 minute drama was sponsored by the Kansas Power Company and narrated by the famous utility spokesman, Reddy Kilowatt, who rode his faithful steed, Copper. The stories featured human interest incidents ranging from the founding of the first Sunday school and church, to the burial of Dora Hand on Boot Hill and the comic adventures of frontier scouts Billy Dixon and Jack Stillwell. The scripts were written by *Dodge City Daily Globe* newspaperman Jay B. Baugh. Cast members, drawn from the ranks of KGNO, the *Globe* and area theater group, included Trohman Robinson, Robert M. "Bob" Olson, Claude Main and Grace Wilcox. To date, no scripts have been located.

Source: *Dodge City Daily Globe*, March 10, 1939.

OLD TRAILS PLOWED UNDER

KARL SCHADOW

The program originated in 1941 from eastern Montana station KRFJ in Miles City and was a production of Lou "Montana" Grill, the editor of the *Miles City Daily Star* and the author of several books on western history. The weekly 30 minute program featured Grill interviewing old timers who had taken part in Montana's frontier history in the 1890s and early 1900s. Miles City billed itself as "the cow capital of the West" so the station's call letters were soon changed to KATL (pronounced "cattle"). Grill's program promoted the founding of the local Range Riders Museum, and his portrayal of the Indians was on such a favorable basis that he was awarded honorary membership in four different tribes. The program, which was heard at 7 P.M. on various evenings, continued into 1942 and was syndicated through 1943.

Source: "Annual Shows of Tomorrow," *Radio Daily*, July 5, 1942.

OLD WAGON TONGUE

KARL SCHADOW *and* JACK FRENCH

A fairly sophisticated 1930s weekly show that dramatized actual events in the history of the West as the basis of its storytelling, the program aired on station KOA, Denver. The program was sponsored by the Kuner-Empson Company. Roscoe K. Stockton headed up a production team that claimed it devoted up to 50 hours researching the factual accuracy of each episode before rehearsals were scheduled. Cast members are not known, but Clarence A. Perregrine was the control room sound engineer. The program was done live before studio audiences of up to 75 patrons who, it was said, were impressed with the methods used to create the sounds of locomotives, stagecoaches, etc.

Source: *Variety*, June 9, 1931, p. 56.

PAT BARNES' BAR Z RANCH

KARL SCHADOW *and* JACK FRENCH

Although a children's western program, this series was more about its humorous characters than it was about typical western adventure. The mild action revolved around how the arrival of a young girl changed life on the ranch. The program was unique in that all the adult parts were played by Pat Barnes, a veteran radio actor. At different times, Barnes portrayed a Chinese cook, a grunting Indian, a nasal cowboy and other characters as needed. For the series' two children's roles, Billy Boy and Bess, the program used child actors, Bruce Bradway and Geraldine Weber. This sustaining series was broadcast from station WENR, Chicago in 1933.

Source: *Variety*, February 7, 1933, p.38.

THE PHANTOM RIDER

JACK FRENCH *and* DAVID S. SIEGEL

NETWORK: None
FORMAT: Half hour, weekly
DURATION: Unknown, circa mid–1940s
AUDIO COPIES EXTANT: 1 (probably audition)
SCRIPTS ARCHIVED: Undetermined

There are few surviving clues to determine the date and background of the lone audio copy of *The Phantom Rider* which starred Tex Ritter. Some sources place it in the 1930s, although it was more likely produced in the mid–1940s, and was possibly a spin-off from *All-Star Western Theatre* (1946 to1949). The evidence for this later estimate is based upon the fact that *The Phantom Rider* was written and produced by Cottonseed Clark and released through Foy Willing and Jack Beekman Enterprises. As Clark and Willing's longest and closest association was *All-Star Western Theatre*, logic would dictate they originated *The Phantom Rider* during that time together in the mid–1940s.

The 30 minute program features hackneyed characters, outlandish plot devices, and an insipid script and certainly did not live up to the laudatory introduction by the announcer who exclaimed the program to be "a thrilling new story packed with the daring adventures of a rough-riding, fast-drawing, quick-thinking western star." The plot centered on a mounted vigilante, his head covered by a white mask, who arrived without warning, "spreading his mysterious brand of justice." He was evidently a cross between the Lone Ranger and Santa Claus since the announcer warned the juvenile audience at the end of the program, "Wherever you go, whatever you do… the Phantom Rider is watching you!"

Tex Ritter, who was always more accomplished as a western singer than a dramatic leading man, portrays three versions of the same individual in this program. First, he is just a drifting cowpoke, bearing the very unlikely name of Blue Gabbet whose thirst can be quenched only with a glass of milk. Later we find out he is a U.S. Marshal, presumably with the same strange name. Finally, to the surprise of no one but the youngest listener, he also turns out to be the Phantom Rider.

The story begins with Gabbet strolling into a saloon in lawless Basin City where he orders a glass of milk. When a local desperado, Lobo Dawson, sneers at his beverage, Gabbet beats him up, shoots the gun out of his hand, and forces Lobo to drink the milk. The fight impresses the local evil ring leader, Boss Kincaid, who hires Gabbet to help him harass honest ranchers.

That evening Lobo and another henchman are confronted by the Phantom Rider who makes them put on white shirts so he can see them better in the moonlight. He threatens to shoot them if they don't obey his commands. Both are terrified. The next night, the Phantom Rider robs the stage coach but takes only the money Kincaid has stolen from local citizens. In the program's conclusion, Gabbet, flashing his U.S. Marshal badge, arrests Dawson and Kincaid and turns them over to the sheriff. When Gabbet disappears, Kincaid asks Dawson if he knows who the Phantom Rider is. "Nope," says Dawson, "but he done one thing that set me to thinking. When he was done, he asked for a glass of milk."

In the absence of any additional information about the show, it may be safe to assume that despite the popularity of Tex Ritter, the first program did not justify a second and that the producers failed to interest stations or possible sponsors in what appeared to be a mediocre series.

Ritter's birth name sounded more like an Easterner (Woodward Maurice Ritter) but he was born in Panola County, TX, on January 12, 1905. After graduating from high school, he attended the University of Texas (1922–1927) which included a year of law school. But his real interest was music, not the legal profession, and one of his first singing jobs on radio was at station KPRC in Houston in 1929. By 1930, after touring with a country and western band, he ended up in New York City where one year later he was in the Broadway cast of *Green Grow the Lilacs*, the play that eventually was the basis for the musical, *Oklahoma!*

After that he alternated between radio and the stage. Ritter was in the radio casts of **Bobby Benson, Cowboy Tom's Round-Up, Maverick Jim**, and **Death Valley Days**. On Broadway, he appeared in *Mother Lode*. His first movie contract was signed in 1936 and he would go on to be in 85 motion pictures, most of which were westerns. He also had a recording contract with Decca Records, who distributed most of his songs. John, one of his two sons, became a popular television actor in the 1960s and 1970s.

In 1964, Ritter became the fifth inductee into the Country Music Hall of Fame. Ten years later, he died in Tennessee on January 2, 1974, while visiting the Nashville jail where he had gone to bail out a fellow band member.

Sources: Audio copy of *Phantom Rider*; Tyler; O'Neal; Bond; Marshall.

PHOENIX SUN RANCH CHUCK WAGON

Jack French *and* David S. Siegel

Network: Syndicated
Format: Half hour, weekly
Duration of Run: 1937 to 1939
Sponsor: Phoenix Valley of the Sun Club
Audio Copies Extant: 13
Scripts Archived: Arizona Archives, www.azarchivesonline.org

This western series was an informative variety show, usually divided into 15 minutes of cowboy songs followed by 15 minutes of a dramatization of Arizona history, featuring a specific city, mountain, pioneer, or event. It was produced in a radio studio in Phoenix (either KTAR or KOY) but created the impression that it was broadcast around an actual chuck wagon, parked in a different location in Arizona each week. After the "Give Me My Boots and Saddle" theme song introduction, the host and narrator, "Arizona Bill" Bender greeted everyone "around the campfire" and the first song began.

The unnamed cast, which from transcriptions appear to be about a dozen, were not identified except by first names or nicknames: Bob, Alkali, Mary Jane, Jim, Sally, Shorty, and Kitty. The country and western singing groups were referred to as The Bunk House

Boys, The Wranglers, and The Top Hands, which may mean there were three different groups, or just one group assigned different names in various programs. While the first half of the program was frequently all music, Bender would occasionally parse out some details of the dramatization between each song.

Scripts were by Stephen Caroyl Shadegg (1909–1990) a Minnesota native who was raised in California and took up residence in Arizona in 1932. As a prolific author, publicist, and short story writer, he was also a dedicated researcher and his scripts show his attention to historic detail. Little is known about the producer and director, Howard Esseray, including the correct spelling of his name.

The dramatizations, encompassing 12 to 15 minutes per program, were narrated by Bender, sometimes in response to questions from one of the women in the cast. The performers in the dramatizations were excellent, in terms of acting, timing, and accents, if required for a specific character. Each script featured one or two separate stories, based upon whatever Arizona location the chuck wagon claimed to be near. For example, one program started at the Casa Grande National Monument, an ancient Pueblo structure near Coolidge, AZ, where Bender gave a detailed summary of its Indian history. After that Bender mentioned the town of Florence, AZ which launched into a dramatization of the story of the infamous swindler, James Addison Reavis. This self-styled "Baron of Arizona" in the late 1800s laid claim to 12 million acres of Arizona, based upon an impressive Spanish land grant that he had forged.

Other dramatizations featured on this series included the gunfight at the OK Corral in Tombstone, the long efforts to authorize, finance, and build the Theodore Roosevelt Dam across the Salt River, the Mormon immigration to northern Colorado and Utah, the Lost Dutchman Mine, and the historic battles between the Apache Indians and the U.S. military forces on the program in which the chuck wagon was supposedly parked on the White Mountain Apache Reservation.

Script writer Shadegg filled his dramatizations with historical facts and interesting anecdotes that enriched the stories he told. In the program about Wickenburg, AZ, "the capital of the dude ranches," Shadegg included the fact that British novelist, J. B. Priestley, wrote his book, *Midnight on the Desert*, while vacationing at a nearby dude ranch in 1936. Regarding Wyatt Earp's arrival in Tombstone, which Shadegg reported occurred on December 1, 1879, the writer described him as "six feet tall, 150 pounds, with two guns, a .45 calibre six-shooter with a 12 inch barrel in one holster and a regular .45 six-shooter in the other." When Shadegg wrote the dramatization of immigrant miner, Henry Wickenburg, he included the fact that the miner was born Heinrich Heinzel on July 4, 1820, in Austria.

It was not uncommon for the show to include park officials (or actors impersonating them) to chat "around the campfire" with the listening audience. Bender got "Jack and Andy," two National Park Rangers, to talk about the history of the Grand Canyon. Other park officials at various monuments offered their comments, and in the episode, "Water for the Valley," the then governor of Arizona, Rawghlie Clement Stanford, made a brief appearance "around the campfire."

No chance was missed to promote Arizona tourism, and most of the sites covered in the dramatizations were those that out-of-state vacationers would be interested in visiting. If any event had been accorded network radio coverage on other shows, Bender found a way to work it into his story, as he did with Easter services at the rim of the

Grand Canyon and the Indian "Smoke Eye Snake Dance" in Prescott, AZ. Annual events in Arizona, including western festivals and rodeos, were frequently mentioned by location and date.

Sound effects on the series, which appeared primitive and minimalist on the early episodes, got much better in later shows, including its crowd scenes, footsteps, animal sounds, gun shots, and even a gigantic rock slide. Despite the presence of several instrumentalists on the show who accompanied the singing groups, most of the musical bridges in the dramas were recorded excerpts from a string section. Shadegg's scripts almost always contained realistic conversation, although occasionally he veered into stilted dialogue, i.e. "'T'is a task to try our strength, but we'll not be stopped by the savages or the terrors of the trail."

But all in all, it was an excellent variety show which skillfully combined cowboy music with rich dramatizations of Arizona history.

Sources: Audio copies of *Phoenix Sun Ranch Chuck Wagon*; Trachtman; *Time*, March 29, 1937 (J.B. Priestley); http://www.miningswindles.com/html/the_baron_of_arizona.html (James Reavis); http://www.srpnet.com/water/dams/roosevelt.aspx (Theodore Roosevelt Dam); www.azarchivesonline.org (Stephen Shadegg Papers).

PISTOL PETE RICE

KARL SCHADOW *and* JACK FRENCH

A radio adaptation from the popular 1930s Street and Smith pulp magazine, *Pete Rice Magazine*, this series featured Pistol Pete Rice, the sheriff of Buzzard Gap, fighting for law and order in the Old West with the aid of his loyal deputies, Misery and Teeny. Broadcast three times a week from station WOR, New York in cooperation with the magazine, the action packed program was promoted with the slogan: "Be proud of America and have America be proud of us."

Source: *Pete Rice Magazine*, November, 1934.

THE PLAINSMAN

JACK FRENCH *and* DAVID S. SIEGEL

NAMES: *The Plainsman, Bill Cody, the Plainsman*
NETWORK: Syndicated
FORMAT: 15 minutes, daily
DURATION OF RUN: Unknown, circa 1934
SPONSOR: Various, depending on station
AUDIO COPIES EXTANT: 2
SCRIPTS ARCHIVED: Undetermined

As with many other syndicated series, in the absence of original disks, it is difficult for vintage radio historians to identify the production dates, cast, production crew, and recording company for *The Plainsman*. Both existing audio copies of the program yield little background information and even the title of the program is uncertain as the initial episode calls itself *The Plainsman*, while episode #2 is titled *Bill Cody, the Plainsman*.

The first two episodes set the scene for what would be an eventual resolution of the story line in 39 episodes, which was the industry standard minimum for marketing a syndicated series. "Buffalo Bill" Cody, under orders from General George Custer, sets out from Fort Hays, KS, to locate and confront a Pawnee medicine man who is building strong alliances among all the Plains tribes of Indians, thus a danger to the whites. This Pawnee is half-white, leading General Custer to describe him as having the "cunning of an Indian and the organization of a white man."

A very young Bill Cody, Junior (whose mother was earlier killed by "savage Indians"), sneaks away from his Aunt Mary and follows his father and the military contingent without their knowledge. He bumps into Calamity Jane and the two are quickly ambushed by hostile Indians. By the second episode, it is apparent that the unknown scriptwriter for this syndication company was weaving a hodgepodge of historical fact and fiction with real and imaginary characters. Two famous Indians are mentioned in the first two episodes, Sitting Bull and Crazy Horse, and might be expected to appear in later episodes.

In the series, Buffalo Bill's sidekicks are Applejack Murphy, played by an actor using an Irish brogue, and Swede Dawson, who has a Scandinavian accent. A third fictional character is an Indian scout, Plenty Buffalo Meat, whose name must have been coined as an inside joke. While history records that Buffalo Bill and General Custer were at Fort Hays sometime, whether or not it was at the same time is a matter of conjecture. But certainly an Army general would not send Cavalry troopers out under the command of Cody, an Army scout, no matter how famous he was.

The introduction of Calamity Jane in the action of the second episode is interesting but not totally unpredictable. Calamity was Martha Jane Cannary (1852–1903) who went through a variety of occupations on the frontier: ox team driver, cook, and prostitute, and who also claimed to be an Indian fighter and Army scout. She was obsessed with James Butler "Wild Bill" Hickok (1837–1876), followed him around the plains, and after his death, claimed they were married. Their real and fictional relationship would probably require that the series' author write him into subsequent issues. However it's certain that her stint as a prostitute on the outskirts of Fort Laramie would never be mentioned in this radio series.

William F. Cody's real family was totally ignored by the scriptwriter. Although he did have four children, none were named Bill Junior. Cody and his wife had three daughters, Orra, Arta, and Irma, plus one son, Kit Carson Cody. Unfortunately, the son died of scarlet fever at age five. The father lived a long time and died at age 70, but his wife outlived him, so none of their children were ever in the custody of an "Aunt Mary."

For a syndicated series, the scripts, while not always rooted in truth, are at least colorful and exciting. Plenty Buffalo Meat refers to Buffalo Bill as "Thunder in Two Hands." This Indian scout can "hear the grass whisper" and therefore learn of events happening on the prairie countless miles away; he is the first to know that Small Bill and Calamity Jane are besieged by marauding Indians.

While none of the actors in this series are recognizable by their voices, all appear to be competent at their job. Since the script guarantees a variety of distinctive character voices, it's easy to follow the scene action even if a half dozen characters are interacting: the hero (Buffalo Bill), his little son, an Irish associate, a woman (Aunt Mary or Calamity Jane), a Swedish assistant, and an Indian.

As with most of the syndicated shows of that era, the sound effects range from satisfactory to inept. The standard and easily executed sounds of hoof beats and door knocks are realistic, while the frequent gun shots are totally unconvincing, probably because they were created with a wooden lathe slapping a leather cushion. Crowd scenes, particularly those of Indians, are unrealistic and usually consist of several "woo-woo-woos" in the background. On the other hand, the music played in the fort, "Oh Susanna," is accurate for the period; Stephen Foster composed the composition in 1848 and it quickly became one of the most popular tunes throughout the West.

Although this was a 15 minute show, only 11 minutes were devoted to the drama since two minutes of instrumental music was recorded at both the beginning and ending of each episode so whoever the sponsor was at any station, a staff announcer could read the commercials as voiceovers with the series music in the background.

Sources: Audio copies of *Plainsman*; Carter; Josephy; Trachtman; www.kshs.org/ kansapedia/fort-hays/11793.

Preview Theater of the Air see *Zorro*

RANCH HOUSE JIM

Jack French *and* David S. Siegel

Network: NBC Blue
Format: 15 minutes
Duration of Run: 1943 to 1944
Sponsor: Ranch House Pancake Flour
Audio Copies Extant: 3
Scripts Archived: Undetermined

The origin of this musical variety western, as well as its duration and standard format, is murky. It is likely that there were two separate, but related, series with the same name, both emanating from Chicago. If so, the first version was only local while the second one aired over NBC Blue affiliates in the Midwest.

As early as 1941, station WLS in Chicago had a local show called *Ranch House Jim* that was headlined by Reggie Cross who had joined that station in 1938. Cross, a talented harmonica player, was on a number of country and western music programs of WLS, frequently paired with guitarist Howard Black; when Black died in 1940, Cross formed a trio, Reggie Cross and his Harmonizers. The group expanded from three to five, and around 1941, they were all on a program called *Ranch House Jim*. How long this musical program was on the air has not yet been confirmed.

By May 1943, *Ranch House Jim* was being heard over stations as far away as New York. It was usually a 15 minute show, airing from 12:15 to 12:30 P.M., two or three times a week. It is believed that the programs consisted only of Cross and his group of country and western musicians.

In December 1943, *Ranch House Jim* picked up a new leading man, Joe "Curley" Bradley, a new station, WENR in Chicago, and a new sponsor, Ranch House Pancake Flour. The program was still a quarter hour, but the time was changed to 3:45 to 4:00 P.M. when it was heard over 22 station affiliates of NBC Blue, three times a week, Monday, Wednesday, and Friday. Cross and his fellow instrumentalists supplied the musical support to Bradley's vocals. The sponsoring flour was but one of several products marketed by Omar, Inc., a grain company in Omaha, NE. The company's symbol, a turbaned mystic who resembled Ibis, a comic book hero, appeared on most of its products, including the 100 pound bags of "Omar All-Mash Chick Starter and Grower."

Joe "Curley" Bradley, left, who portrayed *Ranch House Jim*, *The Singing Marshall*, and *Tom Mix*, with Frank Bresee, who was Little Beaver on *Red Ryder*, rehearsing for a re-creation of a western program, circa 1980 (Frank Bresee collection).

Whether Omar named its flour after the *Ranch House Jim* program is as yet unverified, but it would seem too much of a coincidence having Ranch House Pancake Flour sponsor *Ranch House Jim* if that were not the case. When the initial contract was signed in December 1943 for 26 weeks, the account was managed by the Chicago advertising agency of McFarland, Aveyard & Company.

At some point during this time period, the program began to include a western drama, also starring Bradley. Cross was gradually phased out as Bradley did all the flour commercials ("pancakes as light as a Colorado cloud") and bantered with the other musicians between his songs. Comic relief was provided by a lackadaisical character named Fireball who also sang an occasional spiritual.

It appears that eventually there were three *Ranch House Jim* programs weekly, all of which were 15 minutes each. On Tuesdays and Thursdays, the musical version aired, while the dramatization was broadcast on Saturdays. In each of the latter, Bradley was the central character and he ran the Lazy J Ranch, along with some ranch hands, including Pedro, sharing most of the action with Jim. The tales were simplistic, mixing adventure and comedy, and the sound effects and musical bridges were understated.

In one of the existing episodes, Jim and a new schoolmarm are victims of a stage coach robbery. Later, Jim recovers their losses from the outlaw, but he hides out at his ranch when she tries to kiss him in gratitude. In another existing audio copy, an unscrupulous banker, Jabez Butterworth, hatches a plan to rob a train carrying a gold shipment and puts all the blame on Jim. But Jim and the local sheriff see through the ruse and find the evidence to arrest Butterworth and his cronies.

It is believed that *Ranch House Jim* ran until June 1944, at which time "Curley" Bradley took over the title lead in **The Tom Mix Ralston Straight Shooters**. Omar, Inc. lasted much longer than the western show it sponsored; the company existed as a corporate entity until 1960 when it was absorbed into the Continental Baking Company of Rye, NY.

Sources: Audio copies of *Ranch House Jim*; Harmon, *Radio Mystery*; *Schenectady (NY) Gazette*, May 31, 1943; *Broadcasting*, December 13, 1943; 1960 Annual Report of the Federal Trade Commission, docket 7780; www.bassharp.com/reggie.htm.

RED GOOSE INDIAN TALES

KARL SCHADOW *and* JACK FRENCH

Initially written for a juvenile audience and heard in the early 1930s over station WBBM, a St. Louis CBS affiliate, adults became the target audience when this early program switched to NBC on station WMAQ, an NBC affiliate, airing in mid-evening. A mixture of story-telling with musical interludes, each program in the series started with an old pioneer retelling the adventures of Red Goose, a young brave of the Ojibwa tribe, to his two grandchildren. As his tale unfolded, the dramatization of the story took over. The program was sponsored by the Freedman-Shelby Shoe Company of St. Louis, who promoted their Red Goose brand shoes.

Source: *Variety*, September 8, 1931, p. 112.

Red Horse Ranch see *Life on Red Horse Ranch*

RED RYDER

J. RANDOLPH COX

NAMES: *Red Ryder, The Adventures of Red Ryder*
NETWORK: NBC Blue, Mutual
FORMAT: Half hour, three times a week
DURATION OF RUN: February 3, 1942, to 1951
SPONSOR: Langendorf Bread
AUDIO COPIES EXTANT: Approximately 70
SCRIPTS ARCHIVED: American Radio Archives; http://www.genericradio.com; SPERDVAC

"Oh, bury me not on the lone prairie...." The sound of the theme, known as "The Dying Cowboy," was the opening to this popular radio series. Based on the newspaper comic strip created by Fred Harman (1902–1982), *Red Ryder* ("America's Famous Fighting Cowboy") debuted on February 3, 1942, on the NBC Blue Network. The title is sometimes given as *The Adventures of Red Ryder*. Like its major competition, **The Lone Ranger**, the program aired three times a week, but on Tuesday, Thursday and Saturday instead of

Monday, Wednesday and Friday. It was on the air at 7:30 P.M. (PT) and the last episode aired in 1951.

As a newspaper comic strip, *Red Ryder* began as a Sunday feature on November 6, 1938, and was followed by a daily strip that began the next year on March 27, 1939. Prior to introducing *Red Ryder*, Harman had had some success with another western strip called *Bronc Peeler*. The *Red Ryder* strip lasted for over 20 years until 1964 and was one of the most popular western strips ever syndicated (first by the NEA Services, then the McNaught Syndicate, and finally by King Features). At the height of its popularity it appeared in 750 newspapers. The characters were licensed to appear in the movies (27 feature films and a 12 episode serial), in comic books (151 issues) and in Whitman's Big Little Books (11 titles) and mystery and adventure novel series (7 titles). There was also more than one pilot for an unsold television series. Most of these were the brainchild of Stephen Slesinger, an entrepreneur and agent who worked with Harman and had a talent for product promotion.

The concept of the radio series was simple. Unlike the heroes of other western shows, Red Ryder was not a lawman, although he was occasionally sworn in as a deputy sheriff, or even a full sheriff as circumstances merited. Most of the time Red, so named for his fiery red hair, was a working cowhand. While he appeared to have had his own ranch early in the strip, he was principally working for his aunt, a feisty pioneer known only as the Duchess.

On the very first Sunday comics page Red met a young Navaho Indian named Little Beaver who became his constant companion. Red rode a black stallion named Thunder while Little Beaver's pinto was named Papoose. The strip's cast of recurring characters was filled out with the addition of Beth Wilder, Red's sometime girlfriend, and Ace Hanlon, a gambler and villain who was often accompanied by his sidekick, a man known only as One-Eye. The locale was somewhere in the West, probably Colorado where cartoonist Harman had his studio and ranch. The geographical names most often mentioned included the Duchess' ranch at Painted Valley, with the nearby towns of Devil's Hole, Rimrock and Maverick. Sheriff Newt represented the law. Some of these characters and locales were used on the radio as well.

According to radio historian John Dunning, actor Reed Hadley played Red Ryder from 1942 to 1944. Hadley may be best known for playing the dual role of Diego De La Vega and Zorro in the 1939 Republic serial *Zorro's Fighting Legion*. Hadley was followed in the role by Carlton KaDell in 1945 and from 1946 to 1951 Red Ryder was played by Brooke Temple. All three actors affected a rich western drawl in portraying the hero. On the air, Red Ryder had a quick temper which was seldom referred to on the printed page.

Little Beaver was played by a series of actors: the first was Tommy Cook who had been Little Beaver in the 1940 Republic serial, *The Adventures of Red Ryder*, with Franklin (Frank) Bresee as an alternate from 1942 to 1946, then Henry Blair (1944 to 1947), Johnny McGivern (1947 to 1950), and finally Sammy Ogg in the last two years of the series, 1950 to 1951. The character of Little Beaver had relatively little to do in the series except to come to the rescue of his adult comrade, help in capturing the villain, and utter phrases in Pidgin English such as "You betchum, Red Ryder!" There were a number of episodes in which Little Beaver did not appear and this was sometimes explained by mentioning that he was away at school.

Other regular actors were Arthur Q. Bryan as Roland (Rawhide) Rollinson and

Horace Murphy as Buckskin Blodgett, Red's durable sidekick in many of the later episodes. Gerald Mohr and Mercedes McCambridge also appeared on the program in supporting roles.

The show was produced by Brad Brown, with Paul Franklin as writer/director and Albert Van Antwerp also contributing scripts. Sound effects were handled by Monty Fraser, Bob Turnbull, and James Dick while Ben Alexander and Art Gilmore were the announcers.

Toward the end of the first year, the character of Roland Rollinson was used as comic relief in a few episodes. A genial little fat man who came west from Providence, RI, he eventually returned east to look after his ailing brother. Red received at least one letter from him afterwards in which he said how much he had enjoyed his stay in Painted Valley, but there is no evidence that he ever came back. As played by Bryan, the Rollinson character sounded just like another of the actor's famous voiced characters, Elmer Fudd.

Another figure employed for comic relief was the Chinese cook and handyman, Ching How. He could be depended on to fill the air with a string of Pidgin English that represented the popular concept of what the Chinese language sounded like to western ears. That he was an immigrant to the West was made apparent, but what was also made apparent was that he was a valued member of the staff on the Duchess' ranch. In one early episode, "Trouble in Shawnee" (April 30, 1942), he and his restaurant owner cousin, Lu Sin, were the recipients of Old West racism when they were made to dance to the bullets of the bad men's guns, simply because they were not considered "real Americans." A few words from Red Ryder showed how real Americans should feel about his sort of abuse.

Red Ryder was produced in Hollywood and carried by the NBC Blue Network on the West Coast except for a period when it moved east for about four months in 1946 to appear on the Mutual Network. Originally a sustaining program with no commercials, *Red Ryder* acquired Langendorf Bread as a sponsor with the sixth episode. At some point in the first year the show began using the slogan that *Red Ryder* was a show about "the West that lives forever."

The earliest radio stories were serials in three parts to match the three episodes that aired each week. The very first story, "Trouble on the Shogono Trail" (1942), was taken from the Sunday pages published from January 21 to March 17, 1940, but only the third episode (February 7, 1942) survives in audio form. Prior to its use on the radio the same story had been adapted from the newspaper strip by Russ Winterbotham for *Red Ryder and the Mystery of Whispering Walls*, a hardcover book published by Whitman Publishing Co. of Racine, WI, in 1941. While all three versions tell the same basic story they differ in some respects. The comic strip included the recurring character of Beth Wilder while the book named her Beth Sweet. On radio, the female lead was named Jane Bruce, a character who did not appear in either the newspaper strip or the Whitman book; Bruce was the local schoolteacher and appeared from time to time.

The plot of that first story involved a missing prospector and some cattle rustling near the ghost town of Whispering Walls. Strange noises seemed to come from the bowels of the earth and people saw the shadows of bawling bulls driven by men with whips projected on the walls of the old saloon. The mystery was solved when it was discovered that there was a river underneath the ghost town and the cattle were being transported on barges to a box canyon from which they could be shipped to market. While most of the remaining stories were typical western plots, there were touches that made it possible to distinguish one story from another.

The program featured the familiar western plots involving cattle rustlers, range wars, and vigilantes. Further, conflicts between cattlemen and sheepherders or between ranchers and nesters, or ranchers and homesteaders were featured. There were also other story lines: a rancher needs to raise money so that his wife may have a necessary operation; another needs money to reclaim his ranch; a dam must be blown up in order for the water to be diverted and not flood the valley; and an unscrupulous scoundrel who plots to acquire another man's ranch or gold mine. The program featured some of the most despicable villains known to the fictional West, villains who were equipped with voices that could predict doom to those on the side of law and order with almost sadistic glee.

Some stories dealt with problems concerning the recurring characters. When the time came for Little Beaver to go to school, he rebelled and ran away. It turned out he had gone back to the Reservation to be with his own people, a tribe headed by Chief Clearwater. There he met a young Navaho girl named Poco, a character also found in the newspaper strip. In spite of his usual disinclination to like girls, Little Beaver enjoyed the company of Poco, and when he saw that Poco also needed to go to school, the Navaho boy grudgingly agreed to accompany her. Unfortunately, the character of Poco was used in only a handful of episodes and their relationship never developed to its full potential. The episodes with Little Beaver and Poco were sometimes used to show that the boy was growing up.

Ace Hanlon was a recurring, although infrequent, villain in the comics; months could go by without him raising his head. By contrast, in the radio series Hanlon appeared to be responsible for most of the villainy for the first few months. And, if he was not directly responsible, he was able to manipulate events like a puppeteer pulling the strings of a marionette. In one episode he actually talked the sheriff into letting him out of jail. Hanlon could be caught at the end of one episode and still be free at the beginning of the next one. It may not have made much sense to the continuity, but Ace Hanlon made a superb villain. His gravelly voice in the early episodes was distinctive; another actor reading his lines in later episodes did not have the same effect.

In "Trouble at Iron Horse Junction" (March 5, 1942), someone wanted to prevent the railroad from being completed. It appeared that Ace Hanlon had arranged to have the Pawnee stampede the buffalo, for if there were no buffalo, there would be no food for the railroad workers. There is an interesting historic note in this episode because the railroad workers, referred to as "paddies," all speak with an Irish brogue. It is a fact that immigrant groups like the Irish were used to build the railroads. In this instance Ace Hanlon was not working alone, but was in the pay of someone else who would benefit from the railroad not being built. In "Lone Star Final" (December 19, 1942), there was a change of pace when Ace Hanlon and Red Ryder teamed up to investigate the murder of newspaperman Andrew Becker. It was also to Hanlon's benefit that the paper stop printing stories about his nefarious exploits.

Scripts often contained a preview of the next episode at the end of the current one and sometimes there was even a scene taken from the next episode. To establish a running continuity in the series, there was a reference to the previous episode at the beginning of each new one. After a while it may have seemed somewhat implausible that Red Ryder and Little Beaver should go from one adventure to another in such a short time with scarcely a chance for a rest in between.

Many of the earliest episodes took place far from Painted Valley; while Red and Little Beaver might return to the Duchess' ranch for a bit of relaxation, it was certain they would be called to ride many hundreds of miles to a town that needed their help. The sheriffs in these towns seemed to be in the habit of telegraphing Red Ryder whenever there was trouble. Sometimes they would get there only to learn that the sheriff or marshal had been killed; and then Red would be deputized to represent the law.

In most of the stories there was little doubt about who was responsible for the latest round of trouble, but there were occasional surprises. In "Born to Gunsmoke" (May 26, 1942), a sympathetic character, Rick Backus, suddenly showed signs of irrational behavior and was diagnosed as being emotionally unstable. At the end of the story he was sent to a hospital instead of to jail for his crimes. This seems an unusual plot twist for a series that was marketed to young people.

Red Ryder could always be counted upon to make the right decisions and his fiery temper may have been responsible for his reactions when faced with danger. Gunshots frequently rang out with effective sound effects because most of the characters carried six-guns. The smack of fist against fist or fist against chin was another regular sound effect. Like *The Lone Ranger*, Red Ryder was able to shoot the gun out of his opponent's hands and not shoot to kill, but occasionally someone shot the gun out of the hero's hand.

Some of the episodes were decidedly not the sort of thing to be expected in a western. When the circus came to Devil's Hole (April 23, 1942), the plot involved rival circuses, one of which schemed to put the other out of business. It could just as well have been a bank trying to foreclose on a ranch, but the change of situation made it fresh. It would be four years before the newspaper strip printed a circus story.

In another episode, "The Law Comes to Stovepipe" (January 12, 1943), a traditional plot about a widow needing money to reclaim her ranch turned out to be a humorous story with the introduction of a character named Sticky Fingers McGlute. McGlute, a friend of Buckskin Blodgett, was a professional pickpocket and his presence in the story explained how it was that money and other valuables (including Red's pocketbook) would disappear only to turn up again in McGlute's possession. And in "The Devil's Hole National Bank" (January 7, 1943), Red used the myth of the "dead man's eyes"—the belief that the last thing a dead man saw before expiring would be imprinted on his retina—to lure a killer out of hiding. This myth has been used in a number of works of fiction.

There was a 1944 parody, which never aired, celebrating the birthday of writer/director Paul Franklin that was a spoof on most of the clichés found in this and other western series. From the appropriation of the "William Tell Overture" from *The Lone Ranger* to the gags about the sponsor, to the female sheriff who sounded like Mae West, as well as having Red and his opponent shoot the guns out of each other's hands, the incidents in this episode are memorable.

On September 11, 1948, Red Ryder in the person of actor Brooke Temple paid a visit to the *Abbott and Costello Kids' Show* that aired on Saturday mornings. The five minute western sketch enacted demonstrated how popular the show was at the time and may have helped the ratings of both radio shows.

Perhaps the most famous product to be associated with *Red Ryder* is the Daisy air rifle, the 111 Model 40 Red Ryder Western Carbine. Developed by the Daisy Manufacturing

Company of Plymouth, Michigan, it was in development in 1938 and the first ones were marketed in 1940. It was advertised in comic books and *The American Boy* magazine, among other publications and to this day has become the definitive BB gun. Over the years changes were made to parts of the carbine, but its basic structure remains the same to this day. An original BB gun in mint condition has become a collector's item worth a hundred times more than the $2.95 for which it originally sold. It gained a new sort of immortality in the stories of Jean Shepherd that became the basis for the 1983 movie *A Christmas Story*. In it, young Ralphie asks Santa for a Red Ryder BB gun for Christmas even though his parents (and nearly everyone else) warn him that he'll just shoot his eye out with it. Few viewers of that movie were familiar with the origins of Red Ryder in the comics or on the radio.

An organization derived entirely from the radio show was the Red Ryder Victory Patrol, a club founded in 1942 for patriotic young Americans to encourage them in conservation practices that would help the war effort. Boys and girls could get application cards from their local grocery stores and mail them in. In return they would receive a membership card, a certificate, a secret decoder and a 32 page Red Ryder comic book. The comic book had a page advertising official Victory Patrol equipment like a blackout flashlight (presumably handy in a blackout), a bronco buster belt with 17 cowboy designs, a cowboy coin purse, and a pen in the shape of a bullet. Weighed down with all of this gear, the young member of the patrol could have no end of fun as well as be patriotic.

The decoder was used much like the Secret Squadron decoders connected with the *Captain Midnight* radio serial to decode messages that previewed the action of the following episode. In the radio show there is preserved a simple message for Memorial Day 1942. Four years later in 1946 a coded message answered the question of what was the name of the mountain range where Rip van Winkle fell asleep. No other messages have apparently survived.

Some radio historians contend that the early episodes of *Red Ryder* attracted more listeners than **The Lone Ranger** did. By the time *Red Ryder* debuted in 1942, **The Lone Ranger** had been on the air for a decade, so perhaps *Red Ryder* seemed fresh by comparison. Whatever the case, the redheaded cowboy didn't outlast the masked rider of the plains, but Red lives on in the story of the young boy who asks Santa Claus to bring him a BB gun for Christmas.

Sources: Audio copies of *Red Ryder*; Dunning, *On the Air*; Poling; *Dime Novel Round-Up*, June 2008 and June 2010; *Radio Recall*, March/April, 2011; *Popular Mechanics*, July 1999; *True West*, September/October 1968.

REMINISCENCES OF THE OLD WEST

KARL SCHADOW *and* JACK FRENCH

This was a half hour weekly KOA broadcast out of Denver and sponsored in 1933 to 1935 by Kuner-Empson, a local cannery specializing in groceries and related products. The program was cited as the station's second most popular program, based largely upon its reputation for making regional history more interesting than traditional textbooks. The practice of utilizing carefully researched historical evidence as the basis for well written dramatic sketches influenced public schools in the region to play these programs in some classes. Following one such broadcast about Custer's Last Stand, the station actually received letters from a few students questioning an historical inaccuracy. Usual cast members included Roscoe Stockton, Harker Collins, Fred Hile, and Earle Shaw.

Source: *Variety*, January 1, 1935, p. 90.

THE RETURN OF BILL HART

JACK FRENCH *and* DAVID S. SIEGEL

NETWORK: Unknown
FORMAT: Half hour
DURATION OF RUN: Unknown, circa late 1930s
SPONSOR: Possibly Swift & Company
AUDIO COPIES EXTANT: 1 (Probably audition)
SCRIPTS ARCHIVED: Undetermined

While there may be many good reasons to produce a western radio series, starting such a project with a silent movie script may not have been the best choice. But William S. Hart was never known to back down from a challenge. Sometime in the mid–1930s, Hart decided to try his talents before the radio microphone and re-create one of his silent motion pictures.

Hart was born in Newburgh, NY, on December 6, 1864, four months before Abraham Lincoln was assassinated. He began acting on stage in his early 20s, performing mostly classical roles, including those of Shakespeare, both on Broadway and also in touring companies. In 1914, at the age of 49, he branched into the primitive movie industry. Fascinated by the Old West, he did everything in the silent era of film: acting, directing, screen writing, and producing. His rugged and seemingly realistic westerns, with drab costumes and uplifting moral themes of good versus evil, were very popular at first with audiences. However, by the 1920s, the public's taste in westerns had turned to those of Tom Mix, a flamboyant showman with fancy costumes and stunt riding.

Paramount Pictures released Hart who then produced, with his own money, another silent movie, *Tumbleweeds*, but the box office receipts were disappointing. In 1939 Hart recorded a spoken prologue for the re-release of *Tumbleweeds*. By then he was 75 and the film turned out to be his farewell to Hollywood.

Contemporary records are sketchy regarding what motivated Hart, at the age of 75, to try his hand in radio. *The Return of Bill Hart* exists in only one episode and that surviving copy was taken from a disk in which only the first 25 minutes exist of a half hour recording. The episode is based upon his 1920 silent film, *The Testing Block*, co-starring Eva Novak as Nell, which had a running time of 60 minutes. In the movie, the infamous outlaw, Sierra Bill (played by Hart) leaves his gang when he falls in love with a singing violinist, Nell. He convinces her to marry him and later they have a child. A former member of his gang, Ringe, persuades Nell to leave Bill and come with him. Later he ruins Bill at the gambling tables. Bill ends up in jail but breaks out, determined to seek vengeance on Ringe.

We may never know who adapted this film for radio (it may have been Hart himself) but the script moves at a snail's pace and almost nothing of significance happens in the first 25 minutes. However, the introduction of the program, by the "old-timer," is almost embarrassing to hear by today's standards with its lavish praise of Hart's bygone days as a silent star:

Good evening, folks. This is one large, fine evening for the United States. Bill Hart is coming back. Land sakes alive, Bill, we've sure missed you. Why say, you're the idol of the American boy, that's what you are… and the old folks too. Believe me, Bill, we never missed a picture. And it's sure mighty fine of Swift and Company to make it possible for us to sit home in our easy chairs and ride them old trails over again.

The deadly dull script is not improved by humdrum acting and inept sound effects. The outlaw gang galloping has only one sound man with two coconut halves and each horse whinny sounds more like a man sneezing. Around the campfire, Bill threatens to shoot Hola, the "lazy, good-for-nothin' half-breed" who had gotten into the whiskey keg again, and a few minutes later, Bill knocks unconscious one of his gang who slapped his horse.

Near the end of the program, Bill wants to go to town to see Nell and he spends five minutes around the campfire, trying to borrow some better items of clothing to wear from various members of his gang. Mercifully, the last five minutes of the program do not exist. There is no evidence that this program was ever broadcast and it was a sad conclusion to those twelve years of brilliant movie making by a true genius.

Sources: Audio copy of *Return of Bill Hart*; Katz; Franklin.

RIDING WITH THE TEXAS RANGERS

KARL SCHADOW *and* JACK FRENCH

This 15 minute show aired from station WFAA in Dallas, usually Monday, Wednesday, and Friday, normally in the 5:30 P.M. time slot. It began in July 1935 and continued until at least May 1938. The show, based upon the exploits of the Texas Rangers, was created and written by Glenn G. Addington. The central character was the Old Colonel (voiced by Louis Vada Quince) who told western tales, some of which may have been dramatized. There was also a musical component to the program; the singers were Hal Whitaker, Jack Prigmore, Leonard Ohlson, Harry Hume, Jimmy Hodges, J.P. Scoggins and Hubert Woodward. Kellogg's Cereals sponsored this show through

Riding with the Texas Rangers advertisement, circa 1936 (courtesy Archives of Kellogg Company. Kellogg's is a trademark of Kellogg North America Company, used with permission).

the advertising company of N. W. Ayer & Sons which offered several premiums, including membership in the Junior Texas Ranger Commission.

Source: *Dallas Morning News*, February 5, 1936.

RIN TIN TIN

CHARLIE *and* KATHERINE SUMMERS

NAMES: *The Wonder Dog, Rin Tin Tin, The Adventures of Rin Tin Tin*
NETWORK: NBC Blue, CBS, Mutual
FORMAT: 15 minutes, weekly; half hour, weekly
DURATION OF RUN: April 5, 1930, to June 8, 1933; October 5, 1933, to May 20, 1934; and January 2, 1955, to December 25, 1955
SPONSOR: Ken-L-Ration, Nabisco
AUDIO COPIES EXTANT: 2 half hour episodes (1955)
SCRIPTS ARCHIVED: Undetermined

It is ironic that so very little survives from a series of radio programs based on one of the biggest film stars of the 1920s. The origin of Rin Tin Tin is fairly well-known. The German shepherd puppy was discovered in a bombed-out kennel in Lorraine, France, shortly before the end of World War I by U.S. Army Corporal Lee Duncan, who had found the mother and her five scrawny pups. He took the six dogs back to camp, and kept two of the puppies, a male and a female, while the mother and remaining three pups were given to other soldiers.

Duncan named the two he kept, Rin Tin Tin and Nannette, after the good luck charms the French children had given the American soldiers. Nannette died of pneumonia shortly after her arrival in the United States but Rin Tin Tin survived the trip to California and thrived, becoming strong and graceful. Rin Tin Tin was filmed performing a leap at a show by an acquaintance of Duncan's, who then fixated on the idea of getting his dog into films. "Rinty" was initially cast in *The Man from Hell's River* (1922), but it wasn't until he entered the Warner Bros. lot and replaced an uncooperative wolf that he had his big break. Many silent and a handful of sound films, including a twelve part serial, then followed. It was reported the dog single handedly saved the Warner Bros. studio from bankruptcy as he became one of the biggest box office draws of the 1920s.

The initial version of the radio program was titled *The Wonder Dog*, Rinty's Hollywood advertising moniker. This series, starring Francis X. Bushman and Lee Duncan, aired on the NBC Blue Network Saturday evenings at 8:15 P.M. (ET) premiering on April 5, 1930, as a 15 minute serial. The program then morphed into *Rin Tin Tin* in September 1930 (for a few weeks, the AP radio listings contained both names), and moved to Thursdays at 8:15 P.M. in April 1931. This version starred Don Ameche and Junior McLain. The cast around this time also included radio actress Betty White (no relation to TV's Golden Girl) as the little girl Sally. This run was sponsored by Chappel Brothers' Ken-L-Ration, the first commercial canned dog food, and moved a final time to Thursday at 8:30 P.M. in August, 1932, where it remained until its final broadcast June 8, 1933. The series was revived by CBS on October 5, 1933, running Sunday evenings at 7:45 P.M., again sponsored by Ken-L-Ration, where it ended its run on May 20, 1934. None of the 15 minute episodes from these series have been unearthed.

While some sources claim that Rin Tin Tin voiced himself in this 1930s radio program until his death on August 10, 1932, when his offspring, Rin Tin Tin Jr., took over the role, this seems rather unlikely, at least on an ongoing basis. According to a 1931 *Chicago Daily Tribune* article, it was actually NBC's Tom Corwine who vocally performed the role of the Wonder Dog. The article even refers to a battle scene between the dog and a wild bull, both portrayed by Corwine, who was also credited for making the sounds for objects like rusty pumps and swinging doors.

Susan Orlean, in her 2011 book *Rin Tin Tin: The Life and the Legend*, instead credits a voice actor named Bob Barker (no relation to TV host Bob Barker) with providing Rinty's voice on this early radio program. Barker, a specialist in animal sounds, also voiced the howl of the wolf on *Renfrew of the Mounted*. Orlean describes some of the plots used during this time as being somewhat ludicrous, with elements of fantasy and science-fiction added to the mix. From her description, it appears this serial version of the program may not have been a western-themed show.

It would be two decades before the Wonder Dog would have another series on radio. *The Adventures of Rin Tin Tin* premiered on Mutual January 2, 1955, and is one of only nine programs which originated on television and made the transition to radio, instead of the more common reverse. This series was identical in its scenario to the concurrent running black and white television series; it involved Rusty, the young lone survivor of an Indian attack, and his dog who were rescued and adopted by the 101st Cavalry, stationed at Fort Apache in Arizona. It was designed to be a complement to the television series, driving viewers to the TV and customers to the stores for Rin Tin Tin merchandise.

Each 30 minute program was a complete story, and the two existing episodes are from this series. While some sources credit the television cast as appearing in the radio version, including Lee Aaker as Rusty, James L. Brown as Lt. Rip Masters, and Joe Sawyer as Sgt. Biff O'Hara, the cast and production credits are conspicuously absent in the two surviving episodes. Moreover, the radio program was transcribed (recorded) in New York, instead of California where the television series was filmed. The National Biscuit Company, Nabisco, sponsored this series, promoting its products Shredded Wheat cereal and Milk Bone dog biscuits, tying in nicely with the basic story of a boy and his dog. Announcer Don Morrow received the sole name credit. The radio series ended on Christmas Day 1955 while the television series continued for another three and a half years.

One of the two existing episodes, "The White Buffalo," was an adaptation of the television script of the same name dealing in a somewhat heavy-handed fashion with racial and ethnic tolerance. The radio version contained an unusual spoken word rendition of the title song performed on the television program by James L. Brown with the Trail Winders, which was commercially released on record by MGM. The other existing episode, "The Ambassador," featured a surprisingly strong female character for the 1950s, but also included some rather stereotyped Mexican bandits. Of course, in both examples, the humans, male or female, young or old, needed the assistance of the brave, fleet-footed Rin Tin Tin to save the day.

While the television version of *Rin Tin Tin* was re-run for decades, the radio version sank into obscurity, leaving little more than a footnote in the larger than life story of *The Wonder Dog*. Perhaps if more episodes are ever resurrected, particularly from the 1930s fifteen minute serial version, radio will take a more prominent role in the fascinating life and legend of this amazing dog.

Sources: Audio copies of *Adventures of Rin Tin Tin*; Dunning, *On the Air*; Hickerson,

4th Revised; Orlean; *Daily News of Los Angeles*, February 19, 1988; *Chicago Daily Tribune*, March 8, 1931, p. H4.

THE ROMANCE OF THE RANCHOS

STAN CLAUSSEN

NETWORK: CBS
FORMAT: Half hour, weekly
DURATION OF RUN: September 17, 1941, to May 10, 1942 (repeats on West Coast through 1948)
SPONSOR: Title Insurance and Trust Company of Los Angeles
AUDIO COPIES EXTANT: 35 (complete run)
SCRIPTS ARCHIVED: California Historical Society at University of Southern California

On February 11, 1942, episode 22 of an historical series called *The Romance of the Ranchos* was aired on the CBS Western flagship radio station KNX, Los Angeles. The strong voice of Frank Graham, well known to regular KNX listeners, told the story of Don Hugo Reid, a Scottish businessman who came to the New World in the 1820s, became a merchant in Los Angeles in 1834, and won a land grant from the Mexican government in 1841 that became the Rancho Santa Anita. But what was significant to the regular listeners was that Don Hugo Reid married a cultured Indian woman named Doña Victoria and they had a beautiful daughter named Ignacia. Many Californians knew that the real story of Don Hugo Reid and Victoria had inspired the fictional story of Helen Hunt Jackson's book, *Ramona*.

The Romance of the Ranchos consisted of thirty-five 30 minute programs that aired on the Columbia Pacific Radio Network from September 7, 1941, to May 10, 1942, Sundays at 7:30 P.M., Wednesdays at 7:30, then Sundays at 8:30. The series was inspired by the long, sometimes sad, but always colorful, history of the old Spanish land grants or "ranchos" that had been preserved in the archives of the Title Insurance and Trust Company of Los Angeles. The researcher for the firm, W.W. Robinson, claimed that the company had more than 3,000 volumes dealing with the history of the ranchos.

CBS dramatized this history with scripts by John Dunkel and Les Farber. Music was fashioned from traditional Spanish tunes by John Leopold with Gaylord Carter at the organ and Irwin Yoh on the violin. The program was produced and directed by Ted Bliss and Cliff Howell, with Bob LeMond as the announcer. Frank Graham, "The Wandering Vaquero," narrated each story and read the commercials for the sponsor, The Title Insurance and Trust Company of Los Angeles.

Beginning with the first episode, "Rancho San Rafael" on September 7, 1941, the writers, through the voice of Graham, assured listeners that the object of the series was "romance," a narrative dealing with characters bigger than life whose adventures were remote in time. Another goal of *The Romance of the Ranchos* was to tell listeners the history of the communities in which they lived. For Californians the old missions and the newer buildings built in the Spanish Colonial Revival style were the perfect setting for the adventures of early California, an environment which Californians shared with the residents of other southwestern states in the American West.

Mission and Spanish Revival styles came to California in 1915 when the architect Bertram Goodhue designed the exhibition buildings housing the Panama California Exposition in San Diego's Balboa Park. Soon thereafter the Revival style was incorporated into the design and construction of city halls and courthouses from Santa Barbara to Beverly Hills while its handcrafted beams, wrought ironwork and red roof tiles graced many new haciendas built for the stars of the silent motion picture era.

The characters who populated the era, rich and powerful ranch owners, their strong-willed women, hard-working ranch hands and noble Indians, treated by the priests like heathen children, were familiar to readers of Helen Hunt Jackson's 1884 novel *Ramona*, which she intended to be the *Uncle Tom's Cabin* of mistreated California Indians and to do for the Indians what Harriet Beecher Stowe had done for black slaves.

Instead, *Ramona* inspired a romantic myth that seemed to fit its early California setting well. The heroine, a half Scottish and half Indian orphan girl living in southern California shortly after the Mexican War, is raised in luxury by an indifferent foster mother who expects her to marry her own son, Felipe Moreno. Instead, Ramona falls in love with the son of the local Indian chief, a poor sheepherder named Alessandro. Her foster mother will not allow them to marry, so Ramona and Alessandro elope, and wander through California, suffering rejection and discrimination.

Jackson died of stomach cancer the year after the novel was published so she never enjoyed its eventual widespread acclaim. The novel was so popular it went through 300 printings, and gradually fiction became confused with reality. New Southern Pacific rail lines brought visitors to California who started looking for locations that appeared in the novel. When the railroad brought tourists to Rancho Camulos in Piru, CA, the old Spanish ranch house became the official "Home of Ramona." The Del Valle family, who owned the property associated with the novel, welcomed visitors and sold them wine and oranges with "The Home of Ramona" label. The myth was exploited in other locations, notably "Ramona's Marriage Place" in Old Town San Diego, which had to be rebuilt when the original Estudillo House was sold off piece by piece to tourists. A small adobe near Mission San Gabriel Arcangel, where Don Hugo Reid's wife, Doña Victoria, was trained to be a lady, was supposed to be "Ramona's Birthplace." An outdoor play created by Garret Holme opened in 1923 and is still performed in the "Ramona Bowl" in Hemet, CA.

Four motion picture versions of *Ramona* were produced between 1910 and 1936. In 1910, D.W. Griffith produced a two reel silent version of *Ramona* starring Mary Pickford. Donald Crisp directed a second silent film in 1916, which was praised by *The New York Times* for "excellent photography" and "good work" by the cast. The last silent version was directed by Edwin Carewe in 1928 and opened to good reviews. It starred Dolores Del Rio and Warner Baxter. Mabel Wayne composed the popular song "Ramona" for its promotional tour. By the time the sound version of *Ramona* appeared under the direction of Henry King in 1936, business owners and public officials were already naming schools, streets and theaters after the heroine and her lover. And, although *The New York Times* praised the film for its technicolor technology, a black-wigged Loretta Young as Ramona and movie and radio star Don Ameche as Alessandro could not convince movie goers they were destitute and hopeless lovers, especially when so many Americans were still suffering through the last years of the Great Depression.

Another film that resonated with *The Romance of the Ranchos* listeners was the 1940 film *The Mark of Zorro* which was set in early 19th century California. The cast was loaded with big name actors of the late 1930s: Tyrone Power and Linda Darnell as co-stars, with

Basil Rathbone, Gale Sondergaard and J. Edward Bromberg as villains. Tyrone Power's Don Diego Vega pretends to be the irresponsible rich man's son in the daytime while playing Robin Hood at night as El Zorro, slashing the letter "Z" in whatever surface is handy as his symbol of solidarity with the common folk. Pre-teens going on trick or treat adventures in the 1940s would often dress in black capes, masks and mustaches, wielding cardboard sabers, possibly seeking both justice and candy.

Fiction and fact had so merged in the public mind that California and the whole Southwest obtained a unique identity. The architecture of the missions and the Spanish Revival style got national attention as restoration projects began in the early 20th century. Railroad lines were expanding to bring visitors to blossoming real estate developments. But many who came were disappointed when they found out that "Ramona" was fiction and not fact.

The Buchanan advertising agency left nothing to chance when it launched a campaign to promote radio's *The Romance of the Ranchos* for its sponsor, the Title Insurance and Trust Company of Los Angeles. The series came on the air offering free copies of E. Palmer Conner's 40 page booklet, *The Romance of the Ranchos*, and when the series finished its first run in 1942, host Frank Graham offered a free map of all 52 of the ranchos covered in the series. The series was a big hit and ran another eight years over the Columbia Pacific Network, garnering the City College of New York award in 1945 for the "most effective institutional series" and *Billboard's* third place award in 1946 and 1948 for the best drama on a clear channel station.

In addition to Graham and LeMond, the series featured several other prominent West Coast actors: Pat McGeehan, Lou Merrill, Howard McNear, Herb Butterfield, and Byron Kane. Supporting cast included Jerry Farber, Ann Whitfield, Nestor Paiva, Lou Krugman, Marian Wilkins, Gail Bonney, Horace Murphy, Arthur Q. Bryan, Joseph Kearns, Jim Mather, Howard Duff, Barton Yarborough and Pedro de Cordoba who earlier had portrayed Father Salveierderra in the 1936 film *Ramona*.

Of the 35 episodes broadcast from September 7, 1941, to May 10, 1942, 18 told the history of the land grant ranchos of the early Californians and dealt with four specific social and political groups: the founding fathers and mothers, the interlopers, the speculators and finally the movers and shakers, or the people who brought what the writers of the series called "progress." While improvements in transportation were hailed in most episodes as bellwethers of progress, these efforts were summed up in "Transportation: From the Oxcart to the Airliner," the next to the last episode heard on April 10, 1942. Three additional episodes treated the social life of the rancheros, "Christmas at Mission San Gabriel" (December 24, 1941), the removal of native inhabitants, "Santa Catalina and the Channel Islands" (February 4, 1942), and the checkered history of Los Angeles, "El Pueblo de Nuestra Señora la Reina de los Angeles" (April 26, 1942).

The pattern followed by the first script, "Rancho San Rafael" (September 7, 1941), was typical: the founder of Rancho San Rafael, in the present age, Glendale and Burbank, was Jose Maria Verdugo who married Maria Lopes, obtained the required herd of cattle and received title from the Spanish governor of the department of California in 1784. His descendants become part of the comfortable class of ranch owners known as Californios. The Verdugo family held on to at least part of the land grant until 1904, when the Pacific Electric railway came to Glendale the same day as its last Don, Teodoro Verdugo, was on his death bed.

The second script emphasized another common outcome for the Dons. "Rancho Santa Gertrudes " (September 14, 1941), opened with speculator John G. Downey buying Santa Gertrudes for $3 an acre in 1859 from Lemuel Carpenter, the poor farmer who owned it. Downey later became governor of California and one of the biggest oil strikes in California history made his former ranch land some of the most valuable land in the state.

Many of the problems experienced by the Californios arose from the provinces' isolation from Mexico coupled with its proximity to the westward moving United States. While most Californios tried to be loyal to Mexico, they often accepted travelers and interlopers from Europe and America into their society, especially if they had resources and technical skills. And for the most part, when they asked for assistance from Mexican authorities, such requests were usually turned away. On the other hand, attempts by Mexican officials to bring the Californios into line were often crude and heavy handed.

Thirteen episodes of *The Romance of the Ranchos* were biographical studies, mostly of Europeans and Americans who came to Spanish and Mexican California when it was legally forbidden. Seven of these were men who made new lives for themselves, married into the existing ruling class, and became rancheros and/or businessmen. Two were interlopers: a privateer who eventually became a useful and productive citizen, and the other, a trapper, who was asked to leave but refused to go. Two were short-lived bandits who obtained semblances of legendary status.

The interlopers' lives were dramatized in "The Story of Joseph Chapman" (January 7, 1942), and "The True Life Story of Jedediah Strong Smith" (January 21, 1942). Chapman, a privateer caught and jailed for raiding ranchos, was later accepted as a useful citizen best known as the builder of the original Plaza church in the Pueblo of Los Angeles. Smith, a mountain man and beaver trapper who remarkably crossed the Mojave Desert in 1827, was told to leave California, but instead trapped beaver in the San Joaquin Valley and was arrested in San Jose. Bailed out by a sea captain, Smith continued northward with a small group and was caught in an Indian revolt in Oregon known as the Umqua uprising. Although little regarded after his death, years later he was hailed as one of the pathfinders of the westward movement

Tiburcio Vasquez and Joaquin Murrieta were well known California bandits. Vasquez called himself a "Californiano," a rebel who was dedicated to expelling Americans in the 1870s, 20 years after California became a state. As recounted in "The Tale of Tiburcio Vasquez" (November12,1941), he was trapped by a clever sheriff who hid a posse in an ordinary wagonload of supplies for revelers at a fandango.

"Joaquin Murrieta, The Infamous Robin Hood of the West" (March 29, 1942), was actually, "one of the most blood-thirsty robbers in history," what Frank Graham called "a dark chapter" in *The Romance of the Ranchos*. Murrieta's rage against Americans in the days of the 1849 gold rush was explained by a tragic incident. One day drunken miners raped and murdered his wife and lynched his brother. To take revenge, Murrieta murdered all who participated in the crimes and continued to rob wagon trains afterwards. He was hunted down and executed by self-appointed vigilantes called "California Rangers" in 1853.

Two "movers and shakers" chronicled in the series were Phineas Banning and William Mulholland. Banning was active in the 19th century in transportation and shipping, and

Mulholland planned and saw to the construction of southern California's two principal water aqueducts in the 20th century. Banning came to California from Delaware, so he named the newly established Los Angeles harbor port, "Wilmington" in 1868. He was featured in "Phineas Banning" (March 8, 1942). "William Mulholland and the Southland Water System" (March 22, 1942), told the story of a hydrologist who started out laying pipes that brought precious water to the drought ridden southland. It was his vision that guided the new Department of Water and Power that planned and built both the Owens Valley and Colorado River aqueducts.

"The True Story of Don Hugo Reid" (February 11, 1942), interwove the career of Dona Eulalia Perez de Giullen Marine, the cook, midwife and "keeper of the keys" at San Gabriel Mission and the life of Hugo Reid who left Scotland when his sweetheart Victoria found another love and journeyed to Los Angeles where he hoped to make a better life for himself as a storekeeper. When Reid arrived in Los Angles, Dona Eulalia unexpectedly introduced him to a beautiful Indian widow, also named Victoria, whose husband had died and left her with three children. Hugo became a Roman Catholic, married Victoria, and took out papers to become a naturalized Mexican citizen in 1839. Hugo and Victoria became an almost legendary couple among the Californios and their oldest daughter, Ignacia, was well-known for her intelligence and beauty. When Hugo lost his Rancho late in life, he devoted his time to the study and customs of the Cahuilla Indians and his essays were published in Los Angeles' first newspaper, *The Star*. Elements of Hugo Reid's story subsequently made their way into *Ramona* when Jackson decided to make her fictional heroine the daughter of a Scotsman and an Indian woman.

A fitting conclusion to the series was "The Carrillo Family" (May 10, 1942), which was both a celebration of and tribute to one of the earliest land grant families that continued to fascinate the public in the 1940s. The founder was Juan Ramundo Carrillo, a Spanish army captain who arranged for his descendants to marry into most of the other founding families. A proper romance was brewed up for Juan Antonio Carrillo, who later ran successfully for public office. Not the least of his descendants was Leo Carrillo, his great grandson, who in 1942 was not only a motion picture celebrity but also a public spokesman for many charitable causes of that period.

Sources: Audio copies of *Romance of the Ranchos*; Dunning, *On the Air*; Jackson; James; *Billboard*, November 20,1948; *Long Beach Independent*, November 4, 1941.

ROMANCES OF THE WESTERN RANGE

KARL SCHADOW *and* JACK FRENCH

Originally titled *Sage Brush Heaven* on station KLX and aired from Oakland, CA, this series was written by John H. Hamlin, a prolific author of many western novels and short stories appearing in the pulp magazines of that era. The total run of the show was ten half hour episodes, from April 30 to July 2, 1931. The titles of the programs indicate it was long on humor and romance and short on adventure: "Buckaroos and Bonnets," "Plumb Reckless," and "Cupid's Corral." Ursula Faucit was the director and her cast included Walter Cunha, Elizabeth Mills, Thelma Martell, Celia Parsons, Ruth Lyons, Edward Nick, Stanley Farrar, Andrew De Cot, and Robert Perkins.

Sources: *Oakland Tribune*, April 30, 1931, and July 2, 1931.

ROUNDUP TRAIL

KARL SCHADOW *and* JACK FRENCH

Also known as the *Ken Maynard Show*, this quarter hour juvenile serial aired Monday, Wednesday and Friday at 6:45 P.M. from station KFWB, Hollywood, CA in the mid–1930s. The program opened and closed with sagebrush music. Film cowboy Ken Maynard did his very best to breathe life into the program's somewhat stereotypical plots. Stock characters in the scripts by Owen Crump included: Chink, Pete, an African American cook, and two children visiting from the big city. Roundup Soda sponsored the program and boosted sales by offering Ken's "Buckeroo Club" membership card and various western items to kids who mailed in bottle caps from the four flavors that Roundup sold. Despite its limitations, *Variety* termed the series "For a juvenile program, period is usually good and handled intelligently."

Source: *Variety*, July 25, 1936, p. 9.

THE ROY ROGERS SHOW

IVAN G. SHREVE, JR.

NETWORK: Mutual: 1944 to 1945 and 1948 to 1951; NBC: 1946 to 1947 and 1951 to 1955
FORMAT: Half hour, weekly (25 minutes from August 1952 to December 1953)
DURATION OF RUN: November 21, 1944, to July 21, 1955
SPONSOR: Goodyear 1944 to 1945; Miles Laboratories 1946 to 1947; Quaker Oats 1948
   to 1951; General Mills 1951 to 1953; Chrysler 1954 to 1955
AUDIO COPIES EXTANT: 89
SCRIPTS ARCHIVED: SPERDVAC; http://www.genericradio.com

Only in America could a Cincinnati, OH, boy born Leonard Franklin Slye rise from the humblest of "flatland" beginnings to be crowned "King of the Cowboys." The monarch of the sagebrush in this particular instance is better known to legions of western aficionados as Roy Rogers, whose successful career in film, radio, TV and recorded media made him one of the most instantly recognizable and marketed celebrities of his era.

With his film and recording careers in full swing in the 1940s, one thing Roy Rogers didn't have was a weekly radio show — but he rectified that in the fall of 1944. His rival Gene Autry had already started broadcasting for CBS beginning in 1940 with *Gene Autry's Melody Ranch*, and while Roy wasn't a stranger to performing before a microphone (he had been on radio as far back as 1931 as a member of Uncle Tom Murray's Hollywood Hillbillies), he did suffer the occasional bout of "mike fright." His radio program for Goodyear ("The greatest name in rubber, Goodyear, invites you to meet America's greatest western star, Roy Rogers") premiered on Mutual Thursday nights at 8:30 P.M. on November 21, 1944.

Rogers was born on November 5, 1911, the only son of Andrew ("Andy") and Mattie Womack Slye in a section of Cincinnati where Riverfront Stadium now stands; Rogers joked in later years that he had been born on second base. Andy made his living working in a shoe factory, but in his quest for a better life for his family, he purchased a farm in Duck Run, a small community 12 miles north of Portsmouth. Here the young Roy got his first taste of what it was like to be in the saddle, though his horse riding expertise wouldn't really blossom until his Hollywood years. He also learned to play the guitar and mandolin while singing in the church choir and calling the occasional square dance.

Both of Roy's parents had musical inclinations; his father had once been a professional entertainer on a river steamer, as did the Rogers sisters — a trait not uncommon in rural communities at that time when entertainment was generally self-made. Roy and his family moved back to Cincinnati when he was 17, and he joined his father in the shoe factory. Andy had never completely abandoned this line of work, toiling in a Portsmouth shoe plant to supplement the meager income from the family farm.

The family's decision to set out for California in 1930 would play a large role in the future career path of Roy Rogers; though they would soon discover that the trip west was not unlike the hardships experienced in John Steinbeck's *The Grapes of Wrath.* Roy began to supplement what work he got fruit picking and driving a

Roy Rogers, cowboy star of motion pictures, television and radio (courtesy American Radio Archives at Thousand Oaks Library, Thousand Oaks, California).

gravel truck with the singing and guitar playing skills he had honed in his Ohio days. He teamed up with a cousin, Stanley, to form a group known as the Slye Brothers, and was content to play mostly "pass the hat" gatherings. Later his sister Mary convinced him to enter an Inglewood, CA, talent contest that got him noticed, and hired, by a promoter for the western music group, the Rocky Mountaineers. And although the group's fortunes were not any rosier than those of the Slye Brothers, it was through his work with the Rocky Mountaineers that Rogers was able to make the acquaintance of Bob Nolan and Tim Spencer, two musicians who would later comprise, with Roy, the nucleus of the successful Sons of the Pioneers.

It was as a member of the Pioneers that Roy Rogers got his show business break; the Pioneers began to have chart success with hits such as "Cool Water" and "Tumbling Tumbleweeds," and with that fame they were often in demand to provide background music for movie westerns. Roy and the Pioneers worked a great deal in the B-movies churned out by Republic Studios. There Roy was alternately billed as both "Len Slye" and "Dick Weston." Republic featured the studio's bread-and-butter cowboy, Gene Autry (*The Old Corral, The Big Show, The Old Barn Dance*).

In 1938, when Autry walked out on his movie contract after a dispute with Republic Studios' head, Herbert J. Yates, Roy got the opportunity to audition as Gene's replacement and was soon cast as the lead in *Under Western Stars,* his first starring picture. And because his real name, Leonard Slye, sounded more like one of the villainous bankers that frequently turned up in his pictures, the studio renamed him "Roy Rogers." The surname was a tribute to the late humorist Will Rogers and Roy for its alliterative quality. Rogers would go on to headline 87 B-western movies for the studio between 1938 and 1951, formulaic fare geared primarily to the Saturday matinee juvenile crowd that was his fan base. And yet Roy certainly could handle the occasional serious dramatic foray, witnessed by his change-of-pace villainy in John Wayne's 1940 film, *Dark Command*.

The kid from Cincinnati legally changed his name to "Roy Rogers" in 1942 and acquired an additional title the following year, "King of the Cowboys" when his Republic rival Autry went off to fight in World War II. Roy even starred in a film bearing that title in 1943. Rogers escaped the draft through the luck of the lottery, and while Gene did his service, Roy lived up to his new designation by becoming the number one moneymaking western star from 1943–1954 according to the *Motion Picture Herald*. He also had his share of loyal subjects; nearly 2,000 fan clubs sprung up at

Dale Evans, wife of Roy Rogers, who performed with him on radio, television and in the movies (courtesy Library of American Broadcasting, University of Maryland, College Park).

that time to buy Roy Rogers action figures, comic books, toy guns, western clothing, novels and play sets. Rogers, who saw much of the income from his films, not to mention his public appearances, swallowed up by Republic, was savvy enough to sign a contract in 1940 that gave him the merchandising rights to his name, voice and likeness. It was a smart business decision; Rogers was soon second only to Walt Disney in merchandise that bore his name.

Roy's Goodyear-sponsored radio show was quite similar to ***Gene Autry's Melody Ranch***, featuring jovial banter around the campfire, many musical numbers from Roy, vocalist Pat Friday, the Sons of the Pioneers and Perry Botkin conducting the Goodyear Orchestra. In addition, there would be a brief dramatic or comedic skit. Surviving broadcasts include guests such as veteran radio actress Sara Berner and movie character actor Porter Hall. *The Roy Rogers Show* left the airwaves after one season on Mutual but resurfaced a year later on NBC as a 9 P.M. Saturday evening program sponsored by Miles Laboratories, which promoted its Alka-Seltzer and a host of other healthcare remedies.

By this time in his radio career Roy was joined by two personalities familiar to his fans from his movies. George "Gabby" Hayes, who had been Rogers' loyal sidekick since their first teaming in 1939's *Southward Ho*, would serve as the program's comic relief; a garrulous, grizzled old codger with a large reservoir of fabricated stories and tall tales. The other co-star was actress-singer Dale Evans (Frances Octavia Smith, born October 31, 1912, in Texas) with whom Roy became acquainted when she played his leading lady in the 1944 motion picture *The Cowboy and the Senorita*. Dale didn't always appear in Roy's movie westerns; he was a bit flexible when it came to cinematic romantic interests, but she would soon be by his side over the airwaves, and in real life as well. Rogers' second wife, Arline, had died shortly after giving birth to their son Roy, Jr. ("Dusty") in 1946. After a whirlwind courtship that culminated with his proposal to Evans during a rodeo at Chicago Stadium, Roy and Dale became "Mr. and Mrs. King of the Cowboys" (her fourth marriage) on December 31, 1947. However, Dale decreed that her title of sagebrush royalty was to be "Queen of the West."

The Roy Rogers Show continued its popularity on the airwaves despite taking another year long respite before resurrecting itself on Sunday evenings for Mutual on August 29, 1948, for Quaker Oats or "the Giant of the Cereals," as announcer Art Balinger informed listeners with hyperbolic gusto. The series had discarded its earlier variety show beginnings and transformed itself into a solid half hour of juvenile western adventure, with many of the show's plots involving Roy heroically tangling with outlaws in the form of cattle rustlers, bank robbers, etc. who would dare jeopardize the star's livelihood running the Double-R-Bar Ranch in picturesque Paradise Valley.

Gabby was on hand to help out with the necessary comic relief, and Dale was certainly the target of Roy's romantic endeavors — though the kids in radio land suspected that it was Rogers' golden palomino, Trigger, who was the apple of Roy's eye. Trigger, originally known as Golden Cloud, was purchased by Rogers in 1932 from a rental stable and taught a repertoire of nearly 50 tricks, including simple arithmetic and signing an "X" with a pencil. Roy's trusty steed soon became known as "The Smartest Horse in the Movies," and enjoyed the same cinematic popularity as his master — allowing him to appear on the radio series alongside Roy, Dale, and Gabby and becoming a frequent player in the action. In later shows, Roy introduced his faithful dog Bullet, though his intelligence didn't quite measure up to Trigger's.

The two-fisted western heroics on *The Roy Rogers Show* were once described by *The Christian Science Monitor* as "a little song, a little riding, a little shooting, and a girl to be saved from hazard." It was great fun for the younger cowpokes in the listening audience, but most of the material, scripted at various times by Ray Wilson, Ralph Rose, and Fran Van Hartesveldt, rarely rose above the plots prevalent in the movies Roy was grinding out for Republic at that same time. Though the novelty of having Dale in charge of the neighboring ranch in the Quaker Oats shows might have seemed a little progressive to some, she existed primarily as the damsel in distress for Roy and Gabby to rescue each week, or, if not her, then "her father, or her brother," as a reviewer for *Radio Life* observed in 1948. As the series soldiered on in the 1950s, Dale eventually got out of the ranching business and started running the Eureka Café in nearby Mineral City. Still, all of the action on *The Roy Rogers Show* would always end in time for a song from Roy and Dale, with frequent accompaniment in the Quaker Oats years by Foy Willing and the Riders of the Purple Sage.

Roy Rogers was the last of the "big three" movie cowboys to establish a beachhead in the new medium of television: William "Hopalong Cassidy" Boyd made inroads in 1949 with repeats of his old feature films although his actual TV series didn't start until 1952 and Gene Autry followed in July of 1950. When Rogers made it known that he was anxious to get in on the action, even to the point of producing his show in the same manner as Autry, Republic's Yates thought that television was a passing fad; but that didn't dissuade Yates from selling Roy's movie backlog to television to generate revenue. Determined not to see his movies showcased on the small screen where they would be susceptible to advertisements which he disapproved of (cigarette commercials, for example), Roy filed a temporary restraining order against Republic to block the sale of his films to television.

This legal skirmish led to the performer's departure from Republic Studios; his last film was 1951's *Pals of the Golden West*. The court battle also jeopardized his business relationship with Quaker Oats, who not only stopped sponsorship of his radio program, but refused to consider paying the bills on his proposed television series. Roy, however, was covered on the television venue; he had received $100,000 in front money from NBC to start production on a video version of *The Roy Rogers Show*. General Foods agreed to take over the sponsorship of both the television and radio *Roy Rogers Show*, provided Roy prevailed in his legal proceedings against Republic. But the General Foods people must have had enormous confidence in Roy's legal team because the judge in the trial didn't hand down his permanent injunction against the sale until October 18, 1951, and Rogers' radio program was already on the air for Post cereals two weeks prior. Republic appealed the ruling and the judgment was overturned in 1954, but by that time Roy was riding high in both mediums, so it mattered very little.

To the strains of "It's Roundup Time on the Double-R Bar," Roy continued his radio adventures with Dale and Trigger, defeating outlaws and ne'er-do-wells in the span of a weekly 30 minute session over NBC Friday nights. Bullet, a German shepherd, also became a member of the cast, but sidekick Gabby was replaced by actor Forrest Lewis as Jonah Wilde, a trail scout who prevaricated in the same manner as the esteemed Hayes. Lewis was actually the second actor to replace Gabby; Horace Murphy had played a codger named Clackity during the series' final Quaker Oats season.

In the fall of 1952, Pat Brady joined the radio cast as Roy's comical associate, a role he was already playing on Roy's television show where he was known for his wacky antics and chauffeuring of a rattletrap jeep affectionately dubbed Nellybelle. Brady had known Rogers since Roy's stint with the Sons of the Pioneers; he replaced Roy in that group and appeared in many of the Cowboy King's Republic films, often as zany ranch cook, Sparrow Biffle.

Other notable changes in the lineup of *The Roy Rogers Show* regulars included the addition of the vocal group, The Whippoorwills, and later The Mellomen. A new closing song, "Happy Trails" was added; it was penned by Dale, supposedly composed in 20 minutes, for their television program. It eventually moved up to the beginning of the radio show as well, and was thereafter immortalized as the Rogers' theme song.

The Roy Rogers Show was one of the earliest radio series to be transcribed to accommodate Roy's hectic moviemaking and personal appearance schedules. The show continued on NBC in the 1952-1953 season, moving to Thursday nights at 8 P.M. for the rest of its radio run, except for a brief stint on Tuesdays in August and September of 1953. For the most part, it maintained a half hour presence with the exception of two broadcast runs, August 28, 1952, to August 30, 1953, and October 1 to December 24, 1953, when it was trimmed down to 25 minutes.

Beginning January 28, 1954, *The Roy Rogers Show* gained a new sponsor in Chrysler, touting Dodge automobiles and trucks. This relationship would last until the series ended its radio run on July 21, 1955. The Chrysler sponsorship brought a small change in the show's format. The musical contributions were held to a minimum and the plots began to take on a mystery thriller element not uncommon to detective shows at that time. Some of the program's later shows dealt with such plot lines as investigating a stolen stamp collection and breaking a criminal ring which used railroad refrigerator cars to smuggle diamonds from Mexico. Vintage radio historians suspect that the series' shift may have been an attempt to attract a more adult audience, but it also may have been the inspiration of writers who had grown weary of doing the same old cattle rustling or bank robbing plots that was previously *The Roy Rogers Show*'s forte.

Roy, Dale and the gang called it quits in 1955 as far as radio was concerned, though the television version of *The Roy Rogers Show* would continue until June 23, 1957, and then settled into retirement in both syndicated reruns and as a Saturday morning kid staple from 1961 to 1964. The " King of the Cowboys" and the "Queen of the West" took a stab at a musical variety series in the fall of 1962 in *The Roy Rogers and Dale Evans Show*, but the program didn't last beyond a single season. From that point on, Roy and Dale were content to rest on their laurels and limit themselves to guest appearances in movies and TV shows, with Roy making the occasional foray into country music, with song hits like "Lovenworth" and the wonderfully nostalgic "Hoppy, Gene and Me."

In its approximately ten year run on radio, *The Roy Rogers Show* had no loftier pretensions other than to entertain its target audience, and present a hero who represented the virtues of honesty and integrity, something that its star also did in his personal life, and quite well. It's no wonder that with only a few exceptions, Roy's characters in movies, film and TV were all named Roy Rogers. So it was essential that a man who aspired to be a role model for young, impressionable folks practice what he preached since his name was the product. Even if his depiction of the West strayed from the historical record from time to time, he gave his audiences what they wanted: a true hero in a white hat. Roy Rogers was never more sincere when he signed off each radio broadcast with "Goodbye, good luck, and may the Good Lord take a likin' to ya."

Even his passing in 1998 did nothing to temper the enthusiasm of his fan base. In July 2010, the executors of his Branson, MO, museum auctioned off much of the memorabilia that had been warehoused there and the total receipts of the items came to nearly $3 million.

Sources: Audio copies of *Roy Rogers Show*; Brooks; Cox, *Radio Crime Fighters*; Dunning, *On the Air*; Dunning, *Tune In*; Harmon, *Great Radio Heroes*; Hurst; Katz; Lenius; MacDonald, *Don't Touch*; Maltin; Rothell; www.Christies.com (Roy Rogers museum auction); www.RadioGoldindex.com; www.ThrillingDaysofYesteryearArchives.Blogspot.com; www.WesternClippings.com.

Sage Brush Heaven see *Romances of the Western Range*

Sagebrush Dentist see *Dr. Frackleton's Stories of Cheyenne & Crow Indians*

Santa Fe Trail see *The Lone Indian*

SAUNDERS OF THE CIRCLE X

JACK FRENCH *and* DAVID S. SIEGEL

NETWORK: NBC Blue (West Coast only)
FORMAT: Half hour, weekly
DURATION OF RUN: October 2, 1941, to January 22, 1942
SPONSOR: Sustained
AUDIO COPIES EXTANT: 1
SCRIPTS ARCHIVED: Undetermined

This Thursday evening 30 minute western dramatization was produced in station KGO, the NBC affiliate in San Francisco, and aired only on the West Coast. The linchpin of the series was Samuel Dickson, whom we know wrote all the scripts, and probably also directed and produced the series as he was the head of programming at KGO. Although approximately 16 episodes were broadcast, they were all done live, and the only surviving audio copy is episode #7 which aired November 13, 1941.

The evidence provided in this one program demonstrates that this was not a typical western radio show. It actually started off like a soap opera, with the unnamed announcer summarizing what had transpired in prior episodes on this Arizona ranch. Singapore Bill Saunders was an unlikely character to be the foreman of a cattle ranch for, as he boasted, "I'm a seafaring man and spent most of my life at sea."

His navy vernacular was sometimes not understood by the cowpunchers under his supervision and it occasionally required a translation. In one instance, Saunders ordered his men to "drop anchor." They were briefly confused until one of them explained to the others, "That's jist sailor lingo; he means git off yore horse."

Plot segments of this sole surviving program ranged from poignant to almost silly. In one scene, an old ranch owner, cruelly blinded by a past explosion, suddenly regains his sight in the tender arms of his daughter. Yet in another scene, a cowpoke from the Circle X is inexplicably trapped in quick sand — in the front yard of another ranch. At the conclusion of this episode, the villain leads 20 of his men into the night to walk to a nearby creek where they are to "beat the living daylights out of" three unarmed cowhands of the Circle X who are trespassing.

The sound effects on this show were good, but not great. Infrequently they were confusing wherein a sound was heard distinctly but not explained in the dialogue. Sound effects, both manual (e.g., hoofbeats) and transcribed (e.g., explosions), were utilized in this series. Musical bridges and the main theme were adequate.

The cast consisted primarily of what was known at station KGO as the National Players, a semi-repertory company of San Francisco based radio actors. Singapore Bill, the title lead, was portrayed by John Cuthbertson. Backing him up in this episode were Everett Glass as Joseph Dinnell the villain, Bert Horton as Hank Pepper, Lu Tobin as Thomas Mott the elderly rancher, and Bob Hudson as Pinto, the cheerful cowpoke.

Others in the supporting cast were Bob Tobin and Jack Kirkwood. Ann Langendorf was the voice of Jimmy, Mott's daughter. In her other professional roles, she was the spokesperson for Langendorf Bread, and presumably part of that famous baking family. While Langendorf Bakeries never sponsored *Saunders of the Circle X*, the company was the sponsor for another western frontier radio series, **Red Ryder**, and much later, in the 1950s, it sponsored the *Hopalong Cassidy* television series.

Sources: Audio copy of *Saunders of the Circle X*; Dunning, *On the Air*; Hickerson, *4th Revised*; Schneider.

THE SCARLET CLOAK

JACK FRENCH *and* DAVID S. SIEGEL

NETWORK: None
FORMAT: Half hour
DURATION OF RUN: None
SPONSOR: None
AUDIO COPIES: 1 (audition disk, February 15, 1950)
SCRIPTS ARCHIVED: Unknown

In 1950, advertising dollars and audience choices were beginning to switch from radio to television, especially on the two coasts. This audition recording of a possible radio show was apparently produced to accomplish two goals: 1) obtain sponsorship for a television version, and 2) launch the acting career of longtime radio announcer, Wendell Niles. Although the program was done very well, it failed in both of its objectives since it never reached the video screen and Niles remained an announcer.

Producing a television pilot was an expensive endeavor so there were occasional attempts to "sell" a television series on the basis of a radio audition recording. The announcer for *The Scarlet Cloak* made clear the intent of this audition in his middle program break:

> Let's take just a minute now to mention one or two of the many advantages that this program provides for an astute advertiser. It's a western-type story utilizing the basic success pattern of galloping horses, gun fights, and high adventure. It gives you a dramatic, exciting radio program, but is even more suited to a filmed television series. The performers have been selected for their ability and experience and also for their appearance, so that the television picture will bring you most of the same people you hear on this record. As you listen to the second act, imagine if you will, a television screen where you can watch this believable, exciting, romantic man of action, the wearer of the scarlet cloak and rapier as he rides against the evil to bring hope to the oppressed.

The scenario of this program was basically the story of Zorro with just enough differences to avoid any charges of copyright infringement. Niles played Brad Carver (an obvious surname for a man whose primary weapon was a rapier) who takes over his dead father's secret identity of El Diablo, a fighter for justice in old Monterey. Wearing a scarlet cloak, a black sombrero and a rapier, he gallops forth to challenge all evildoers. The only person who knows that Carver is El Diablo is his Mexican servant, Sancho, who still calls

Carver by his childhood nickname, Bradito. The love interest in the story is Maria Alvarez, the daughter of a wealthy land owner.

Overall, this is a solid production. The script by Joel Murcott moves along at a good pace and all the sound effects are both convincing and well-timed. Dee Englebach, director, and Vic Hunter, producer, got the most out of their cast, including Paul Frees and Gerald Mohr, as well as their production staff. Lyn Murray handled the music well and the use of a solitary guitar for most of the musical bridges was very effective.

But despite its strengths, there were no takers from among television executives and the series never got beyond the audition stage. Wendell Niles, who had been the announcer on over a dozen network shows (*When a Girl Marries, The Bob Hope Show, Adventures of Philip Marlowe, Hollywood Star Time, Fitch Bandwagon*, etc.) would remain an announcer and never became an actor.

It's possible that *The Scarlet Cloak*, as a Zorro clone, never became a television show because some in the industry knew that the agent for Johnston McCulley (Zorro's creator) had been offering the television and movie rights for Zorro since 1950. Eventually in 1953, Walt Disney signed a contract with that agent to bring Zorro to the video screen. However, with Disney's usual lengthy preparation, his Zorro, with Guy Williams in the lead, did not reach network screens until the 1957-1958 season. By that time, *The Scarlet Cloak* had been long forgotten.

Sources: Audio copy of *Scarlet Cloak*; Dunning, *On the Air*; Curtis.

SEAL OF THE DON
JACK FRENCH *and* DAVID S. SIEGEL

NETWORK: Syndicated
FORMAT: 15 minutes, daily
DURATION OF RUN: 1930s
SPONSOR: Hancock Oil, plus local sponsors
AUDIO COPIES EXTANT: 2
SCRIPTS ARCHIVED: Undetermined

The Conquest Alliance Company of New York City, which marketed dozens of transcribed shows in the 1930s, made no secret that *Seal of the Don* was its attempt to tap into the popularity of the Zorro character. In its catalog, Conquest boasted "the story closely parallels that of Douglas Fairbanks' most successful picture, *The Mark of Zorro*." But while the radio series did feature a sword-wielding hero fighting Mexican oppression in the 1800s in California, its Don Hancock was no Zorro.

The original Zorro debuted in a five installment series, "The Curse of Capistrano" which began in the August 9, 1919, edition of the pulp fiction magazine *All-Story Weekly*. Created by Johnston McCulley, a former newspaper man from Illinois who became a successful and prolific freelance writer, this masked hero achieved great popularity very quickly. One year after his initial appearance, Douglas Fairbanks, Sr. portrayed Zorro (and his alter ego, Don Diego) in a popular silent film, *The Mark of Zorro*, which Fairbanks also wrote and produced. Coincidentally, Fairbanks and McCulley were born the same year, 1883.

Radio scriptwriter Eugene J. Carman, probably under orders not to infringe on the Zorro character or movie's copyright protection, dropped the idea of the secret identity of the avenger. Every character in the series knew that Don Hancock (shamelessly named after the primary sponsor) was fighting the Mexican government forces, led by evil Captain Garcia, who were oppressing the local peons as well as the resident Americanos. Instead of a carved "Z" on any flat surface, Don Hancock's trademark was a seal embedded in the hilt of his dagger.

The series was produced for Conquest by the Charles H. Mayne Company and directed by Jack Joy. He managed to cast several good actors, who would later become prominent network names: Gale Gordon, True Boardman, and Barbara Jean Luddy. Joy filled out the supporting cast with Charles Carroll, Mora Martin, Theodore Osborne, Owen Crump, Eugene Carman, and Cyrus Kendall.

Syndicated shows nearly always used music in public domain in order to escape having to make royalty payments and *Seal of the Don* was no exception. The theme, "Tango in D," a classical piece composed by Issac Manuel Albéniz (1860–1909) of Spain and played on a guitar, ran for at least a minute at both the beginning and the end of each episode (for the overlay of commercials). Although Conquest had given the name of the original sponsor (Hancock) to the leading character, the company was unabashed in marketing the series to any radio station looking for a modest priced western. They advertised that the minimum contract was for 39 episodes, which was the total they had recorded.

The overall scenario and individual episode plots (based on audio of episodes in private collections) were cumbersome, trying to combine adventure, mystery, and romance. Story lines included armed robberies, illegal searches, a stolen painting, mysterious visitors, unexpected murders, jailing of the innocent, military aggression, and escapes from jail. The Mexican characters spoke English with pseudo-Spanish accents while the Americanos (including Don Hancock) sprinkled their conversation with Spanish words: sí, gracias, señor, bueno, caballero, carumba, and vino. For some unknown reason, they always bid farewell by saying "Vaya con Dios" (Go with God) rather than the traditional Spanish "adios" or "hasta la vista."

Nearly everyone, including some of the peons, spoke in a stilted formal manner, e.g., "His death shall not go unavenged; I leave at once." The love interest between Don Hancock and the governor's daughter, Dolores, was a minor thread in the scenario throughout the 39 episodes. Youthful listeners of the program were probably grateful for that.

Sources: Audio copies of *Seal of the Don*; Curtis; Franklin; Conquest Alliance Company, Inc. New York, NY, undated (circa 1935) catalogue of syndicated shows.

The Sheriff see ***Death Valley Days***

THE SINGING BANDIT

Doug Hopkinson

NETWORK: Syndicated
FORMAT: 15 minutes, weekly on Monday afternoons
DURATION OF RUN: February 1939 to March 1939
SPONSOR: Unknown
AUDIO COPIES EXTANT: 7
SCRIPTS ARCHIVED: Undetermined

Each *Singing Bandit* program began with the sound of thundering hoofbeats, accompanied by gunshots, and the cry of "Aquí Vengo!" three times in succession. This syndicated series featured stories of a Mexican vaquero during the time of the California gold rush. However, the locations of these stories varied widely, from New Mexico to St. Louis to the Redwood Forest as well as on rancheros, in the desert and in mining towns. The plots usually dealt with murder, robbery and natural disasters.

The cast, as listed on the audition disk, included: Jay Novello (title role), Marjorie Bainbridge (feminine lead), Tristram Coffin, Bob Burleson, Carmencita (Latin-American soprano), Alfredo Garmo (Castillian tenor), Elena Wolfskill, Luke Berry, Shorty Malone, Banjo Harry and Black Beaver. Music for the series was written by José Arias and performed by 12 troubadours. All of the shows were written and produced by Robert E. Callahan and directed by R. Calvert Hawes. Callahan also had these same duties with another radio series, **The Lone Indian**.

The daring Mexican vaquero was known as The Spider to some and The Singing Bandit to others, but his actual name was Pancho Gonzalez. He dressed in black velvet, had gold-plated revolvers and rode a black horse with a silver beaded saddle. A secondary character, a half-breed Indian who called himself The Red Spider caused many problems for Pancho by robbing and killing and then claiming to be Pancho Gonzales, The Singing Bandit. This gave Pancho the undeserved reputation of being an outlaw.

The programs all followed a simple formula. Pioneers on a trail found themselves in troublesome circumstances, and although Pancho was suspected or accused of a crime, he helped them in the end. Some programs featured a beautiful, young woman, who was of course attracted to the hero. A few programs featured musical numbers of ranchero type music and richly toned solos and duets sung in both Spanish and English, while other episodes had no singing at all.

The Singing Bandit had drama, adventure and romance, all seasoned with southwestern flavoring and justice in the end. It was much more fictional in nature than Callahan's previous radio programs which were based more on actual history and had something factual in them to teach the listener. Indians rarely appeared in these shows, although one episode featured a fierce Indian chief. Nearly every program had Mexican characters, ranchero music, and some Spanish language.

A few of the programs were apparently all music, as suggested by their titles such as "California Fiesta." Other titles point to criminal activity and presumably the guilty were brought to justice by the hero. These would be: "Stage Holdup," "Death Fire," and "Three Americanos in Calaboosa."

This series was very similar to Callahan's **Santa Fe Trail** in that both programs told stories of frontier pioneers, their caravans, and the troubles they experienced. But they differed in format since there was no narrator in *The Singing Bandit*; these programs explained themselves without the presence of a narrator. Another obvious difference was the reduction of Indian involvement in the stories compared to **Santa Fe Trail**, where Indians were prominent.

There was another connection between *The Singing Bandit* and **Santa Fe Trail**: In September, 1938, *Variety* reported that Anthony Rivers was signed to do the lead of The Singing Bandit in the syndicated series **Santa Fe Trail** which was being produced by Bob Callahan. This suggested that Callahan's early plans were to introduce this new character in his **Santa Fe Trail** series, but later decided to spin it off as a separate series entirely — and apparently with Rivers.

The Singing Bandit first aired on radio station KMTR, Los Angeles, Monday, February 13, 1939, in a 3:00 P.M. slot. It continued in the same Monday afternoon slot through March 27, 1939, but then was cancelled. According to information obtained from the audition disk, there were 26 programs produced with 100 planned for production. However, only seven broadcast listings have been confirmed and only seven shows are extant today. It is interesting to note that four weeks after the last broadcast of *The Singing Bandit*, KMTR began broadcasting *Indian Trails* (a previous Callahan radio production) and this after a long absence from the airwaves of 16 months. The reasons behind the short life of *The Singing Bandit* remain as yet unexplained.

Sources: Audio copies of *Singing Bandit*, *Lone Indian*, and *Santa Fe Trail*; Callahan; *Variety*, September 30, 1938.

THE SINGING MARSHAL

JACK FRENCH

NAMES: *The Singing Marshal, Curley Bradley, the Singing Marshal*
NETWORK: Mutual
FORMAT: Half hour, usually weekly
DURATION OF RUN: July 1950 to December 1951
SPONSOR: Sustaining
AUDIO COPIES EXTANT: 2 (and one partial)
SCRIPTS ARCHIVED: American Radio Archives

When Ralston Purina ended its long term sponsorship of the ***Tom Mix*** radio program in June 1950, the company would not permit Mutual to resume airing it as a sustainer. So Mutual merely reformatted it as *The Singing Marshal* and kept it on the airwaves from July 1950 to December 1951. Although it evolved somewhat over those 18 months, the new program was virtually a carbon copy of the old one.

In the original series, Joe "Curley" Bradley played Tom Mix, U. S. Marshal and owner of the T-M Bar Ranch in the modern West. His sidekick was Sheriff Mike Shaw, the voice of Leo Curley, and the comedy relief on the program was a stereotyped African American ranch cook, Wash, portrayed by Caucasian actor, Forrest Lewis. But on *The Singing Marshal*, Bradley got to use his own name; he was a U. S. Marshal and owner of the Circle B Ranch. This time Leo Curley played Red Rivers, the foreman on the ranch, and the humorous cook was Prosperity, again the voice of Forrest Lewis.

To complete the cycle, announcer Don Gordon and producer/director Mary Afflick filled the identical roles on *The Singing Marshal* that they had on the ***Tom Mix*** show. There were also family ties; Bradley and Afflick in real life were then husband and wife. Most of the supporting cast and production crew at Chicago station WGN where the series was produced had been regulars on the ***Tom Mix*** program.

The series was transcribed and the Mutual affiliates could run it any day in any time slot of their choice. Some stations broadcast it only once a week; others aired it two or three times weekly. While it usually aired in the juvenile-friendly period of 4 to 6 P.M. (during which time Mutual also aired ***Bobby Benson*** and ***Straight Arrow***) some affiliates broadcasted *The Singing Marshal* only on Saturday mornings. When the show ended in December 1951, several stations had it scheduled at 8 P.M. on Sunday nights.

The program's strengths and weaknesses can be assessed based on the three surviving, undated, audio copies. They are the full half hour each of "Big Jim Bradley" and "The Bewildered Banker" and the first 15 minutes of "Black Arrow Canyon." Jim Bradley's story tells of this famous fictional lawman and his shootout with the outlaw, Bad Danny Dean, in which both men die. This leaves Curley, a youngster, and his widowed mother, to mourn violence and killing. In "The Bewildered Banker," a con man and a bank president hatch a plot in which two other men rob the bank. But the bank officer and his co-conspirator reap the ill-gotten gains — until Curley Bradley exposes their nefarious plot.

The plot is set in motion in "Black Arrow Canyon" when an elderly prospector is shot to death and his killers try to destroy the corpse under a stampeding cattle herd. The trail of the outlaws leads Bradley and Rivers to a dead end canyon where years ago a large band of renegade Indians, chased by the U.S. cavalry, disappeared in the canyon without a trace.

All three of these programs are well paced and possess mystery, excitement, and humor. The sound effects are executed skillfully while the organist (probably Harold Turner) does commendable work with the musical themes and bridges. Every program begins with the announcer inviting listeners to hear: "This western adventure with the champion of range land justice, whose bullets sing as true as the songs from his heart."

Many talented Chicago actors filled out the supporting roles during the run of this series, including Maurice Copeland, Ken Nordine and Muriel Bremner, with Cornelius Peeples in the juvenile roles. Two prominent actors, who had the lead role in other shows portrayed occasional minor characters in *The Singing Marshal*: Everett Clarke, who briefly played *The Whistler*, and Jim Goss, the long-term voice of Uncle Jim Fairfield on *Jack Armstrong*.

The stereotyped character of Prosperity was phased out and the new ranch cook was a no-nonsense grandmother, Acey, played by Viola Burwick. She was as comfortable firing a six-gun as she was pulling baked bread out of the oven; her constant bantering with Red Rivers must have been enjoyed by the listeners. In the announcer's role, John Mallows occasionally substituted for Don Gordon. At least two different writers contributed over the 18 month run: Kay Chase, who began on Chicago soap operas, and John Kelley, a former radio director of *Family Theater*.

Despite the title of the series, the marshal didn't do much singing. Bradley would briefly hum his signature tune when closing in to capture the bad guy. If a script ran short on time, Bradley might offer a brief song to tag on at the end. But the excitement, mystery, and humor of the show were the real emphasis, just as they had been on the **Tom Mix** show.

Sources: Audio copies of *Singing Marshal*; Dunning, *On the Air*; Hickerson, *4th Revised*; Harmon, *Radio Mystery*; *Brooklyn Eagle*, July 9, 1950; *Birmingham (NY) Press*, December 15, 1951.

SIX GUN JUSTICE

KARL SCHADOW *and* JACK FRENCH

This CBS series, which aired weekly, was written by Wilbur Hall and had its debut in April 1935. Half of each episode was a dramatization of the cowboy's struggle to protect herds of cattle from unscrupulous rustlers while the remainder was cowboy music. Jim Dance, the hero, was played by William Johnstone while Ray Collins portrayed the villain,

Jeff Ownesley. The romantic interest was Maureen Catheart, voiced by Barbara Weeks, and a nearby rancher, Mrs. Pete, was played by Gladys Hurlburt. Carson Robinson portrayed Desolation. Among the musical talents who performed during the non-dramatic half of the program were: Tex Ritter, the Buckaroos, the Mitchell brothers and Pearl Pickens. The program aired evenings until October 1935.

Source: *The Daily Capital*, Topeka, KS, July 31, 1935, p. 11.

THE SIX SHOOTER

FREDERIC S. BERNEY

NETWORK: NBC
FORMAT: Half hour, weekly
DURATION OF RUN: July 15, 1953, to June 24, 1954
SPONSOR: Coleman Heaters and sustaining
AUDIO COPIES EXTANT: 39 shows (complete run)
SCRIPTS ARCHIVED: Undetermined

The Six Shooter radio program was supposed to be about the history of Britt Ponset, "the Texas plainsman who wandered through the western territories, leaving behind a trail of still-remembered legends" as the announcer claimed. In actuality, it was a series of stories of a remarkable, but fictitious, prairie drifter, in scripts written by Frank Burt.

This NBC series started on September 20, 1953, however it had earlier origins. On April 13, 1952, *Hollywood Star Playhouse*, a weekly half hour anthology that featured original scripts, presented a radio drama called "The Six Shooter." In the starring role was James Stewart. The story began with a Wells Fargo station holdup in which the evidence pointed to the sheriff's son. Britt and the sheriff, played by William Conrad, rode out to find the real robber. As it turned out, the robber was not the sheriff's son.

Following the *Hollywood Star Playhouse* episode, an audition transcription was recorded on July 15, 1953. The story was based upon the script utilized on *Hollywood Star Playhouse*. The only difference was that the opening part of the robbery was deleted and this audition disk began with Ponset riding into town. At the half way point in the story, when there would normally be a commercial break, James Stewart announced that he accepted the role of the Six Shooter because he believed that the program portrayed honest stories of the West and the character of Britt Ponset typified the greatness that built America. He also stated that this was his first starring role in a radio series. At the end of the recording, Stewart does not mention any specific sponsor, only that his sponsor has a good product that is well known and the listener should try it. (This was a customary statement on audition records.)

The broadcast date of the first show was September 20, 1953; the title of the script was "Jenny" and it included a significant change in the program's introduction. In the audition script, the opening was: "The man in the saddle is angular and long legged. His skin is sun dyed brown. The gun in his holster is gray steel and rainbow mother of pearl, its handle unmarked. The gun has killed and the man has killed. People call them both the Six Shooter." However, in the debut NBC broadcast, and for the rest of the program's run, the sentence "The gun has killed and the man has killed" was deleted. Obviously this was done to make the main character appear more respectable and responsible.

Ponset was an interesting character. He was not a lawman, just a roving cowpoke, yet he got involved in righting wrongs, catching evildoers, and helping those in trouble. Stewart played his role in a very earnest but easy-going manner. Money was not important to Ponset, who earned a living doing occasional jobs for ranchers handling cattle round-ups or part time work on the railroad. Trouble tended to come to him, rather than Ponset looking for it.

Stewart (and the scripts) portrayed Ponset as a sincere and understanding person, one who realizes that everything is not measured in black and white or simply good and bad. Also he was not necessarily the hero who always bests the bad guy; in at least two episodes, he was held at gunpoint until someone else saved the day.

In another episode, a friend of Ponset's had once been in jail on a bank robbery charge but had escaped. Ponset sees him in a distant town and learns that the townspeople know his friend by a different name. The old friend is now living a decent life, is married, and his wife is expecting their child. At the end of the program, Ponset decides that there is no point letting the local sheriff know that his friend is still wanted by the law. He feels that the man has changed and that the law is looking for a gun-carrying bank robber, and not the decent citizen his friend has become.

The program was originally sponsored by Coleman Heaters but by October 18th, the fifth program in the series, Coleman was no longer a sponsor and thereafter it was a sustaining program by NBC. The program also underwent a time slot change, from Sunday night at 8 P.M. to Thursday night at 8 P.M. as of April 1, 1954. The series had two announcers; the first was Hal Gibney, and then on January 24, 1954, John Wald became the new announcer.

The Six Shooter was an anthology of western stories with Ponset as the central character to hold the plots together. Other than Ponset's horse Scar, there were no regular re-occurring roles. This allowed the program to provide a variety of work for several supporting actors who were among the best on the West Coast: William Conrad, Parley Baer, Herb Ellis, Harry Bartell, Sam Edwards, Alan Reed, and Virginia Gregg. Most of these also had prominent roles on the great CBS western programs of that era, including *Gunsmoke* and *Fort Laramie*.

The adventurous stories were not always about finding and arresting outlaws. In one story, "More Than Kin" (December 13, 1953), a group of Shakespearean actors are hoping for their big break and Ponset helps bring them together with P. T. Barnum. In another, "Sheriff Billy" (November 29, 1953), Ponset becomes involved with a young man who is searching for his father. However, unknown to his son, the father is an outlaw and tries to keep this knowledge from the son.

While all the scripts were realistic, they were able to alternate adventure programs with poignant relationship tales and also, on occasion, pure comedies. Scriptwriter Frank Burt did not ignore the seasons either. For the December 20, 1953, broadcast, "Britt Ponset's Christmas," he penned a western updating of Dickens' classic "A Christmas Carol" in which Ponset finds a runaway orphan boy on the trail who is trying to avoid Christmas. Around his campfire, Ponset recycles the Dickens tale, reset in the frontier of that era, substituting ranchers and cowboys for the original London characters. By the end of the story, the youngster willingly returns to his elderly guardian so they can share Christmas.

Burt was not adverse to plucking an ancient fairy tale and recasting it with western prairie folk. In his script entitled "When the Shoe Doesn't Fit" (June 17, 1954), Britt happens upon a family consisting of a mean old stepmother, her two ugly daughters, and a shoe that doesn't fit them in a re-telling of Cinderella's trials and triumph.

The sound effects on this series were excellent, both the manual ones and those from transcription disks. Musical bridges were well executed and maintained the tone of the various events within the program. The series' main theme, the work of musician Basil Adlam, was "Highland Lament," a haunting melody of the plains. Radio audiences found the theme so compelling that at the end of one program, the announcer stated that the station had received letters from listeners wanting to know more about the theme music played at the opening and closing of the program.

While not as popular as other westerns, i.e., *Gunsmoke* and *Have Gun — Will Travel*, *The Six Shooter* remains one of the few radio programs in the mid–1950s to have a major movie star as its lead actor. By the time his radio program debuted, James Stewart was a well-established movie actor. Obviously what he earned on the movie set significantly dwarfed the modest salary he had to accept on *The Six Shooter*, a sustained radio series.

The series lasted less than a year, a total of 39 weekly episodes. In its final program, "Myra Barker" broadcast on June 24, 1954, Ponset falls in love and proposes to a young lady. But by the conclusion of the episode, they both realize that married life at this time is not possible as long as he still has wrongs to right and people to save. So in the end, just as other proverbial cowboys had done, Britt Ponset rode off alone into the sunset.

Sources: Audio copies of *Six Shooter*; Dunning, *On the Air*; Hickerson, *4th Revised*; Katz; Swartz.

SKY KING

MAGGIE THOMPSON

NETWORK: ABC, Mutual
FORMAT: 15 minutes, daily serial; 30 minute, self-contained episodes
DURATION OF RUN: October 28, 1946, to June 3, 1954
SPONSOR: Swift, Peter Pan Peanut Butter and sustaining
AUDIO COPIES EXTANT: 15
SCRIPTS ARCHIVED: Undetermined

The range of *Sky King* was not so much that of sagebrush and cactus as it was the sky itself, or so it seemed for the early run of the radio show. However, *Sky King* on radio followed what seemed to be the standard plot set-up of most of the children's adventure series of the day: a protagonist meets with a mystery, the mystery endangers many, the mystery is solved, and the heroic protagonist and his associates are saved.

Sky King was initially produced in Chicago as a 15 minute-per-episode serial but later changed into half hour shows. It first aired on ABC from October 28, 1946, to August 29, 1947, as 15 minute episodes weekdays, briefly sponsored by Swift, but mostly sustained, containing public service messages.

It was on ABC from September 2, 1947, to June 2, 1950, as 30 minute shows, usually alternating with *Jack Armstrong* or *The Sea Hound* and sponsored by Peter Pan Peanut Butter. Lastly, it aired on Mutual from September 12, 1950, to June 3, 1954, as a 30 minute show twice a week, again sponsored by Peter Pan Peanut Butter.

The main scenario involved Schuyler ("Sky") King, an ex–Navy pilot and modern-day Arizona rancher, the owner of the Flying Crown Ranch. His palomino horse was named Yellow Fury. (This was an amazing similarity to **Straight Arrow** who rode a palomino named Fury.) King flew two airplanes: Songbird, his primary plane, and Flying Arrow. He captured outlaws, outwitted international terrorists, and solved mysteries, accompanied by his niece Penny, his nephew Clipper, and sometimes his elderly ranch foreman, Jim Bell, and Jim's wife, Martha. Sky was initially played by Roy Engel, and later by Jack Lester, Earl Nightingale, and John Reed King. Penny was voiced by Beryl Vaughn while Clipper was portrayed by Jack Bivens and Johnny Coons. Jim Bell was played by Cliff Soubier. The announcer was Myron Wallace, later to achieve fame as the hard-hitting television personality Mike Wallace.

The show's music was provided by an organ, both for the main theme and bridges. Sound effects were complex, but handled well both manually and with transcribed disks. Airplane engines, hoof beats, explosions, crowd scenes, gun shots, footsteps, and background noises were commonplace on this series.

Not yet positively confirmed, the authorship of the series has been credited to several writers. Robert A. Burtt and Wilfred "Bill" G. Moore, who scripted both *Captain Midnight* and *Hop Harrigan*, may well have been the original scriptwriters on this series. Roy Winsor (1912–1987) who wrote a number of radio and television programs may also have been the head writer for years. One of the least likely candidates to be listed as a *Sky King* writer was Abe Burrows (1910–1985) since he was primarily a gag writer for several CBS shows. If and when the original scripts are located, the mystery of who wrote these adventures will be solved.

For young female listeners, one of the attractions of western stories during the 1940s and 1950s was the very nature of those adventures' possibilities of emancipation. If a girl had a gun and a horse, it was possible to be as powerful and as fast as a boy — or even a man. But in general, while girls would accept a program with a male protagonist, boys would usually avoid a story in which a female takes center stage. So in radio westerns, females tended to be the endangered, the helpless, or the comic relief. Penny's role seemed mostly to utter such lines as, "Oh, Sky, we're safe! We're safe!" or "Oh, Sky, Sky, what can we do now?" or to provide occasional exposition, "Gene McCall will get out of jail now, won't he, sheriff?" Therefore it was encouraging to female listeners when Sky King's niece occasionally played an important part on the radio adventures.

In his book, *The Great Radio Heroes*, vintage radio historian Jim Harmon summarized the half hour plots as:

> Always starting and concluding with western elements such as cattle stampedes, gunfights, and hard-riding horseback chases, the middle of Sky King's story might concern a flight to Europe to track down a Paris stool pigeon with some information, then a flight across Africa in the prop-driven Songbird, or the jet (Flying) Arrow, a crash landing, Sky and Clipper swinging Tarzan-like through the trees, fighting off hostile natives, reaching Algiers to be treated to intrigue there, and, finally, returning to America for a cowboy shoot-out in the streets of Grover, Arizona.

In fact, this western occasionally veered into science fiction, as in one story taking place in Ecuador where Sky and his companions flee a tribe of giants only to encounter another tribe of little blue men.

While the radio series was still airing, *Sky King* jumped to television and, on three different networks over the years, would be on the small screen from April 5, 1952, to March 8, 1959. The role of Schuyler King was played by Kirby Grant (1911–1985). Gloria Winters had the role of Penny, and Ron Hagerthy was Clipper, but his character lasted only one TV season. The television series had two sponsors: Peter Pan Peanut Butter and Nabisco breakfast cereals.

Changes were made in the course of the transition to television. Penny and Clipper, who came across on radio as pre-teens, were played on TV by actors in their early 20s, so they were young adults eager to learn from their uncle but able to act on their own. The Songbird was equipped with a machine gun on the radio show and many of its flight plans included jaunts to other continents. On the radio, it wasn't unusual for King and the kids to be world travelers. Surviving episodes, for example, find them in Marseilles, France, and Quito, Ecuador. However on the television show, the focus was on the Arizona ranch and nearby territory.

Amusingly, announcer Wallace took time out on the sustained radio show in 1947 to encourage a series of safety messages with the repeated mantra: "All the time — everywhere — be cautious! Take care!" He warned juvenile listeners to be careful with knives and guns and "Don't be a fellow or girl who takes chances." Of course, after that, it was back to what kids tuned in for: adventures featuring adults and children running on a cliff-side path in a jungle, trying to avoid attacking savages.

Both the radio and the television series of *Sky King* offered dozens of premiums, available for proof of purchase of Peter Pan Peanut Butter or Nabisco cereals, plus a few coins. Rings were, by far, the most frequently offered. Over the years, there was a radar signal ring, a mystery picture ring, a magni-glo writing ring, an Aztec emerald calendar ring, a Navaho treasure ring, a kaleidoscope ring, an electronic television picture ring and a tele-blinker ring. But there were also a variety of other premiums of interest to juvenile fans of the show: a signal scope, a belt buckle with a secret compartment, a detecto microscope, a stamping kit, a set of plastic figures representing the cast, and a pilot's lapel pin.

Today, fond memories of this western radio show that let kids' imaginations fly free can be reinforced in all the collectibles that still exist in various premiums. Fans today can still make a sandwich with Peter Pan Peanut Butter and let their imagination take to the air again with America's favorite flying rancher and the episodes that survive.

Sources: Audio copies of *Sky King*; Dunning, *On the Air*; Hake; Harmon, *Great Radio Heroes*; Hickerson, *4th Revised*; Overstreet, *Overstreet Toy Ring*; Schaden; Tumbusch.

Songs of the B-Bar-B see *Bobby Benson*

SPIRIT OF THE PIONEERS

KARL SCHADOW

Historical events of the Pikes Peak region were heard on the Colorado Springs station, KVOR during several months in 1937. Broadcast on Sundays at 5:30 P.M., the dramas were written and produced by KVOR program director Wauhillau LaHay. She recruited groups from five area organizations to partake in *Spirit of the Pioneers*, one of the most popular programs heard on KVOR in the 1930s. The groups included an American Legion post and area college and high school groups. The program was sponsored by the Jardine & Knight Plumbing and Heating Co. which offered a $200 prize to the group with the best performances. The contest was won by the American Legion group, which was organized and directed by Zelle Wade. Stories of lesser known events were dramatized including: the story of the first white man to visit the Pikes Peak Region, the tale of Winfield Scott Stratton's gold strike, the exciting capture and imprisonment of Colorado Springs founder, William Jackson Palmer, as a spy in the Civil War, the story of the first habitation built on Pikes Peak, and the discovery of the Cave of the Winds. To date, no scripts or audio copies have been unearthed.

Source: *Colorado Springs Gazette & Telegraph*, May 23, 1937.

STRAIGHT ARROW

WILLIAM HARPER

NETWORK: Don Lee Network, Mutual
FORMAT: Half hour, two or three times weekly
DURATION OF RUN: May 6, 1948, to June 21, 1951
SPONSOR: National Biscuit Company (Shredded Wheat)
AUDIO COPIES EXTANT: 6 complete shows, with portions of several others
SCRIPTS ARCHIVED: American Heritage Center

This juvenile western was the first one on network radio since *Lone Wolf Tribe* in the 1930s to feature an Indian in the leading role. Each program began, and ended, with the sponsor's Shredded Wheat cereal woven into a simple but effective commercial. Milton Charles, on the studio organ, would replicate the drum sound of an Indian tom-tom while announcer Frank Bingman intoned rhythmically:

> N — A — B — I — S — C — O,
> Nabisco is the name to know,
> For a breakfast you can't beat,
> Eat Nabisco Shredded Wheat!

Following this introduction, Bingman would explain the premise of the series:

> To friends and neighbors alike, Steve Adams appeared to be nothing more than the young owner of the Broken Bow cattle spread. But when danger threatened innocent people and when evildoers plotted against justice — then Steve Adams, rancher, disappeared — and in his place came a mysterious stalwart Indian, wearing the dress and war paint of a Comanche — riding the great golden palomino — galloping out of the darkness to take up the cause of law and order throughout the west — comes the legendary figure of Straight Arrow!

The documented beginning of *Straight Arrow* was January 5, 1948, when writer Sheldon Stark turned a script of his American Indian hero over to the advertising agency of McCann-Erickson. The National Biscuit Company (Nabisco) had engaged McCann-Erickson to develop a promotion of its Shredded Wheat cereal to appeal to a younger market.

Stark, who would eventually write all the scripts for the radio show, had returned to his hometown in New York in 1941 after a stint with radio station WXYZ in Detroit. There he assisted Fran Striker, the acknowledged creator of ***The Lone Ranger*** and at that time head of the WXYZ's script department. Stark wrote scripts for *Green Hornet*, *Challenge of the Yukon*, and ***The Lone Ranger*** as well as other shows. The many nuances between *Straight Arrow* and ***The Lone Ranger*** were not denied years later when Stark was confronted with the similarities.

Under the guidance of veteran director Carlo de Angelo, Stark's *Straight Arrow* script was produced in a New York City studio and auditioned for McCann-Erickson and Nabisco, both of which approved. Nabisco subsequently became both sponsor and owner of the *Straight Arrow* property. McCann-Erickson's Hollywood office was given the responsibility of auditioning the actors and producing the shows. Stark remained in New York, never seeing a production, having only several telephone conversations with Ted Robertson who was hired shortly after the show began as both producer and director.

Years later, Lois Culver, Howard's widow, recalled a late 1940s article in *Radio and Television Life* in which Ted Robertson remarked, "The main idea we want to achieve is to help people get the correct perspective on Indian history, and in our stories we emphasize the Indian as a constructive force in our country." This was echoed on the radio special, *Straight Arrow Pow-Wow*, a promotional presentation that introduced *Straight Arrow* on the nationwide Mutual Broadcasting System in February of 1949 by Indian actor Iron Eyes Cody who said: "This is the first show that has put the Indian in correct light." To insure this concept, all the scripts were subject to scrutiny by Nabisco's lawyers. Nabisco even went to the extent of encouraging contributions to the American Indian Funds in its May 25, 1950, program. For their efforts *Straight Arrow* was written into the *Congressional Record* and Stark received a citation from the Iroquois Federation for his scripts.

Following the pilot show approval, Stark turned in the first Hollywood script on April 5, 1948, and then completed six scripts before the show reached the air waves on May 6, 1948. Heading up the cast were Howard Culver, in the dual role of Straight Arrow and Steve Adams, while radio and entertainer veteran Fred Howard (Wright) won the role of Packy McCloud, sidekick to both Straight Arrow and Steve Adams (and the only person who knew they were one in the same). Gwen Delano, a seasoned actress of both stage and radio, became Mesquite Molly, housekeeper of the Broken Bow Ranch. Frank Bingman was chosen as announcer and narrator, while the talented Milton Charles took over as musical director and organist.

The show had the luxury of the services of the best trio in producing its sound effects: Ray Kemper, Tom Hanley, and Bill James. They were also the sound effects team for the popular series *Voyage of the Scarlet Queen* and would later achieve great acclaim at CBS for their superb work on the adult westerns, **Gunsmoke**, **Fort Laramie**, and **Have Gun — Will Travel**.

Straight Arrow's supporting cast, chosen from some of the best radio actors in the Los Angeles area, was excellent and included: Parley Baer, John Dehner, Vic Perrin, Virginia Gregg, Sam Edwards, Jack Moyles, Lillian Buyeff, Herb Ellis, Jack Kruschen, Barney Phillips, Dick Crenna and many more over the years.

The 30 minute programs aired Thursday evenings, 8 P.M. over the Mutual West Coast affiliate, Don Lee Network, and were produced in the studio of its key station, KHJ Los Angeles, for a scheduled trial period of 18 weeks. McCann-Erickson Hollywood's Radio-TV Division's senior producer, J. Neil Reagan (President Ronald Reagan's older brother), was the initial producer/director for the series. The increase in sales of Nabisco Shredded Wheat convinced the sponsor to extend the show for an additional 21 weeks for a total of 39 weeks prior to the nationwide hook-up.

By the time the show aired over the Mutual nationwide berth, the program was well honed with all the players comfortable in their respective roles. The massive promotional efforts of Nabisco's 28 sale offices in key cities and 241 branches as well as the 409 Mutual stations were set into motion for the February 7, 1949, Monday evening, 8 P.M., premiere of *Straight Arrow*. The show aired three times a week, Mondays, Tuesdays and Thursdays at 5 P.M.

The show quickly soared to the number one juvenile program and eventually broke into the top ten of all programming, making it the first children's show to achieve this ranking. Premiums, merchandise items, comic book and newspaper strips were launched to promote and continue interest in the show as well as to reap revenue from the success of the radio series. In 1949, however, after a poor response to the Straight Arrow Tie Clip premium offer, Nabisco discontinued the program's sponsorship and *Straight Arrow* remained on the air Monday evenings only on a sustaining basis for 13 weeks, a not uncommon practice as Nabisco owned complete control of the property and a new sponsor could not be signed up.

A combination of factors, however, led to Nabisco's resuming sponsorship of the program with a special show on Sunday, September 18, 1949: the nationwide focus on American Indian Day, September 23, 1949, the fact of *Straight Arrow* having been read into the *Congressional Record* and the airing of Mutual's *The Song of the Tom-tom*, a salute to American Indians scheduled that aired on September 23, 1949. The program then continued its earlier three-day-a-week schedule until February 7, 1950, after which it was aired only twice a week, on Tuesdays and Thursdays at 5 P.M.

While it may have not been clear to its juvenile listeners, Straight Arrow was not a white man dressed up like an Indian. Straight Arrow was a full-blooded Comanche who disguised himself as a white rancher named Steve Adams. And, although there never was an "origin story" during the radio series to explain this, the spin-off *Straight Arrow* comic book later explained that a Comanche orphan was raised by a white family named Adams and grew up to be Straight Arrow.

When the show debuted on the network, the Comanche warrior rode a nameless palomino and would do so for the first 11 weeks. Then the sponsor held a contest for the juvenile listeners to name Straight Arrow's horse. The winning entry was "Fury" and thereafter, the steed was always called by that name.

The show was set in the Old West of covered wagons, stage coach robberies, buck-board wagons, and roving herds of buffalo. This placed it in contrast to **Bobby Benson and the B-Bar-B Riders**, with which *Straight Arrow* alternated time slots during the week, as the latter series was set in the modern West of fast cars and airplanes.

Virtually every episode started out with Steve Adams and Packy McCloud encountering some trouble, law breaking, or wrongs that needed to be righted. This would require that the rancher go to Sundown Valley, a short distance from his Broken Bow ranch house, where a secret entrance, known only to him and Packy, led to a subterranean cave. There was Fury, waiting patiently, with Straight Arrow's Comanche attire, war paint, bow, and quiver hanging on the walls. A quick change would be accomplished and Straight Arrow would be astride Fury. With a war whoop bouncing off the cave walls, Fury would gallop out of the cave, with Straight Arrow riding bareback.

Like Clayton "Bud" Collyer who deepened his voice when he switched from Clark Kent to Superman on *The Adventures of Superman*, Culver modulated his voice when he switched to Straight Arrow. To assist him to keep his dual roles separate, Culver would mark his scripts, circling Steve's lines with a blue pencil and Straight Arrow's in red.

The show's geographic location was revealed through existing radio scripts. In the first show, "Stage from Calvaydos" (May 6, 1948), references were made to the "Sangre Cristo" mountains (spelled out on maps as Sangre de Cristo), a sub range of the Rockies that extended from New Mexico into Colorado. In nine episodes, April 20, 1950, through May 18, 1950, Colorado was mentioned by name as the site of events by the evildoers to block settlers from entering this northwestern region in a desperate attempt to stall statehood. In those episodes, Roger Lynch, the self-declared "ruler" of the region, feared statehood would usurp his power base and his hoped for empire lost. The action appeared to have taken place in a valley with the San Juan Mountains on the west and the Sangre de Cristo on the east and the "Sangre Cristo" mountains were described as being in the vicinity of both Steve Adams' ranch, Broken Bow and Straight Arrow's secret cave.

In the show's 200th episode dated May 18, 1950, Frank Bingman helped set the time frame for the series in the 1870s when he says: "The new territory in the northwest had voted to seek admission to the United States"; Colorado achieved statehood on August 1, 1876.

While there were occasional mysteries to be solved in this frontier series, the majority of the adventures involved fairly standard plot devices in juvenile westerns. There were stage coach robbers to be apprehended, claim jumpers to be thwarted, land swindlers to be stopped, victimized widows and children to be comforted, and outlaws to be brought to justice.

To accomplish these deeds took more than just Steve Adams slipping out of his disguise as a rancher and donning the war paint and attire of his Comanche heritage. Straight Arrow was capable of doing feats which Steve Adams was apparently unable to do, especially tracking down the culprits by reading signs that would escape the eyes of a white man. This was not to say that Steve Adams was less of a man, for on occasion he too, could handle a dangerous situation and stand up for justice. Usually the ride to Sundown Valley and the secret cave was when Adams was no longer effective in his disguise as rancher and a Comanche could bring about a successful conclusion e.g., soliciting the aide of other Indians.

One program refers to the fact that there are "good men and bad, good Indians and bad" but every episode emphasized the necessity of fair play and justice. There were Mexicans, Swedes, French, Irish and other ethnic groups in the scripts but none spoken of in derogatory terms. The American Indian was often referred to as "injuns, redskins" or some other slang expression by both good citizens and unsavory characters. Of course, the bad guys deprecated the Indian while the town folks or others expressed an uncertainty about the American Indian, such as being unreliable, unfaithful or some other negative comment. However, through the efforts of Steve Adams and Straight Arrow, the Indian overcame the belittling and rose to the occasion in a heroic manner; the focus was always on righting wrongs and achieving justice.

Nabisco authorized a *Straight Arrow* comic book series. Primarily written by Gardner Fox, with drawings by Fred "Ted" Meagher, the first issue was February/March 1950. Eventually 55 editions would be published, finally ending in March 1956, nearly five years after the radio show's demise. The same publisher, Magazine Enterprises, also put out a comic book in 1954 entitled *Straight Arrow's Fury*, but the palomino's debut was also his last issue.

Through the efforts of McCann-Erickson, *Straight Arrow* became a promoter for Shredded Wheat cereal. Life sized cardboard cut-outs of the Comanche warrior were distributed to grocers throughout the nation and they were placed prominently in the cereal aisles of many stores. The agency also designed the "Injun-Uity cards" which were three gray cardboard dividers in each box of Shredded Wheat inserted between the four rows of wheat biscuits. These collectible cards, with graphics and text, explained "Indian Skills and Crafts."

In addition, Nabisco offered premiums that were requested by mail from young fans of *Straight Arrow*; most of merchandise had an American Indian theme. These items included the following: bandana, headband, tie clip, war drum, powder horn, nugget ring, shoulder patch, cereal bowl and mug, and arrowhead light. Many of these premiums were advertised on the back covers of the *Straight Arrow* comic books.

There also was a daily and Sunday comic strip of Straight Arrow distributed through the Bell-McClure Syndicate. The strips began in June 1950 and were illustrated by John Belfi and Joe Certa, with Martin Demuth as principle letterer; Gardner Fox wrote the scripts. It was a short run, ending on July 30, 1951, shortly after the radio series was cancelled.

The show's cancellation was abrupt, ending on June 21, 1951, after a total of 292 broadcasts. Various reasons could be cited, but the most logical one was the same one that caused the death of most dramatic radio shows in the 1950s: the switch of fan loyalty to the new medium of television.

Sources: Audio copies of *Straight Arrow*; Dunning, *On the Air*; Hake, *Official Price*; Harper; Overstreet, *Overstreet Comic Book*; Interviews with Lois Culver by author.

STRAY HOLLISTER

Karl Schadow *and* Jack French

Relatively little is known about this 15 minute western syndicated series which aired from 1935 to the early 1940s. The main character, Stray Hollister, was a veteran range detective, who worked closely with the local sheriff and Brad Turner, a ranger, to promote justice and thwart evil. The program usually aired around 6 P.M., either three or four times weekly. Stations airing it in 1937-1938 included KEHE in Los Angeles and KLO in Ogden, UT.

Source: *Los Angeles Times*, January 24, 1938.

SUNDAY AT THE HY-G RANCH

Karl Schadow *and* Jack French

This 15 minute regional show aired from station WOAI in San Antonio, TX, and, as the name would suggest, was sponsored by Hydro Gas. It was written and directed by Phil Alexander, who also acted in it. The 1939 program was a combination of comic dramatization and music, with the staff orchestra under Emilio Cacers, backing up the soloists. In addition to Alexander, who played Little Joe, a second actor played three roles: Allen Chapman was the voice of the Old Timer, the ranch owner, and the African American cook. *Variety* praised the series as "fast moving, full of action, music and drama."

Source: *Variety*, November 15, 1939.

TALES FROM THE DIAMOND K

J. DAVID GOLDIN

NETWORK: Syndicated
FORMAT: 15 minutes, daily
DURATION OF RUN: 1951
SPONSOR: Ken Maynard shirts and records
AUDIO COPIES EXTANT: 36 (of 39 recorded, plus an audition disk)
SCRIPTS ARCHIVED: Undetermined

This was a unique radio show, hosted by a unique personality who was not the nicest guy in the world; certainly one with whom you would try to avoid an argument. Ken Maynard, the star and only performer on this program, was born in 1895 in Vevay, IN and attended high school in Columbus, IN. There were no ranches there, but he learned to ride a horse, worked his way westward, and by 1923 had appeared in a silent movie. By the time talking pictures were released, Ken was a singing cowboy. His movie publicist claimed Ken was a rodeo champion who was born in Texas, served in the Army in World War I and was a former gold miner. None of this was true. However, he could ride a horse and sing; apparently that was enough.

Singing cowboys became popular because they appealed to women who weren't too thrilled about going to western movies and it was a lot cheaper to film a buckaroo with a guitar than a horse chase. Ken Maynard (his real name) preceded Gene Autry and Roy Rogers in serenading a señorita, although his voice was somewhat high pitched. A claim could be made that Ken was the first "singing cowboy." He recorded eight sides for Columbia in 1930 of songs from his early sound films, but as sales were dismal, only two were ever released. He did give Gene Autry his first break in 1934 by allowing him to sing in his film, *On Old Santa Fe.*

While starring in his westerns, Ken commanded $10,000 per week from 1934 right through 1940. He also ran a circus for about a year with the evocative name of "The Diamond K Wild West Circus and Indian Congress." But, as his age got higher and his waistline got larger, his career and paychecks got smaller. The sad truth is that many people considered Ken to be a liar, a drunk, a bully, and a braggart. Playing opposite Ken in four of his films, actress Cecilia Parker later said, "I finally laid it right out for him. I said, 'You pay my salary but if you can't behave yourself and curb your language, you're going to have to get yourself another actress.'"

Yet moviegoers loved him on the screen. In real life, his best friend was his palomino horse Tarzan, purchased in 1925 for $50. Ken could ride really well and Tarzan was just the horse that could make him look like the ideal screen cowboy. There's no record of Ken ever getting into an argument with Tarzan, but the horse eventually got second billing in all Ken's films. At age 14, about 1940, Tarzan passed away and was replaced by Tarzan II, also named after the Edgar Rice Burroughs character. That famous novelist took umbrage at Ken's use of the name of his famous character; a lawsuit dragged on for years, and was settled out of court.

Ken was arrested for assault more than once, sued for divorce, probably twice, and accused of a drunken hit-and-run incident. The film crews who worked with him were cursed, abused, and threatened. Despite his profanity and his fists, he made 93 movies from 1923 to 1972, when he shot his last movie, *The Marshal of Windy Hollow.* By 1972

Ken was broke, living in a trailer, and was drunk a good part of the time. The *Windy Hollow* film was shot with almost no budget, no talent, and was mercifully never released.

In 1951, Ken recorded 39 episodes of *Tales from the Diamond K* as a children's series. Unlike his earlier juvenile series from the 1930s, **Roundup Trail**, that consisted of stereotypical plots, *Tales from the Diamond K* was pure simplicity and required nothing in front of the microphone except Ken. Each 15 minute show was a western yarn simply told by Ken, and they were good stories, well-told; Ken did not sing. It's hard to imagine a radio program with a lower production cost. There is no clue as to the writer of the series. The program was meant to be heard five times a week in the afternoon. There were no actors, no music, and no sound effects except Tarzan whinnied "Hello" right after Ken greeted his listeners. Most of the western tales involved gold mines, buried treasure, or lost fortunes and occasionally Ken and Tarzan were part of the story line. Ken referred to the announcer several times, as "Charlie," but Don Stanley identified himself as the announcer on the audition recording for the series.

The series was produced by a firm called Peterson, Schaefer, and Buck, Inc., of which nothing is known. It may even have been an ad hoc company formed just for *Tales from the Diamond K*. The whole show involved a direct mail offer of Ken Maynard products. (While the details about the first mail order offers on radio are not known, during the 1940s such offers weren't that uncommon.)

The show was an example of what came to be called a "P.I. Deal," made famous at XERA and other "border blaster" radio stations in Mexico. "P.I." stood for "per inquiry" and that's how the stations were paid. *Tales from the Diamond K* was supplied to the station at no cost, a product was offered, and the money from the listeners was sent directly to the radio station. A portion of the receipts was sent to the Peterson, Schaefer and Buck firm, who fulfilled the order and shipped the product. The balance was kept by the radio station. This was fairly sophisticated marketing at this time, and one of the likely requirements was that Ken would get a piece of the action since he received no money up front for performing. Peterson, Schaefer, and Buck did have to pay for studio time, for pressing the transcriptions for the radio stations to play, as well as for selling the deal to the radio stations, plus creating and shipping the product.

Two products were offered on the show: Ken Maynard "K-shirts" and Ken Maynard personalized phonograph records. A "K-shirt" was a regular "T" shirt, but it was colored "desert brown" and boasted a "flaming red picture of Ken Maynard and his horse Tarzan on the front. This was not a bad idea to capitalize on Ken's fame that still lingered with the younger generation. The shirts came in sizes 2 to 12, and were an unusual product for the 1950s. Today, T-shirts with writing and pictures on the front are commonplace.

The personalized phonograph records were a brilliant idea. The product was a set of two 8-inch "vinylite" records containing two brief stories by Ken. Vinylite was a trademarked vinyl chloride plastic that had been invented during the war and which later became popular with the recording industry for the newly invented lightweight 78s, LPs, and 45s. They were red in color and were so thin one could see through them.

The record would begin with Ken saying, "Hello Andy. This is Ken Maynard with a story just for you!" He addresses each kid by his first name, whether the listener is Mary, John, Percival, or whoever. Ken tells a different story on each of the two records "for just a dollar bill." The two stories are titled "The Killer Stallion," and "Fargo Red and the Dangerous Double-Cross." Eight-inch records at 78 rpm play about two minutes on each side. Ken tells the story in his own voice, except for one whinny from Tarzan, with no sound effects or music.

Obviously Ken did not record separate disks for each juvenile customer. The records were most probably produced in the following manner: With the newly common tape recorder, it would have been no problem for Ken to just say the opening sentence with each first name required, and then have all the opening lines put on one reel of tape. The engineer would play back the openings on tape on one recorder followed by the stories on tape on a second machine. The sequence would be fed onto a disk cutter for the first side of the record. The conclusion of the story on the second side of the record was not customized. This system would work, but it was labor intensive and expensive. The recordings still had to be pressed, or cut, packaged, and mailed. On the show, Ken apologized to his listeners for the necessity of asking for $1 for the shirt or the records. He said it was a requirement because "the fellow that makes 'em ain't a millionaire."

In his lifetime, Ken married and divorced several times, and at the end, he was a lonely pauper, residing in the Motion Picture Home in Woodland Hills, CA. Ken died there in 1973 of alcoholism and malnutrition. It was later revealed that Gene Autry and Ken's brother, Kermit, were supporting him in his last years.

Sources: Audio copies of *Tales from the Diamond K*; George-Warren; Gossett; Harmon, *Radio & TV Premiums*; Hickerson, *4th Revised*; Hurst; Katz; Rothel; http://b-westerns.com.

TALES OF PIONEER DAYS
DAVID S. SIEGEL

Although no audio copies of this program have been located, the editors have identified the source of 61 scripts of this 15 minute program, broadcast on either KTAR or KOY out of Phoenix between 1936 and 1937. Written by Stephen C. Shadegg, who also wrote **Phoenix Sun Ranch Chuck Wagon**, the programs are a single person narration of stories about Arizona history, people and places, with a brief introduction by an announcer. The scripts range from a retelling of a massacre that took place on the San Carlos reservation, to the creation of the Territory of Arizona, the story of the Spanish explorer Cabeza de Vaca who explored Arizona in the 16th century, the history of the Arizona normal schools and the establishment of a Phoenix bakery in 1881 when the city was only 11 years old and the home to more than 1,500 residents. Many of the scripts, as well as the research that clearly went into writing them, were later adapted by Shadegg for his **Phoenix Sun Ranch** program. For example, the 1937 *Tales* script, "Lost Dutchman Mine" was recycled and became the "Superstition Mountains" episode on **Phoenix Sun Ranch** series.

Sources: www.azarchivesonline.org (Stephen Shadegg Papers); February 2013 phone interview with archives staff.

TALES OF THE TEXAS RANGERS
IVAN G. SHREVE, JR.

NETWORK: NBC
FORMAT: Half hour, weekly
DURATION OF RUN: July 8, 1950, to September 14, 1952

SPONSOR: Briefly sponsored by General Mills (Wheaties), July–August 1950, then sustained
AUDIO COPIES EXTANT: 92 shows (including April 10, 1950, audition)
SCRIPTS ARCHIVED: Undetermined

The overall concept of *Tales of the Texas Rangers* was presented in the manner of a crime anthology: dramatizations of actual closed cases by that agency, covering a 20 year span from 1928 to 1948. The lead investigator was represented through the personification of a fictional ranger, Jace Pearson. The program's attention to historical fact and its realistic detail distinguished the program from many other radio western series airing during the period of the early 1950s, including the fact that it was set against the backdrop of a more modern West.

Texas Rangers have a rich history. In 1823 the "Father of Texas," Stephen F. Austin, organized small groups of armed men for the purpose of protecting Texas colonists from Indian and/or Mexican incursions and in doing so, instituted what is now known as one of the oldest law enforcement bodies in North America: the Texas Rangers. Originally hired to serve as scouts, guides and other armed forces (for which its members were paid with land), the Rangers were formerly constituted in 1835 by Daniel Parker as a paramilitary force. Though briefly disbanded during the Civil War's Reconstruction period, they were later brought back upon the reinstitution of home government and their duties included investigating crimes, tracking down fugitives, and protecting the Governor of that sovereign state. At one time, the membership of the Rangers was limited to fifty men. All candidates had to meet qualifications of maturity, intelligence, physical stamina, and provide their own horse. In recent years the Rangers membership totaled approximately 150.

The mystique of the Texas Rangers, who are in some ways an American version of the French Foreign Legion, has long provided inspiration in various areas of the pop culture media. They have been featured in films including the 1936 and 1951 feature films *The Texas Rangers*, the 1941 Republic cliffhanger serial, *King of the Texas Rangers*, and a 1942 to 1945 series of 22 B-westerns entitled *The Texas Rangers* produced at PRC Studios. More recently there was a popular television series starring martial arts actor Chuck Norris in *Walker, Texas Ranger* (1993–2001). On radio, the most famous Texas Ranger was a young man who had the misfortune of being ambushed by the notorious outlaw Butch Cavendish and his gang. When the other Rangers, including his brother, perished in the sneak attack, he alone survived with the help of an Indian named Tonto who later assisted him in the "fight for law and order in the early western United States." That young Ranger was, of course, the Lone Ranger.

The Lone Ranger had been weaving a fabric of western legends three times weekly since its premiere broadcast on January 31, 1933. Seventeen years later, new stories about the bravery of the Texas Rangers would entertain radio audiences, thanks to character actor Stacy Keach, Sr., a noted film and radio thespian. (His sons Stacy, Jr. and James also had careers in show business.) Keach created what eventually became the radio series *Tales of the Texas Rangers*, although in its embryonic stage it had originally been planned as a feature film. With writer Joel Murcott in tow, Keach was able to convince the publicity shy Rangers that a radio series would not only be viable, but would provide excellent publicity for the law enforcement body. It was stipulated that the organization would have to approve each script, similar to such shows as *This is Your FBI*. Producer/director Keach and Murcott then traveled to the Lone Star State for further background study and to get the agency's approval.

Keach and Murcott received assistance in their research when they made the acquaintance of Captain Manuel Trazazas "Lone Wolf" Gonzaullas, a 30 year veteran of the Rangers who was reverently known as "the last of the old quick draw artists." Considering that he had killed 31 men in the line of duty, with the notches on his gun to prove it, it was not a boast made lightly. Gonzaullas would serve as a consultant and technical advisor on the series. He functioned as the two men's liaison as they traveled 1,500 miles throughout Texas, observing actual investigations involving the Texas Rangers and getting a feel for the enormity and diversity of the state.

The lead role of Jace Pearson was given to Joel McCrea, an actor who had been appearing in movies since the late 1920s and was known to movie going audiences for solid performances in films such as *These Three* (1936), *Dead End* (1937), *Foreign Correspondent* (1940), *Sullivan's Travels* (1941), *The Palm Beach Story* (1942), and *The More the Merrier* (1943). McCrea also had a real affinity for westerns, and had appeared in *Barbary Coast* (1935), *Wells Fargo* (1937), and *Union Pacific* (1939). From his appearance in *The Virginian* (1946) until the end of his career 30 years later, he appeared only in westerns.

Landing McCrea for the series was a feather in the cap for all involved, though by the time the show went on the air it was not unusual for many Hollywood celebrities to perform on radio. These stars included Alan Ladd (*Box 13*), Brian Donlevy (*Dangerous Assignment*), and Humphrey Bogart and Lauren Bacall (*Bold Venture*). An audition record for *Tales of the Texas Rangers* was cut on April 10, 1950, and by July of that year it was scheduled on NBC on Saturday nights at 9:30 P.M. On October 8, 1950, the show moved to Sundays at 8:30 P.M., and then shifted to an earlier time slot at 6:00 P.M. beginning September 30, 1951.

Tales of the Texas Rangers is remembered by vintage radio fans for its stirring opening, with announcer Hal Gibney trumpeting excitedly: "Texas! More than 260,000 square miles! And 50 men who make up the most famous and oldest law enforcement body in North America!" This enthusiastic announcement was also accompanied by "The Eyes of Texas Are upon You" which is also known as "The Texas Ranger March." It has a similar melody to the folk tune "I've Been Working on the Railroad."

While *Tales of the Texas Rangers* featured familiar western trappings, it was first and foremost a police procedural show, beginning with the assignment of a case by Captain Stinson, played by Tony Barrett, the only other regular character on the show, who traded narration with McCrea. Ranger Pearson needed a "horseless carriage" to travel that 260,000 square mileage, though he frequently pulled behind his automobile a horse trailer housing a dark steed named Charcoal, affectionately referred to by Jace as Chalky. Charcoal, whose hoofbeats were provided by sound effects man Monty Fraser, came in handy whenever Pearson had to go after a suspect in areas not navigable by car.

Although Murcott was the head writer, he had a fine support staff, comprised at various times by writers Irwin Ashkenazi, Arthur Brown, Jr., Adrian Gendeaux, Will Gould, Charles E. Israel, Robert A. White and Bob Wright. Working with the materials from the Rangers' closed cases, they were able to construct scripts that were realistic, compelling and entertaining.

Pearson also relied on modern methods of crime detection in his investigations, notably forensic science and psychological analysis, but he never strayed far from the traditional means of old fashioned tracking and dogged legwork. Like the Royal Canadian Mounted Police, the doggedly determined Pearson would eventually get his man by the time the program's half hour was up, and then McCrea would provide the audience with some Texas Ranger trivia. Next, announcer Gibney informed the curious listener as to what sort of justice had been meted out to the guilty party in each episode, usually in the form of incarceration at the Texas State Penitentiary at Huntsville; on the show, Huntsville would eventually become shorthand for "prison."

Tales of the Texas Rangers bore a strong resemblance to another show that had redefined radio crime drama beginning in 1949: the popular *Dragnet*. *Tales* could very well be nicknamed "Dragnet in the saddle." From its premiere on June 3, 1949, Jack Webb's seminal police show broke all of the previous law enforcement rules with an emphasis on how police work was often boring and tedious, and yet such methodical attention to detail as well as tireless legwork was the key to solving cases. *Tales of the Texas Rangers* announcer Gibney did double duty on *Dragnet*, in tandem with George Fenneman, and *Dragnet* actors like Virginia Gregg, Sam Edwards, Lillian Buyeff, Herb Ellis and many others regularly performed on both programs.

Pearson's investigations also involved the similar sordid crimes investigated by Joe Friday and his various partners: murders, robberies, prison breakouts, etc. But *Tales* did distinguish itself by concentrating more on dramatization in its stories, as opposed to *Dragnet*'s clinically cold "just the facts" approach. *Dragnet* made its cops the focal point of each drama, whereas on *Tales* it was possible to have characters engaged in the episode's action or conversation before Pearson's arrival on the scene. In addition, Gibney would remind listeners that the Texas Ranger tale to follow was "based on fact... only names, dates, and places are fictitious for obvious reasons."

With the performances and scripts of *Tales of the Texas Rangers* generally hitting the high mark set by *Dragnet*, why was the radio run of *Tales* relatively brief? *Dragnet* was able to secure the sponsorship of Fatima, and later Chesterfield, cigarettes rather quickly after its premiere. *Tales*, on the other hand, lost its Wheaties/General Mills sponsorship only two months after its debut, putting the show's commercial spokesman, Frank Martin, out of work as well. The last Wheaties sponsored broadcast, "The Open Range" (August 26, 1950), even included a spot with writer Murcott asking listeners to buy the cereal "just to show us you like the show." But apparently they didn't.

The show was thereafter sustained by NBC, and while the early history of radio made allowances for some shows to be "kept" by their networks, by the time *Tales* made it to the airwaves, shows without sponsorship were doomed, due to the increasing competition from television. McCrea was certainly working for less money than he usually received for film work, but even he couldn't do the series indefinitely at modest wages. A similar situation faced **The Six Shooter**, the 1953-1954 radio western starring James Stewart. The difficulty in finding a sponsor for that series limited it to a single season, although some of that stemmed from Stewart's unwillingness to allow his program to be associated with cigarette companies, some of which were interested in its sponsorship. In retrospect, *Tales of the Texas Rangers* was luckier than the Stewart program in that it managed to hang on longer. But ultimately low ratings and its lack of sponsorship sadly sidelined the series; its last episode aired on September 14, 1952.

Beginning September 3, 1955, *Tales of the Texas Rangers* arrived on television as a half hour series produced by Screen Gems which aired Saturday mornings on CBS-TV. Jace Pearson was played by Willard Parker in the role that McCrea made famous on radio. In the TV incarnation, Pearson took on a partner, Clay Morgan, portrayed by Harry

Lauter, a marked departure from the radio series where the Pearson character had no regular associate, generally relying on the cooperation of local police departments or sheriff's offices. The video version also emphasized more western elements, e.g., shootouts and chases, with episodes alternating between modern day investigations and historical cases set 100 years earlier. Its Saturday morning scheduling signaled that TV's *Tales* was geared more towards juvenile audiences, and after two years of episode production (ending May 25, 1957) the series was later rerun over ABC-TV in several evening time slots from September 1957 to May 1959.

Sources: Audio copies of *Tales of the Texas Rangers*; Brooks, Cox, *Radio Crime Fighters*; Dunning, *On the Air*; Dunning, *Tune in*; Maltin; Katz; http://www.Radiogoldindex.com; http://www.TexasRanger.org.

TENDERFOOT

KARL SCHADOW *and* JACK FRENCH

A juvenile series broadcast three times a week on approximately 30 stations in the ABC Network, the series lasted for several months during 1936. The programs revolved around the adventures of Pete, the tenderfoot, who displayed his skills as both a cowpuncher and bronco buster when a rodeo came to town. The character of Pete was played by Billy Malkemus, a radio actor who had also portrayed roles in other juvenile adventure network programs (*Skippy* and *Little Orphan Annie*) and soap operas (*Princess Pat* and *Just Plain Bill*).

Source: *The Hammond* (IN) *Times*, November 4, 1936.

TENNESSEE JED

DONALD RAMLOW

NETWORK: Mutual (WOR), ABC
FORMAT: 15 minutes, weekdays
DURATION OF RUN: May 14, 1945, to August 17, 1945, 5:00 P.M. Mutual (WOR); September 3, 1945, to August 29, 1947, 5:45 P.M. ABC (WJZ); September 1, 1947, to November 7, 1947, 5:00 P.M. ABC (WJZ)
SPONSOR: Tip Top Bread (Ward Baking Company), plus local sponsors including Beverly Peanut Butter (Safeway Products)
AUDIO COPIES EXTANT: 24 (18 in circulation and 6 in a private collection)
SCRIPTS ARCHIVED: J. Walter Thompson Archives, Duke University

Tennessee Jed initially appeared as a summer weekly show carried over the Mutual Broadcasting System (WOR, in New York City), beginning on May 14, 1945. The initial run ended on August 17 and was replaced by the program *House of Mystery*. Two weeks later, on September 3, the show reappeared on ABC (WJZ, in New York City), staying on the air until the early part of November. There were no major changes between the Mutual and ABC versions of the series. The lead character of Jed Sloan was similar to other radio heroes of the airwaves, honest and forthright in all ways. This was important to the Tip Top Bread sponsor, since *Tennessee Jed* was not intended to be an adult western. Jed was targeted directly at young listeners who tuned into radio programs between 5:00 P.M. and 6:00 P.M.

Little information is currently known about the first actor, Johnny Thomas, who is credited with playing the lead role of Tennessee "Jed" Sloan. Only 24 episodes are estimated to exist out of approximately 650 performances, allowing for a modest interpretation of the series. Some archival material refers to a Johnny Thomas, who appeared on the shows *True Detective Mysteries*, *The Second Husband* and *Snow Village Sketches*. However, as there was a second radio actor with the name of John Thomas, at this time further investigation is needed to verify this information. Thomas was later replaced by Don MacLaughlin, who performed on many radio and television programs, most notably *David Harding, Counterspy*. MacLaughlin's greatest overall claim to fame may have been his role as Chris Hughes, the male lead on *As the World Turns* on CBS-TV, a role he played from 1956 for 30 years until his death in 1986.

The fact that *Tennessee Jed* was a juvenile western was made very clear during its second season in 1946 when its sponsor participated in a joint radio contest with the advertisers for *Terry and the Pirates*, **Sky King**, and *Jack Armstrong, the All-American Boy*. Listeners were asked to submit letters of 50 words or less indicating "Which Program I Prefer." Recipients would then become eligible to win bicycles and radios, in addition to many other items. Only people under the age of 16 were eligible to win the prizes and almost 300,000 listeners submitted letters. *Tennessee Jed*'s sponsor also utilized radio premiums, another tried and true method of tracking the size of the juvenile listening audience. Among the items offered were: a mirror ring, magnet ring, transfer tattoos, magic trick book, photo of Jed, and a lariat puzzle. There was even a single issue of a *Tennessee Jed* comic book released in 1945.

The broadcast version of the series differed somewhat from the promotional materials initially released in advance of the first episode. An early news release promoted the plot as "a story of a boy from Tennessee who sets out to explore the great Southwest." However, most of the story lines in the existing circulating shows place the focus on an adult Jed and his heroic adventures. The show was produced by Paul Defur and directed by William "Bill" Hamilton who also directed *Hannibal Cobb* and *Ethel and Albert*.

The earliest circulating show is from August 10, 1945, one of the last shows in the Mutual run. The opening began with a yodel and segued into the lines "There he goes, Tennessee!" at which point a rifle shot echoes out, and the announcer yells "Got him! Deeeeaaaad Center." The announcing style for this episode and other early episodes was very interesting because of the stylized clipped way in which the announcer introduced the story. The program's use of music was also unique in that the musical bridges were sung with lyrics that advanced the storyline of the current adventure. The performer doing the yodeling and singing of the various songs throughout the series was Elton Britt (James Elton Baker) (1913–1972). Britt was a popular country singer who received a gold record for his song "There's a Star Spangled Banner Waving Somewhere." Interestingly, an article in the March 23, 1946, issue of *Billboard* indicated that the sponsors wanted to keep the identity of the singer a secret, but that because so many people recognized his voice there was no sense trying to keep it a secret.

The early announcer for the series was Layman Cameron, who also announced for the popular radio shows *Hill Country Jamboree* and *Hill Country Hit Parade*. Cameron was also a professional musical performer who worked with Britt at one time in a group entitled the Mentholatum Mountaineers. Later announcers included Larry Elliott, who had previously been the announcer for *Fred Allen's Texaco Star Theater*, and Court Benson, who also performed as an actor on many radio shows, including *Suspense* and *X-Minus One*. Benson was married to Grace Matthews, an actress in her own right; she portrayed Margo Lane on *The Shadow* during the late 1940s.

The stories on *Tennessee Jed* ranged from adventures involving the Circle S Ranch to stories of famous historical figures. A major storyline for the series involved the discovery that the villain Nick Dalton was attempting to rekindle the war between the states which, he believed, would allow him to take over the U.S. government. Later episodes focused on attempts to kill Tennessee or steal his "great horse, Smokey." The show, while targeted at younger listeners, had its fair share of serious violence.

One of the meanest characters on the show was the Rat, a character that delighted in eliminating anyone who was a threat to himself or his boss, Nick Dalton. The Rat killed two people in cold blood during the Civil War conspiracy storyline, with both of them begging for their lives. The first victim died by shooting and the second, as he put it, "quietly." When the Rat returned from killing the second victim and Dalton told him that he hadn't heard a shot, the Rat replied, "Of course not, I like variety." The Rat was played by Allan John Melvin (1923–2008), who appeared on many radio shows and was known for his ability to mimic the voices of other people. His characterization of the Rat was reminiscent of a cross between Peter Lorre and Walter Brennan. Fans of television would recognize him for his recurring roles on *The Phil Silvers Show*, *The Partridge Family* and *All in the Family*. Allan also did numerous voiceovers for commercials and cartoon shows.

Many well-known radio actors had supporting roles on the series. Sheriff Jackson was portrayed by Humphrey Davis (1912–1987), a busy New York actor who appeared on many East Coast radio shows including *Nick Carter, Detective*, *Philo Vance* and *Sherlock Holmes*. Jim Boles (1914–1977) appeared as the new deputy in the series. Boles was especially known for his appearances on the Carlton E. Morse programs *I Love a Mystery* and *One Man's Family*. Raymond Edward Johnson (1911–2001) played the character of Masters, a gambler. Johnson appeared in many radio shows but is best known for his role of Raymond, the host of *Inner Sanctum Mysteries*. Ed Begley (1901–1970) played the character of Blackie and was known for his many roles on radio, Broadway, television and film; he won a Best Supporting Actor Academy Award for his appearance in the movie *Sweet Bird of Youth*. Chief Gray Eagle was portrayed by Juano Hernández (1896–1970), a busy and highly acclaimed actor who appeared on *The Shadow*, *Mandrake, The Magician* and the very popular series, *The Cavalcade of America*. Hernández also performed on Broadway and appeared in many television shows and films. Other supporting actors who appeared on the series were: Nora Marlowe, John McGovern, Blanchard McKee, George Petrie, Larry Robinson, and Cecil H. Roy.

The early script writing for the series was by Howard Carraway, who also produced a variety of radio productions during the 1940s. Carraway was replaced by Sheldon Stark around April 1946, and was replaced in turn by the writer Tom Taggart who started writing for the series in 1947. A letter dated February 1947, written by Taggart that appears in the book *Listening: A Collection of Critical Articles on Radio*, stated that with the approval of the sponsors he began to introduce historical figures into the story, even including dialogue from plays by Shakespeare. Some of the other figures included Mark Twain, Walt Whitman and Ulysses S. Grant. According to Taggart this was done to give *Tennessee Jed* "historical accuracy." Taggart left the series later that year. Ashley Buck was also a writer for the series in addition to penning scripts for *Casey Crime Photographer* and *When We Were Young*.

Tennessee Jed had a successful run of over two years, but eventually left the airwaves in November 1947, being replaced by *The Adventures of Dick Tracy*. Some radio stations around the country continued to re-run episodes for a while, but the last original production was broadcast on November 7, 1947.

Sources: Audio copies of *Tennessee Jed*; Buxton; Dunning, *Tune In*; Williams; Siegel, *Resource*; *Billboard*, March 23 and October 19, 1946; *New York Times*, May 13,1945 and July 1,1947; *Radio Daily*, July 8, 1946; *Broadcasting*, February 4 and March 25, 1946; www.ancientfaces.com; www.philsilversshow.com; www.encylopediaofarkansas.net; www.americanradiohistory.com; www.americanradiohistory.com.

TOM MIX

JACK FRENCH

NAMES: *The Adventures of Tom Mix, The Tom Mix Straight-Shooters*
NETWORK: NBC Red (1933 to 1942), Mutual (1944 to 1950)
FORMAT: 15 minutes, 2 to 5 times weekly
DURATION OF RUN: September 25, 1933, to March 27, 1942; June 5, 1944, to June 23, 1950
SPONSOR: Ralston Purina Company
AUDIO COPIES EXTANT: 25
SCRIPTS ARCHIVED: Library of American Broadcasting; American Radio Archives; SPERD-VAC

Tom Mix was one of the most popular movie stars of the silent era in the 1920s and had continued success in the 1930s with the Sells-Floto Circus and other personal appearances. However, he had nothing to do with the long running radio series that bore his name other than signing his royalty checks from the Ralston Purina Company of St. Louis, MO.

The radio series was the creation of a young representative of the Gardner Advertising Company, also of St. Louis, by the name of Charles E. Claggett. In 1933 Claggett was determined to get the Ralston account. He and a young lady from his firm took an informal survey of local school children, aged 6 to 14, to determine their top hero. Tom Mix was the overwhelming choice.

Claggett proposed a western radio series using Mix's name and Elmer G. Marshutz, the president of Gardner Advertising, went to California and got Mix's signature on a contract, which, according to Ralston lore, was scribbled on the back of an envelope. After William Danforth, president of Ralston, agreed to sponsor the new show, Claggett went to New York City and obtained air time on the NBC Red Network.

For his new series, Claggett hired Roland Martini to write the scripts and he cast Artells Dickson in the title role. Dickson, who was born in Oklahoma in 1898, was a veteran performer, principally a singer and stage actor, with experience on the Chautauqua Circuit. His sidekick on the show, who was also the narrator, was the Old Wrangler, portrayed by Percy Hemus, a 55-year-old native of New Zealand. In the early years of the show, the Old Wrangler opened every program by exclaiming: "It's Round-up time, so let's git a-going!" That phrase would become so popular it was the slogan of some of the Navy's PT squadrons in World War II.

The setting of the show was the T-M Bar Ranch which Tom owned and operated, near the fictional town of Dobie, TX. But Tom and the Old Wrangler spent little time there as they were constantly summoned away to solve baffling crimes and mysteries. One of their mysteries took them as far away as the Bay of Whales in New England. They worked all types of cases: federal, state, and local. Neither they, nor their writers, gave any thought to, or were worried about, legal jurisdiction.

Filling out the supporting cast that first year were Winifred Toomey, Andy Donnelly, Florence Freeman, Bruno Wick, Wilfred Lytell and Stanley Davis. Two of the actors would find great success later in the soap opera world of Chicago radio: Freeman would go on to play the title leads in both *Young Widder Brown* and *Wendy Warren and the News* while Davis not only was the producer and director of the long running *The Romance of Helen Trent*, he also sang the theme song.

From the very beginning, radio premiums were a large part of the promotion of the series, usually in exchange for a Ralston cereal box top and a few coins. During first season of 1933–1934 Ralston offered: Tom Mix photos, a shoulder patch, a booklet on the life of Tom Mix, and several items of western clothing and accessories. Ralston and Gardner did everything possible to tie Hollywood's Tom Mix to their radio show. In one radio premium post card, Tom and his horse, Tony, were pictured with the radio cast.

Tom Mix was interwoven with nearly every premium, including the "lucky horseshoe nail ring" which was "just like the one Tom wears himself." Some of the recipients who ordered this premium may have been surprised, however, when they opened the package because instead of a ring, the package contained a horseshoe nail with instructions on how to make the ring: "Use a poker or iron bar as an anvil. Place the horseshoe nail on it. Hold the end of the nail with a pair of pliers. Bend it by hammering until it is the exact size for your finger." Obviously, youngsters of that era were of sterner stuff than they are today.

On radio, there was nothing that Tom Mix could not do — draw faster than anyone, fight and beat the strongest opponent, fly a plane without instruments, tame the wildest horse, and in one episode he bested a chess master in three moves. He never killed a man. Each violent outlaw was rendered helpless when Mix outdrew him and fired a shot which grazed the villain's temple, knocking him unconscious. "Just creased his skull" Tom would comment over his fallen foe.

The production remained in New York City until mid–1937 when it moved to Chicago. The change was done primarily to get the program into the Central Time Zone which was more convenient for scheduling a juvenile adventure show that was heard from coast to coast. The only original performer who accepted the move to the Windy City was the oldest one in the cast, Percy Hemus. In Illinois, the new Tom Mix was Jack Holden, who was also a popular announcer on the *National Barn Dance* at radio station WLS. Jane Webb played Tom's ward, Jane, while a succession of young boys, including Hugh Rowlands and George Gobel, voiced another juvenile sidekick, Jimmy. Gobel, of course, became a television comedy star in 1954.

Another Chicago cast member was Harold "Hal" Peary, a versatile dialectician who would sometimes play two or three different characters in the same episode. By 1939, Peary was also playing Gildersleeve, the neighbor of *Fibber McGee and Molly*, where his popularity would earn him his own show in 1941. Others in the *Tom Mix* cast were Willard

Cast and crew of the *Tom Mix* show at 1947 party, clockwise from left foreground: Leo Curley (Mike Shaw); Bob Cline, sound effects; Harold Turner, organist; Forrest Lewis (Wash); Joe "Curley" Bradley (Tom Mix); Charles Claggett, producer and advertising agency representative; Mary Afflick, director; George Kuentz, sound effects; Don Gordon, announcer; and Carl Anderson, studio engineer (Jack French collection).

Waterman, Sidney Ellstrom, Charles MacDougal, and a singing trio, The Ranch Boys, consisting of Joe "Curley" Bradley, Jack Ross, and Ken "Shorty" Carson.

The young listeners of both genders were referred to as "Straight Shooters" and were addressed by that term by Tom Mix and whoever was the announcer. That term eventually became part of the title of the program. There even was a "Straight Shooter's Pledge" that Tom expected his listeners to follow. It included eating and drinking healthy food and beverages, playing fair and square at work, school and play, plus keeping a keen and alert mind and a strong healthy body. In addition, the pledge included a promise to eat Ralston cereal at least three times a week.

The series was a modern western in which Tom could be racing in a speeding roadster or flying a small airplane, but usually he was riding his horse Tony. Each program emphasized mystery and adventure, with Tom and the Old Wrangler pursuing cattle rustlers, bank robbers, and even international spies.

While the *Tom Mix* show was very popular with its juvenile audience, in terms of both listenership and orders for the increasing number of radio premiums, the admiration was not universal. *Variety* thought much less of the program and criticized it as early as

1936: "It's difficult to see much appeal to the program ... from any angle. Story is meaningless, inane, and every time the homestead gets in trouble, the Ranch Boys ... yodel off some so-called cowboy harmony."

Such reviews did not bother Claggett who was in charge of all phases of the program. He picked the director and all of the cast members, oversaw the scriptwriters, and supervised the selection of the continuing line of radio premiums. He knew the series was well liked by his target audience, juvenile boys and girls, and that's what counted with the officials at Ralston.

While Tom Mix was a U.S. marshal on his radio series, there was one attempt to change his occupation in February 1937. Someone, either at Ralston or Gardner, decided that Tom Mix and the Old Wrangler should be

Tom Mix supporting cast members clowning around at the microphone, circa 1940, from left: Hugh Rowlands, Jack Ross, and Harold "Hal" Peary (Jack French collection).

FBI Agents or "G-Men." NBC sent a letter to FBI Director J. Edgar Hoover, asking if he had any objections to this and assured Mr. Hoover that nothing in the scripts "would be said which would not be to the credit of the G-Men." Regardless of Hoover's response, the idea was subsequently dropped and Tom did not trade in his Marshal badge for G-Men credentials.

By 1939 when many of the kids in the audience routinely recognized the voice of Tom Mix (Jack Holden) as the announcer on the *National Barn Dance*, Claggett instructed Holden to give up the announcer's job. When Holden refused, Claggett fired him. Auditions were held for the vacancy and Russell Thorson, a tall, slim actor, became the next Tom Mix. He would play the part through 1942, two years after the death of the real Tom Mix.

An automobile accident claimed the life of Hollywood's prominent cowboy on October 12, 1940, on a highway near Florence, AZ. Driving his Cord roadster, he may have been speeding when he hit a patch of road work which sent him skidding into a gully. A steel trunk in the back seat plunged forward, snapping his neck and killing him instantly. He was 60 years old. The news flashed across the wire services and caused great consternation for both Ralston and Gardner officials. It was finally decided to merely mention the death in a dignified manner on the show and continue the radio series. That decision would keep Tom's show-biz career active for another decade.

While the show remained high in the ratings and the orders for the various premiums (wooden pistol, badge ring, periscope, signal flashlight, pocket knife, etc.) continued to pour in, Ralston decided to cancel the series for the year 1943. The reason? Daylight Savings Time. Over the objections of Claggett and his associates at Gardner, Ralston officials discontinued the *Tom Mix* program because they were convinced youngsters would not give up their playtime in the sun to listen to the radio. Ralston was wrong, of course, but it would take a year to get *Tom Mix* back on the air, in June 1944, after moving to the Mutual Network.

During the Mutual run, the leading roles were performed by two different actors. Joe "Curley" Bradley, who had been playing a significant supporting cast member, Pecos, in the NBC series, was elevated to portraying Tom Mix in the Mutual version. Percy Hemus had died in December 1943 at age 65 so the part of the Old Wrangler was eliminated. Tom's new sidekick was Sheriff Mike Shaw, voiced by a rotund ex-vaudevillian, Leo Curley.

Every episode had two or three Ralston commercials. Prior to Bradley winning the role of Tom, the commercials were usually read by the announcer and/or the Old Wrangler. Bradley had a fine baritone singing voice, so when he took over as Tom, he would sing the opening commercial on every show to the tune of "When the Bloom is on the Sage (When it's Roundup Time in Texas)." The lyrics varied, depending upon the season; Bradley sang about Hot Ralston in the cold months and about Shredded Ralston in the warmer periods.

There was also some reshuffling in the supporting cast, retaining a few from the NBC version, and hiring some new performers. The role of Wash, the ranch cook, went to Forrest Lewis, replacing Vance McCune; Lewis also doubled as Doc Green. Jane Webb continued to play her namesake, Jane, while Templeton Fox played other female roles. In addition, Betty Lou Gerson, Willard Waterman, and Cheer Brentson voiced, respectively, Chloe, Longbow Billy, and Drusilla Drake. Don Gordon, who had taken the announcer's job from Lynn Brandt, was retained on the Mutual show. Mary Afflick directed the series. She and Bradley pursued an off-mike romance and she eventually became the third of his four wives.

There were two sound effects men on the program, Bob Cline and George Kuentz, both talented fellows. The sound effects they created, both manual and from transcription disks, were convincing, timely, and skillfully executed. Carl Anderson was the regular studio engineer. All of the music on the show came from Harold Turner, who played both the studio organ and piano. Over the years, Turner also had his own musical programs on radio station WGN.

The series had no resemblance to real life. As a U.S. marshal, Tom Mix never reported to a supervisor, nor turned in a time sheet or a voucher, and never went to his office. Sheriff Mike Shaw was never at his county jail, never served a summons, and never ran for election. The two bachelors just enjoyed each other's company at the T-M Bar Ranch and broke away only when mystery or adventure beckoned. Usually each new storyline would contain a new radio premium, carefully woven into the plot.

None of the writers over the years, Roland Martini, Charles Tazewell or George

In center, left to right, Ralston-Purina president William H. Danforth, Margaret Marshutz (daughter of the head of Gardner Advertising, the firm which managed the *Tom Mix* radio show for Ralston) and Tom Mix, all holding Ralston products in publicity shot, circa 1936 (Jack French collection).

Lowther, intended for their scripts to be realistic or even logical. It was far more important for them to be exciting, interesting, and maintaining the attention of a juvenile audience. The episodic adventures averaged two to five weeks to wrap up a storyline, each one ending with a new one beginning in the same program. Tom and Mike usually were confronted with mysteries involving villains or spies with fanciful names and unusual powers.

One of the villains was called the Black Cat and he had the unexplained ability to jump great distances between buildings. Two other evildoers were the Woman in Gray, who used mental telepathy to bend victims to her will, and the Scarlet Scarecrow, who covered up his kidnappings by using post-hypnotic suggestion on the witnesses.

Large missing things were frequently employed in the storyline, e.g., an entire herd of cattle might disappear into thin air. One lengthy mystery was predicated upon an entire "vanishing village." Occasionally the scripts veered into science fiction. In one such mystery, a house disappeared, then reappeared, both caused by an ancient spirit inhabiting a giant cactus called the Green Man.

Literary figures also found their way into Tom and Mike's strange adventures. "The Story Book Mystery" began with the arrival of a man upon whose shoulder rested a parrot;

the stranger claimed to be Robinson Crusoe. In another storyline which aired one December, a jovial, portly prospector with white whiskers appeared unannounced at the T-M Bar Ranch to stay a while. A few days later, a large red sleigh was found in one of the ranch's out buildings. Both the chubby visitor and the sleigh disappeared the day before Christmas Eve.

On rare occasions, a real person would appear as himself on the show. In the April 29, 1947, episode of the mystery story "Hurricane Horse," George "Babe" Ruth was on the program. The writers set up a scenario where Ruth was headed to Hollywood to help supervise the filming of the movie, *The Babe Ruth Story*. Tom and Mike met the gravelly voiced baseball legend at the Dobie railroad station and they chatted with Ruth for about five minutes. They thus promoted both the upcoming motion picture with William Bendix, as well as the newly formed Babe Ruth Foundation to fight juvenile delinquency. This would be one of Ruth's last radio appearances; he died of cancer and pneumonia on August 16, 1948, at the age of 53.

But despite all the mystery, adventure, and "mile a minute thrills" that announcer Don Gordon promised at the beginning of each program, the series was not devoid of humor. Much of the show's humor involved the character of Wash, the African American ranch cook and handy man, played by Caucasian Forrest Lewis. A reoccurring joke on the series had Wash rushing out of the ranch office on some errand: "Ah goes, Ah flies, Ah… (sound of body falling on floor) Ooo, someday Ah jist gotta fix that rug." From time to time, Wash would dub himself "Shamrock Holmes" and attempt to assist Tom and Mike with the solution of a difficult case, and his antics and observations became very humorous.

The Mike Shaw character was also a source of humor. Some of it was derived from his unique expressions of indignation or surprise: two of his favorite ones were "sassafras and sourdough" and "tumbleweeds and Texas ticks." Occasionally Mike would be the subject of a running gag stretched over several episodes. One such storyline involving a mix-up at a lonely hearts club, had Mike pursued amorously by a 300 pound elderly spinster named Prunella Crabapple.

Through the late 1940s, the *Tom Mix* show continued on, although the numbers of its juvenile audience were gradually diminished by the inroads of television, especially on the East and West Coasts. The writers struggled to come up with new ideas for stories that would maintain the interest of the young Straight Shooters. For a while, the writers "broke the fourth wall" by having Tom and Mike discussing hurrying back to the studio to do their radio show.

Some of their youngest listeners were even more confused when one entire episode consisted of the two lawmen at the microphone, getting ready to do their program. Suddenly an armed Italian gang broke into the studio and held the cast and production crew hostage for the full 15 minutes. The episode ended when the gang ordered Don Gordon to give the signature sign-off. In the next episode, Tom and Mike commented on the audacity of the event which kept them off the air. This must have put the grade school age audience in a quandary, pondering reality versus fictional drama.

But it got worse. A new storyline contained a most outlandish premise: Straight Shooters were invited to send in their names and telephone numbers and Tom Mix would pick some lucky winners and call them — during a live broadcast. Tom's writers may have borrowed this technique from ABC radio's *Stop the Music* which used this method to soar in the ratings beginning in 1948.

Of course, it was easier for an audience participation program to do this, as opposed to a western fictional dramatization. Moreover, Curley Bradley as Tom Mix was not phoning the youngster merely to chat; he would make the call when he needed help or advice with an ongoing difficulty. It was absolutely preposterous and embarrassing for the great Tom Mix to telephone some kid to help him out of a tough spot.

During one particular episode, Tom was trapped alone by an arch villain in a furnished room with no doors or windows. The villain telephoned Tom and told him he knew about Tom's relationship with his Straight Shooters so he agreed to let Tom make one telephone call. A few minutes later Tom Mix was ad-libbing with an eight-year-old girl on the air. She suggested a couple of ways to activate a secret panel, including twisting a table leg, but nothing worked. Tom thanked her, hung up, and then, by pushing an entire wall sideways, made his escape.

By late 1949, other juvenile radio fiction had switched from 15 minute serial adventures into half hour complete stories. Ralston and Gardner Advertising were unable to agree on adopting this new format and the *Tom Mix* show was discontinued. Don Gordon ended the last episode by saying, "In the heart and imagination of the world, Tom Mix rides on, and lives on, forever."

Mutual thought that Bradley and Curley could still maintain audience interest so they launched a 30 minute sustaining show. Since Ralston still had the Tom Mix contract, this new show featured Curley Bradley under his own name as **The Singing Marshal** while Leo Curley portrayed his sidekick, Red Rivers. This new series lasted just 16 months.

Ralston continued its promotional relationship with a long dead Tom Mix by using his name and likeness in premiums after the radio show ended — including, ironically, a miniature toy television set. The 17 year run of the *Tom Mix* radio show had forged a permanent alliance with the Ralston Purina Company. In the 1980s, three decades after the show ended, Ralston resumed offering Tom Mix premiums, including cereal bowls, wristwatches, and membership kits in the Straight Shooters Club.

Sources: Audio copies of the *Tom Mix*; Cox, *Great Radio Soap*; Dunning, *On the Air*; Hake; Harmon, *Radio Mystery*; Hickerson, *4th Revised*; Katz; Mix, *Fabulous Tom*; Mix, *Life and Legend*; Correspondence of K. H. Berkeley, NBC Network, to J. Edgar Hoover, February 13, 1937; *Ralston Purina Magazine*, July/August 1979; Ralston Straight Shooters Manual (radio premium) circa 1934; *Variety*, October 23, 1935, and October 21, 1936.

TOMAHAWK TRAIL

KARL SCHADOW *and* JACK FRENCH

This series aired in 1937 over radio station WBBM, Chicago at 5:45 P.M., Mondays through Fridays. The 15 minute serial concerned a white boy and girl captured by Indians, some of whom were depicted as having evil intentions. The creators assuaged parents, who might find the content too frightening for younger listeners, by coordinating scripts with Irving Crump, the editor of *Boys Life Magazine*. Tom Shirley, as both the announcer and the narrator, had a voice with a welcoming tone that kept the action exciting without being terrifying. Other cast members included Al Brown, Charles Flynn, Earl George and Dolores Gillen. The program was sponsored by Kraftone Cheese and developed by the J. Walter Thompson advertising company. The program aired from April to July 1937 and the sponsor distributed thousands of wolf tails and good luck rings in exchange for gift certificates found in Kraftone Cheese cans.

Source: *Variety*, May 26, 1937, p. 30.

TOMMY GALE OF THE BOX T RANCH

JACK FRENCH *and* DAVID S. SIEGEL

NETWORK: Syndicated
FORMAT: 15 minutes
DURATION OF RUN: Broadcast unlikely
SPONSOR: None known
AUDIO COPIES EXTANT: 1 (first episode)
SCRIPTS ARCHIVED: Undetermined

The only surviving remnants of this juvenile western program consist of one disk with two copies of the same initial episode and a copyright filing with the Library of Congress in 1941 by creator and writer Robert E. Callahan who was the author and director of other western series, including *The Lone Indian* and *The Singing Bandit*. Whether or not this likely audition disk was ever aired is unknown at this time.

The reason for two copies of the same initial episode is that in the first one, the unnamed announcer lost his place briefly in the introduction, uttered an expletive which ruined the take, although the recording went forward to the conclusion. As was the syndication custom in that era, none of the actors or production staff were identified in the recording. It can be surmised that it was produced on the West Coast as Callahan was usually located there and did most of his radio work in California.

There are only four speaking parts in the first episode, three of whom form the typical triangle of many of the juvenile radio adventure series: the young but competent kid, the strong protective adult, and the likable geezer. This combination was utilized in many similar shows, including *Bobby Benson*, *Red Ryder*, and the early years of *Tom Mix*.

In this program, Tommy Gale is an orphan who had just lost his job at the Chicago Stock Yards. There he meets two cowboys, Tex Larrabee and Salty O'Brien, who have just sold their herd of cattle. Tex, who is the stalwart foreman of the Box T Ranch, is also a singing cowboy and at the beginning of the program, he warbles his song about his dead horse, "Good Bye, Pinto." Salty, a chuckling old timer, fills the air with colorful conversational declarations, i.e., "Leapin' Horntoads! I'll be a hog-tied brother of a walleyed calf!"

The fourth character heard in this episode is the owner of the ranch, Judge George Montgomery. When this script was being written, the actor who achieved some fame under the professional name of George Montgomery was still acting in small roles under his birth name, George Letz. So Callahan's choice of a name for the ranch owner was not significant at that time. Three characters are mentioned in the episode but do not actually appear as speaking parts: Ace Scanlon, the villain, Ma, the matriarch at the ranch, and little Jane whose pet pony has just returned to the ranch without her.

Characteristic of the many juvenile adventure series, the kid in the leading role drove the plot since he was the smartest one in the room and the adults followed his instructions: When Tex loses his wallet containing $24,000 because the lining in his pocket is ripped,

Tommy finds the wallet and returns it, refusing to accept a tip. Then, when an emergency comes up and Tex, Salty and the Judge have to get back to the ranch and the train ride would be too slow, Tommy offers to drive them in a car, but if this will not be fast enough, Tommy then suggests they charter a plane and the Judge agrees.

Sound effects on the show were minimal but realistic and musical bridges were short but sufficient. All of the actors performed well and showed their microphone experience, including the youngster portraying Tommy.

Sources: Audio copy of *Tommy Gale of the Box T Ranch*; Katz; *Los Angeles Times*, December 20, 1933, pg. A4; http://www.radiogoldindex.com.

TRIPLE BAR X DAYS AND NIGHTS

JACK FRENCH

A half hour Sunday evening program on NBC Blue, the series was on the air from 1933 to 1934. The show combined cowboy songs with dramatized fiction of the west. The frontier tales featured "strong men and brave women" and were aimed at a family listening audience. White's Cod Liver Oil (in both liquid form and concentrated tablets) sponsored the series and generally ran its commercials only at the beginning and end of each show. *Variety* reviewed the program and concluded: "Good production, casting and presentation."

Source: *Variety*, November 14, 1933, p. 34.

UNDER WESTERN SKIES

KARL SCHADOW

This series began as a 30 minute local production on November 10, 1937, from Pittsburg's KDKA and achieved network status on NBC Blue on January 26, 1938, where it aired until May 10, 1938, when it reverted to a local program, ending in 1939. The program's creator, Derby Sproul, had spent two years writing and producing **Light on the West** on KOA in Denver. Each episode was a complete story written or adapted by Sproul with mystery or comedy plots of mining, railroads, the forestry service and ranch life. Cast members were: Jay Orrison, Delle Gillis, Charles Webster, Leon Churchon, R. P. Griffith, William Hetzel, William Wallace, Stephanie Diamond, John Johns, Helen Wayne, Leon Ward, Richard Poe, Frank Frielong, Jack Anderson, George Hyde, Dorothy Bushy, Paul Shannon, Marion Potter, Portia Matthews and Elmer Waltman. The production crew included: Spar Hull (narrator), Bill Hinds (announcer), John Shiliano (sound effects), Jack Taylor (animal imitator), Bernie Armstrong (organist), Bert Egizi (orchestra director for local run), Maurice Spitalny (orchestra director for the network run) and Carl Weininger (music writer). The series consistently received high ratings in national publications.

Source: *Billboard*, April 2, 1938.

WESTERN CARAVAN

JACK FRENCH *and* DAVID S. SIEGEL

NETWORK: NBC
FORMAT: Half hour, Sundays
DURATION OF RUN: June 25, 1950, to October 15, 1950

SPONSOR: Pepsodent Toothpaste
AUDIO COPIES EXTANT: 5
SCRIPTS ARCHIVED: Undetermined

Various sources attribute different dates to this short lived mid–1950s western drama. Two audio copies in general circulation (the others are available in the Library of Congress) are dated by collectors as August 11, 1950 (a Friday), and September 20, 1950 (a Wednesday). However, both of these dates must be in error as contemporary newspaper listings confirm that the show was heard only on Sunday evenings. East Coast newspapers list the program premiering on June 25, 1950, and on the October 15, 1950, episode, it was announced this would be the last episode so these are probably the inclusive dates of its brief run.

The leading roles were filled by western musicians, not traditional radio actors. The star, Tex Williams, was born Sollie Paul Williams on August 23, 1917, in Ramsey, IL. As a teenager, he played in a country and western band in Washington state and by the early 1940s he was the lead vocalist and played guitar with Spade Cooley's band. About 1946, Williams formed a trio with Deuce Spriggins and Smokey Rogers which was called Western Caravan. Beginning in 1949, the trio appeared in a series of twelve short musical pictures produced by Universal International. From there it was just a short leap to the radio microphone, using their group name as the title of their series for NBC.

Based on listening to the audio copies in general circulation, this brief series was a combination of music, drama, comedy and mystery, none of which had any relevance to the real West of the prairie frontier era that it was portraying. Some of the scenes, although played straight, were just plain silly. In one program, the trio shoots a helpless coyote, accidentally causing a stampede of 10,000 cattle nearby which they hadn't seen on the prairie. After the stampede is quelled, the cattle owner wants to hire all three, but Yancey, the trail foreman, refuses, saying, "I don't hire any man unless I whip him in a fight." He and Tex fight and the foreman is badly beaten. The owner then makes Tex his new foreman, explaining, "I won't have any foreman who can't whip every cowboy working for me."

The script gets even more outlandish. Yancey convinces all the cowhands to quit the drive because of the danger of marauding Apache nearby. Tex threatens to kill Yancey and any other man who tries to leave the cattle. They relent. Next, when a dangerous river blocks the trail, Tex's plan is to drive the reluctant cattle into the deep river. When they drown, the cowboys drive more cattle after them, until the herd is walking on dead cattle to reach the other side. Obviously such a simplistic and unrealistic western program could capture and retain only the attention of a juvenile audience.

Williams, Spriggins, and Rogers, while primarily singers, acquit themselves fairly well, despite the limitations of the scripts. Three other people are given name credit on the programs: Robert Armbruster for the music with Hal Gibney and Eddie King as announcers.

After the radio series ended, Williams continued with modest success in the movies, record industry, television, and even operated his own night club, Tex Williams Village. While some of his songs became somewhat popular, none of them approached the ratings of his "Smoke, Smoke, Smoke (That Cigarette)" which was ranked number one for the year 1947 by *Billboard* on its country chart. Despite the title, the song was a strong anti-smoking message. How ironic that the vocalist who made that song so well-known would eventually die of cancer, as Williams did on October 11, 1985, in California.

Sources: Audio copies of *Western Caravan*; Marshall; *Brooklyn Eagle*, June 25, 1950; *Binghamton (NY) Press*, July 30, 1950; http://www.sing365.com.

WHEN THE WEST WAS YOUNG

JACK FRENCH *and* STEWART WRIGHT

NETWORK: Armed Forces Radio & Television Service (AFRTS)
FORMAT: Half hour, weekly
DURATION OF RUN: Circa 1966 to 1968
SPONSOR: None
AUDIO COPIES EXTANT: 3
SCRIPTS ARCHIVED: University of California at Northridge (1)

Although documentation is incomplete for this series, it was obviously a companion piece to *Horizons West* as it has the same director, one of the same writers, the same sound man, and most of the supporting cast appears in both series. It was produced by AFRTS in Los Angeles, CA, possibly in the same location used for *Horizons West*, Studio B of Capitol Records. The show was recorded at least three years after *Horizons West* based on a time marker inserted into the script at the end of one chapter: the script mentions the death of three war correspondents, including Georgette "Dickey" Chapelle, who was killed in Vietnam when she stepped on a land mine on November 4, 1965.

The writers on this series, including William Tundberg and Milton P. Kahn, based their western frontier dramatizations around real people in U. S. history but they deliberately chose historical figures who would not be well known to their listeners, e.g., Richard Pratt, Esther Hobart Morris and Mark Kellogg. Frequently the scripts would not reveal the historical significance of the person until the closing minutes of the program.

The 30 minute show began with a minute or two of significant dialogue from the script, followed by the music theme which would diminish as the announcer began his introduction:

Stand up high and face the west! And see their footprints span a continent before you … footprints that were made when the west was young. *[Music sting]* This is the story of one of those who sought new frontiers and found them when the west was young, shaping them into the greater part of a nation. Their deeds and their accomplishments have been recorded by history, but their spirit remains as constant, young, and progressive as the country that is indebted to them. *[Music up]*

The production values on this series were very high with crisp writing, excellent acting, fine direction, and realistic sound effects. William "Bill" Lally, as producer and director, must have been justifiably proud of the product. Since this was an anthology with a different historical person as the central figure, Lally chose different people as leads, e. g., Harry Bartell as Mark Kellogg, Lurene Tuttle as Esther Morris, and Herb Ellis as Richard Pratt.

Lally's supporting cast for this series consisted of a cadre of West Coast network veterans, many of whom he had utilized in producing *Horizons West*. They included Parley Baer, Howard Culver, Philip Pine, Lillian Buyeff, Brian Adams, Wright King, Stanley Farrar, Jack Carroll, Don Messick, Jack Edwards, Don Doolittle, Jane Webb, Jack Kruschen and Tyler McVey. The announcer was Bob LeMond, who had an extensive resume in that capacity; he was also the announcer on *Lights Out*, *My Friend Irma*, *Hollywood Showcase* and a dozen other network programs.

Radio sound effects by the 1960s had progressed from largely manual sounds to transcribed ones. Moreover, some of these could be "overlaid" on recorded dialogue. Therefore, complicated programs like this series, which years prior might have required three or four people to create all the sounds, could now be done by one experienced man. For *When the West Was Young* that person was Gene Twombly who had learned his craft doing sound effects on the **Gene Autry Show**, *The Whistler*, and *The Jack Benny Show*.

The scripts, while aimed at an adult audience, were still palatable to juvenile listeners. Stories were chosen to avoid gun fighters, law enforcement officials, and military heroes of the western frontier and instead concentrated on lesser known historical figures, including women and minorities, who were presented in a positive way.

The episode which ends with Custer's Last Stand at the Little Big Horn in 1876 is told through the diary of the *Bismarck Tribune* correspondent, Mark Kellogg, who traveled with the U.S. Cavalry on this ill-fated excursion as a representative of the *New York Herald*. Kellogg, as both narrator and participant, relates to the audience his observations on the weather, the terrain, the mood of the soldiers, and even the impatience of his editor. The script does not even name Custer or the Little Big Horn until the closing minutes.

Another episode involved "cultures in conflict" as Army Captain Richard Pratt commanded a contingent of African American "Buffalo Soldiers" who, in 1875, escorted a large number of Indian prisoners on a train. In the ensuing drama, listeners learn of the strengths and weaknesses of all three races and are provided with a realistic summary of how they interact in this period of American history. The surprise, revealed in the program's conclusion, was that in 1879 Pratt founded a school for Indians at Carlyle, PA which later became famous because of Pop Warner and Jim Thorpe.

A third program was a tribute to the strength of women on the frontier in terms of fighting for their rights of citizenship. A group of Wyoming women, led by Esther Hobart Morris, none of whom could legally vote or hold political office, coerce their husbands (by threatening a boycott in the kitchen and bedroom) into supporting women's suffrage. Their determination, organized pressure, and steadfastness prevails in 1869 when the territory of Wyoming gives full voting rights to women, some 50 years before women in the rest of the country were given those privileges.

Milton Geiger, a radio and television writer, contributed one script to this series entitled "Booth: The Fiery Star," a dramatization of the career of actor Edwin Booth, the older brother of John Wilkes Booth, Lincoln's assassin. While this script is archived at California State University in Northridge, no audio copy has yet surfaced. The total number of episodes in this series is still unknown, but believed to be approximately twelve.

Sources: Audio copies of *When the West Was Young*; Brown; Utley; Milton Geiger papers, Special Collections, California State University at Northridge; http://home.epix.net/~landis/histry.html; http://www.sameshield.com; http://www.wisconsinhistory.org/topics/chapelle.

WILD BILL ELLIOTT

JACK FRENCH *and* DAVID S. SIEGEL

NETWORK: ABC (proposed series)
FORMAT: 15 minutes
DURATION OF RUN: Probably never aired

AUDIO COPIES EXTANT: 5

SCRIPTS ARCHIVED: Undetermined

In the summer of 1948, the ABC Network attempted to secure sponsorship from the Quaker Oats Company of a new quarter hour juvenile western series starring Republic Studios cowboy star, Wild Bill Elliott. ABC recorded at least five transcriptions in this project, some of which were complete episodes and one with just isolated scenes to introduce the characters in the series. Apparently no agreement was reached with Quaker Oats, or any other company, and no evidence has surfaced yet to confirm that the series was ever broadcast.

Not a great deal is known about this proposed program, other than it was recorded at ABC Studios in Los Angeles, CA. Only two of the approximately one dozen performers in it are identified: Bill Elliott and Owen James, the announcer. The director, scriptwriter, sound effects person, and organist are equally unknown. The series was obviously aimed at a juvenile listening audience, so unfortunately, that meant Elliott was paired with a "pint sized saddle partner," Buddy Fillmore. Although the announcer terms him "teen-aged," the young actor playing him sounds more like a 10-year-old.

Writers of juvenile adventure series loved to pair the adult hero with one or two youngsters as sidekicks who were sometimes explained as wards or nephews and nieces. Examples of this dynamic can be found in *The Sparrow and the Hawk*, **Tom Mix**, **Rin Tin Tin**, and **Red Ryder**. Occasionally, as in this series, the relationship between the hero and his tagalong is never explained in the script. Presumably, the youngster in the program provided juvenile listeners with someone with whom they could identify.

But this strategy usually failed on two counts. First, few children in the radio audience identified with the kid on the program; they were too interested in the hero. Secondly, the presence of a juvenile as an almost equal partner was simply not believable in a realistic sense. However, the *Wild Bill Elliott* show was not intended to be an accurate portrayal of the western frontier. Any astute listener could determine that from the announcer's introduction of rancher, Wild Bill: "He loves kids and fair play as much as he detests knavery and untrustworthiness. And in turn, Bill is loved by children, the underprivileged, and even the very animals he raises."

Elliott was born Gordon A. Nance in 1904 in Missouri, the son of a cattle broker. He grew up on a ranch and even won a few rodeo events before Hollywood beckoned. By 1925 he was getting bit parts in silent movies. After a few more years, he was cast in fairly decent film roles, changed his name to Gordon Elliott, and after some successful western motion pictures, modified his name again, this time to Wild Bill Elliott.

By the time he started recording this radio series, he'd had major roles in over four dozen western movies, first with Columbia Pictures and then with Republic Studios, where he starred in 24 films. In 16 of the latter, he played Red Ryder, even though he and the studio refused to make him look anything like the popular Red Ryder of the comic books; that fictional cow puncher always wore a white hat and traditional two-gun holsters. Elliott instead wore a black hat and on his waist, his holsters were backwards so his six-guns were butt forward.

As the 1950s and television approached, the fortunes of Republic Studios began to fade. That meant fewer western films were being released and there was less work for the studio's cadre of cowboy stars. For whatever his reasons, Elliott decided that he was going to try to make some money in radio but this involved getting sponsorship for a series and there is no evidence that that ever happened; Elliott's personality, which did not transition well from the silver screen to radio, may have been one reason for his failure to attract a sponsor.

In most movie scenes, Elliott possessed an almost grim poker face and spoke his lines in a laconic way, nearly languid. On a galloping horse or in a corral fist fight, this was not noticeable, but with only a radio microphone to project his emotions, his character comes across rather flat. This is especially evident since the actors in the supporting roles are both energetic and interesting. His youthful sidekick, Buddy, brims with enthusiasm. The grandfather, a newspaper editor, is both bombastic ("Great Gilded Glory!") and highly animated. A third actor, portraying Longhorn Jones, does a respectable imitation of Walter Brennan which is entertaining.

The sound effects were minimal, mostly consisting of hoofbeats, but certainly adequate for a juvenile western. Musical bridges and the main themes were the work of a skilled organist. Elliott's signature movie line was "I'm a peaceable man" so it was also woven into the radio program. The combination of an interesting script (stage coaches vanish on hard ground into thin air), fairly good acting backed up with adequate sound effects and music could have resulted in sponsorship and air time. But it didn't.

Sources: Audio copies of *Wild Bill Elliott*; Hickerson, *4th Revised*; Hurst; Katz; Mac-Donald, *Don't Touch*; http://www.radiogoldindex.com.

WILD BILL HICKOK

Bob Burnham

NETWORK: Mutual
FORMAT: Half hour, weekly
DURATION OF RUN: April 1, 1951, to February 12, 1956
SPONSOR: Kellogg's cereals and sustained
AUDIO COPIES EXTANT: 25
SCRIPTS ARCHIVED: Undetermined

While fact and fiction are blurred in the life and career of the real Wild Bill Hickok, it's safe to conclude that he had absolutely no similarities to the character on television and radio that bore his name. The original "Wild Bill" (James Butler Hickok, 1837–1876) was a frontier scout, an inveterate gambler, an occasional lawman, a callous gunslinger and killer, and an unabashed alcoholic who, at age 39, was killed in a saloon.

Wild Bill Hickok appeared first as a syndicated radio program on Mutual in 1951 and then on CBS-TV from 1955 to 1958 and also on ABC-TV from 1957 to 1958. For a while, both radio and television versions ran concurrently, but when the radio series ended in 1956, the television show remained popular and stayed on the air for another two years. Both the radio and television series featured the same two leads: Wild Bill was played by Guy Madison (born Robert Ozell Moseley) who had appeared in a large number of western film roles starting in 1944 and had won a Golden Globe special award for best western star in 1954, and Andy Devine, the gravelly voiced B-movie hero, played Jingles, Wild Bill's comedic sidekick.

Devine would open each episode by yelling "Wiiiiiiiiiiiiild Billlllllll Hickok!" He also generally delivered the opening commercial as well on the sponsored shows and narrated the programs, calling them "rootin' tootin'" adventures.

Several notable West Coast actors appeared on the show, including Cliff Arquette,

Ralph Moody, Howard McNear, Charlie Lung, Paul Frees, Will Wright, Barney Phillips, Tyler McVey, Forrest Lewis, Clayton Post, Ken Christy, and Jack Moyles. Charlie Lyon, whose voice was familiar to radio listeners as the announcer for *Yours Truly, Johnny Dollar* was the show's announcer.

Sound effects for the series were handled by Bill James, one of the most talented in that profession on the West Coast. Teamed with Ray Kemper and Tom Hanley, this trio was responsible for the sound artistry on **Gunsmoke, Fort Laramie**, and other great CBS radio shows. On *Wild Bill Hickok*, James used both manual and transcribed sounds of cattle, horses, hoofbeats, sheep, and goats. Crowd scenes and fights were particularly realistic, complete with breaking furniture. Occasionally director Paul Pierce would give James a few lines resulting in name credit in an episode.

All of the music on the show, both the main theme and scene bridges, came from the organ with Richard Aurandt at the keyboard. One of the busiest radio musicians in Hollywood, Aurandt played for several adventure shows, including *Yours Truly, Johnny Dollar* and *Adventures of Philip Marlowe* and soap operas, including *Masquerade*. He also composed the main themes for some radio series, including the majestic one on *Voyage of the Scarlet Queen*.

During the time Kellogg sponsored the radio show, the company featured photos of Madison and Devine on the front of their cereal boxes of Sugar Pops and offered juvenile listeners a series of badges, photo buttons, and miniature rifles and pistols. When the transcribed show was aired in Canada, Madison and Devine extolled Kellogg's Rice Crispies in the commercials as "Canada's Only Talking Cereal."

Both the television series and the radio shows were clearly intended for a juvenile audience. Wild Bill and Jingles, respectively riding steeds named Buckshot and Joker, wandered throughout the West and outfought outlaws, solved bank robberies, prevented cattle rustling, and generally brought justice to the rangeland they traveled through. While gunplay was used on many occasions, many of the fights with the evildoers were settled with fisticuffs. The scenario of the series had Hickok as a U.S. Marshal and Jingles as his deputy. However neither of them ever engaged in the routine of a real marshal; they never went to a federal office, reported to a superior, guarded a court room, or filled out an expense report.

Some juvenile westerns had little humor in their scripts, such as **The Lone Ranger** and **Tennessee Jed**, while other programs, such as **The Cisco Kid** and **Bobby Benson** did incorporate fun and comedy into their shows. The *Wild Bill Hickok* series was similar to the latter with Jingles being the source of much of the comedy. Voiced by the rotund Devine, Jingles conveyed mischief, fun, and surprises in their adventures. Sometimes Jingles appeared to the bumbling, klutzy sidekick, but of course, the two saddle pals would always find a way out of whatever predicament Devine's character had gotten them into.

Sources: Audio copies of *Wild Bill Hickok*; Brooks; Dunning, *On the Air*; Hake; Hickerson, *4th Revised*; Katz; Raine.

WINNING THE WEST

Karl Schadow *and* Jack French

One of radio's early western oriented programs, *Winning the West* celebrated the exploits of the early pioneers who settled on America's western frontier. It was written by

NBC staffer, Wilbur Hall, who claimed to be an authority on the Old West. The series, which debuted in 1933 and ran for three years, originated from San Francisco and was sponsored by the Occidental Life Insurance Company of California. Starring in the cast were Charles MacAlister, Helen Musselman, and Frank Provo.

Source: *Broadcast Weekly*, November 5–11, 1933.

A WOMAN OF AMERICA

Martin Grams, Jr.

Network: NBC
Format: 15 minutes, five days a week
Duration of Run: January 25, 1943, to June 21, 1946
Sponsor: Proctor & Gamble (promoting Ivory Snow)
Audio Copies Extant: 2 shows, July 23 and August 10, 1945
Scripts Archived: General Foods Archives at the Library of Congress; Proctor & Gamble, Cincinnati, OH

A significant western soap opera, *A Woman of America*, was the dramatic story of a young widow's struggle against the forces that caused her husband's untimely death and her unrelenting determination to find happiness in the frontier West. Airing during World War II, the series championed the opportunities for freedom and justice which represented the true American spirit. The program opened with a fictional young widow, Prudence Dane, and her two small children setting out from Pennsylvania in 1865 with a group of pioneers in a covered wagon train bound for Kansas. The program was introduced by Margaret Dane, the "great granddaughter of Prudence Dane" who stressed that today the women of America were once again fighting side by side with their men — in the factories, on the farms, in their homes, even on the field of battle itself, they were responding by the millions to America's needs.

Each episode opened with the theme song "Westward Ho," a composition of Hugo Reisenfeld first written for the 1923 silent film *The Covered Wagon* and played on the studio organ. The same song would be used as the theme for *Bobby Benson and the B-Bar-B Riders* when that program debuted on Mutual in 1949. As with most soap operas, the sound effects were minimal and if the organist could not mimic the desired sound effect on the keyboard, it was usually eliminated.

The show's scenario involved all the trials and hardships of traveling across the country via the Oregon Trail, including battles with hostile Indians, the danger of typhoid, blackmailing schemers who tried to strike their fortune before reaching Kansas, and harsh winter storms. When food rations were low, tempers flared and the men responsible for hunting wild game were frequently wounded or sick. Prudence was not afraid to arm herself and fetch food for the camp. When the troubles mounted and those in the team feared the worst, the character of Julia King often sang to help the others keep their minds off their troubles. In one episode, King confessed to a friend that she really sang to keep others from suspecting she herself was afraid. The singing was performed by Dorothy Kirsten.

Ultimately the wagon trains reached their destination where greedy landlords, conniving saloon girls and reckless ranchers began offering new problems for the Dane clan. Prudence helped write a number of crusading stories for the local newspaper. She played cupid when love wasn't prevailing. And when the sheriff had to ride out of town on business, Prudence was forced once again to arm herself against drunken cowpokes. This was a milestone in her career because she gained respect from the town citizens and, as the result of an election, the town was renamed Danesville.

Although this was a 15 minute show, there was only 10 minutes of scripted drama since two and a half minutes at the beginning and the end were devoted to the commercials. Proctor & Gamble promoted only Ivory Snow on this series, "the strong dishwashing detergent that's mild on your hands." Many of the Ivory Snow commercials on this program were sung to the tune of "Jingle Bells."

What made *A Woman of America* unique compared to most soap operas of the day was not just the western setting, but the fact that commercial time was occasionally supplemented with patriotic reminders with guest speakers. For the broadcast of October 6, 1943, Bill Orndorff of New York City, a former aerial gunner in the Royal Canadian Air Force, told of his Wellington bomber crashing. He bailed out and landed in Nazi occupied territory. He described, briefly, his seven weeks among the enemy until he made his escape. He closed his speech with a plea for conservation of waste kitchen fat.

In lieu of the commercial for the broadcast of October 10, 1943, Gwen Priestwood, author of *Through Japanese Barbed Wire*, gave a detailed account of her escape from a Japanese prison, Camp Stanley. And, for the broadcast of March 8, 1944, Gunner's First Mate Second Class George Lambert of Chillicothe, OH, described his experience on two ships that were torpedoed and sunk. For his heroism he was awarded the Silver Star and a citation from President Roosevelt. His citation was read over the air.

Other non-commercial messages included a prayer and a Thanksgiving tribute from the cast at the close of the Thanksgiving broadcast of November 23, and the August 8, 1945, broadcast that featured only seven minutes of drama because it was interrupted by a special news broadcast by Morgan Beatty from Washington with details about Russia declaring war on Japan.

After the network received numerous letters addressing the concern that the drama of the day was never completed and that a summary was never provided the next day to fill in what the listeners failed to hear, the sponsor used the letters as leverage insisting the network reimburse the cost of airtime they were contractually obligated to pay. The network put up resistance for an estimated seven days, claiming the sponsor's seven minutes were sufficient (especially since a commercial was aired sometime during those seven minutes), but eventually it dropped its position and consented to the sponsor's request.

Anne Seymour, who starred as Prudence and Margaret Dane, received a Stage Door Canteen Award after two years of service. During her off hours, in between home and her time in front of the radio microphone, she worked in the Canteen's kitchen making coffee — and maintained a production schedule of 400 cups an hour. Her efforts were praised during the closing of a broadcast in late June of 1944.

Over the years, Seymour was backed up with a very large supporting cast including: Ginger Jones, Cecil Roy, Kenneth Lynch, James Monks, Staats Cotsworth, Lawrence Robinson, Rosemary Garbel, Santos Ortega, Kenny Delmar, Cliff Carpenter, Joan Tetzel, Linda Carlon, Irene Hubbard, Edwin Jerome, and Jack Manning.

Others in the supporting cast were: Ian Martin, Everett Sloan, Arthur Vinton, Ed Begley, Jo Boland, Cameron Prud'Homme, Ed Latimer, Bartlett Robinson, James Van Dyke, Marilyn Erskine, Chester Stratton, and Donald Ormond.

The remaining cast members consisted of: Florence Freeman, Carol Peterson, Donald Loughlin, Frances Woodbury, Helen Claire, Nancy Douglas, Joseph Curtin, Joan Banks, Betty Philson, Barry Hopkins, Kay Miller, Juano Hernandez, Maurice Ellis, Luis Van Rooten, Jose Ferrer, Jackson Beck, and Louise Larabee.

The series was directed by Don Cope and the scriptwriter was Merrill Denison, who was replaced in September of 1944 by Doria Folliott. Shortly after the war ended, Folliott decided to change the format of the series. (Some evidence suggests that when Proctor & Gamble dropped its relationship with Benton & Bowles on September 17, 1945, its new agency, Dancer-Fitzgerald-Sample, disliked the program and insisted on revamping the series from a frontier background to a modern day setting.) Beginning with the September 11, 1945, broadcast, the series switched to the 20th century and to the great-great grandchildren of Prudence Dane in the town that she had founded, Danesville. Everyone was gathered around the town square to greet Captain John Dane Barker who was coming home from the war. His mother, Prudence Dane Barker, was Prudence Dane's great-grandchild.

Playing the lead of Prudence Dane Barker in the new format was Florence Freeman, who played prominent parts in radio dramas since her debut in 1935. During her tenure on *A Woman of America*, Freeman was also playing the title lead in *Wendy Warren and the News*. Freeman was a college graduate and taught for a year before deciding to become an actress. Her real life resembled somewhat that of the character she played on the air; she was the wife of a rabbi, had two daughters, and spent years failing to remodel her house by herself until she acquired the assistance of her entire family.

The new cast, backing up Freeman, included: Ogden Miles, Nancy Douglas, James Van Dyke, Edgar Stehli, Bartlett Robinson, Frances Carlon, Robert Haag, Barry Thompson, Michael Fitzmaurice, and Adelaide Hawley.

On the final broadcast of the series, June 21, 1946, Prudence Dane Barker celebrated her birthday with a happy family reunion and a closing speech to the audience by Prudence.

Initially, Proctor & Gamble was uncertain whether the series would be worth the cost of sponsorship. The initial contract was for 22 weeks, from January 25 to June 25, 1943, but before the end of May, executives at Benton & Bowles, the advertising agency representing P&G, convinced the company to extend sponsorship in increments of 52 weeks, and the series was renewed every year thereafter. The only stipulation P&G requested in return for the extension was a later time slot.

With the series broadcast live, a later time slot allowed exposure on the West Coast but NBC was contractually unable to provide them a later time slot until September 27, 1943, when the series moved from 10:45 A.M. to 3:00 P.M. When *A Woman of America* concluded in 1945, P&G retained the same time slot for a soap opera formerly broadcast on the Mutual Broadcasting Company, *Life Can Be Beautiful*.

Sources: Audio copies of *A Woman of America*; Cox, *Great Radio Soap Operas*; *Herald-Statesman*, Yonkers, NY, November 14, 1944; NBC press releases, June 24, 1944, and January 10, 1945; *New York Times*, July 3, 1944; Proctor & Gamble Archives in Cincinnati, Ohio; *Schenectady (NY) Gazette*, June 18, 1943; Scripts on microfilm at the Recorded Sound Division of the Library of Congress.

The Wonder Dog see ***Rin Tin Tin***

ZANE GREY THEATER

S<small>TAN</small> C<small>LAUSSEN</small>

N<small>AMES</small>: *Zane Grey Theater, The Zane Grey Show*
N<small>ETWORK</small>: Don Lee Mutual
F<small>ORMAT</small>: Half hour, weekly
D<small>URATION OF</small> R<small>UN</small>: September 23, 1947, to February 24, 1948
S<small>PONSOR</small>: Sustaining
A<small>UDIO</small> C<small>OPIES</small> E<small>XTANT</small>: 1 complete, 2 others containing only first half
S<small>CRIPTS</small> A<small>RCHIVED</small>: Undetermined

Less than a decade after the death of popular adventure novelist Zane Grey, a radio show bearing his name debuted on Mutual. It would be heard Tuesday evenings from September 23, 1947, to February 24, 1948. It was originally produced in Hollywood and later from New York. Vic Perrin played the lead cowboy, Tex Thorne, in Hollywood while Don MacLaughlin played Thorne in the New York version. The announcer described Tex as "a high country drifter on the wild frontier where strong men lived by the strong law of personal justice."

Harry Zimmerman composed the music and conducted the live orchestra. Paul Franklin wrote the scripts and directed in Hollywood, just as he was doing for another western radio series, **Red Ryder**. When the show moved to New York, Emmett Paul directed. The producer was Stephen Slesinger. Franklin tried to incorporate the general themes of Zane Grey into his scripts and occasionally simplified some of the plots from the Grey novels. Grey (1872–1939) wrote over 60 novels, many dealing with the western frontier, and his novels sold more than 13,000,000 copies in his lifetime. His books were melodramatic with little depth of characterization; he preferred stock villains and self-sufficient heroes in the saddle. His main characters were steadfast and faithful to the "code of the West" and both shy and chivalrous in the presence of the opposite sex.

His 1912 novel, *Riders of the Purple Sage*, is often cited as his breakthrough story of the American West. And while the novel was set in Great Basin country, frontier life took second place to the struggle of young June Withersteen to escape Mormon polygamy and eventually find true love outside the Mormon Church with the help of outsiders; the couple is hunted down until the pair finds a hidden valley with no access to the outside world. Most of Grey's plots before his Hollywood years were highly romanticized but after he moved to the West Coast, he made his own motion pictures for a short interval, and then wrote western stories and novels for adaptation by filmmakers.

The radio series was set in a cow town called Purple Sage, which the announcer assured listeners was "sprawled along the roaring frontier while rutted trails rumbled under the frequent movement west and constant clanking of wagons and mules urged on by men seeking rainbow's end; where beckoning fingers of the sunset etched purple on the great slopes of the unconquered Rockies."

Each program opened with "Oh, Susannah!" played on a banjo after which the narrator announced: "The adventures of Tex Thorne, based on the works of Zane Grey." While it is not known how many of Grey's actual plots Franklin borrowed for his scripts, it is apparent that he did use portions of Grey's 1915 novel, *The Border Legion*, set in Idaho, in which a rancher's daughter, Joan Randle, falls in love with a cold-hearted gunslinger named Jack Kells. The novel was made into no less than three motion pictures.

Franklin's episode "The Duel," which aired September 30, 1947, has rancher Sam Crockett objecting to trigger-happy Jack Bemis, who wants to court Crockett's daughter, Mary. Tex, who delivers mail on his horse Topaz, fails to bring peace between the two men, and during a later fight, Bemis wounds the old rancher. (In what would appear to be an inconsistency in the script, Franklin has Tex delivering mail which would imply that he cannot be illiterate. However, the script also has him confessing to Miss Tyler that he "cannot write.")

Tex is present when the town marshal tries to arrest Bemis, who almost escapes after killing the marshal. Eventually Tex concludes that Bemis, who keeps saying "Don't call me crazy," may indeed be mentally unstable. Later, Bemis escapes from jail, goes to the Crockett ranch, and at gunpoint, insists that Mary run away with him and become his wife. Tex shoots Bemis in the leg, takes him into custody, and insures that his mental problems are brought up during his trial so he is sentenced to life in a prison hospital.

In his book *Who Shot the Sheriff?* J. Fred Mac Donald writes that there were "varieties of adultness" in early westerns. And in the case of *The Zane Grey Theater*, the mental instability of Jack Bemis must stand out as an early instance of adult programming, even if most of the plot is almost completely driven by frequent gunfire.

The other relationship in this story is the cautious affection of a restaurant owner, Miss Tyler, for Tex Thorne although Thorne confides to an associate, "But for me, [I'm] footloose and jist following the tumbleweeds, and no female woman is dapping a rope on my carcass."

Sound effects on the series were generally realistic and consisted mostly of hoof beats, gunshots, and in the case of some fights, broken furniture. Zimmerman does a good job with his orchestra and both the main theme and the musical bridges demonstrate variety and were appropriate to the script.

Vic Perrin and other performers in *Zane Grey Theater* actively participated in the evolution from juvenile to adult westerns. Richard Le Grand, Earle Ross, Howard Mc Near and others in the supporting cast also appeared in **Red Ryder** and other network shows and many would be heard in **Gunsmoke** a few years later. Perrin also had a major role in **Fort Laramie** as Sergeant Gorce and Don MacLaughlin played a federal agent in the popular show *Counterspy* and was almost typecast as the "wise doctor" in *The Road of Life* and several other soap operas. He also played Dr. Chris Hughes in *As the World Turns* on TV for almost 20 years.

Sources: Audio copies of *Zane Grey Theatre*; Dunning, *On the Air*; Hart; Mac Donald, *Who Shot*; http://www.zanegreyinc.com.

ZORRO

Jack French *and* David S. Siegel

NAME: *Preview Theater of the Air*
NETWORK: Regional from KFWB, Los Angeles
FORMAT: Half hour
DURATION OF RUN: One performance (October 24, 1947)
SPONSOR: Sustained
AUDIO COPIES EXTANT: 1
SCRIPTS ARCHIVED: Undetermined

NAME: *The Adventures of Zorro*
NETWORK: Syndicated
FORMAT: 15 minutes, weekdays
DURATION OF RUN: 1947 to 1949
SPONSOR: Various, local
AUDIO COPIES EXTANT: 2
SCRIPTS ARCHIVED: Undetermined

The dashing, athletic masked hero of old California, created by Johnson McCulley in 1919, made his mark prominently in every phase of popular culture, with the possible exception of radio. Zorro has been the subject of dozens of films, including serials, several television series, some of which were animated cartoons, and a host of related toys and other products including his costume, sword and whip. In her extremely thorough 1998 book, *Zorro Unmasked: The Official History*, Sandra Curtis, the creative director of Zorro Productions, lists every published story, stage play, movie, and television appearance of this fascinating horseman. In this inventory, she mentions only one radio program featuring Zorro: a five part series on the BBC that aired in the United Kingdom in July 1997.

However, Zorro was present on the U.S. airwaves during the Golden Age of Radio, albeit his efforts were not a major factor in broadcasting. Zorro was the subject of at least three different programs, and also inspired two copy-cat versions: **Seal of the Don** and **The Scarlet Cloak.** One of the first public notices of Zorro on radio was in the January 15, 1940, issue of the magazine *Broadcast Advertising* that noted that the Aerogram Corporation of Hollywood had purchased the radio rights to the character of Zorro and that production would begin soon on 65 quarter hour episodes. However, to date, no audio copies or scripts from this possible series have been uncovered.

From approximately June to December 1947, Warner Bros., who owned radio station KFWB in Los Angeles, broadcast a program on Friday evenings called *Preview Theater of the Air.* Each week a different show would be auditioned, usually with a Hollywood star in the cast, and if the program was well received, that show might evolve into a regular series. Typical offerings were "For Men Only" with Jane Russell and Wally Brown and "The 13th Juror" with Otto Kruger and Hans Conried.

On October 24, 1947, *Preview Theater of the Air* broadcast "The Adventures of Zorro" with Hyman "Hy" Averback in the title role. The script was written by Maria Little while Robert M. Light directed this Mitchell Gertz production. The music was composed by Irving Gertz and Gil Warren was the announcer. The story dealt with Zorro's rescue of an innocent friar, Padre Felipe, from the evil Captain Ramone and his bumbling henchman, Sergeant Pedro Gonzales. A daughter of a wealthy land owner, Señorita Lolita, was romanced by both Zorro and his alter ego, Don Diego. The program was skillfully written and the cast supporting Averback was convincing. Sound effects (swordplay, hoofbeats, fight scenes, etc.) were all done well and enhanced the action.

Mitchell Gertz (1911–1961), using the same writer and director, next produced a Zorro syndicated series of 15 minute programs, although the total number of episodes is still unconfirmed. It is safe to assume the total was not less than 26, as this was the minimum number for syndication marketing in that era. Thus far, only episodes #1 and #9 currently exist in audio form. The series was recorded in the 1947-1948 period under the name of *The Adventures of Zorro*. Gertz's company, Transcription Recordings, with offices on Sunset Boulevard in Hollywood, advertised the availability of this series in the 1949 edition of *Radio Annual*, but this announcement did not state the number of episodes being offered.

Each episode of *The Adventures of Zorro* opened with Zorro warning his protagonist, "On guard!" followed by sound effects of swordplay. The exchange was finished with "swish-swish-swish" and Zorro concluding "And that, for robbing a poor man of his bread." Episode #1 uses the same script of the program that aired on *Preview Theater of the Air* and is a virtual repeat of the first half of that 30 minute program.

By episode #9, Captain Ramone has arrested Don Carlos and his daughter, Lolita, on charges of treason. Zorro meets with the other landowners and they agree to help him rescue the two. Both episodes are a good balance of well-paced scripts, fine acting, and realistic sound effects. The only possible drawback to its enjoyment by juvenile male listeners would be the frequent love scenes between Lolita and Zorro, which traditionally turned young lads away.

The scriptwriter, Maria Little (1914–1967), would go on to become a successful TV writer and story editor on *Lassie*, *Gentle Ben* and *Flipper*. The composer, Irving Gertz (1915–2008) was the younger brother of Mitchell and lived to be 93. He had a productive career scoring music for dozens of motion pictures, including *Destination Murder*, *Top Gun*, and *The Incredible Shrinking Man* as well as the television series *Land of the Giants* and *Voyage to the Bottom of the Sea*.

Based upon the success of Disney's Zorro on ABC-TV (1957–1959), Buena Vista released a series of Zorro albums, each of which were approximately 9–10 minutes in playing time. The television cast was used in some of the roles, and each record began, and ended, with the Zorro theme song from the video version. Over the next 50 years, some confusion has arisen over these audio copies and as a result some Internet dealers and their customers erroneously believe that these recorded adventures were originally radio shows, which they never were.

Sources: Audio copies of *Preview Theater of the Air* and *Adventures of Zorro*; Brooks; Radio Annual of 1949; Curtis; *New York Times*, November 20, 2008; Personal correspondence with John Gertz of Zorro Productions, January 2013.

Appendix 1: Series with Insufficient Data to Classify or Describe

There are many radio programs with western sounding titles that the editors identified during the course of their research that are not included in the main section of the book, either because the editors were not able to locate information to describe the program or because, upon further investigation, the program, despite its title, turned out not to be a true western show. For example, the editors stopped researching a show called *Calamity Jane* after learning it was a program about a feisty female reporter in modern days played by Agnes Moorehead. Similarly, upon further research, we learned that *Win Your Spurs* was a talent contest narrated by Hoot Gibson.

Some of the programs listed below may have been all music or even documentary lectures on the West with no dramatization. In any case, the editors are listing them in this Appendix, with the extent of the available information, to make a record of their existence in the hope that the future will reveal more about their place in American broadcasting history.

Adventures in Navaho Land, 1930s, KAWM, Gallup, NM
The Alamo, NBC, 1930s
American Indian, 1937, KSEI, Pocatello, ID
The American Indian, 1950, syndicated
Chisholm Trail, 1940s, syndicated
Circle C Ranch, KVOO in Tulsa, 5 times weekly, 5:15 to 5:30 P.M.
Covered Wagon Adventure Trails, WMT, Cedar Rapids, IA, 3 times weekly, Saturday, 5:45 P.M.
Dakota Days, 1930s, KABR, Aberdeen, SD
Early California Drama, 1936, KFWB, 6:45 P.M. Tuesday and Thursday, 15 minutes
The Forty-Niners, 1935-36, 3 times weekly, syndicated
Frontier Days, 1930s, NBC
Gold Rush Days, KFRC, 1936-37, three times weekly, 15 minutes, 9:30 P.M.
Indian Legends, 1930s, KIUP, Durango, CO
Indian Legends, 1935, 3 times weekly, WLS
Indian Lore, 1930s, WAPI, Birmingham, AL
Indians All, 1930s, NBC
Legends of the Southwest, 1930s, KVOR
Life of Buffalo Bill, 1940s ?

The Long, Long Trail, 1930s, KIDO

Night on the Prairie, 1930s, KGNC, Amarillo, TX

The Old Oregon Trail, 1930s, KIDO

Out of the West, 1930s ?

Over Southwest Trails, 1930s, KTSM, El Paso, TX

Pals of the Prairie, 1930s ?

Parade of the Pioneers, 1930s, KGGM, Albuquerque, NM

Partners of the Trail, 1930s, KIDO

Phantom Indian, syndicated ?

Pioneer Stories, 1930s, KSL, Salt Lake City

Pioneer Stories, 1930s, syndicated by World Broadcasting System

Pioneer Trails, 1936-37, KSL, Salt Lake City

Pioneer Trails, KWSC, Pullman, WA, 1938

Prairie Jane, syndicated, 1930s

Radio Rides the Range, 1930s ?

Riders of the Range, 1930s, KDYL, Salt Lake City

Riders of the Rio Grande, 1930s, KFPY, Spokane

Roamin' Through the Rockies, 1930s, KLZ, Denver (Might be all music)

Roy Starkey's Circle S Ranch, 1948-49, 30 minutes, WHAS, Louisville

Saga of the Southwest, 1930s ?

Sage in the Hills, 1940s, Texas State Network

Sons of the Lone Star, 1938, NBC, 5 times weekly 7 P.M., aired from San Francisco

Sons of the Plains, 1930s ?

Tales of California, 1930s, KGO-KPO, San Francisco

Tales of the Plains, 1940s ?

Telling the West About the West, 1936–37, twice weekly on KTAR, Phoenix and KSL, Salt Lake City

Thunder in the West, KMBC, 1930s

Trails, Rails, and Waterways, 1940s ?

Triple B Ranch, 1930s ?

Troop D, syndicated by Gotham Radio, 1948-49 (Tales of U.S. Cavalry)

The Vigilantes Ride Again, 1930s, KGIR, Butte, MT

Wagons West, 1930s, KFAC, Los Angeles

Way Out West, 1930s, KONO, San Antonio, TX

West of Cheyenne, 1938, WLW, Cincinnati (Might be all music)

The West Remembers, CBS, 1939, 30 minutes, Saturdays 8:15 P.M.

Western Frontiers, 1930s, KRE, Berkeley, CA

Western Trails, 1930s, KDKA, Pittsburgh

Westward Ho! 1930s, KFAC

Westward Ho! 1930s, KFOR, Lincoln, NE

Westward Ho! 1930s, KLO, Ogden, UT

Westward Ho! 1948-49, Curley Bradley and organist Irma Glen, syndicated

Whence Came the Red Man, KMBC, 1935

Wyoming Ranch Life, 1930, WRC, Washington, DC, Saturdays, 3 to 3:15 P.M.

Young Forty-Niners, 1933, WENR, Chicago

Appendix 2: Time Line of Western Programs

The following time line includes only the major title by which the program was known, or the title when the program was first aired. Subsequent or alternate titles are shown only in the main text. An asterisk (*) after the date indicates the year the audition disk was recorded. There is no documentation that the program was ever broadcast.

First Year Aired	Program
1929	The Empire Builders
1930	Death Valley Days
1930	Rin Tin Tin
1931	Colorado Cowboys
1931	Covered Wagon Days
1931	Lone Wolf Tribe
1931	Romance of the Western Range
1932	Bobby Benson and H-Bar-O Rangers
1932	Historical Southern California
1932	The Lone Indian
1933	Cowboy Tom's Round-Up
1933	Eagle Wing, the Navaho
1933	Gold Rush
1933	The Lone Ranger
1933	Maverick Jim
1933	Pat Barnes' Bar Z Ranch
1933	Reminiscences of the Old West
1933	Tom Mix
1933	Triple Bar X Days and Nights
1933	Winning the West
1934	The Desert Kid
1934	Plainsman
1935	Frontier Fighters

First Year Aired	Program
1935	Life on Red Horse Ranch
1935	Light on the West
1935	Night Hawk Rides
1935	Riding with the Texas Rangers
1935	Six Gun Justice
1935	Stray Hollister
1936	Hoofbeats
1936	Tales of Pioneer Days
1936	Tenderfoot
1937	Cactus Kate
1937	Gunsmoke Law
1937	Phoenix Sun Ranch Chuck Wagon
1937	Spirit of the Pioneers
1937	Tomahawk Trail
1937	Under Western Skies
1938	Dude Ranch
1938	Lightning Jim
1939	Dr. Frackelton's Stories of Cheyenne & Crow Indians
1939	Old Dodge Dramas
1939	Singing Bandit
1939	Sunday at the Hy-G Ranch

First Year Aired	Program	First Year Aired	Program
1930s	The Black Ghost	1947	California Caravan
1930s	Covered Wagon Days	1947	Cisco Kid (Series 2)
1930s	Old Wagon Tongue	1947	Zane Grey Theater
1930s	Pistol Pete Rice	1947	Zorro
1930s	Red Goose Indian Tales	1948	Arizona Adventure
1930s*	Return of Bill Hart	1948	Straight Arrow
1930s	Roundup Trail	1948*	Wild Bill Elliott
1930s	Seal of the Don	1949	The Adventures of Champion
ca. 1940	Chief Gray Wolf	1949	Bobby Benson and the B-Bar-B Riders
1940 ?*	Boots and Saddles	1949	Frontier Town
1940	Gene Autry's Melody Ranch	1949	Hopalong Cassidy
1940	Lone Journey	1949	Little Hunter
1940s*	Phantom Rider	1950	Darrow of the Diamond X
1941	Justice Rides the Range	1950	Hashknife Hartley
1941	Old Trails Plowed Under	1950*	The Scarlet Cloak
1941	Romance of the Ranchos	1950	The Singing Marshal
1941	Saunders of the Circle X	1950	Tales of the Texas Rangers
1941*	Tommy Gale of the Box T Ranch	1950	Western Caravan
1942	Cisco Kid (Series 1)	1951	Tales from the Diamond K
1942	Red Ryder	1951	Wild Bill Hickok
1943	Grapevine Ranch	1952*	Adventures of Annie Oakley and Tagg
1943	Ranch House Jim	1952	Gunsmoke
1943	Woman of America	1953	The American Trail
1944	The Roy Rogers Show	1953	The Six Shooter
1945	Buffalo Bill Bates	1954	Dr. Sixgun
1945	Cimarron Tavern	1956	Fort Laramie
1945	Destiny Trails	1958	Frontier Gentleman
1945	Tennessee Jed	1958	Have Gun—Will Travel
1946	All-Star Western Theatre	1958	Luke Slaughter of Tombstone
1946	Hawk Durango/Hawk Larabee	1962	Horizons West
1946*	Law West of the Pecos	1966	When the West Was Young
1946	Sky King		
1947*	The Andy Devine Show		
1947*	Bob Sterling, American Ranger		

Appendix 3: Western Programs on Mainstream Radio

Stories about the West were not exclusive to particular series. The western adventure story was attractive enough to be adapted by many anthology programs, sometimes based on fact, e.g., *Cavalcade of America*, and more often based on fiction, e.g., *Escape*.

Listed below are examples from some of the Golden Age's most popular programs.

Series	Date Aired	Program Title
Academy Awards Theater	5/4/46	"Stagecoach"
Catholic Hour	5/4/41	"Winning the West"
Cavalcade of America	6/16/37	"Heroes of Texas"
	3/9/38	"Buffalo Bill"
Crime Classics	1/6/49	"The Younger Brothers"
	10/21/53	"Billy Bonnie Bloodletter (a.k.a. Billy the Kid)"
Escape	12/6/49	"Command"
	12/22/50	"Wild Jack Rhett"
	11/30/52	"Pagosa"
Hallmark Hall of Fame	9/13/53	"San Houston"
	9/27/53	"Marcus Whitman"
	1/3/54	"Tom Mix"
	12/6/54	"Wyatt Earp"
Hollywood Star Playhouse	4/13/52	"The Six Shooter"
Lux Radio Theater	2/2/36	"Green Grow the Lilacs (Plot of Oklahoma)"
	3/9/36	"Girl of Golden West"
	9/27/37	"Cimarron"
	9/23/40	"The Westerner"
	6/16/41	"The Lady From Cheyenne"
	3/13/44	"In Old Oklahoma"
	11/5/45	"Destry Rides Again" (Max Brand novel)
	3/7/49	"Red River"
	1/22/51	"Broken Arrow"

Series	Date Aired	Program Title
Lux Radio Theater [cont.]	3/12/51	"She Wore a Yellow Ribbon"
	6/4/51	"A Ticket to Tomahawk"
	11/12/51	"Winchester 73"
	12/29/52	"Westward the Women"
Radio Reader's Digest	11/28/43	"Braves on the Warpath"
Richard Diamond, Private Detective	9/27/50	"The Oklahoma Cowboy"
Romance	8/6/51 & 12/12/53	"Pagosa"
	9/5/54	"The Postmistress of Laurel Run"
	11/26/55	"Ladies Day at Medicine Hat"
Screen Director's Playhouse	3/3/50	"The Paleface"
	6/7/51	"The Gunfighter"
Screen Guild Theater	8/21/44	"The Ghost Goes West"
	9/18/44	"The Oxbow Incident"
	4/30/45	"Ramona"
	6/24/46	"The Barbary Coast"
Sears Radio Theater	1979–1980	Monday night was "western" night
Studio One	10/21/47	"Singing Guns"
Theater of Romance	2/20/45	"Destry Rides Again"
You Are There	5/2/48	"The Surrender of Sitting Bull"
	3/27/49	"The Oklahoma Land Run"

Appendix 4: Sources for Audio Copies of Western Programs

Recordings of the programs listed in this book, as well as recordings of other Golden Age of Radio programs, are available from a variety of sources, some free and readily available and others for sale. Still other recordings are available only in private collections or are available only under certain circumstances. Depending on the source, an inventory of the holdings may be searchable online. This appendix is not meant to be a definitive list, especially for Internet sites where, depending on the program, a keyword search by title may suggest multiple sites. Also, many of the old time radio clubs have audio lending libraries that, in addition to recordings of programs, also have copies of interviews of former radio personalities, many of whom were connected with western drama programs. (For a listing of available interviews, see Siegel, *Remembering Radio* in the Bibliography.)

Source	Web site	Notes
Digital Deli	www.digitaldeliftp.com	Free downloads
Internet Archive	www.archive.org/details/oldtimeradio	Free downloads
Library of American Broadcasting/University of Maryland	www.lib.umd.edu/special/collections	By appointment
Library of Congress, Recorded Sound Reference Center	www.loc.gov/rr/record	By appointment
Library of Congress, Links to other sound archives	www.loc.gov/rr/record/nrpb/nrpb-archives.html	Links to various other institutions
Media Heritage	www.mediahertiage.com	By appointment
Old Time Radio Fans	www.oldtimeradiofans.com	Free downloads
OTR Network library	www.otr.net	Free downloads
Otrcat.com	www.otrcat.com/westerns-c-120.html	Free downloads
Radio Archives	www.radioarchives.com	For sale
Radio Spirits	www.radiospirits.com	For sale
Radiogoldindex	www.radiogoldindex.com	Private collection
Satellite Media Production	http://oldietv.com	For sale
SPERDVAC	www.sperdvac.org	Lending library
The Vintage Radio Place	otrsite.com	For sale

Appendix 5: Sources for Scripts of Western Programs

When scripts for a specific program have been located, their location(s) have been shown as part of the program's write-up.

Listed below are some of the major non–Internet sources for archival scripts. For Internet sources, use the keyword function to search by program title. Additionally, *A Resource Guide to the Golden Age of Radio: Special Collections, Bibliography and the Internet* by David S. and Susan Siegel (Book Hunter Press, 2006) lists sources for scripts.

Source	Location	Web Site
American Heritage Center	University of Wyoming, Laramie, WY	www.uwyo.edu/ahc
American Radio Archives	Thousand Oaks Library, Thousand Oaks, CA	www.americanradioarchives.com
Broadcast Arts Library	Fort Worth, TX	broadcastartslibrary.com
Generic Radio Workshop	Web site	www.genericradio.com
J. Walter Thompson Collection	Duke University, Durham, NC	www.library.duke.edu
Library of American Broadcasting	University of Maryland, College Park, MD	www.lib.umd.edu/special/collections
Library of Congress	Manuscript Division	www.loc.gov/rr/mss
Media Heritage	West Chester, OH	www.mediaheritage.com
SPERDVAC	Van Nuys, CA	www.sperdvac.org
Wisconsin Historical Society	Madison, WI	www.arcat.library.wisc.edu/

Bibliography

Books

Alicoate, Jack, ed. *Radio Annual*(s). New York: Radio Daily, 1945, 1946, 1947, 1949.

Autry, Gene. *Back in the Saddle Again*. New York: Doubleday, 1978.

Barabas, SuzAnne, and Gabor Barabas. *Gunsmoke: A Complete History*. Jefferson, NC: McFarland, 1990.

Barbour, Alan G. *The Thrill of It All*. New York: Collier, 1971.

Beller, Susan Provost. *Medical Practices in the Civil War*. Blue Ash, OH: Betterway, 1992.

Bickel, Mary E. *Geo. W. Trendle, Creator and Producer of: The Lone Ranger, The Green Hornet, Sgt. Preston of the Yukon, The American Agent, and Other Successes*. New York: Exposition, 1971.

Boemer, Marilyn Lawrence. *The Children's Hour*. Metuchen, NJ: Scarecrow, 1989.

Bond, Johnny. *The Tex Ritter Story*. New York: Chapel Music, 1976.

Brooks, Tim, and Earle Marsh. *The Complete Directory to Prime Time Network and Cable TV Shows, 9th ed*. New York: Ballentine, 2007.

Brown, Dee. *The Gentle Tamers*, 6th ed. Lincoln: University of Nebraska Press, 1981.

Buxton, Frank, and Bill Owen. *The Big Broadcast*. New York: Viking, 1966.

Callahan, Robert E. *Heart of an Indian: A Gripping Story Based Upon a Great American Truth*. New York: F.H. Hitchcock, 1927.

Carlock, Robert H. *Early Days of the Aztec Land and Cattle Company*. Tuscon, AZ: Westernlore, 1994.

Carter, Robert A. *Buffalo Bill Cody: The Man Behind the Legend*. Edison, NJ: Castle, 2005.

Clark, Cottonseed. *Cottonseed Clark's Bushwood Poetry and Philosophy*. New York: Bourne, 1950.

Cox, Jim. *Great Radio Soap Operas*. Jefferson, NC: McFarland, 1999.

_____. *Historical Dictionary of American Radio Soap Operas*. Lanham, MD: Scarecrow, 2005.

_____. *Radio Crime Fighters*. Jefferson, NC: McFarland, 2002.

Curtis, Sandra. *Zorro Unmasked: The Official History*. New York: Hyperion, 1998.

DeLong, Thomas A. *Radio Stars*. Jefferson, NC: McFarland, 1996.

Dinan, John A. *The Pulp Western*. Albany, GA: Bear Manor, 2003.

Dixon, Peter. *Bobby Benson on the H-Bar-O Ranch*. Racine, WI: Whitman, 1934.

_____. *Radio Sketches and How to Write Them*. New York: Frederick A. Stokes, 1936.

Drew, Bernard A. *Hopalong Cassidy: The Clarence E. Mulford Story*. Metuchen, NJ: Scarecrow, 1991.

_____. *Jingle of the Silver Spurs: The Hopalong Cassidy Radio Program, 1950–52*. Boalsburg, PA: Bear Manor, 2005.

Dunning, John. *On the Air: The Encyclopedia of Old-Time Radio*. New York: Oxford University Press, 1998.

_____. *Tune In Yesterday*. Englewood Cliffs, NJ: Prentice-Hall, 1976.

Felbinger, Lee. J. *The Lone Ranger Pictorial Scrapbook*. Green Lane, PA: Countryside, 1979.

Forbis, William H. *The Cowboys (The Old West Series)*. Alexandria, VA: Time-Life, 1973.

Franklin, Joe. *Classics of the Silent Screen*. New York: Citadel, 1959.

French, Jack. *Frontier Gentleman Program Guides*. Little Falls, NJ: Radio Spirits, 2008.

_____. *Private Eyelashes: Radio's Lady Detectives*. Boalsburg, PA: Bear Manor Media, 2004.

George-Warren, Holly. *Public Cowboy No. 1: The Life and Times of Gene Autry*. New York: Oxford University Press, 2007.

Goodstone, Tony. *The Pulps*. New York: Bonanza, 1970.

Gossett, Sue, Bobby J. Copeland and Neil Summers. *Trail Talk*. Madison, NC: Empire, 1996.

Grams, Martin, Jr. and Les Rayburn. *The Have Gun—Will Travel Companion.* Churchville, MD: OTR, 2001.

Hake, Ted. *Official Price Guide to Pop Culture Memorabilia.* New York: House of Collectibles, 2008.

Harmon, Jim. *The Great Radio Heroes,* rev. ed. Jefferson, NC: McFarland, 2001.

_____. *Radio & TV Premiums.* Iola, WI: Krause, 1997.

_____. *Radio Mystery and Adventure and Its Appearances in Film, Television and Other Media.* Jefferson, NC: McFarland, 1992.

Harper, William H. *Straight Arrow: The Definitive Radio Log and Resource Guide.* Albany, GA: Bear Manor, 2007.

Hart, James D. *The Oxford Companion to American Literature,* 4th ed. New York: Oxford University Press, 1965.

Harvey, Sir Paul, ed. *The Oxford Companion to English Literature,* 4th ed. New York: Oxford University Press, 1969.

Heide, Robert, and John Gilman. *Box-Office Buckaroos: The Cowboy Hero from the Wild West Show to the Silver Screen.* New York: Abbeville, 1982.

Hickerson, Jay. *4th Revised Ultimate History of Network Radio Programs.* Hamden, CT: Presto, 2010.

_____. *New Ultimate History of Network Radio Programming and Guide to All Circulating Shows.* Hamden, CT: Self-published, 2009.

Hogg, Ian V. *The Illustrated Encyclopedia of Firearms.* Secaucus, NJ: Chartwell, 1991.

Holland, Dave. *From Out of the Past: A Pictorial History of the Lone Ranger.* Granada Hills, CA: Holland House, 1989.

Howard, Harold P. *Sacajawea.* Norman: University of Oklahoma Press, 1971.

Hurst, Richard M. *Republic Studios: Between Poverty Row and the Majors.* Lanham, MD: Scarecrow, 2007.

Jackson, Helen Hunt. *Ramona.* New York: Little, Brown, 1945.

James, George Wharton. *Through Ramona's Country.* Boston: Little, Brown, 1909.

Jones, Reginald, Jr. *The Mystery of the Masked Man's Music.* Metuchen, NJ: Scarecrow, 1987.

Josephy, Alvin M., Jr., ed. *The American Heritage History of the Great West.* New York: American Heritage, 1965.

Katz, Ephraim. *The Film Encyclopedia,* 2nd ed. New York: HarperPerennial, 1994.

Kramer, Ronald. *Pioneer Mikes: A History of Radio and Television in Oregon.* Ashland, OR: Western States Museum of Broadcasting and JPR Foundation, 2009.

Lawton, Sherman Paxton. *Radio Continuity Types.* Boston: Expression, 1938.

Lenius, Ron. *The Ultimate Roy Rogers Collection.* Iola, WI: Krause, 2001.

Lesser, Robert. *Pulp Art.* New York: Metro, 1997.

MacDonald, J. Fred. *Don't Touch That Dial! Radio Programming in American Life From 1920 to 1960.* Chicago: Nelson-Hall, 1979.

_____. *Who Shot the Sheriff? The Rise and Fall of the Television Western,* Santa Barbara, CA: Praeger, 1987.

Maltin, Leonard. *The Great American Broadcast.* New York: Penguin Putnam, 1997.

Marshall, Rick. *The Encyclopedia of Country & Western Music.* New York: Bison, 1985.

McDaniel, Ruel. *Vinegarroon: The Saga of Judge Roy Bean.* Kingsport, TN: Southern, 1936.

Menke, Frank G., Suzanne Treat and Pete Palmer. *The Encyclopedia of Sports,* 6th ed. Garden City, NY: Doubleday, 1977.

Mix, Olive Stokes. *The Fabulous Tom Mix.* Englewood Cliffs, NJ: Prentice Hall, 1957.

Mix, Paul. *Life and Legend of Tom Mix.* New York: A.S. Barnes, 1972.

Mott, Robert L. *Radio Sound Effects.* Jefferson, NC: McFarland, 1993.

Newark, Peter. *Cowboys.* London: Bison, 1982.

Nivens, Francis M. *The Cisco Kid: American Hero, Hispanic Roots.* Tempe, AZ: Bilingual Press of Arizona State University, 2008.

_____. *The Films of The Cisco Kid.* Waynesville, NC: World of Yesterday, 1998.

Nivens, Francis M., and Beverly and Jim Rogers Museum of Lone Pine Film History. *Hopalong Cassidy: On the Page, On the Screen.* Lone Pine, CA: Riverside, 2008.

Norris, M.G. *The Tom Mix Book.* Waynesville, NC: World of Yesterday, 1989.

O'Neal, Bill. *Tex Ritter: America's Most Beloved Cowboy.* Waco, TX: Eakin, 1998

Orlean, Susan. *Rin Tin Tin: The Life and the Legend.* New York: Simon and Schuster, 2011.

Osgood, Dick. *WYXIE Wonderland.* Bowling Green, OH: Bowling Green University Popular Press, 1981.

Overstreet, Robert M. *The Overstreet Comic Book Price Guide.* New York: HarperCollins, 2000.

_____. *The Overstreet Toy Ring Price Guide,* 3rd ed. Timonium, MD: Gemstone, 1997.

Phillips, Robert W. *Roy Rogers: A Biography, Radio History, Television and Bibliography.* Jefferson, NC: McFarland, 1995.

Raine, William MacLeod. *Famous Sheriffs and Western Outlaws.* New York: Doubleday Doran, 1929.

Rogers, Roy, and Dale Evans with Carlton Stowers. *Happy Trails: The Story of Roy Rogers and Dale Evans.* Waco, TX: Word, 1979.

Rothel, David. *The Singing Cowboys,* San Diego, CA: A.S. Barnes, 1978.

_____. *Who Was That Masked Man? The Story of the Lone Ranger*. New York: A. S. Barnes, 1981.

Salomonson, Terry. *The Lone Ranger Log*. Howell, MI: Self-published, 2004.

_____. *The Western Logs. Revised and Updated*. Howell, MI: Self-published, 1998.

Schaden, Chuck. *Speaking of Radio: Chuck Schaden's Conversations with the Stars of the Golden Age of Radio*. Morton Grove, IL: Nostalgia Digest, 2003.

Schneider, John F., *Bay Area Radio*. Mount Pleasant, SC: Arcadia, 2012.

Siegel, David S., and Susan Siegel. *A Resource Guide to the Golden Age of Radio: Special Collections, Bibliography and the Internet*. Yorktown Heights, NY: Book Hunter, 2006.

_____. *Radio Scripts in Print: Books Featuring 1,700 Golden Age of Radio Scripts*. Yorktown Heights, NY: Book Hunter, 2006.

_____. *Remembering Radio: An Oral History of Old-Time Radio*. Albany, GA: Bear Manor, 2010.

Striker, Fran Jr. *His Typewriter Grew Spurs... A Biography of Fran Striker—Writer: Documenting the Lone Ranger's Ride on the Radiowaves of the World*. Landsdale, PA: Questco, 1983.

Summers, Harrison. *A 30 Year History of Programs Carried on National Radio Networks in the United States, 1926–1956*. New York: Arno, 1971.

Swartz, Jon D., and Robert C. Reinehr. *Handbook of Old-Time Radio*. Metuchen, NJ: Scarecrow, 1993.

Trachtman, Paul. *The Gunfighters (The Old West Series)*. Alexandria, VA: Time-Life, 1974.

Tumbusch, Tom. *Illustrated Radio Premium Catalog and Price Guide*. Dayton, OH: Tomart, 1989.

Tyler, Ron, ed. *New Handbook of Texas*. Denton: Texas State Historical Association, 1996.

Urwin, Gregory J.W. *The United States Cavalry: An Illustrated History*. New York: Blandford, 1983.

Utley, Robert M. *Cavalier in Buckskin: George Armstrong Custer*. Norman: University of Oklahoma Press, 1988.

Van Hise, James. *The Story of the Lone Ranger: Who Was That Masked Man?* Las Vegas: Pioneer, 1990.

Variety Radio Directory. Annual Edition. New York: Variety, 1940-41.

Wheeler, Keith. *The Chroniclers (The Old West Series)*. Alexandria, VA: Time-Life, 1976.

Williams, Albert Nathaniel. *Listening: A Collection of Critical Articles On Radio*. Freeport, NY: Books for Libraries, 1948.

Wright, Stewart M. *Gunsmoke: The Myth of the Prime Time Repeats*. Lakewood, CO: Privately printed, 2005.

Wylie, Max. *Best Broadcasts of 1940-41*. New York: McGraw-Hill, 1942.

Articles

Beckett, Charles. "From Gunsmoke to Fort Laramie." *Return with Us Now*, January/February 2012.

Cox, J. Randolph. "Red Ryder Once Again: The Merchandising of a Hero." *Dime Novel Round-Up*, June 2010.

_____. "Red Ryder Rides Again!" *Dime Novel Round-Up*, June 2008.

Crosby, John. "There Are More Eggheads Than You Think." *Radio and Television Life*, May 6, 1953.

Ellett, Ryan. "The Radio Career of Gomer Cool." *Radio Recall*, February, 2011.

Foote, Timothy. "1846: The Way We Were." *Smithsonian Magazine*, April 1996.

French, Jack. "Cowpoke from Colorado." *Radio Recall*, March/April 1991.

_____. "The Story Behind Her Soap Opera Success." *Nostalgia Digest*, Winter 2011.

Gould, Jack. "Gunsmoke: A Western Well Off the Beaten Path." *Ralston Purina Magazine*, July/August 1979.

Gromer, Cliff. "It's a Daisy." *Popular Mechanics*, July 1999.

Harman, Fred. "New Tracks in Old Trails." *True West*, September/October, 1968.

Moser, Whet. "RIP Sol Saks, 'Bewitched' Creator." *Chicagomag.com*, April 22, 2011.

Pelgram, Jane. "Behind the Scenes—No. 7 of a Series: Norman Macdonnell." *Return With Us Now*, May 8, 1949.

Poling, James. "Ryder of the Comic Page." *Collier's*, August 14, 1948.

Wright, Stewart. "Norman Macdonnell's Gunsmoke Stock Company." *Radiogram*, December 2005.

_____. "The Reluctant Westerner." *Return With Us Now*, Vol. 30, No. 11, November 2005.

_____. "Revisiting the Frontier Gentleman." *Old Radio Times*, March 2006.

_____. "We Offer You... Escape." *Radio Recall*, Vol. 28, August and October 2011.

Magazines

The following magazines routinely covered the broadcast industry during the Golden Age of Radio.

Billboard

Broadcast Weekly

Broadcasting (searchable online at americanradiohistory.com/Broadcasting_Individual_Issues_Guide.htm)

Broadcasting/Telecasting

otrr.org/pg06b_magazines.htm (online copies of many radio magazines)

Radio and Television Life

Radio Daily
Radio Guide
Radio Life
Radiogram
TV Radio Mirror

Newspapers

The "radio listings" pages of the following newspapers are helpful in identifying regional broadcast dates. See Source citations for local newspapers.
Chicago Tribune
Los Angeles Times
The New York Times
Variety

Program Logs

audio-classics.com
digitaldeliftp.com
radiogoldindex.com
otrr.org
otrsite.com/radiolog

Websites

A selected list of websites that provide a broad range of information about the Golden Age of Radio and related subjects. Web sites that deal only with specific programs are included in the appropriate Source citations.
archive.org
audio-classics.com
b-westerns.com
classicthemes.com (Musical themes)
digitaldeliiftp.com
forums.oldradio.net
genericradio.com
goldenage-wtic.org (Interviews with radio personalities)
imdb.com (Movie and television information)
old-time.com
otr.com
otrr.org
pacificariadioarchives.org (Interviews with radio personalities)
radioGoldindex.com: Comprehensive database of radio broadcasts
thrillingdetective.com

About the Contributors

Frederic S. **Berney** began recording radio shows in 1952 at age 13. He started his own recording studio while in high school, which eventually became a full service audio and video company. In 1964 he produced his first feature film, *Once Upon a Coffee House*, which starred a young Joan Rivers. He is an old time radio collector and dealer, and is the president of the Metropolitan Washington OTR Club. He lives near Frederick, Maryland.

Bob **Burnham** began in the late 1970s as co-editor and columnist for *Collector's Corner* magazine and later authored several "how-to" booklets on the technical aspects of preserving and duplicating sound. He contributed to *NARA News* as a columnist and for the past 40 years has been a vendor of OTR products. He has received the Allen Rockford Award and the Stone/Waterman Award. A broadcast engineer in Detroit, he is an engineer in the Michigan school system.

Stan **Claussen** has written extensively on the golden age of radio. He is the audio theater producer at the American Museum of Radio and Electricity in Bellingham, Washington, and also an instructor of radio history and drama in the Academy of Lifelong Learning program at Western Washington University. He is also an actor and has performed in radio re-creations in Seattle.

J. Randolph **Cox** is the editor of the *Dime Novel Round-Up* and professor emeritus (library), St. Olaf College, Northfield, Minnesota. A noted authority on detective Nick Carter, Cox's publications include *The Dime Novel Companion*, *Flashgun Casey, Crime Photographer*, and writings about magician/author Walter B. Gibson.

Ryan **Ellett**, a Kansas public school teacher, founded the online popular publication *The Old Radio Times*. In 2008 he received the Stone/Waterman Award. He has rescued several historical radio shows from obscurity and his first book, *Encyclopedia of Black Radio in the United States, 1921–1955*, was published by McFarland.

Jack **French** is a former Navy officer and retired FBI agent who has been researching radio history for the past 40 years. He is the former editor of *NARA News* and current editor of *Radio Recall*. He has been honored for his radio research and writing with the Allen Rockford Award, the Stone/Waterman Award, the Warren Award and the Ray Stanich Award. He was inducted into the Radio Once More Hall of Fame in 2011. He lives in northern Virginia.

J. David **Goldin** had a network radio engineering career with CBS, NBC, and Mutual. Since 1994, he has donated more than 10,000 16-inch disks to Marr Sound Archives at the University of Missouri–Kansas City. He maintains a database of old time radio programs; his website www.radiogoldindex.com lists more than 102,500 programs. He lives in Sandy Hook, Connecticut.

Martin **Grams**, Jr., is the author or co-author of more than 20 books about old time radio including *The Have Gun—Will Travel Companion* and *The Shadow: The History and Mystery of the Radio Program, 1930–1954*. The recipient of the 1999 Ray Stanich Award, the 2005 Stone/Waterman Award, and the 2010 Rondo Award for Best Book of the Year, he is a frequent contributor to the *Old Time Radio Digest* and *Radiogram*.

William **Harper**, as a 10-year-old, appeared on *Don McNeill's Breakfast Club* in the summer of 1951. He has edited a newsletter, *Pow-Wow*, and is author of the book *Straight Arrow: The Definitive Radio Log and Resource Guide for that Legendary Indian Figure on the Trail of Justice*. He lives in North Augusta, South Carolina.

Doug **Hopkinson** began collecting, researching and writing about the Golden Age of radio in 1994 and has uncovered the background of such little-known shows as *Cecil & Sally*, *Og, Son of Fire* and *Baron Keyes' Air Castle*. His articles have appeared in *Radiogram*, the *Old Radio Times* and on several Internet sites. He lives in the Chicago area.

Bobb **Lynes** of southern California served as an artist/illustrator in the Air Force and has worked at Los Angeles area motion picture and television venues. He has been broadcasting old time radio programs since 1975 from KCSN in Northridge, California, and on www.KPFK.org. He has been a radio actor and was the announcer on NPR's *Doc Savage* series in 1985. A recipient of the Rockford Award, he co-wrote (with Frank Bresee) and illustrated the book *Radio's Golden Years*.

William **Nadel** is a radio and media historian who has authored or co-authored more than 100 liner notes for re-issued CD boxed sets of classic vintage radio programs. He comes by his interest in westerns through members of his family, who include O. Henry, the creator of the *Cisco Kid*. He lives in the Bronx, New York.

Donald **Ramlow** has directed more than 300 radio re-creations since 1982 at old time radio conventions. Among the performers he has directed are Kim Hunter and William Windom, in addition to Parley Baer, Peg Lynch and Will Hutchins. He co-founded All-Ears Theater and has lectured on radio history throughout the Kalamazoo region. He lives in Michigan.

Terry **Salomonson** has aired shows from his collection on radio, taught a college course in vintage radio, compiles radio logs and conducts interviews with radio celebrities. His work has earned five awards. He has written dozens of articles and is the co-author (with Martin Grams, Jr.) of the book *The Green Hornet: A History of Radio, Motion Pictures, Comics, and Television*. He lives in Howell, Michigan.

Karl **Schadow** is a freelance radio historian living in Virginia. He specializes in the history and background of *The Shadow* and has also written about many obscure radio programs, including *Dark Fantasy*, *The Spirit*, *Peter Quill*, and the four soap operas Mutual debuted in 1941. He is the recipient of the 2011 Ray Stanich Award.

Ivan G. **Shreve**, Jr., of Athens, Georgia, has been collecting and researching old time radio for 40 years. His blog "Thrilling Days of Yesterday" includes information on vintage radio, television and movies. He also writes program notes for boxed CD sets of old time radio programs.

David S. **Siegel**, a retired superintendent of schools, has been collecting radio broadcasts, scripts, magazines, books and ephemera for 50+ years. He is the editor, author or co-author of seven books about old time radio: *The Witch's Tale*, *Remembering Radio*, *Flashgun Casey*, *Crime Photographer*, *A Resource Guide to the Golden Age of Radio*, *Radio Scripts in Print*, and *Radio and the Jews*, as well as numerous articles. The recipient of both the Allen Rockford and Ray Stanich awards, he lives in Yorktown Heights, New York.

Charlie and Katherine **Summers** are a Pennsylvania father and daughter team involved in old time radio collecting, preserving and researching. She is believed to be the youngest actress to have performed in a re-creation at the Friends of Old Time Radio Convention in Newark, New Jersey. He is a long time collector of the Golden Age of radio and is the listmaster of the Internet OTR Digest, which goes out daily.

Maggie **Thompson** is a writer and editor of the *Comics Buyer's Guide*. While she has focused professionally on the popular culture field of comic books, her favorite hobby is old time radio. She is the recipient of the Jack Kirby Award in 1985 and the Allen Rockford Award in 2006, and lives in Wisconsin.

Barbara **Watkins** lives in the Los Angeles area, where she has co-hosted an old time radio program for three decades. She is the co-founder of a group producing new radio drama for more than 17 years. One of seven experts chosen by John Dunning to help with his *On the Air: The Encyclopedia of Old-Time Radio*, she is a radio columnist and a recipient of the Rockford Award.

Stewart **Wright**, a retired cartographer and geographic researcher who lives in Colorado, has been collecting vintage radio shows for 40 years, and writing about a range of radio topics for more than 20, especially *Gunsmoke* and other westerns. He is an active member of various vintage radio clubs.

Index

Page numbers in **bold italics** indicate pages with illustrations.